*To all the brave men and women who served in
the Battle of the Bulge, especially those who
didn't return home. We salute you with gratitude.*

CONTENTS

INTRODUCTION

The Veterans of the Battle of the Bulge, Inc. (VBOB) is a membership organization instituted to: Perpetuate the memory of the sacrifices involved during the Battle of the Bulge; preserve historical data and sites relating to the Battle of the Bulge; foster international peace and goodwill; and promote friendship among the survivors of the Battle of the Bulge and their descendants.

The purpose for creating and publishing this book is to help preserve the legacy of those brave men and women who served the United States of America during the largest land battle ever fought by the US Army, the Battle of the Bulge.

The book contains stories written by individuals who only knew about the job they where supposed to do, and they did it in magnificent fashion until the Nazis were defeated. These same stories were published in *The Bulge Bugle*, a quarterly publication of the Veterans of the Battle of the Bulge, Inc. We can never repay them for their courage and sacrifices, but we can make sure they are always remembered.

To read over 1,000 stories that are in *The Bulge Bugle* visit our web site at www.battleofthebugle.org. Click on the Research link and select Newsletter Archives.

A CLOSE CALL

Don Addor

10th Armored Division, 20th Armored Infantry Battalion

This was our second night in the crossroad town of Noville, Belgium. I had been sent here with Team Desobry to hold the town from the Germans at "any or all costs," while the defenses for Bastogne were being set up.

I and three buddies serving in the 20th AIB Headquarters of the 10th Armored Division were told to stand by with the major's half-track in a three story old stone house on the comer of the main intersection in the town. The house was built on a slope so that in the back the first floor was at ground level, but in the front was one story up looking out over the "main street."

This gave us a great view of the row of stone houses across the street, but beyond that the fog was too heavy to see anything. During the day we had taken quite a pounding from the enemy's artillery and tank fire. The row of buildings and barns out front had been hit so often that only the burned shell remained by nightfall.

I should say here that we had chosen to sleep in a small vegetable cellar that made for lumpy, but safe sleeping as the thick stone walls were under ground. Now there were nice double beds up stairs in this house. They even had clean sheets and blankets on them. Who ever had lived here had left in one big hurry as there was even a nice dinner laid out on the dining room table.

That night I had volunteered for the first shift of guard duty. The rest of the guys went down into the vegetable cellar and their sleeping bags laid out on a large turnip bin and the cobblestone floor. Not very comfortable but safe! I pulled a big overstuffed easy chair over in front of the big window facing the row of burning houses across the street. I was far enough back that I could not be seen. We had a sniper some place in town. However, I had a great view of the foggy, misty night outside. I thought it was kind of like watching a big movie screen from a seat in the balcony.

The houses out there reminded me of huge jack-o-lanterns lit up by the flames inside. The fires reflected on the wet cobblestone street making an eerie and haunting sight. There were several vehicles also burning at the side of the street to add their bit to the dancing reflection from the houses. The house across from where I was seated was a burned-out shell, but flames still leaped from the debris that had fallen to the first floor. The entire roof was gone, leaving two stone peaks facing me. The peak closest to me had a few layers of stone missing and lying in the street below. The point of the rear peak was complete right to its pointed end.

The whole scene seemed unreal, but an occasional burst of gunfire and a shell exploding somewhere not too far away, reminded me that this was the real thing, not a Hollywood set. As I gazed out the window mesmerized by the flames a shell hit the rear peak and blew it away.

Almost simultaneously these thoughts ran through my mind: Wow!; if that peak had not been there the shell would have landed in my lap; they hardly ever sent just one shell at a time. I leaped out of my comfy chair and headed for the safety of the root cellar.

About eight feet from the cellar's door, I heard that second shell tear though the stone outer wall and come crashing across the floor above me. I took a dive and entered the storage room head first plowing down about 12 wooden steps. When I hit the floor everyone was awake. The shell had not exploded, but still had made a lot o f noise crashing across the floor and through the furniture.

We all hunkered down with fingers cross waiting for the explosion. We waited and waited, but none came. We thought that maybe the shell had a proximity or time fuse so no one ventured out of our little "bunker" until daylight. By then we were fairly sure that there would be no explosion, but wondered what the hell had happened. With the sun shining through the windows up stairs things did not seem so grim. Actually it wasn't sunshine we saw, just its light that had filtered through the still dense fog. Everything was all right in the living and dining room. I told Sarge that the shell had come through the wall upstairs. I added that as I was sliding across the floor on my nose. I could hear it smashing things above me.

I volunteered to go up and take a look. Sarge said that he would come with me. When we looked into the front bedroom we saw a mess. There was a shell-shaped hole cut right through the stone wall just a few inches above the floor. A small table and a chair lay in splinters. The big bed had been split right down the middle and there it was buried halfway into the interior wall.

We gave it a good looking over, but didn't touch anything. We also put our ears close to it, but could hear no ticking sound or anything else. Even though it looked mean and nasty stuck in that wall, we both came to the conclusion that it was a genuine dud. We had been getting a lot of them lately.

Sarge and I went back down and told the guys what had happened and that there seemed to be nothing to worry about, at least from that shell. We did not stay in Noville much longer, but I never sat in that chair in front of that window again.

CHRISTMAS 1944 – TOO WHITE, TOO COLD

Don Addor
10th Armored Division, 20th Armored Infantry Battalion

Since I joined VBOB I have read a lot stories from different members on how they spent Christmas of 1944. For all of us, this holiday was truly celebrated in a different manner than usual. A white Christmas that was too white and too cold!

I, too, shall never forget Christmas of 1944, but for a different reason than stated in the tales I have read in *The Bulge Bugle*. I was with the 20th Armored Infantry Battalion, 10th Armored Division. We were on RR down in France when General Patton ordered us north to Bastogne. I would up on an outpost in Noville with orders to stop the German's advance at any cost while defenses at Bastogne were set up.

This Team Desobry did for about two and a half days. On the 20th of December we were told, "That we were no longer needed and could withdraw back to Bastogne. That is if we could make it!" We pulled out of the devastated town and headed into the thick fog for Bastogne. At Foy we were ambushed by German armored forces and received many casualties.

I was one of those casualties. I had been knocked down by a mortar shell and when I got back up, I was hit by burp gun fire. The bullets tore the field jacket off of my back and three went through my right leg. Two went through my shin bone and the other through the artery in my calf. Blood streamed out of my right leg making a big puddle in the grass of that Belgian cow pasture. I thought I had had it but a voice from above said, "You're not dead yet!" After some difficulties, I finally got a tourniquet to work and the blood stopped flowing. I looked around me and I was all alone, except for the dead, sitting in the fog behind the German lines about a mile outside of Bastogne—that city was also behind the lines. After what seemed like hours a jeep came down the road. It turned out to be the major's jeep and driver with a medic from the 101st paratroopers.

They had been lost in the fog dodging Germans for over a day. When they finally got back to Noville it was deserted. I told them what had happened and directed them the way back to Bastogne. When I got to our battalion aid station, I passed out. Sometime later, I came to in some kind of rocking tunnel.

When I tried to get up, the medic, hooking another bottle of plasma over my head, pushed me back and told me I was on a hospital train on my way to a hospital in Paris. I retained consciousness after that. I guess all of those blood transfusions and other liquids had done their work.

Rolling down the hospital hallway, I noticed Christmas decorations hanging from the ceiling. A life sized cardboard Santa smiled at me as we turned a corner and entered a ward. This was the first time I had thought about Christmas since we had made that mad dash from lower France to Bastogne. I asked a nurse what day it was and she said, "Why it's Christmas Eve!" Before I could ask her anything else, the doctor arrived at my bed side to examine my leg.

Somewhere along the line, a cast had been put on it. I looked down and saw that my toes sticking out of the cast were an awful bluish black. The doctor gently lifted my cast and the bottom slushed out all over the nice clean sheets. A terrible smell hit my nose. I had smelled that smell before from the dead. It was the smell of death.

The doctor came over to me with a very solemn face. I saw he was struggling for words, so I said, "Gangrene?" He replied, "Yes." He went on to tell me that it had to be amputated as soon as possible. He added that he hated to do it on Christmas morning. He would send the chaplain to talk with me.

I told him I would be glad to talk with the chaplain, but I looked at the operation as a gift of life. I also told him that I had been so close to death twice that I was happy to be alive and in good hands. I don't know if he understood me or not. One has to actually be in combat and experience death all around to really understand.

The next morning bright and early, I was off to the operating room. I was trying to take a last look at my leg when the nurse stuck a needle in my arm. I was out by the count of three so never got that last look.

The next thing I knew was a nurse pulling a thermometer out of my mouth. I was hot and sweating, so I said to her, "I guess it's pretty high." She answered, "Why, no. It's almost normal!" She examined the bed and discovered that I had seven heavy army blankets on me. I could not feel them as there was a wire cage keeping them off of my body. She explained that the way back from the operating room crossed an open courtyard. Paris was having a very cold, white Christmas so thus all of the covers.

We both had a good laugh. Then, she asked me if I would like a drink. I said I was not thirsty and she said, "Not that kind of drink." I had two Scotch and waters to celebrate Christmas 1944. She said the officers in the hospital had saved their liquor ration so the patients could have a holiday toast. "Merry Christmas!"

IN A SMALL CHURCH

Michael V. Altamura
750th Tank Battalion, Service Company

We were in a picturesque, snow-covered valley in Belgium during the Battle of the Bulge in December of 1944. It was Sunday morning. A small Catholic church stood on a slight slope overlooking the snow-covered fir trees. At the other end of the valley was a coal-fueled electric power plant. Every once in a while a German buzz bomb came over attempting to knock out the power plant. A group of tankers and infantrymen decided to attend church that Sunday morning. We stood in the back of the church with our guns slung over our shoulders as the priest gave the mass in Latin. The congregation was kneeling in prayer.

We heard the "put-put" of a buzz bomb overhead, and then the sound cut off. When the sound ceased, we knew the rocket engine had stopped propelling the airborne buzz bomb and it would fall, exploding when it hit the ground. The congregation looked upwards as if to accept their fate. The priest's intonations stopped. We stood in the rear as if accepting our fate. The bomb hit pretty close to the church. The ground shook; a few of the stained glass windows cracked. No one moved or said a word; the priest resumed his mass in Latin. I thank God for sparing us that Sunday morning in a small Belgian church during the Ardennes battle.

750TH TANK BATTALION

Michael V. Altamura
750th Tank Battalion, Service Company

The 750th Tank Battalion had the lowest percentage of vehicles abandoned in combat on the western front and as a result was chosen to share in the honor of occupying the former Nazi citadel in Cologne.

Sgt. Eddie Oryll, who was killed in action during a German bomber raid while we were repairing one of our M-4 tanks, and I were assigned a half-track. We would accompany the battalion maintenance tank retriever and assist in retrieval of our 750th Tank Battalion unit tanks which were damaged by the enemy.

One of my jobs was to check for enemy placed booby traps in the abandoned M-4 tanks and deactivate them if possible. Most of the time it was the better part of valor to slip a block of dynamite and blow up the tank with the German booby traps; as it was virtually impossible to deactivate the ingenious German booby traps. Capt. Shiner our battalion maintenance commander would give me the command to blow the tank with a block of dynamite when I noticed the trip wires and explosive which had been placed in the tank. If you pulled on a wire or cut a wire, the explosion would be set off.

During World War II, soldiers would name their planes, tanks and half-tracks. Some were named after girlfriends, mothers, home towns, etc. Sgt. Eddie Oryll and I decided to name our half-track "Skunk Hollow" after the home town of the 1940s newspaper cartoon characters' (Little Abner and Daisy Mae) fictional home town. Each 750th Tank Battalion letter company A, B, C, D, headquarters and service company vehicle's name had to start with the alphabet letter of that company. Ours was "S" (service company).

Since the three of us were assigned to the half-track and often went for weeks without baths, clean clothes, and passed gas often due to the Army food and K-rations, we decided that "Skunk Hollow" not only described our situation but also fit the aroma that prevailed in the confined front seats of the half-track. After the war, I was once asked by a friend, "How was the war?" I replied, "It stank."

CHRISTMAS 1944

Alfred A. Alvarez
1st Infantry Division, 16th Infantry Regiment, Company C

All my little cherubs bounced around my lap. "Grandpop, Grandpop," tell us a Christmas Story.

I remembered a long time ago, during that terrible war of my youth. My thoughts were on the Christmas of 1944, where in snowy Belgium the cruel and relentless foe had surged forth and blown us completely aside. During that dark December, when as a newly-minted corporal, I acquired some strange traveling companions.

Out of a shell-splintered forest emerged Magnes, a young New Jersey Jewish soldier equally lost from his unit. Upon entering a destroyed village we met Trios, a black soldier and new arrival on the front.

Seeing that they both looked to me and my two stripes for guidance, I said "Let's head North," by following that North star. So off we trudged in the eerie winter darkness. We hoped desperately we were headed toward friendly folks, and we needed shelter in this bitter cold.

Sister Rose Marie

"I think I see a light," Magnes said.

"Where?" I asked.

"There," Magnes said, "to the right."

A little beacon was blinking in the falling snow. Taking heart, we cautiously stumbled toward an old farm house. It seemed vacant, so we scratched up a small fire.

Suddenly while staring at the fire and taking stock of our rations, we all became conscious of a squeak. Then we gazed in unison as the trapdoor in the floor began to open. We were tense, expecting an enemy. What relief and total surprise to see a nun.

Initially she may have been frightened by what appeared to her as three apparitions that were enhanced by cellar lighting and illuminating us like demons.

Then as more cellar light played on us, she saw the helplessness on our dirty, young faces. She focused her gaze at me and the crucifix I wore on my helmet band.

"Christian?" she said to me.

"Yes, Sister," I replied.

"We're all Christians, Sister," my Jewish friend said.

No longer were we the enemy, just three lost teenagers under the relentless confident, yet questioning gaze of a domineering Sister of the Benedictine order.

The Sister smiled in a schoolmarm manner. She asked if we could help her. Beckoning us downstairs, we followed somewhat meekly and clumped down the cellar ladder.

The room below must have been some kind of an animal shelter with shelves on the walls, as well as the floor, laden with straw, hay, and an abundant nitrogen smell.

In the meager light of a lantern we could make out cows, sheep, pigs, dogs—all responding loudly to our invasion. As the light penetrated to the far reaches of the cellar, it reflected on the eyes of a small group of children. Moving the lantern about, we uncovered a number of coal-smudged-cheeked children. Literally, they were angels with dirty faces cowering in fear around a young mother and her new-born baby.

Hiding from the war, they had sheltered here in the dry, warm cellar. They had not eaten in some time.

We checked our pockets. We came up with an orange. They squealed with delight as they ate and the orange juice dripped from their lips. Then they wanted to eat the orange skins. Sister Rose Marie quietly and firmly stopped the children from yelling and grabbing when Magnes opened a Hershey chocolate bar. He wanted to break it into many little sweet portions for all.

"No," Sister Rose Marie said, "we'll wait until later."

Not to be outdone, Trios distributed some of his loose change, mostly copper pennies to their delightful amazement. Surely, Saint Nick's elves were among them.

Sister Rose Marie had us stoke the fire, gather more wood, arrange more beds, cover the windows to keep out the cold and any possible enemy.

We got ready for bed, but first the children would have a winter washing and feast. We heated snow in some buckets and poured the hot water in our mess gear. With this, we washed many grimy faces and hands.

"Get in your beds and go to sleep," Sister Rose Marie told the children. "There's nothing to worry about, the Americans are here."

Sister Rose Marie, while berating us for destroying the village, now laughed at us three city boys attempting to milk a non-receptive cow. All our efforts brought amusing glances from our farm knowledgeable audience.

Sister Rose Marie then rolled up her sleeves and proceeded to show us how to milk. She filled our helmets with the steamy warm milk. We at least assisted in mixing it with shavings from our chocolate ration bars and in no time produced a foamy hot cocoa for the children and the young mother.

Silent Night

We American soldiers and these German ladies and children exchanged more looks and you could see that we were experiencing a wondrous moment. Here were all the children, clean, all snug in their blankets of hay and straw, sipping hot cocoa and clutching their pennies. They were wonderfully happy and safe.

Adding to the moment, Sister Rose Marie led them in singing, thanking us for their beautiful evening. We listened to their Christmas carols in German. It was warm and amazing to realize that "Silent Night" in German was the same as we had heard in the States.

As we accompanied them in English, we were transported back to our home towns. A snowy Belgium night was Chelsea, Massachusetts. Christmas here was Christmas there. It was the same all over the world.

The new day commenced with a promise. The bombardment had quieted. It was time to leave, so we said our sad goodbyes. We marched away from that snowy farmhouse near Bastogne, Belgium. Our trek through the deep snow brought us back to the safety of our lines.

"Maybe the Christmas story isn't about the place and possibly not the time," I told my inquisitive grandchildren. It's really about that special spirit of the simple goodness of we gentlefolk, during our moments of wonder. "Just giving of ourselves out of love."

When you go to war pray once
When you go to sea pray twice.
When you marry pray three times.
—Slavic Proverb

TASK FORCE DAVISSON

Alfred A. Alvarez
1st Infantry Division, 16th Infantry Regiment, Company C

"Recon, you find 'em; engineers, you fix 'em; tanks, you fight 'em; and TDs, you finish 'em!" With these emphatic, but crystal clear adjurations, LTC Henry L. Davisson set the tempo for his task force sub ordnance commanders. It was 16 December 1944, and the yet-to-be-named "Ardennes Offensive" had exploded. This Kraut's massive tank penetration now was creating this northern shoulder of what was to be its acquired sobriquet, "The Battle of the Bulge."

In response, hastily thrown together units from the vaunted 1st Infantry Division (The Big Red One), would acquire its title "from the aggressive commander of the 634th Tank Destroyer Battalion." Task Force Davisson was thus quickly formed as a lightly armored, tank-killing reaction force! Major Olson, the "TDF" S3 designated the line of march, handed out strip-maps for a southward reconnaissance.

Our armored convoy consisted of the 1st Recon Troop heading out with puny 37 mm armed M-8 Greyhound armored cars. Intermingled came the 1st Combat Engineer Battalion's A Company, riding its soft-skinned vehicles. Now came D Company of the 745th Tank Battalion with its measly Lt. Whippert tanks armed also with 7 mm guns, but back up by its 75 mm assault gun platoon. Spread out and looking for targets came C Company of the 634th Tank Destroyer Battalion with their 9mm rifles, claiming the ability to compete with German armor. All probably supported by "The King of the Battlefield," our four-man "P.O. Charlie" Artillery Observation party (with the commo capability to call down Divarty and Corps Arty "barrages or serenades").

Our battery veterans of the "Lucky 7th" Arty Bn, who had fought German armor in Tunisia, Algeria, the beach at Sicily, and in the fields of Normandy, spoke out in warning to our little observer party: "Be ready. This TF Davisson is outgunned by the huge Panthers and King Tiger monsters reported coming your way. Remember, your tank-destroying force needs to equal or outgun those battle-tested German Behemoths and also mount sufficient armor to protect themselves from the superior German anti-tank weapons. In other words, you better be "killer tanks" rather than tank killers. If not, you will have to stop 'em with indirect 105 mm or 155 mm arty concentrations."

Despite these knowledgeable words, we heard only the spurrings of Col. Davisson. Quickly, the "TFD" saddled up and cautiously commenced traveling south through snowy Belgium. The lengthy convoy slid out of Sourbrodt and Robertville and clanked into Walk and Waimes, small villages recently vacated by U.S. medical units.

The weather was frigid cold and damp, but the fog was dissipating, and for once, Arty would have wonderfully clear observation! Here we were, "The Lucky 7th's" forward observation party on high ground, salivating at the abundance of lucrative targets! Spotting from our town's church steeple with our 20-power scopes, German convoys, to include tanks, traveling west across our front from 863-020 to 863-024—an artillery man's dream! Compounding our good fortune, our previously secretive ammo employing "the proximity fuse" constructed around its nose plug, which activated when the emitted radio beam encountered an object within 15 yards! We were going to have the proverbial field day... and we deserved it!

Our parent organization, "The Fighting First," was still recuperating from its horrific bloodletting in "The Hurtin Forest" this past November, where the Krauts had grounded us into Hurtgen Forest and past! Surely now was to be payback time... but the war gods frowned and said no... not yet!

The American artillery ammunition supplies across the entire 1st Army front were dangerously low, contriving to place "quotas" on all "shoots"! Our radio pleas to FDC for fire missions received a "wait out"! Our frantic telephone messages informed us their priority was to our east. There, our sister regiment, the 26th Infantry "Blue Spaders," were in continuous battle with German armored thrust at Bullingen and Butgenbach. There, LTC Derrill, M. Daniels, and his 2nd Battalion would successfully blunt the German Col. Pieper's rampaging westward drive and dream! That portion of the northern shoulder would remain firm!

So now it was to be our turn. The German 1st SS Panzers, frantically searching for a route on the Rollbahnen to the west, then side slipped and proceeded to smash at us; TFD now intermixed with 3rd Battalion 16th Infantry at Waimes. Our front erupted with tank fire and reported infantry advancing plus intensified artillery fire in our immediate front. Our first indication was a flying buzz bomb smashing into the battery area and WIAs three gunners—CpI Homer A Jerome, T/5 Raymond A. Fink, and PFC Erlo Baton. We were further alerted by a commotion reported on our eastern outpost which luckily forewarned everyone in town! Speeding down the only street in Waimes came two G.I. jeeps overloaded with Krauts. Firing madly and careening widely to escape our firing gallery response, they crashed off the road on the west side of the village.

Col. Davisson then ordered, "Recon, send a squad to investigate and recover the bodies and/or the vehicles." Lt Cagerosi, our FO, took over the viewing scopes from our lofty OP as the submachine-armed recon squad gingerly approached the overturned vehicles. They sprayed the area, righted a jeep, and returned with a WIA spread-eagled on the hood! Another German captive was shoved into the co-pilot's seat, hands on his head. Arriving at the town square, now crowded with a rubbernecking GI throng, the Jerry prisoners held center stage! Looking like "right out of Hollywood" with his peaked hat and black leather topcoat and gloves, in excellent English, he demanded medical attention for his men! In response, someone in the crowd belted him with a rifle butt! He was saved from further harm by the NCO's who held back the provoked soldiers. It appeared that in breaking through our outpost, the Germans had hailed in English, then fired and killed the wounded, surprised guards. These angry crowd members were old-time buddies of the soldier killed by this "ruse-de-guerre"!

Later, with his head now bandaged, the German officer was carted off to the 16th Infantry Regimental S-2, where subsequent interrogation divulged he was an officer-courier transporting the photographic proof of this German explosive and successful penetration through the American lines. The following day, angered regimental staff members descended and oversaw a search of the snowy jeep accident area and found this valuable film!

These important photos, immediately developed at the rear headquarters, received prominent world attention as the classic "Bulge" combat film showing smiling German paratroopers as "successful warriors in action"!

With our shooting priority reestablished and our observation still A-OK, our arty observer party initiated fire missions with visibly outstanding results! Lt. Anthony Cangelosi, our latest FO, who would break the "bad luck cycle" of officer casualties and proceed to "make it" to the war's end in Czechoslovakia, took targets under fire. First, we fired on "enemy troops forming for attack," then followed a mission on enemy vehicles. Finally, we observed for a Divarty TOT on an enemy assembly area. With the horizon ablaze, we continued with harassing fires throughout the night. Cpl Maurice Vacher was our instrument corporal who would be promoted and get the Purple Heart the following week. He would return, bandaged, with three new stripes and stories of great chow in the medical rear. Me, now a T/5 (corporal's pay without the authority) and my cohort, T/5 Rene Cote, our dependable driver, rounded out our crew. At first light, all of us, now professionals after six months on the combat scene, poured destruction on the advancing white-painted enemy armor and accompanying white-clad infantry. After four missions and 275 rounds expended, we reported "enemy activity ceased and one tank burning!"

Later, during a slow afternoon, Capt Fred F. Chirigotis, from the 745th Tanks, asked for our indirect fire observing so they could "use up" their 75 mm ammo. With a total expenditure, their tanks would be able to acquire new 76 mm tubes! Jumping at the chance, I got some invaluable and exhilarating shooting experience and contributed some damage, too! During another quiet period, on Cote's watch, he asked, "What the hell are those guys doing?" An engineering squad seemed to be laying a hasty mine field in the road leading south in the Town of Faymonville. Apparently, these engineers must have been short of mines because the engineering sergeant had his squad scrounge up dinner plates from the nearby Belgium homes. His squad, laden with this ample supply of dishes, were pacing off the distances and placing plates face down on the road and adjoining fields. As viewers, our interest peaked. "Look at him now. He's putting some real mines amongst those kitchen plates!" Finally, the squad members covered these actual metallic mines with large porcelain dinner platters. "Very clever, these Americans!" Those porcelain covers will inhibit the mine metallic detectors." Later that afternoon, as it showed, our forward area was dimpled with the ingenious defensive preparation.

German counter fire re-intensified and seemed to be directed at our high ground and steeple, so we moved into town to the second floor of the town hall or barroom... "kaboom!" The biggest tank you ever saw blew our jeep to kingdom come. No one was hurt, but we sure were happy we had gone to church the previous Sunday. We countered with "purple smoke," our air strike marking rounds as FDC insisted, "No aircraft available." A couple more rounds that "landed first, then whistled after" and whew, he backed out of view somewhere back into Faymonville. The troops were understandably quiet as we hurriedly plastered the town with HE and WP and set numerous fires, everyone privately hoping he was through with us good guys!

Our Chief of Detail and my boss S/Sgt Joseph Desforge and Motor Sergeant "Shorty" Hofer came up during darkness with a replacement jeep. Besides replacing our food and extra radio batteries, they told us we were stopping an enemy armored attack on the northern shoulder of something called "the Battle of the Bulge." After that illuminating information, we settled back in, but encountered some new problems. Our "posit" rounds were exploding at their maximum ordinate as premature bursts over our heads. Apparently, the sensitive fuses were set off by clouds! As if that was not enough, Sgt Ringer's howitzer, back in the firing battery area, had a muzzle burst and the gun was destroyed, but luckily, with no gunner casualties. Probably the intense cold on the metal tube and the sudden heat of the morning firing caused it. My remembrance of this December is the bitter cold, with all the troops occupied with ways of keeping warm. The approved method was putting on layers of any clothing. Many brainy GIs wrapped blanket strips over straw around their boots and created an incredibly large footprint in the snow—anything for insulation to stave off trench foot while occupying their foxholes.

During our lengthy and boring time on watch, someone mentioned, "Today's Christmas. This'll make our third Christmas overseas for our 'Lucky 7th Arty Bn.'" Cote reminisces about Christmas 1942 in Africa and on the moors in England on Christmas of 1943. Lt. Cangelosi celebrated by knocking out an MG position at 864-013 with two direct hits! The doughs cheered and waved their arms and weapons, stamping their cold feet, too, in their exposed foxholes. Afterward, when I sneaked down to the chow line in an adjoining cellar, the cooks told us "Boomers" (artillery observers), "You're doing a bang-up job." But more importantly, he slipped me an extra helping of meat and potatoes!

From Christmas to New Years, it was just continuous fire—at "enemy troops in the open" and "enemy tanks." Our records show we averaged over 1,800 rounds per day during the last days of December 1944. This wall of steel both harassed and hampered the enemy's efforts to exploit and enlarge his armored thrust. Our uninterrupted night defensive fires, requested by our supported 16th Infantry, commenced with the coming of darkness and carried over until daybreak. Even so, another strong tank counterattack was repulsed in the vicinity of 053-013 (railroad tracks near Steinbach, Belgium) by the direct fire of the 634th Tank Destroyers and 74th Tankers. The blackened hulks of destroyed German tanks stood out against the snow. The bodies of German infantry were not as easily discerned. New Year's Day opened with hordes of German aircraft strafing our positions. As usual the poor bloody infantry suffered the casualties, and as always, it's the new replacements. We "Boomers" hid in our cellars as the bomb explosions rattled around us, watching the lieutenant celebrate by drinking his liquor ration as we underaged peons looked on.

Rumors were now flying that we would attack Faymonville the first week of January 1945. So we took under fire all possible EN positions in the town. Methodically, we increased the destruction by dropping HE rounds through the roofs, then followed up with WP to burn the houses. Most of them, however, were constructed of stone and resisted all our bombardments. Still, slowly, Faymonville was not systematically pulverized.

During that first week of January, we carefully, in conjunction with the mortars, fired in support of a patrol attempting to retrieve the body of Lt McLaughin, of L Company, KIA'd days previously.

Lt Cangelosi "had the word" and got us ready by checking our equipment, clothing, and footwear. "I want constant commo while on the attack," he said. "The infantry is going to get us on high ground every chance they can and protect us, too." That's good, but for me, first I must get and be warm. Layering of clothing was the answer. So it's long underwear, shirts, jackets, many trousers, ponchos, wrapped blanket strips over straw, and joining the "monster footprint brigade." With a French Foreign Legion "kepi" look, I covered my helmet with a white pillow slip with a flap covering my neck. Then I enclosed myself in a white bed sheet, a snow cape, and emerged through the slit for my head. Finally, I connected up the radio and set it on a German wooden sled with a 50-foot on/off switch for the lieutenant's use. We were "ready for Freddy." Threw some cardboard ammo cartons filled with coffee, sugar, and cans of cream on the sled and loaded my pockets with "goodies." Now, as the last preparation, I ate everything I could of rations: crackers, cheese, meat and beans, cocoa, sugar, candy—anything for energy. "Now bring on those Krauts. I'm warm, full, and have dry feet. I can shoot, scoot, and communicate."

On 14 January 1945 with heavy snow falling, the 16th infantry's 3rd Battalion, commanded by LTC Charles T. Horner, co-mingled with portions of TF Davisson's tanks assaulted Faymonville. We (with me pulling the radio sled) accompanied I Company, then later L Company. As we slowly trudged into the northeast portion of Faymonville, mines in the snow took out some of A Company's 745th tanks, but the doughs continued despite incoming mortars. The first reports were 2 KIA and 15 WIA for our 3rd Battalion. We stopped at nightfall and ran a line to the nearest company. To hear reports of 70 casualties for the 3rd Battalion. We fired harassing missions and kept everyone awake. The next morning dawned crisp and sunny, and Lt Cangelosi returned from battalion briefing; "We are going to take Schopen, the next town to the southeast. Let's move it." Trudging again through the snow, we encountered some woods where MG fire erupted. Lt Cangelosi quieted it with an HE concentration. We held up in these woods with no fires, no hot chow, and tried stomping our feet all night to stay warm. Only good thing was a can of sliced peaches (kept warm in my armpit) for breakfast from my food stash. The following day (maybe the 15th of January), we accompanied the 3rd Battalions's L Company, which seemed to be in reserve since we stepped in the footprints of the lead company. The snow was knee deep and snowing fiercely with drifts piling up. Someone passed the word down the line, "We are in a blizzard." Observation was impossible—we cannot see anything, but better still, the Germans cannot see us either. My day consisted of struggling through the snow, laying a line back on the road, and finally meeting our artillery liaison wire crew; then splicing the line with frozen fingers and hearing the two parties conversing. We tried bumming rides on the only vehicles moving, "Weasels," some type of a lightweight covered track vehicle. They seem to be ambulances carrying WIA and flying their Red Cross flags, everyone on the road now piled on a tank dozer for a slippery, dangerous ride back, and I followed my line back into a house. Thank God the troops had fired up a stove, and it was crowded and cozy. While Lt Cangelosi and Sgt Vacher observed upstairs, I dried up and tried heating my radio batteries on the stove to restore their strength; "Eureka, I think it works." The artillery liaison bunch gave me the bad news that "Jonsey," A Battery radioman, was KIA'd when we hit Faymonville. The word was he was hit by a sniper. We were losing a lot of doughs, but they were strangers to me. Jonsey was an artillery buddy doing my same job on the RO. I had just returned a quarter-mile of commo wire I'd borrowed from him.

We continued through the snow at the proverbial "snail's pace," the doughs plodding through snowdrifts, the tanks sliding and slipping off the roads. Noticed some oops had wrapped barbed wire around their boots for traction; they claimed it worked. My salvation was my sled and wrapped boots. The lieutenant was pleased with his constant commo as I dragged the sled.

We entered Moderschied and fired normal missions on enemy troops, and then strangely, we gave them four missions of propaganda shells. We continued with 13 missions on enemy troops at CPs and OPs with approximately 70 hits on houses containing troops, with resulting fires. Then we continued with harassing fires throughout the night—nobody sleeps.

The next morning—don't know the date—we commenced preparation fires prior to forward displacement, meaning "move out and drag the sled." It seemed to be getting lighter in weight—probably from eating the rations and throwing away the used batteries.

Great news! The 16th Infantry was squeezed out of the advance by the 18th Infantry, so for us, immediate support became general support, and another team took over. We were lucky—the food just about ran out. Sgt Vacher quartered us in a large barn while Lt Cangelosi checked with 3rd Battalion for hot scoop. We cleaned up the equipment, gassed up the jeep, set up a stove, and cooked some liberated food.

We were in heaven: no observation duties, in a warm barn, bellies full, just radio watch and waiting for the lieutenant to take us home... "kaboom!" A round came through an opening in the front wall and out the back wall—with a startling, crackling explosion that showered us with debris. Straw flew everywhere, and we were covered with shards of wood, powdered stone, and animal droppings. No one was physically hurt, but someone had to change their laundry. We moved next door to another barn, smaller, but with stone walls.

It was 31 January 1945, and we were pulling radio watch only while putting in land lines to artillery liaison. Listening on the artillery net, we heard a rare command given to the guns: "Battery C, continuous fire to the right at 5 second intervals with a converged sheath" for an expenditure of 45 rounds at the same target. Contact by telephone to my old buddies at Artillery Battalion FOC discloses that a subsequent 18th Infantry patrol reports a German 6-gun battery of 150 mm abandoned their positions and guns at the coordinates of that strange concentration.

It was the beginning of February; the sun came out, and it seemed that Task Force Davisson, having halted, then chased the Germans out of Belgium, then simply faded away with the spring thaw!

RECURRING MEMORIES

Arma E. Andon

26 Infantry Division, 328th Infantry Regiment, Company H

The recent edition of your fine publication *The Bulge Bugle* contained a review by Harold E. Raugh, Jr., reprinted from World War II magazine—February,

2001, on General Manton S. Eddy. The article brought back some memories which frankly over the years cross my mind quite often and particularly during the period of the Bulge.

I was CO of H Company from the time we went overseas until I was seriously wounded on March 13th in Serrig, Germany, on Mockers Hill.

Both incidents were during the Bulge period. The first had to do with an attack where I was with the leading rifle company which was my policy throughout the campaign.

We had entered a small village and noted a garage on the right side of the road adjoining a house and for some reason I said to our communications sergeant, "Let's take a look." We used his bayonet and a knife which I carried to check for booby traps, etc., and, none found, we opened the door and there was my life's dream. There sat a Mercedes Phaeton command car similar to the ones the German High Command officers and Hitler used. I immediately radioed for our motor sergeant to bring a crew and put this in with our other vehicles. Muddy it up and put in some of our heavy weapons and make the vehicle look as innocuous as possible and a prayer to keep me alive so I could take the car with me after the war.

Things went well for the next few days with nothing said by either the battalion or regimental commanders, or division. The men were fully cooperative as they took pride in our new vehicle.

Then about the fourth or fifth day, while on a march, I saw coming a jeep with two stars followed by a command car with two stars and knew immediately we were the target.

Sure enough, out stepped General Manton Eddy and I saluted, gave him my number, and after some small talk, he said, "Captain, I note you have a non-issue vehicle." I said, "Yes, General, but we are utilizing it to carry additional weapons and ammunition." He then asked me if we were using government-issued fuel and I said, "Yes." He then cited the rules and said he would have to appropriate the vehicle on behalf of the U.S. Army. So, we kissed our dream car away and candidly felt it would have happened by a high command sooner or later.

However! On or about early January and January the 4th is my birthday, so this happened on the 2nd I believe. Our battalion was approaching Wiltz, at the time occupied by the enemy, and we were on high ground in a heavily wooded area and it was now dusk and we set-up an OP which was right out of the text book. We overlooked the entire city and the enemy in plain sight. Between the artillery observer and our team we were in business. I issued orders saying there would be no movement during day time and the night shift would be relieved just before day light and no one to be allowed to go out during day light. Previous experience dictated that this order be followed to the letter and I would take all responsibility in the event higher rank wanted to visit the OP.

The next morning I was up early, having checked that all was okay at the OP with transfer of men and supplies for the day. I started back about 50 yards from the route to the OP when up came a one star and said, "Captain, I want to go out to the OP." I said, "Sir, no one goes out," and proceeded to explain our past experiences. He said, "Do you know who I am?" I said, "Yes, you are General Ross, artillery commander," and with that up came the Assistant Division Commander, General Harlan Hartness. We started again to explain the reason, when up came Division Commander General Paul, asking what was going on.

I started again to explain and all at once all three generals saluted and I said to myself "Boy, they finally recognized my position." But that was a split second as behind me was General Manton S. Eddy, who said, "Carry on. Captain, and gentlemen, I want to see you."

So those are my General Manton S. Eddy stories and I will never forget either one.

MOVING TO WERBOMONT, BELGIUM

Eddie Arn
30th Infantry Division, 119th Infantry Regiment, F Company

The whole move to our de-trucking point, near Aywaille, Belgium couldn't have been more than 100 miles. Nevertheless, it took all night.

We must have moved around Aachen in some way because I don't recall going through that battered city. The roads were clogged with fleeing civilians, military vehicles, and frantic GIs of all ranks and types... heading away from Belgium or wherever.

"Axis Sally" (from Berlin) announced on my vehicle's radio that the "fanatical 30th Division... Roosevelt's SS Troops... is going to try to rescue the First Army." We would hold up for minutes on end. Without the use of headlights, the chaos was simply augmented. Truly, a memorable night. My frayed nerves screamed.

At any rate, cold, stiff Fox Company stalwarts climbed out of the trucks at day light and we proceeded on foot. I would be dishonest with anybody who might read this narrative if I indicated that I knew where we were... for I didn't. I simply formed a "column of ducks" and headed down "a road." My compass indicated that we were proceeding south. To me, that was as good a direction as any.

The CO of Fox Company wasn't about to share his concern with anybody. Outwardly, he attempted to maintain an assured confidence but at the same time he hoped that someone would come along soon and inform him as to what he was supposed to do and where. The road took a southeasterly direction.

During that memorable December morning (I have no idea how far we had moved down that highway) our battalion commander's jeep roared up. Spreading his map on the hood of his jeep he pointed to a spot. "Arn, here is where you are." He indicated that we were south of the Ambleve River and were moving toward a place called Werbomont, on the Liege-Bastogne Highway...

...at this point my memoirs are pretty frank and I shall not refer to my actual wording at all for a variety of reasons. Suffice it to say, my Battalion CO indicated where he wanted me to be by nightfall. He did not tolerate arguments and I gave him none but I made up my own mind as to what I would try to do if possible. The CO did say that "there is evidence that there is a counter-offensive underway of considerable strength and we must contain it fast! Now... move!" And his jeep scurried away.

The CO had given me a beat-up map of sorts... thank goodness. I located a town called Chevron, east of Werbomont about eight miles. If we were lucky, I hoped to reach Chevron by nightfall. Bear in mind that I had no idea what friendly elements might be on either of my flanks—if any at all. I noted that the road we were on seemed to follow a very small river named Grand Mont Rivulet, at a lower level and to our right flank. Wooded hillside sloped down to the edge of the road on our left and to the tiny stream's banks on the other side. It was a damned scary situation and I had forbidding thoughts as to what might be in store for my rifle company.

I placed a small squad of men from Ken Austin's third platoon out ahead of our column by several hundred yards. We related to the squad leader by walkie-talkie. The idea was to expose only a few people when a contact with the Krauts would come about.

It must be remembered that the whereabouts of the enemy were completely unknown to me or to anybody else.

I can't recall anything happening in Werbomont. Neither did we find any Americans there. I felt very, very lonely—if that's the word for it. Lonely, I guess, in a military sense.

A radio message from Battalion HQ assured me that Werbomont would be "occupied by Americans soon" and to "get the hell moving."

Without knowing it at the time, it is now clearly evident, Fox Company was way "out on a limb" and ahead of all other people in the Second Battalion. The Third Battalion was supposed to be in Stoumont, about four miles northeast on the north bank of the Ambleve but nobody really could give me any accurate information.

A directional change was now made by our lead squad. It had reached a point on the main road where it and the Grand Mont Rivulet turned south. The squad leader stayed on the main road. Had we taken a secondary road due east, we would have reached Chevron in short order. With as little information as he had, I would have followed the main road also but that squad leader's decision may have altered F Company's history a bit as we shall soon see.

Operating on Arn's schedule—not battalion's—and without incident so far, Austin's people reached one or two buildings on the western edge of what was to prove to be a "wide spot in the road" called Neufmoulin where the Grand Mont Rivulet joined Lienne Creek.

Night had fallen and I was still back down that highway in the middle of the column. There were two or three sharp curves in the road between me and the hamlet. I had no way of viewing the place properly in the gloom of the night. Caution was the word.

By runner, I ordered Austin to cease forward movement and set up a road block. I also ordered the machine gun section forward and under Austin's control. Austin's bazooka man was there too. My valiant and able Third Platoon Leader was to let me know when I could move the rest of the company into Neufmoulin. I was not about to commit all my people into a crowded situation without knowing more about our situation. Austin's advice was awaited. With men relaxed, as only GI's could relax, all along the highway, I strained my ears for enemy movement in the woods above and below the road... on our flanks.

Battalion HQ, of course, was continually screaming over the SCR to keep moving. I could easily have wrung some rear echelon necks—given some time—which I didn't have. I would do this "my way." My radio man, Sgt. Alex Harvey, grinned—as always—with my stubborn maneuvering with Battalion.

I remind the reader that it was now very dark. One could scarcely see beyond his nose. I could hear that small stream's gurgling down below me. Where was the enemy? Did they have infantry in those thick woods? I suddenly decided to request a tank destroyer from Bn. To this day, I don't know why I made that decision. I was assured that one was on the way. What disposal should I make of my men still down the road behind me and in front of me? Why doesn't Austin get on the stick?

Suddenly, Austin was on his walkie talkie, "Jesus Christ, sir... there are tanks... I think... moving toward us from the east." I could hear the clanking sound also. "What should I do?" queried an anxious platoon leader.

"Do you think they have any idea that you are where you are?"

"No, sir, I think they're coming on in... in the dark... and just firing away!"

"Good! Don't expose your position! Stay under cover! Hold your fire. I have asked for a TD and Bn. assures me it is on its way. If the Krauts come on through maybe we can get a crack at their lead tank. Meanwhile, Ken, I'll order Beaudoin's platoon (the same Ray Beaudoin, who as a Pfc had brought me forward to Fox Company—five months before—in Normandy and who was now a battlefield-promoted Second Lieutenant (by me) in command of our Second Platoon) up on the high ground above this rat hole and see what he can do from there in support or in a flanking movement."

I sent Ray and his men on their way. Thank God, they knew how to move in the dark for they had done so many times before.

We could hear distinctly now the mumble and clank of the Kraut vehicles. They had ceased firing apparently assuming there was no resistance.

But another sound was more welcome... from our rear.

It was an American TD. I stepped up on the highway. The commander "unbuttoned." I gave him the situation as best I could. The first of two or three curves in the highway was just ahead of where I had established the company CP by the side of the road.

"Take a position on this side of that first curve," I yelled. "Shut your motor off and when the lead tank, which we're letting through, rounds that curve... let him have it."

I had not developed too much faith in tank destroyers because, generally not always, they had a tendency to hold back and be a bit timid. They were also very vulnerable to enemy fire... more so than conventional tanks which might explain their attitude in part.

From the sound... I couldn't see very well in the dark... and with Austin following orders... a Kraut vehicle lumbered around that last curve. At least I surmised it had and then I knew it had for the TD's muzzle blast was terrific and nearly blinded me as I tumbled partway down the slope on my side and almost into the Grand Mont Rivulet.

It was a German half-track and not a tank and the TD's shell had destroyed it completely thus blocking the road perfectly. I couldn't have asked for anything more efficient and I could have kissed that TD commander which I am sure he wouldn't have appreciated at all.

Within seconds I heard a blast from one of the company's bazookas in Neufmoulin. And then another mingled with M-1 small arms fire, etc. I discovered later than one of Beaudoin's bazooka men, Pfc. Mason Armstrong, had worked his way from the high ground north of the town into the second story of a residence and had fired down on two Kraut half-tracks... knocking out both.

Austin's and Beaudoin's men could be heard from above and on the left in Neufmoulin. Quickly, I decided that this was an advance enemy recon unit without too much support for the small engagement was soon over. At any rate, surviving vehicles could be heard on the other side of the Lienne withdrawing to the east, evidently assuming that they had bumped into a position of some strength.

I ordered Austin and Beaudoin to establish a road block at the eastern edge of Neufmoulin beyond the bridge over the junction of the Grand Mont Rivulet and Lienne Creek. At dawn both of these capable, veteran officers reported back to me that the block was established.

Then something of further note happened and I shall never forget it either.

Just as I was preparing to move into Neufmoulin with the remainder of Fox Company, I heard a jeep coming down the highway behind me. I nearly fell down into the river when the jeep pulled up and a tall, lean paratroop officer leaped out with two stars showing on his helmet.

"Who's in command here?"

"I am, sir, Lt. Arn, F Company, 119th Regiment, 30th Division... at your service."

"I'm Jim Gavin of the 82nd Airborne Division" and he waved away my salute with a grin. "Looks to me, Lt., like you've had quite a night of it here."

"Yes, sir, we have but my men have now secured the position and we are about to complete its occupation."

"Good, you'll be pleased to know that my people will be relieving you here and moving through your positions shortly. We're on the ground now in this emergency. I'll go on up ahead and have a look around if that's all right with you, Lt."

"Yes sir!" I responded with wide-eyed admiration.

Major General James Gavin, CO of the entire and very famous 82nd Airborne Division, out ahead of the whole division with a jeep and a driver!

I was dumfounded and so were my men there with me.

I still recall, with amusement, Austin's voice on the WT—as I hadn't contacted him as yet—"Sir, I wish to suggest that you have me relieved. I'm going nuts. There's a two star general coming into town in a jeep. I can't believe it. Do you think I've had it?"

"No, Ken," I assured my able platoon leader, "you're okay. That's General Gavin of the 82nd Airborne. Be sure and give him the VIP treatment although he strikes me as a guy who doesn't desire that sort of attention at all."

I still recall this little confrontation in Neufmoulin with great pride... pride in the superb quality of my people. Our little, under-strength rifle company, way out ahead of anyone else in the battalion had actually halted—at least in our sector—the westward push of a forward element of the enemy.

I was to find out later that said "forward enemy" was a part of famous SS Oberstrumbannfuhrer Joachim Peiper's 1st SS Division of Sepp Dietrich's Sixth Panzer Army. No more formidable or capable leader could be found in the entire German counter-offensive!

His immediate objective was Werbomont and from there to the Meuse River. At least one of his units never made it and it took F Company, in an exposed, all-alone, forward position to get the job done.

A most meaningful and poignant memory for an aging CO.

AT BASTOGNE: THE FIRST TANK BATTLE
DECEMBER 16–23, 1944

Dustin M. Aughenbaugh
10th Armored Division, Combat Command B,
55th Armored Engineer Battalion, Company C

Company C, 55th Armored Engineer Battalion, Combat Command B, (CCB) 10th Armored Division was part of General Patton's 3rd Army advancing in the vicinity of the Saar-Moselle Triangle, prior to the 16th of December 1944. As the divisional engineers, it was our job, with the help of infantry and/or recon units, to see that our armored columns could bypass or breech obstacles in the armored attack; at least that is what I had been trained and taught at the Engineer School at Ft Belvoir, Virginia, and at the 10th Armored Division training at Camp Gordon, Georgia. We held pretty much to that type of action.

During the early afternoon of the 16th of December, 1944, while our tank column was advancing in the Ardennes we were suddenly pulled out of an attack and started moving north toward Luxembourg. That morning we had heard that something big was happening north of our position so sudden changes like this were normal. I asked the lieutenant, tank commander, what was happening; he replied, "Don't know, we were just ordered to move north; it looks like we are heading to Luxembourg." He suggested I go back to the half-track and take it easy for a while. Generally, one or two of us engineers rode with the lead tanks during an advance, besides I felt a hell of a lot safer up there than in the half-track. We traveled the rest of the day and all night with an occasional stop along the way, and to add to the problem, it was a bitter cold and snowy day.

We arrived in the Bastogne area on December 17th, about 36 hours before the main elements of the 101st Airborne began to arrive on December 19th. Combat Command B, commanded by Col. Roberts, consisted of three tank columns (totaling about 70 tanks, 3,500 men with about 18 units of the 609th Tank Destroyer Battalion, our own mobile artillery, armored infantry, AAA and other supporting units). As I understand, when the 101st Airborne arrived on December 19th, CCB was then attached to Gen. McAuliffe's command of the 101st Airborne.

Our armored column, known as Desobry's Column, took up positions and prepared to defend the approaches to Noville which was about 3 miles (or more) north of Bastogne. The other two columns, known as Cherry and O'Karc, took up offensive positions to the east at Longvilly and Wardin. This way we established an MLD for the area and about this same time, enemy tank fire started falling near our positions. You could see the German tanks moving over the ridge through the fog or blowing snow. Fortunately, they were either Mark 4s or Panthers, but you had to keep your head down and on that frozen ground it was difficult. Our TDs with their "76" rifles did a very accurate job that first day. As I remember, with high German initial losses, it forced them to withdraw back over the ridge. I did not see many enemy ground troops with their armor in that attack; however, the Krauts were laying down a lot of machine gun and small arms fire which made preparing the MLD almost impossible. Most of our work was done after dark on the night of the 17th of December. I was a demolition man, so at night we kept busy with preparing obstacles and mostly, laying mines all of which made life a little exciting. Our 6 lb. mines were so ineffective they couldn't blow dirt off of the enemy tank tracks, so we, engineers and few armored infantry, would generally try to stack the mines or add 6 lbs. or more of additional TNT to the mine to make them as effective as the Krauts telemines, that is if we had time to dig the holes or rig them with prima cord.

On December 19th, our (Desobry's) tank column pulled back west of Noville to form part of the Bastogne circle on the north and east side of Bastogne. In the process of withdrawing to the MLD, Lt. Col. Desobry with most of the command post were wounded and taken prisoner. About this same time the men of the 101st were moving in with our tank teams to help secure the circle around Bastogne. It was years later that I learned that at the same time, CCB of the 9th Armored Division was providing armor on the west and south sides of the Bastogne Circle. To me, it was just another battle in another area. I did not know I was in Belgium let alone the town name which meant nothing to me; of course, later on, while in the hospital, I heard about this big battle of the war and I didn't know I was even involved.

I had been wounded by machine gun fire in early November during the Metz offensive, and after escaping from the convalescent hospital, I managed to return to my unit just two weeks prior to the Bulge. Then on the night of December 20th I was wounded with shrapnel, so I remember very little of the battle conditions after that night; but, I do remember that first clear day when all of our planes were overhead making us feel good.

Gen. McAuliffe later paid us a great compliment when he said, "It always seems regrettable to me that CCB of the 10th Armored Division didn't get the credit it deserved in the Battle of Bastogne. The 10th Armored Division was in there the day before we were and had some very hard fighting. We would never have been able to get into Bastogne if it had not been for the defensive fighting... of the 10th Armored Division."

A SOLDIER AND A PERFECT STRANGER
AND A DAY IN HISTORY THAT WILL LIVE FOREVER!

J. David Bailey
106th Infantry Division, 422nd Infantry Regiment

It was 60 years ago on December 2004 that my regiment of the 106th Infantry Division was plundered in the Battle of the Bulge. As one of the few survivors of 5,000 men of the 422nd Infantry Regiment, I had lost directions as I wandered into a small Belgium village called Anthisnes (Providence of Liege.)

Being homeless, without rations and needing shelter, it was only natural to seek help in this remote European village in friendly territory. I knocked on the closest entry I could find. On that December morning during the Christmas season, a young nineteen-year-old Belgian girl named Adele Orban opened her door and heart to me. Indeed, I truly believe that in this life someone guides and watches over us, and their protective spirit is "always" present.

Yes, it was my guardian angel who had pre-arranged this unusual encounter between David and Adele. We both came from two separate worlds; however, we did indeed share a mutual concern—the ravages of war! Our friendship has lasted over half a century and with such a strong bond we consider ourselves now to be more like brother and sister.

As a young soldier I had the memorable experience of participating in the most decisive battle on the western front during World War II. Also, I was able to share that reality with my new Belgian friends, recently liberated from German hands by our own Army. It was a remarkable experience that happened during my lifetime and a reminder that indeed truth sometimes can be stranger than fiction!

The Battle of the Bulge lasted longer than any battle in our nation's history with the largest number of casualties. The official historian of the U.S. Army, Charles MacDonald, stated that it was the greatest battle in American history.

America's World War II generation did save the world, not for glory, not for honor, and not for lasting tribute. For my buddies who did not return they deserve our blessings.

NIGHT PATROL

Samuel W. Ballinger
26th Infantry Division, 328th Infantry Regiment, Company E

My story begins during the frigid, snowy days in early December 1944 when I was a 23-year-old Corporal whose outfit was billeted in the University City of Metz in southeast France, which is about halfway between Luxembourg and the City of Nancy, also located in France. As a member of General Patton's Third Army, 26th Infantry Division, 328th Regiment, Company E, my outfit was taking special training to crack through the German Siegfried Line. The famed 26th Division, called the Yankee Division, was a very well respected battle-hardened Division.

On December 16, 1944 about seventy-five (75) miles north of Metz the Germans launched a major surprise attack. The German strategy was to separate the Americans in the South and the other allied armies in the North. Their primary target was to take the busy allied supply port at Antwerp. This was of course Hitler's last desperate attempt. The well-trained and heavily armed Panzer divisions advanced and created a Bulge in our lines as they had pushed their way to Bastogne, Belgium.

The 26th Infantry Division, Yankee Division, learned on the night of December 19th that it was going to take part in what future historians would probably describe as one of the most important strategic maneuvers of Gen George S. Patton Jr.'s Third U.S. Army. We moved from the area of Metz and the Saar basin to the virtually unprotected front being opened by the new German counter-attack at the north around Bastogne and the Sure River. It was a lightning-like maneuver and we moved so quickly that we even took a truckload of German POWs. There simply wasn't time to dispose of them through channels, before taking off.

The cloudy weather actually helped. If the Germans had air out, they would have slaughtered the long bumper-to-bumper troop movement. MPs kept the heavy traffic moving. The speed paid off. The Third Army reached its new assembly areas less than 24 hours later and went into action against the surprised Germans within the next two days. General Patton's Third Army stopped the enemy advance and relieved the exhausted American Forces that were defending the critical crossroads at the besieged city of Bastogne. The 101st Airborne Division that defended the city was completely surrounded.

My outfit had arrived at an area between Arlon, Belgium and the small village of Eschdorf, Luxembourg. My little world so to speak was the fox-hole of an infantryman. I recall how the engineers came to our assistance and set off quarter pound blocks of TNT to break open the ground so we could dig foxholes. My story took place near a small village called Eschdorf, Luxembourg where my outfit was located. Luxembourg is a small country situated just southeast of Belgium; it's on the German border, only a dot on the map, but a memory in my heart that has haunted me for over sixty years.

On December 22nd or 23rd, two or three days before Christmas Day, I was on a night patrol to locate the enemy. The Germans also had their own patrols. The night was dark, dreary and extremely cold. The frozen snow responded with a crunch as we worked our way through the midnight darkness. All patrols were supposed to be led by an officer, usually a Lieutenant; however, many officers had become casualties and replacements seldom arrived. The night patrol that horrendous night consisted of a Staff Sergeant, a Corporal, (Sam Ballinger), and a PFC (Bill Elgrim). I had been in the front line for sixty-eight straight days and had only known two Lieutenants in my Company E. The first one was killed when a sniper shot him right in the Gold Bar on his helmet. The second just disappeared!

We proceeded to search for and locate the enemy, not to engage them.

The frigid night cut through our clothing and our feet and hands were almost numb. The M1 rifle was heavy enough; but carrying it felt like a ton. Keeping our rifles and equipment quiet during the windy and swirling snow became an awesome problem. An occasional moonbeam threatened to reveal our omniscient presence; at times shadows were all around us adding to their fearsome experience. Whose shadows, was the big question? We could only see silhouettes. Our overcoats, gloves and regular garrison army shoes and leggings barely did the job. We did not have the combat boots that many of the GI's in the rear echelon had. At this point we had not been re-supplied. So on we went with poor equipment, only an M1 rifle and one hand grenade each. As we carefully maneuvered through the evergreen trees, the thought of Christmas and a tree at home became embraced in my thoughts. It was quickly suppressed as the night sounds filled the brain. The frigid weather can do many things; it absolutely disgusted me. My feet and hands became so very cold. I knew that I had better shake the "I'll be home for Christmas," thoughts. Was my family thinking about me amid their Christmas decorations? Did he survive? Is he living in some bombed out city? Where is he?

After we had advanced beyond the evergreens, we went down and then up a steep ravine that had a frozen ditch at the bottom. That really tired us. We were only in our first thirty minutes of the patrol and we all felt the fatigue. We trudged on until we came to a narrow road that was lined with European type concrete utility poles. They served as our landmarks because everything was just all white or black. We were unable to make out any details or features. We only knew where we were by reading road signs; no one could tell us. After we followed the utility poles for about 45 minutes, we heard a loud vehicle approaching us from behind and coming around a curve in the road. Instinctively we dove into the roadside ditch and we were covered with snow, inside and out. We noticed the cross on the enemy half-track as it roared by.

We were not spotted. The ditch was deep and covered with wintered shrubs; they stopped our fall. After some time, we finally got up and now we were really cold because the snow had fallen down our backs, but we had to continue.

We shook with shivers from the cold and fear and checked our weapons.

We realized that the enemy half-track was most probably on patrol the same as they.

When we got back onto the road and after a few more miles, we heard another vehicle approaching. Now there was no ditch to dive into so we ran as fast as we could through the heavy snow, across a small field and into the forest. This wasn't a good night! Wow, good heavens, it was like diving into a hornet's nest. All of a sudden it seemed like the whole damned German army was camped there. The sharp, snapping sounds of bullets started flying everywhere. We got separated and ran farther into the woods, back toward our lines. As we ran, we stumbled and smashed into trees as the incessant fire continued. Wild enemy bullets and grenades snapped off the snow that covered the evergreen branches above our heads. While we were in the hollow, we knew that the Germans were on both sides of us, with a ridge between us.

The firing continued. Bullets were whizzing by just over our heads. "I didn't even have time to think that we had found the enemy and we had done our job", he said. Having been separated from his Staff Sergeant and PFC Bill Elgrim, I finally came to an opening in the forest when I saw a dark form of a man with his rifle pointed in his direction. I quickly raised my rifle and it seems that the two of us were frozen in this position. We didn't know if we were friend or foe. I finally noticed the outline of an American helmet and then called out "Elgrim." An equally scared voice answered, "Ballinger," what a relief! The sight of his rifle pointed at me, to this day often keeps me awake.

Apparently my Sergeant had run into the woods first. Most probably the Sergeant thought himself to be a bigger target. It's only a guess; in any event he never appeared again. Our only conclusion was that the Sergeant was now among the missing in action. We never heard of him again. At this point, now we were all fired up with adrenalin. It's strange how the body chemistry can cause a person to rise to an occasion. All of a sudden we felt warm; yet we still shivered. We trudged along the several miles back to our CP. Upon our arrival we were cold, relieved, hungry, exhausted and our feet were freezing. We now knew where the enemy was and our ranking officers could plan a strategy of attack or defend ourselves, the patrol had been a success!

Subsequent to receiving our reconnaissance information, the officers' plan of attack was initiated. We did not rest long. The very next night we attacked the village of Eschdorf which was another almost fatal time for me in this Bulge Campaign. Later, the village of Bar-le-Duc a few miles southeast of Metz became my new home. I was in an American Hospital with frozen feet.

BUGLE BOY OF COMPANY B
A DECEMBER SURPRISE!

William H. Barker
99th Infantry Division, 324th Engineer Combat Battalion, Company B

On December 16 my assignment was "kitchen police." At 4:00 a.m., I am assisting the cooks preparing our breakfast. The menu was pancakes, syrup, sausage and coffee. Breakfast was all set up in the courtyard of our farm-house ready to receive our company of 200 men. Suddenly at 5:25 a.m., along a 30-mile front, we encountered an intense two-hour barrage of all caliber of artillery and mortar fire, which saturated the troops on the line. At first we thought it was our artillery dueling with the enemy. Without breakfast, all personnel of Company B (cooks, drivers, specialists, etc.), with the exception of a handful of us, were immediately trucked northeast of Krinkelt to a place called Rath Hill. The 324th Engineer Combat Battalion (absent Company C) is now operating as an infantry battalion taking or-ders from the regimental commander. Our Headquarters Company along with Company A joined us in the defense of Rath Hill. Stripped of all arms including our truck-mounted 30 and 50 caliber machine guns, the com-pany's trucks and drivers rejoined my small group at Bullingen. At least we got breakfast while dodging the incoming artillery. Our refuge is the farmhouse cellar when needed; however, dug foxholes were ready if we had to defend ourselves. Our arms consisted of carbines and rifles with limited ammunition. All the good stuff, such as bazooka, explosives and machine guns, are with the men defending Rath Hill.

On December 13 to 15, our 395th Regimental Combat Team, attached to the 2nd Infantry Division, went on the offensive toward the Roer River Dams. Although successful at penetrating the Siegfried Line and gaining its immediate objectives, the assault of the SS Sixth Panzer Army and the Fifteenth German Army on the 99th Division's 22 mile front, the 2nd Infantry Division and our 395th Regimental Combat Team canceled its offensive and reverted to defense of the Bulge north shoulder.

The Bulge is the result of enemy penetration further south directly west of the Schnee Eifel (the Eifel was the principal staging area for German forces before the December 16 offensive). The Rath Hill defense by the combat engineers played an important advantage as the 395th Regimental Combat Team and 2nd Infantry Division needed the road network to get in its defensive position on Elsenborn Ridge. Company C of the 324th Combat Engineers rejoined our defense line at Rath Hill until all could safely take up their respective positions on the main Elsenborn Ridge line. During the initial three-day period of the German offensive, enemy losses exceeded 400 killed as a result of maniac charges against the engineer battalion's defenses, the northern shoulder of the Bulge at the Elsenborn Ridge, held forcing the Germans southwesterly. With their timetable severely disrupted, the enemy abandoned the direct route to strike toward the Meuse River and on to Brussels and Antwerp with the Sixth SS Panzer Army on the right driving through to Liege and the Fifth Panzer Army thrusting toward Namur.

Meanwhile, my small group spent the night of December 16 in the farmhouse at Bullingen. During the night, an enemy tank stopped at a road junction some 100 yards away from our farmhouse. They stopped, looked at the road signs, carried on a brief conversation and proceeded directly on the Bullingen-Butgenbach highway. This roadway passed through the center of Bullingen in a northeasterly direction then veered westward toward Butgenbach. After reporting the event we took refuge in the farmhouse cellar remaining quiet since we lacked communications or firepower to resist. More tanks passed during the night as we met some of them the following morning, December 17. At daybreak, we noticed enemy infantry crossing open fields near our farmhouse. Within a five minute period, we were ordered to load everything on our several vehicles. Most trucks were hauling trailers.

We tossed duffel bags of company personnel on anything that would hold them. My duffel bag, with my trusty plastic bugle and a watch given to me by my parents at my high school graduation, found its way onto one of our trailers. In the rush, my last trip was to the kitchen area. I selected a #10 tin can that had no markings. Lucky for me, I tossed the can on the truck I occupied as we sped off in the direction of Butgenbach while under artillery fire and menaced by the approaching infantry. Our immediate task was to keep our vehicles and other valuable items from the enemy rather than attempt to defend Bullingen.

It is about 7:00 a.m., when we sped out of Bullingen on December 17. After going about three miles toward Dom Butgenbach, we encountered at least two Tiger tanks blocking our way on the Bullingen-Butgenbach highway. The narrow road circled around very hilly terrain with sharp curves, steep inclines and embankments making a rapid turnaround almost impossible. On the right edge of the highway, mature trees hampered our maneuvers. Turning around was very tricky as most trucks were pulling trailers. The decision to dump all trailers by pushing them down the steep embankment eased our turnaround situation. Of course, I lost all of my belongings (and bugle) as they were in my duffel bag and on one of the trailers. We ignored the snow and very cold weather since our column was constantly under fire. The curvature of the hill provided some shelter from parts of the hostile action. All trucks and jeeps made the turnaround and we sped off this time in the direction of Bullingen.

As we approached Bullingen from the west our convoy took the same northeasterly Bullingen-Krinkelt highway our trucks used the day before. Not certain what we would find, we stopped at the Town of Wirtzfeld. Insane as it may seem, I patrol a small bridge with but a few rounds of ammunition while the lieutenant seeks instructions. When the convoy returns, we rejoin my company defending Rath Hill northeast of Krinkelt-Rocherath area. After spending a few hours on the front lines with our engineer company on December 17, our group and its vehicles assemble on an open hillside about 1,500 yards behind the engineers' defensive positions on Elsenborn Ridge. The engineer battalion abandoned Rath Hill and withdrew to its final defensive

Elsenborn Ridge position once all elements of the 395th Regimental Combat Team and 2nd Infantry Division were in place to defend the north shoulder of the Bulge on Elsenborn Ridge. The 1st Infantry Division secured the right flank of the 99th and 2nd Infantry Divisions and the Town of Butgenbach. This placement completes the north shoulder defense line that thwarted the German campaign toward Antwerp.

The Christmas season of 1944 was unique for all of us. The cold and snow only added to the drama. The main assignment consisted of destroying the vehicles, rendering them useless to the enemy should that be necessary. The vehicles and equipment are booby-trapped and explosives set, except for a few jeeps for our get-away. The division chaplain's jeep is my assignment. The defense lines held. Life slipped into a routine quickly. Constant artillery firing is deafening. The nights were ablaze with flashes from these guns. We feel secure with all this activity. The cold, lack of sleep, frost bite and army rations brought visions of past Christmases. A warm fire, great feasts, family and singing in worship are dreams that kept our spirits high.

On Christmas Day, I remembered that I saved that #10 tin can of 'something.' After many searches, I found the can and we held a ritual opening. To all of our amazement, it was a can of peanut butter! A great treat for all of us. It makes good covering on the army K-ration biscuits or for eating just from the can. A few did not like peanut butter leaving more for the rest of us. It took a while for supplies to catch up with our needs. The peanut butter caper paid off handsomely. It lasted to New Year's Day! We all pooled our money and bought spirits from local Belgian farmers. Most of these spirits went to our company on the front line.

The German threat and offensive to Antwerp ended when the U.S. Third Army under General George Patton broke through to Bastogne on Christmas Day.

The January, 1945, allied offensive eliminated the Bulge and pressed ahead toward the Rhineland. During this period, the 99th Division remained in the Belgium Ardennes to be re-equipped, rested and our engineer battalion resumed its normal function of support for its infantry regiments. We spent many more days building log huts and roads for a rest area.

According to our Commanding General Walter E. Lauer, the engineers lost over 100 officers and men, about 15 percent of its normal strength. In my little group, we all stayed throughout the Battle of the Bulge, although suffering from frostbite, sleep and hunger. At home, little was reported about the north shoulder as it was classified a 'secret' and not released until long after the battle. Luckily, I won a three-day pass to Paris, France, just before the 99th Infantry Division resumed its drive toward the Rhine River.

Once I understood the enormity of the situation that faced us on December 16 and 17 of 1944, the youthful, carefree innocence of a 19-year-old Indiana lad disappeared; my life was forever changed.

Rumors often circulated about other units' actions; they meant little to me until faced with our own possible capture or destruction. Depending on others if taken lightly can put you in a bind. How did such a massive force assemble without being detected by the Allies? The intelligence gathering information we sent to higher headquarters is ignored because of their preconceived beliefs and overconfidence. Why would the enemy attack through such difficult terrain? History shows it is often the route of invaders.

OUR FIRST CLOSE-UP ENCOUNTER

Armand F. Boisseau
172nd/941st Field Artillery Battalions

I would like to share my small story with you and the rest of our Bulge veterans. Hopefully I'll hear from other veterans who were there, and may know more about my battalion's history. After 60 years my memory is no longer what it used to be. My son has researched as much as he could with some success but we believe there's more to the unit's history. This much we do know, the 1st Battalion, 941st Field Artillery, was built from the 172nd Field Artillery Regiment and the 773rd Field Artillery Battalion was built of elements from both the 172nd and the 941st.

It all started when our outfit was assigned to the 1st Army, V Corps, V Corps Artillery, 406th Field Artillery Group, 30th Division Artillery serving in the 1st Battalion, Headquarters Battery, 941st Field Artillery (heavy), commanded by Lt. Col. John F. Ahem.

We were ordered out to advance on the German positions marshaling along the Belgium-German border, in direct support of the 38th Cavalry Reconnaissance Squadron (mechz) and advanced units of the 30th Infantry Division from 16 to 21 December 1944. We set up firing positions in the vicinity of towns called Venwegen, Monschau, Eupen, Hofen, Niveze, Longfaye, Hockai, and Cockaifagne. Our call sign was "Vineyard," and I was assigned to Headquarters Battery as forward lineman and assistant switchboard operator on the wire detail. From time to time we would set up OPs and assist after-action artillery surveying teams.

G2 HQ had advised the battalion commanders of the (186th, 941st and 955th) to take heed about enemy infiltrations. We're told some specialized English-speaking Germans were dressed as American MPs and regular GIs disrupting communications and sabotaging roadways. The Ardennes was so heavily rugged it was not well suited for towing 155s and the new 4.5" guns. Everywhere we went there were large fields of ice/snow, cold/freezing rain and thick sticking mud. We all endured the cold—first it would snow then snow again. It seemed never to stop for days on end. To this day, cold weather does not set well with me.

We all hoped this campaign would be over by Christmas. I had just spent my 24th birthday anniversary (December) with two buddies huddled underneath a burned out, destroyed truck in the freezing snow/rain hoping to win the war soon and go home. It was not to be; the Germans launched their major offensive against the allies early 16 December 1944 and hit us hard.

There was a full scale assault against our own positions, temporarily repulsed by forward elements of the 38th Calvary, some ack-ack guns, a few 105s. It gave the rest of the battalion time to advance in the opposite direction, to regroup and return fire, covering the retreat of the forward elements that were holding the line. Not sure about the 186th and the 955th Field Artillery Battalions—where they were at this time I do not know. In the Ardennes

Forest of Belgium we learned the Germans broke through many thinly held American lines and drove toward the English Channel heading for the Town/Port of Antwerp nearly destroying two American divisions in their path.

The fighting was fierce, our battalion would constantly move out, set-up firing positions, discharge hundreds of rounds, move out, set-up and fire again. This would go on day in and day out for two-three weeks without a warm break. The battalion commander would remind us from time to time to think about the infantry and armored units up on the front lines slugging it out with German tanks and elite well trained mechanized infantry, saying, "If you think you got it bad, think about the boys up front." The colonel was a good man. We all liked him a lot.

Interestingly enough, after reading the story about the 146th Engineer Combat Battalion in the August 2004 issue of *The Bulge Bugle* newsletter, we too were tasked with augmenting some men from the 941st Field Artillery to the 38th Cavalry Reconnaissance Squadron (Mechz). It was a successful attempt to block and delay the advance of the ruthless Col. Peiper's 1st SS Panzer Division and advanced elements of the 326 Volksgrenadiers. Two of the 15 men who were out of Services Battery were from my hometown—Homer Hewitt and George Landry, of Manchester, New Hampshire. We learned they all earned the "Distinguished Service Badge" for their actions. Once again word came down that it was Col. Pipier's forces that had intercepted and captured a large group of U.S. soldiers, most of whom were artillerymen driving south along with elements of the 7th Armored Division. Under orders they were herded into a large snow-covered meadow and gunned down with machine guns and automatic weapons and left to freeze in the snow.

The men of the wire details out of Headquarters were Henry Plante, Horace Abbercrombie, John Busse, Peter Olean, George Pasqual, Hank Henderson, John Busse, Knee-high and myself to name just a few who were under supportive vigilance of Camile Cevalier, Harvey Lessard, Lester Bloom and Ralph Hooper. We were always under constant threat of German snipers, land mines and booby traps. Each time we were sent out to lay or repair broken communications wire, we all had to keep a watchful eye for these personal hazards. I later received the Purple Heart for wounds received when our weapons carrier hit a German AT land mine, killing one and wounding four.

Our first up close encounter with German armor scared the living daylights out of us all. The wire detail was out running new lines up forward to a new OP. Headquarters had marked the roadway (if tracked snow and mud dug out by heavy armor and trucks constitute a road) guiding us to the OP. All morning we would see our small truck and armor convoys passing us while we were working on the wire placement. We later would hear an echoing sound coming from the thick dense forest just ahead and from both sides of us, metal clanking and squealing sounds muffled with low rumbling engine moving around just on the other side of the tree lines. We believed it was our guys moving into defensive positions, perhaps digging in, waiting for others from division. We just kept on working. It was snowing cold, wet and muddy.

We were taking a quick smoke break while heating up a couple of cans of beans (we would place them on the exhaust manifold of our running truck). Then, we heard heavy artillery and mortar barrages. Next came machine gun and rifle fire. It got closer and closer—still, we were unaware of the danger we were in. One of the guys said, "Armand, we should saddle-up and get out of here." Good idea! As we started to load our tools into the truck, we turned to the tree line and saw GIs running out from the forest slipping, tripping and falling, running as fast as they could, howling at the top of their lungs, "Tanks, German Tanks!"

This was the first time we saw German Tanks in action; what we saw earlier were burned and destroyed hulks of either Mark II or III Panzers, but here we would learn were the heavy Mark V Panthers and Mark VI Tigers. They were the biggest armored machines we've ever seen, cannons blasting machine guns firing crashing through the tree lines. Armed only with side arms and carbines we were no match for what was heading our way, so we did the next and only best thing...bug the hell out!! No time to pick up, dropped everything, even left the truck running in place. (We had a utility trailer and extra spools of wire hanging off of both). We finally made Headquarters and reported what happened, then learned that the Germans had broken through our lines and were pushing us back.

The whole battalion started bugging out, jeeps, weapons carriers, 6x6s, M3 Half-tracks towing 105s and trailers, M5 High-Speed tractors towing big boys the 155s and the new 4.5" gums. Ack-Ack gun crews, ambulances, medics, and maintenance and service personnel. MPs directing traffic, security teams setting up machine gun and mortar emplacements (serving as a first line of defense) against the advancing Germans. It didn't appear to be chaos, more like "well orchestrated" confusion, everybody had a job to do and that's what we were doing. The Battalion had trained for this State-side while on field maneuvers in Florida, Mississippi, Louisiana, Texas and desert training in southern California at Camp Iron Mountain.

Once the Battalion regrouped, set up new firing positions, posted heavy security, new Ops and informed Division, we were ready for fire missions. Orders to fire came, the 941st had three batteries four guns each—(12) guns total let loose with such a tremendous explosion of fire and defending thunder it felt like the earth around us was coming apart at the seams; the roar of these guns echoed for many miles around. I can't say, let alone know, what damage we did, but this is for sure: (1) we blasted the Germans advancement three times harder than what they dished out to us, and (2) we made plenty of foxholes for our own GIs to fight out of.

An after action report from S2 revealed the 941st field artillery had expended over 15,300 rounds into the advancing Germans for the month of December 1944 with only four battle casualties. No idea what the other two Battalions (186th and the 955th) had also fired, but it would be safe to say at least the same if not more. The German army had surely paid dearly for this mistake, and we were very glad to have obliged them with extreme predigests. Within three months (November, December and January) we set up headquarters and firing positions through towns known as Hemmeres, Courtil, Tillet, Venwegen, Mont, Vossenack, Rohren, Wiltzfeld, Rotgen, Honsfeld and Winterscheid. If there were others I've long forgotten their names.

I wish to express my most sincere humble appreciation for being able to serve with the men of the 941st Field Artillery. If not for their courage and dedication, I feel I would not be here alive today writing this letter. For all VBoBs, it's an honor to have served with you. It was a good fight and hopefully, with God's grace, not worth repeating. A special thanks to Harry Plante (deceased) and Horace "Abbie" Abbercrumby of Headquarters Battery—two men who taught me well and became my good friends. I welcome all who can correspond, helping to validate your story—good, bad, or indifferent. Would appreciate hearing from anyone who served in the 187th and 406th Field Artillery Groups as well as the 186th, 941st and 955th Field Artillery Battalions. As we used to say in the Guard, "Load with Cannister."

VIVID MEMORIES

Delbert E. Bordner
26th Infantry Division, 328th Infantry Regiment, Company C

On December 13, 1944, our division was relieved by the 87th Division after two months and seven days of active combat. We moved to Metz, France, for R&R and to get our ranks replenished. I was a 60mm mortar squad leader in Company C's weapons Platoon. I received four men to fill out my five-man squad, as I was the only one that was left when we were relieved.

The R&R didn't last long because on December 20 1944 we were heading north to attack the Bulge.

In late November, 1944, my squad leader, Teddy Witowski, received a battle field commission to 2nd Lieutenant and became our platoon leader. I was promoted to squad leader.

About the same time, another friend, Paul Moize, a rifle squad S/Sgt, received a battle field commission to 2nd Lieutenant, and promoted to a platoon leader.

The first few days of the Bulge were chaotic with fire fights in all directions. Our CO, Capt. Ed Kuligowski, became a POW. Paul Moize, who had just received his battlefield commission, was promoted to 1st Lieutenant and became our CO. All of our original officers had either been killed, wounded, captured, or transferred. In my opinion, the promotion of Paul Moize was one of the best decisions I can recall.

Christmas Eve and Christmas Day I will never forget. The attack started the evening of December 24, 1944, lasted all night, and the town was cleared (Arsdorf, Luxembourg) by about noon on the 25th. I don't know how it was accomplished, but our cooks got a turkey dinner, with all the trimmings, to us Christmas night.

The date of January 9, 1945 was a red letter day for me. That's when my luck ran out.

We were in a thick forest near Wiltz, Luxembourg in deep snow and sub-zero weather. Our 60mm mortars were of no use in the forest, so our three mortar squads became bazooka teams.

Our 328th History Book indicates that on January 9, 1945, the 1st Battalion advanced 1,000 meters against determined enemy resistance—this I don't know.

My bazooka team was attached to the lead rifle platoons. We had possibly moved out about 25 meters when I received a bullet in the neck. A medic administered first aid and I was evacuated. I always remember back at a hospital the surgeon telling me that I was a lucky man because the bullet missed my spine by about 1/2 inch.

Floyd Brown and I were roommates at Boston College in the ASTP. When the program closed, we both ended up in the mortar section of the same platoon of the 328th. We both became squad leaders at the same time. Floyd also had a bazooka team on January 9th. Later in the day, he was severely wounded by artillery shrapnel and nearly lost a leg. He was evacuated back to the States and was hospitalized for over two years.

I was in the hospital and rehab for about two months before I rejoined my company. When I returned Paul Moize was now a captain. He placed me in charge of the mortar section until the war ended.

I left the company in November, 1945. By this time Paul Moize was a major assigned to another battalion. Not bad, staff sergeant to major in about ten months. He was an outstanding leader. It was an honor and privilege to serve with the gallant warriors of the Yankee Division.

BREAKING THE SILENCE

James A. Bowers
18th Infantry Division, Company I

[Being a good neighbor, Bineke Oort helped James A. Bowers put together some of his recollections from WWII and sent them in for our publication. We have excerpted that portion which applies to the Battle of the Bulge.]

By the end of November, regardless of countless losses and all the hardship, the overall picture looked favorable for the Allied Forces. The Germans had been pushed back and taken the important city of Aachen. It was a quiet December on the front. Many Americans were taking a well-deserved rest and recreation. They had been transported back from the front into a Belgium camp and were tired from months of nearly non-stop fighting. It seemed to many that the war was just weeks from being over. But they were wrong. Hitler, in his last gamble and act of desperation, had devised a massive counter offensive to defeat the Allied Forces. The plan was to split the Allies and push through to the North Sea port of Antwerp.

On December 16, the Germans moved in full force to the total surprise of all those on the battlegrounds. They pushed in with parachutists, bombs, tanks and of course with hordes of foot soldiers. What followed was the bloodiest and fiercest battle of the ground war in Europe, later known as "The Battle of the Bulge," a month long fight in Belgium which took the lives of 80,000 American soldiers. More than one million soldiers fought in that battle, half a million Americans and 600,000 Germans.

As far as Jim's personal experiences, although he described the whole war experience as hell, several ordeals stand out. One time there were three days and four nights of continuous walking and fighting in three feet deep snow, without any food. At some point Jim was hit so badly by rifle bullets that he couldn't get up anymore. He fell asleep in the snow. His sergeant, seeing Jim's mess kit on his back riddled with bullet holes, thought Jim was dead. He nudged him with his boot to make sure. Jim stirred and was told to get up and move on, which he did with much difficulty. Miraculously Jim escaped the constant barrage of gun fire. He got shrapnel in his chest but was able to remove them himself. One time a bullet ripped off the shoulder strap of his pack but Jim survived.

While most of his buddies were killed, Jim experienced many miraculous close calls.

There was the time when his Sergeant commanded him to dig his foxhole under a tree. Jim had the intuition not to do that and he dug a few yards away. His sergeant threatened he would be court-marshalled after the war for insubordination, but Jim persisted. Not long after that a bomb shell hit exactly the spot where he had been told to dig. Jim and others prayed every day but he said at moments like that he prayed even harder. Christmas was lonely with Jim spending the day alone in a foxhole. His fellow men were spread out over the snow-covered fields, each one by himself in his hole. The plan was for turkey, but it was not until the next day that someone brought Jim his treat. It was cold and dirty because someone had dropped it. Jim, grinning, said it tasted good anyway.

It was hard not being able to get out of the same clothes. The exception had been Thanksgiving when Jim got a change of clothes. But for the next change he had to wait five months!

BULGE MEMORIES

Nathaniel E. Broadhead
1st Infantry Division, 26th Infantry Regiment, Company F

On Nov. 23 we left the harbor of New York City and headed for London, England. We landed, changed ships to cross the English Channel and arrived in France at Normandy Beach where it was raining so hard. We had to put up our pup tents in the rain. On Dec. 14 we got in boxcars and headed for the front lines, where we heard "Boys, the Battle of the Bulge has broke through and on its way, and we were almost there."

Dec. 23 was my first night in combat. We headed for the front lines, and on that night out in front lines we heard the Germans up on the hill above us cranking their tanks and beginning to get ready to make an attack. We had to go back and inform, and they said, "Boys, jump in that foxhole right over there." So we didn't know that two soldiers had been killed in that foxhole. The German tank was on its way, and it was about 20 yards from our foxhole. Our artillery came and knocked it out. The Germans attacked us all night.

The next morning was Christmas Eve and about 10 a.m. the sergeant crawled up beside our foxhole and said, "We want you to come down back to the barn under the hill." We went down to the barn under the hill and we thought, Boy, we got it made; we were going to be behind the front lines now. But when we got down there, we found out that the two machine gun squads had gotten knocked out that night. We were now meeting with the sergeant who was in charge of the machine gun squad that had been wiped out. He said "boys, you are now my machine gunners but I can't take you up until dark tonight." All day the artillery was falling like rain, and all around us there were cows in the barn, they were moaning and groaning, and the shrapnel was hitting them all day long.

That night about 9 o'clock the sergeant came in and he called out and said, "Nathaniel Broadhead." I wouldn't answer so he called my name again. So then I answered him and he said, "You are now the machine gunner."

I remember during training they said the average life of a machine gunner in combat was a minute and a half. And, here I knew that God himself could take me through it. He brought us up to the front line and put is in a foxhole that was already dug where the machine gun crew was killed. We crawled in the foxhole and began to take turns watching, one hour on and one hour off. We were not sleeping much that night.

Finally, around 2 or 3 o'clock, the sergeant came through and said he was checking the line to see if anybody got killed or wounded or anything. He come up to my foxhole and said he spotted a German patrol coming. He jumped in the foxhole with me, and when the German patrol came by, he killed the six Germans right in front of my eyes. That was my second night in combat. I only knew then that God himself was the only one who could take Nathaniel Broadhead through this terrible fight. But for my country, and for my state, and to remember my people, I was willing to do it.

The next day was Christmas Day. All night we fought in snow that was almost waist deep, sleeping in the foxholes with snow all over you. Stand guard an hour and then you'd have to jump on your old coat to make it get down where you could get back in the foxhole.

That day, Christmas Day, about 8:30 that night they got a chance to bring us up what they call Christmas Dinner, and that night we realized canned stuff was better than chicken and turkey on Christmas Day. For 32 days we stayed in those foxholes and held those lines. The snow was so deep you could hardly move. Finally they told us to move out and so we left the foxholes. Thirty minutes later there was a direct hit in the foxhole we just left. God could have brought us out of it.

December 31 was time to begin to think about making attacks and moving on forward, and they told us we were going to take a town, the next step was taking this town. We began to make the attack. The snow was waist deep almost, you'd be bogging knee-deep in the snow, and we came up on this stream at 3 o'clock in the morning. We had to make a crossing over a small stream, but it was frozen over. As we crossed the stream the ice broke and my snow galoshes filled up with water. We were making an attack so you cannot stop to change socks. From 3:00am until 12 noon I had to walk with my shoes full of water. Three days later I changed my socks and when I began to take my socks off, my toenails wanted to come off with them. But with God's help I could stay in there and fight on.

So we began to make another attack. They told us before we started that this is would be a rough town to take. We had three towns to take before we could get to the large town. We had 200 men when we started and we only had just a group of us, a few of us left. In the rifle squad and my machine gun squad together we had six men left. While we were trying to take this town the Germans began to crossfire on us with two machine guns. The machine guns were cross-firing with tracer bullets. The sergeant looked over— hollered over at us and said, "Boys, you see it like I do. You're either going to get captured or killed. Now you take your choice." If you want to run out, you will be killed; if you stay here, they will capture you." And he said, "Well, if you go for it, I am going." And another one of the boys said he was going, and us three together, we ran and made it out with God's help. The other three boys stayed there, two of the boys were captured and the other was killed. We found him when we went back that night to take the town.

It had been two days and we hadn't had anything to eat, and I felt like I was just about to crack up. I felt so nervous and shaky and weak. We had taken the town that night by the help of some other soldiers. The next morning I felt I've just gone my limit, I can't go no more. All of a sudden, I looked out of the window and here comes a jeep with a sheep trailer behind it loaded down with c-rations. Boy, our hopes got up and boy, we said we got it made now. We were getting something to eat here! Just as the driver jumped out of the jeep and ran in the building, an 88, a big tank shell, hit that trailer load of c-rations. There wasn't one can left. We were so hungry!

We were preparing to take a town, which required a river crossing and this is extremely dangerous because the enemy has all the advantages. I had the machine gun set up ready to go when all of a sudden we looked up at this shell coming. I ducked into my foxhole and left my machine gun setting right on the top of the ground. The machine gun took a direct hit; there was shrapnel everywhere, but I did not receive a scratch.

After crossing this river, we had a factory to take. We finally made it across but we had a big wall to go over and I had a boy who was real short and couldn't jump high. I helped him get over the wall, and when we got over the Germans were everywhere. For about 30 or 40 minutes we were lost, and I remember the password that night, it was "Red Apple." When you met up with somebody you had to have yourself ready to shoot or whatever you had to do to protect yourself. When the word "red" was said you answered with "apple." We took the town that night, and the next morning we got to the factory and oh, it was so bad.

We'd taken another town and I was trying to take a house there, and all of a sudden, just as I was going in a door, a big tank shot an 88 shell into the area right over the door, and it knocked me to the ground. When I got up I felt something in my britches, so I pulled my britches out of my boots and the shrapnel began to come out on the floor. I didn't have a scratch, and I thanked God.

We heard the Germans had dropped the big bunch of paratroopers there in the forest and all of a sudden they called us and wanted us to go in and flush them out. It was a big forest, and no tanks could get in. Finally we went in and for about a day and a half we fought to take this forest and push out these paratroopers. We lost a tremendous amount of men in this forest that day. They called it hell.

One town that we went into had a sniper that we couldn't locate. Finally we went into a building and all we found were two women in the middle of the living room, rocking away in big rocking chairs—two little old ladies. One of these ladies had a big German rifle behind the door casing, and she would open that door case and get that rifle and kill a couple of boys and then she'd sit the gun back inside and close it down so that nobody could locate it.

THE BULGE

Clarence L. Buckman
106th Infantry Division, HQs

Let's start when I left Boston Harbor in October 1944, on the USS Wakefield (cruise ship, Manhattan), destination Liverpool, England. I am trying to re-call dates from my memory, but I do recall not staying in Liverpool for long. We picked up our equipment and we left England, were put on a Landing Craft Infantry and headed for Europe. The English Channel was a little rough and land mines were afloat, so we were delayed while mine sweepers were called in to clear the way.

We landed in France and went by trucks to an area outside of St. Vith, Belgium, and we set up our two man tents for the night. It started to snow about 11:00 PM and sometime in the night we were greeted by a German patrol, as they left a note on our tent (written in the snow) "Welcome 106th to the front." The next few days we were sent to St. Vith to our headquarters, which was set up in a Catholic Church.

My wire crew was sent to Schoenberg, Belgium, where we set up in a home near four (4) corners of the town on a river. This was around the 10th of December, 1944. We conducted our operations from here. Laid wire for the division on the evening of the 15th, from 11:00 pm to about 1:00 am. We were bombarded by a V-2 rocket, which landed about 300 yards from where we were working. The explosion was so great that it blew us and the truck we were working with off the road and into the ditch. No one in our company or any trucks were hurt or damaged. When we returned, I was told to get some sleep, as I was to operate the switchboard early in the morning around 4 am.

When I started my watch, the Germans were shelling the City of Schoenberg. The commander in St. Vith called and told us that we were under attack, but we were to hold our position until 5 am. We stayed until 6 am at which time our Sgt. told us to start packing the gear and shut down operations.

Now as we were leaving for St. Vith, a German tiger tank was coming down the hill with his gun pointed directly at us. An 81st Engineer sergeant climbed onto that tank and put a grenade down its turret and stopped them from firing. We then proceeded to St. Vith and arrived at our headquarters. That same night we were surrounded by the Germans! Army headquarters sent the Airborne troops to get us out. Note: My life and many others will always be thankful for their help.

I was later sent to the North into the Netherlands with six new 2nd Lieutenants (field commissioned). Our F/Sgt. from headquarters was one of them. Later I went to Velamen, then to Stuttgart, Manlier, Wenham, Frankfurt, and onto Paris, France. I was assigned to the 17th base Post Office (parcel post and rewrap). When Germany surrendered and the shooting ceased, I was able to see a lot of Germany and France, while traveling for and with the Army.

PS: Memory not as good these days and I know that I have missed a lot, but hope this helps.

CHRISTMAS DINNER IN THE ARDENNES

Joseph W. Bulkeley
10th Armored Division, 61st Armored Infantry Battalion, Company B

We armored guys had the word that Ike Eisenhower had vowed every GI in the ETO would have Christmas dinner, no matter how or no matter what. And we had ours at three o'clock on the morning of December 26, 1944. The weather was so cold we ate out of our mess kits with our mittens on and the cranberry sauce in our mess kits had developed a thin coating of ice. But, the food was good and after we ate we found a hay barn and climbed up into a loft to sleep. Before we dropped off we snuggled down in the hay and lit up cigarettes—why we didn't end up a gang of fried GIs, I'll never know. How many of you who were there that Christmas night remember that there was a full moon that threw gigantic shadows over the snowy fields on either side of the road?

The armored division of 1942–44 trained two full years before we went overseas, so being with the 10th Armored was like "home away from home." To this day I don't remember if I belonged to Combat Command A or Combat Command B. One or the other–A or B–went to Bastogne when the 10th left the Saar River area where George Patton was planning a drive. One combat command went straight up to Bastogne (and got there ahead of the Screaming Eagles) and my combat command went to Luxembourg. So I was in Luxembourg that Christmas night.

We men of "B" Company were not too happy that Christmas Eve because the Germans had dropped a heavy barrage on the section of forest where we were dug in and we lost Andy Klein that Christmas Eve. Andy's wife had knitted him a winter scarf and sent it overseas. Andy wore the scarf and with all his heavy clothes, he looked like Uncle Wiggley from the Cabbage Patch with it on. Andy was in his foxhole that Christmas Eve and a tree burst hit the tree close to his foxhole and a tiny piece of metal no bigger than a hang nail went through his steel helmet and helmet liner and his cloth cap and into his brain and Andy never knew what hit him. When we found him we first thought he had dropped off to sleep.

But maybe I have let the point of this recollection get away from me. The point is that as the armored division had trained two years before leaving the Land of Uncle Sam, we were like family and we cried when we found Andy because we had lost a brother.

BEFORE, DURING, AND AFTER THE BULGE

Girard Calehuff
87th Infantry Division, 345th Infantry Regiment, Company D

The 345th had its baptism of fire at Metz France when it took over from the 2nd Infantry Regiment of the 5th Division in the attack on the fortress system around Metz, France. D Company was billeted in a private home near the rail station and I picked up a Metz-Saarbrucken ticket as a memento. I still have it somewhere.

Fort St. Quentin surrendered on 7 Dec 44 and Fort Plappeville the following day. Credit for the action was given to the 5th Division due to the minimal involvement of the 345th in the actions. Baptism of Fire for the Regiment and Division actually occurred at Fort Jeanne D'Arc on 8 Dec 44 and the division's first casualties were sustained. The Fort surrendered to the 26th Division on 15 Dec 44 shortly after the 345th was reassigned to the Saar Valley Campaign on 12 Dec 44.

Moronville Farms, The Saar, France 15–23 Dec 1944

This was the 345th's first real experience with front-line conditions and over the next week we fought our way across the French/German border in the Saar Valley into Medelsheim Germany. Heavy casualties were experienced for the first time. Memories of this week were usually associated with fighting the elements as much as fighting the enemy. Persistent rain and snow produced the first cases of trench foot. D Company managed to avoid this problem for the most part due to the efforts of the company commander, Captain John Muir. Captain Muir had established the practice that company cooks would deliver a hot meal and clean socks to each group in Company D immediately after sundown and pick up a pair of dirty socks from each soldier. The socks were washed & dried in the rear area for redistribution with the next hot meal. Captain Muir was very positive regarding the hot meal each day and we missed very few during the entire course of the war. Company cooks did not have an easy time under him.

Battle of the Bulge, 25 Dec 1944

The regiment had been pulled out of the Saar to be an active reserve against the German Offensive thru Belgium and Luxembourg now known as The Battle of the Bulge. We had left the Saar during a rain/snowstorm with temperatures in the mid-teens. It was miserable. Christmas Day 1944 was especially memorable. aA the storm lifted, it was bright and clear, and we watched the continuous streams of aircraft being directed to attack the German forces in the breakthrough area. We cheered them on as we thoroughly enjoyed an endless pancake breakfast prepared by our cooks and bakers who had moved out ahead of us to have a memorable breakfast ready on arrival. Breakfast morphed into a full load Christmas Dinner as we recirculated thru the chow line, pausing only to wash our mess kits on occasion. We proceeded on to Reims where we were refitted and brought up to strength in preparation for our assignment directed at reducing the Bulge in the Allied lines. We were also transferred to General Patton's Third Army for the duration of the war. On 28 Dec 1944, our first assignment was to secure the critical road junction at Pironpre, attacking thru Moircy and Jenneville.

Moircy, Belgium, 29-30 Dec 1944

The attack on Moircy is clearly described on pages 68–69 of the 345th Regimental History and I'll elaborate on it to include that part where I and others of "D" company were intimately involved. Our Mortar section was assigned to accompany and support Companies A, B, and C, 345th Infantry Regiment on the attack. Following a day of fierce fighting, Moircy was taken, the Germans had withdrawn and many of the battalion had moved into attached barns in the village to regroup, eat and rest. The mortar section had caught up with the main body of the battalion and had joined with them in the protection [from the elements] of the barns.

The Germans had launched a fierce counterattack first at Jenneville, then at Moircy and under the weight of the action, battalion command ordered a withdrawal from Moircy to allow artillery to open fire on the German troops in the city. Our first indication of the change in fortunes was a frantic message from one of the sentries that "A German tank is in the village square and is firing down the streets at any movement." An order to withdraw had been issued. However the radio with our group had been damaged and we never received the message. We quickly were brought up to date on orders and everyone took off on their own on what might be unkindly described as a route. Some from rifle companies B and C and some of D Company never got the message and remained in the town all night.

I had gone a very short distance from the barn that I had occupied with the others when I realized that our mortar was still in the barn. No one had thought to bring it out and it would be surely needed when we regrouped. Joe Noortheok, one of the mortar section realized the situation at the same time and we reversed course and went back to the guns. I picked up the entire three piece mortar and Joe picked up two or three mortar shell packs in addition to our own personal packs. We were weighted down.

Each piece of a three piece, 81mm mortar weighs about 45 pounds and is considered a load for one squad member. I had picked up approximately a load weighing close to 135 pounds and Joe had about the same load in ammo for the mortar. We went about two or three miles out from Moircy and ran into Captain John Muir, D Company Commander, standing in the middle of the road. He had recognized the situation and organized a defensive position on the high ground outside the town. The enemy meanwhile decided to pull out of Moircy during the remainder of the night.

Carrying that weight (135 pounds) never bothered me too much. However, I can remember some episodes of back pain later in the war, but they never lasted too long and did not, to my recollection, slow me up a lot. I never claimed any problems associated with my back at discharge.

Later following the war, I had severe back problems in my late 20s. The pains were so intense that I could only lie on the floor and would need assistance to get up. I blamed the back problem on work that I was doing for my company, The Agricultural Instrument Company. I never connected it with my wartime experiences. After my back problems were behind me I found out during a regular medical checkup that the part of my spine in the area where the nerves were being pinched had fused together and essentially eliminated the problem. I seldom have problems today.

The 345th continued to fight hard in a number of small towns, Rondu, Bonnerue, Tillet and others in this part of Belgium, reducing the Bulge and clearing out stragglers, until mid-January when it was transferred a "front line rest area."

Echternach, Luxembourg, 15 Jan 1944

We were on the high ground on the west bank of the Sauer River and the Germans occupied the high ground on the east bank. The city of Echternach was accepted to be 'No Man's Land' although the Germans controlled one small corner of the city and the Americans the major part. Action consisted of firing occasional mortar shells at likely targets and patrolling each night, scouting out the territory and taking any prisoners that were careless. The Germans did the same and it was suggested that the Americans would patrol until one or two in the morning and the Germans would have the field until daybreak. Casualties and firefights were minimal. In a sense, the Germans were also using the sector as a frontline rest area and no one wanted to rock the boat.

I was a forward observer for our mortar squad and thoroughly bored with the lack of activity. An offer to join one of the night patrols or Tiger Patrols was accepted and it was carried off without incident or a shot being fired. A bottle of wine was liberated in the process. However, the rest of my friends in D Company began to question my sanity by exposing myself to unnecessary peril.

Neuenstein, Germany, 2 Mar 1944

Following our stay at Echternach, the 345th moved thru the recently taken city of St. Vith to resume the attack near the town of Heuem, just East of St Vith, in early to mid Feb 1944. Hard fighting in difficult weather brought us into the vicinity of Neuenstein/Neuendorf, Germany in early March. During a very short lull in the fighting, I decided to look up Jackson, the son of one of my dad's friends in hometown, Williamsport, PA. Jackson was a medic in another company in our regiment. Dad, in a letter, had asked me to look in on Jackson from time to time as he [Jackson] was really not comfortable in the infantry and his father was concerned.

By this time I had been promoted to Instrument Corporal for D Company and this position gave me a tremendous amount of freedom as no one really knew what I was doing at any time and really didn't care as long as all of the instruments and communications were functioning. Jackson's company was about a mile or so away and I managed a visit. On my way back to D Company, the Germans started shelling our positions and some of the shells were creating "air bursts" as they were set off by tree branches in the thickly wooded area. It was not an attractive situation to be out in the open while all this was occurring.

Fortunately a tank was parked nearby and, for protection against the shell bursts, I dove underneath. When the shelling stopped, I began to sort out the situation. It was only then that I realized that I had been wounded and could not use my left arm. While I was not aware of the complete damage to my body, this concern took second place to another and potentially more serious situation. The tank had started up and the crew was not aware that I was underneath it without the ability to extricate myself. Fortunately another soldier passing nearby heard my yelling and helped drag me out from under the tank.

A medic station was close by and I made my way to it with a stream of blood coming out of my left jacket sleeve. It appeared, on first glance, that the left side of my body had sustained serious wounds. On stripping off my jacket and shirt, it was revealed that shrapnel, probably from a mortar tree burst, had penetrated my left shoulder and left chest. However they were not severe enough to explain the stream of blood that was exiting my jacket sleeve. The source of this stream was a wound in my throat, just in front of my Adams apple. The passing shrapnel had nicked a blood vessel but did no damage to the really important items i.e., esophagus, spinal cord and the like.

I was cleaned up, temporarily bandaged and sent to the Battalion Aid Station. This I did, walking under my own power, with enough energy to stop by D Company Command Post to report that I would be out of action for a short time. At the Aid Station, after evaluation, I was strapped in an ambulance and sedated for the trip to a rear area aid station and then to a hospital unit where the shrapnel was removed from my shoulder. Those pieces in my left chest remain even today and show up on X-ray photos where I usually have to offer an explanation. Occasionally I think they trigger the metal detectors at the airport but this is rare.

Recuperation took place in a hospital back in Bar-le-Duc France. After four weeks I was sent back to my unit, D-345, which was unusual for the time as wounded were usually attached to units with the greatest need. Returning to one's old unit was fortunate as you knew the group and was not an outsider. The war was winding down and this probably had some leverage.

During my absence, the 345 had made the dash to the Rhine, crossing the Moselle in the process. Finally I caught up with my unit, which had raced across Germany following the Rhine crossing which had occurred at Boppard near Koblenz. In mid-April joined them near Crawinkel in time for the dash to Plauen and Falkenstein near the Czech border with Germany which was our station at the end of the war.

We settled in to garrison life again, marching and drilling to impress the locals with our discipline and parade ground abilities. It was more like a troop of Sad Sacks than seasoned soldiers. Our lines were crooked and we had problems keeping in step. The final denouement came when our CO decided to carry out an "Inspection Arms." Our last effort at this was in England some eight months earlier. Our weapons had changed, we had to be instructed on the new arms, and when the inspecting officer almost had his head/hand shot off when a soldier messed up the sequence and chambered a round prior to pulling the trigger, we had to be re-instructed. If this skill demonstration had only happened once, it would be understandable. Recurring three times in one inspection was too much. The maneuver was terminated and we were left to impress the citizens with our youth and handsome appearance instead of our military bearing.

Early July found us shipping back to the United States to Fort Benning for a 30-day leave and retraining for the invasion of Japan. The two A-bombs made this moot and we were discharged when our discharge points allowed this action.

A SUDDEN CHANGE OF PLANS

Frank Chambers
75th Infantry Division, 291st Infantry Regiment

Time: December 10, 1944
Place: On English Channel, Port of Southampton, England
Aboard LST—Destination: Mainland of Europe.

The grappling hooks of the sturdy chains firmly gripped the undercarriage of the trucks and cannons. Every vehicle was securely anchored to the steel flooring of the landing ship tank (LST). The castoff from the dock was imminent. The journey across the notorious English Channel to the European mainland would be launched within minutes.

The motorized units of the Cannon Company, 291st Infantry Regiment, 75th Infantry Division were corralled in the underbelly of this specialized Army transport. The ship's crew had carefully secured each unit, hoping to prevent any damage during the Channel crossing. With space at a premium, the units were anchored only with inches to spare in order to utilize the valuable cargo area.

The truck driver from the Cannon Company had observed his 2½ ton "Jimmy 6 x 6" being driven into the jaws of the LST. It now bore the military designation of "75-291" which was inscribed on the front right bumper with "CN 14" on the left. Across the hood of the truck was stenciled "U.S.A. 436981," which served as the "birth certificate" of this vehicle.

Just two days earlier, the 291st Regiment, including the Cannon Company, had motored across southern England from their assembly camp in Wales. The regiment had departed New York harbor and "Waved Goodbye to the Lady," the Statue of Liberty, on October 22, 1944. Their ship was named the

U.S. Army Transport Edmund B. Alexander and debarked at Swansea, Wales in early November. Those several weeks in Wales provided time to prepare the trucks and cannons for combat service.

These preparations included the truck driver being assigned to CN 14 that would carry the entire Cannon gun crew and tow the 105mm cannon. The journey to Southampton had given the driver the best opportunity to test the ability of his truck while fully loaded. The response of the truck was critical as combat would undoubtedly demand every horsepower from its six-cylinder motor. The driver felt very comfortable with his truck's performance as it sat waiting in the hold of the LST.

After being assigned to the bunk area of the LST, the motor sergeant assembled his drivers for their latest orders. In his hand the sergeant held several packets of sea sick tablets. The loading dock crew had strongly recommended to the sergeant that each driver be given a tablet to prevent severe discomfort during the overnight Channel crossing. According to the sergeant's conversation with the dock crew, they had witnessed extreme cases of seasickness on previous Channel crossings.

The driver of CN 14 quickly swallowed his tablet and climbed onto the top of his three-tiered bunk. The headroom would not permit sitting upright so he carefully stretched out in his limited space. He heard the bells of the LST clanging their signal that the ship was preparing to depart from the English shore. During the first minutes after departure, the sailing appeared to be quite smooth. The driver and his buddies settled in and were soon dozing off. Those seasick tablets were beginning to take effect and the bunk area became very quiet. A steady drone of the ship's motors was like a lullaby to the troops.

Sometime later in the passage, the truck driver was awakened by being tossed from side to side in his bunk and actually banging his head on the ceiling. He remembered loud cursing and other expletives from his bunk mates throughout the night. On his part the sea sick tablet had prevented him from any great discomfort except a bruise or two from contact with the bunk's railing.

In a few hours the ship's speaker system gave the wakeup call. The LST was not moving. The driver and his buddies of Cannon Company assembled on deck for roll call. Across the bow of the ship severely damaged dock buildings could be seen. On one building was a "hand-made" sign indicating that they docked at the French port of LeHarve. Evidently this port had only recently been re-occupied by the Allied forces. The country of France had been occupied by the German military since 1940.

The next important task of the Cannon Company drivers was to enter the hold of the LST where their trucks and equipment were stored. As they eagerly descended the metal stairs, they beheld a shocking sight: several of the trucks and cannons had broken their chains during the Channel crossing. Some tires were flattened and doors crumpled. Again many expletives filled the air as the drivers searched for their respective vehicles.

CN 14 was near the side of the ship, firmly anchored to the deck with no apparent damage. The driver called his crew to load up for the trip down the LST ramp with the cannon in tow. In a few moments they would be on the mainland of Europe nearing the combat zone.

As the truck slowly nosed onto the LeHarve dock, complete devastation met the crew's eyes. Only a narrow path had been bulldozed through the debris to permit movement of troops and supplies. It was very evident that this vital port had been wrested from the German army within recent days. The troops on CN 14 were now face to face with the realities of war.

The Cannon Company caravan of the 291st Regiment slowly moved through the devastated city of LeHarve into the French countryside. The troops on CN 14 were certainly relieved to depart the LST and to be on solid ground. No more rocking and rolling or shouting of expletives from being tossed around in those narrow bunks and other mayhem during the Channel crossing. All the homes in this main port city seemed to be abandoned. No citizens were in sight. The truck driver had this question uppermost in his mind: "Where did the people go?"

Several miles down the highway the trucks entered the city of Rouen. Circling the city square, the Lieutenant occupying the passenger seat of CN 14 pointed to the prominent statue of the revered Joan of Arc. After they left Rouen the convoy of military vehicles motored several miles and arrived at another city—a city of military tents.

It was now December 14, 1944. The 291st Regt. had entered a bivouac camp in fields near Yvetot and Duclair, France. Located 50 kilometers north of LeHarve, the area was best described by the troops as "a swirling sea of mud." The sunny plains of France had been thoroughly churned by the feet and vehicles of thousands assembling there for deployment to the battlefields. A few wooden planks had been placed in the walking paths but they were completely swallowed by the mire. No overshoes had yet been issued to the troops so keeping a "GI shine" on combat boots was almost a lost cause. Thank goodness each soldier had been issued two pair of boots. One pair was always carefully shined and put in a safe place for that unexpected inspection. Those overshoes were back in a warehouse, waiting for orders to be issued to the troops.

It was a true trial of the troop's survival in the mud and mire of the camp. The truck driver was fortunate because his truck was often ordered to bring supplies to the camp from area army warehouses. He could avoid most of the mess while in the truck cab away from the camp. Other side benefits were that truck drivers were often exempt from guard duty and KP (kitchen police) since they were on call 24 hours a day. The truck driver frequently was at the wheel while his assistant caught a few winks of sleep in the passenger's seat and vice versa.

A lot of army scuttlebutt abounded in the camp as to the next destination. Many felt that Hitler was at the end of his rope. Intensive Allied bombings had seriously cut into his supply of fuel for planes and tanks. Fighting a war on two fronts had severely limited the supply of available manpower. Some sources were quoted as encountering captured German males as young as 16 and as old as 70 being held in American prisoner of war camps. There was a lot of talk that the 75th Division would be assigned to a quiet front bordering Germany to relieve those units that had been on the front lines for more than 6 months… since June 6th. Unofficially no action would be expected until next spring after the rivers subsided. This was accepted as the "Plans" for the next several weeks. The troops were always seeking news concerning the latest "Plans"… better known as the previously mentioned scuttlebutt. The 75th

Division was even rumored to be stationed in the Netherlands to wait out the winter in reasonably comfortable quarters. Maybe a few passes to Paris or London during Christmas could be forthcoming.

On the evening of December 16th, the truck driver was conversing in the proverbial chow line with a friend from Company headquarters. The friend casually mentioned that something had happened that morning up in the Belgian Ardennes Forest. The German army had made a minor breakthrough of the American lines. Surely it could not be serious because Hitler's army was supposedly too weak to mount any type of offensive action.

As December 17th dawned, the 75th troops began their daily tasks. Chow, writing letters, cleaning equipment and similar duties were routinely on the agenda. Maybe they could apply for a few hours leave to see the Paris sights. Perhaps army life was not so bad after all. The truck driver was handed a "trip ticket" to make a run to a LeHarve warehouse. This was his authorization to leave the camp and travel the area highways. An army vehicle must have the permit to travel from the camp with a specific destination listed. The army military police (MP) were very strict and the truck driver was stopped on several occasions during each trip. Obviously there was to be no pure "joy riding" in a military vehicle.

As the truck driver returned to his home base that afternoon, breaking news had struck the camp like a bolt of lightning. The skirmish up in the Ardennes was extremely serious. Thousands of German soldiers and tanks had overrun the American troops with many hundreds being killed or captured. To add to the utter confusion, troops from the German army were rumored to be headed towards Paris to capture General Eisenhower, the Supreme Allied Commander, in his headquarters near Paris.

As the afternoon turned into night, a great uneasiness fell over the entire camp. Surely the Germans did not have the resources to cause such a serious problem. Allied intelligence claimed that Hitler did not have the men or tanks or planes to mount a campaign of this magnitude. Then, adding the rumor that General Eisenhower was in danger caused more anxiety since the 75th Division was directly in the path of the German army's possible route to Paris. The big question was, "Where did Hitler get all of these troops and tanks?"

December 18th brought more unbelievable news: Nazi forces had crashed across the Ardennes, capturing many towns and villages in Belgium and Luxembourg. With orders from Hitler to take no prisoners, hundreds of Allied troops, mostly Americans, had been massacred. By the afternoon of the 18th, orders had been issued to the troops of the 75th Division to prepare to move out at a moment's notice.

This was certainly a "sudden change of plans." Previous plans for a quiet winter of "border watching" were quickly shelved. The 250 mile journey north into the Ardennes was to begin at daybreak. There was no sleep that night. All supplies and equipment had to be prepared for the movement. The mud and mire of the camp further complicated the task. Foot soldiers of the 75th were transported to an area train station for the northern journey and loaded onto the infamous "40 and 8" railroad boxcars of the last war fame. This designation referred to the cars' capacity of 40 men or 8 horses.

The truck driver of CN 14 and his crew were "ready to roll" at the break of dawn. The sun could not be seen because of the heavy overcast. Snow had begun to fall during the night. Everyone was happy to leave the mud behind, but their exact destination was unknown. The convoy headed north with a lot of apprehension. With a brief rest stop every 2 hours—the cooks had provided containers of black coffee—the caravan approached the Belgian border. Darkness descended quickly because of the heavy overcast. The snowfall was much heavier by the hour. No overshoes had been issued to the troops. The temperature was plummeting. Traveling in a war zone at night was a challenge. No headlights on the trucks could be turned on. Only those tiny 3 inch by 3/4 inch blackout lights were permitted. They could barely be discerned when closely following the vehicle ahead. The truck driver and his assistant intently peered through the windshield of CN 14 for painstaking hours in their journey to the unknown.

As the convoy proceeded through the darkness, an amazing spectacle suddenly appeared: brilliant flashes of light continually reflected from the low clouds. First impression was a summer electrical storm with vivid bolts of lightning but no—it was December. That impression suddenly turned into reality. Those piercing flashes of light were bursting shells from heavy artillery fire, just a few miles ahead! The Cannon Company was nearing the front lines of battle!

The truck driver's heart was about to burst from his chest. His body was seized by a cold chill and then by a drenching sweat. Those ominous flashes reminded him of those old movies from the last war showing cannon fire and hand-to-hand combat. What lay ahead? Would he survive? Traveling a few more miles, he could hear the artillery fire and feel the concussion of the exploding shells. He admitted to himself that he was really frightened but there was no hesitation on his part. There was a job to do! His assistant driver in the passenger's seat had not spoken for several minutes. He, too, was mesmerized by the spectacular sight unfolding through the truck's windshield. The convoy slowly moved into the forests of the Ardennes, ever nearer the front lines of combat.

That sudden change of plans had thrust the crew of CN 14—and their buddies of the 75th Infantry Division—into the throes of war now known in history as "The Battle of the Bulge!"

WAVE GOODBYE TO THE LADY

Frank Chambers
75th Infantry Division, 291st Infantry Regiment

Time: October 22, 1944
Place: Troop ship departing New York harbor

A somber collection of GIs pushed against the railing of their troop ship. The U.S. Army Transport Edmund B. Alexander was slowly cruising from the New York harbor into the Atlantic Ocean. Not a sound could be heard from the troops. Only the gentle lapping of the waves against the ship's stern broke the stillness of this bright October morning. Suddenly a quiet tremulous voice penetrated the silence with: "There she is guys! Wave Goodbye to the Lady!"

The "Lady"—the Statue of Liberty—was gliding by on the starboard railing. The Lady began to fade into the skyline of New York City as the troops waved those khaki clothed arms in their salute to the Lady.

A second voice which was somewhat stronger than the first shouted: "Three cheers for the Lady" and the entire deck erupted into an explosion of three great "hurrahs" that echoed across the entire harbor. Even the ship's captain could be seen saluting from his post high on the ship's bridge.

As the deck became quiet again, the seriousness of this voyage once more claimed the minds of the GIs. One in particular said to his shipmate, "When will we see the Lady again?"

His buddy responded, "I just hope and pray that we will actually see her again."

These heartfelt sentiments were shared by the soldiers of the 291st Regiment of the 75th Infantry Division. They had just departed Camp Shanks near New York City and were bound for Europe. You can be assured that all the troops were harboring those same questions as expressed by those two shipmates: Would they survive this voyage? Would they survive the battles that were underway in Europe? What was their destiny?

As the troop transport sliced through the blue waters on its eastward journey, one soldier, a truck driver attached to the Cannon Company of the 291st Regiment, was having flashbacks of his past six months Army experience.

He recalled being awakened very early on the morning of the past June 6th to a blast from the loud speakers in his barracks back in Kentucky: "The Allies have landed in France. The invasion of Europe has begun!" He and his barracks buddies let out a cheer—a very subdued cheer—knowing that soldiers like themselves were now in extreme danger.

The sergeant at the end of the bunk rows quietly said, "Well, I guess we missed that one! Will probably be needed for the next invasion! Maybe Southern France or someplace like that." The 75th had been undergoing intensive training since April at Camp Breckenridge in western Kentucky preparing for combat duty. Rumors were rampant that the 75th was being trained to take part in the invasion of Europe. The Army thrived on rumors. Few, if anyone, could foresee the strategy that would be needed to subdue

Hitler and his Nazi crowd that had overwhelmed most of Europe.

All these streams of reminiscence wove through the mind of the soldier truck driver as he gazed across the beautiful Atlantic Ocean. Fluffy clouds floated lazily over the ship. The ocean appeared as smooth as a table top. Just a few whitecaps broke the surface.

The ships in this convoy were proceeding on a "zigzag" path to thwart any attack from German U-boats. Additional security was supplied by several Navy destroyers patrolling the convoy's perimeter. The truck driver soldier felt safe yet apprehensive. Just what the future might hold in the coming weeks and months was foremost on his mind.

While lounging on the deck, the 291st soldiers heard a shout from one of the sailors standing guard on the railing: "Here she comes." He pointed to just a speck on the horizon to the rear. He elaborated that it was the famous Queen Mary on her usual solo voyage as a converted troop carrier. The Queen always sailed without escort since her speed assured her safety from enemy submarines. The soldiers continued to watch as this majestic vessel moved rapidly through the seas. In a few hours the Queen was ahead of the convoy and eventually out of sight destined for its European port of call. Every morning the soldiers assembled on deck for exercises to keep in top physical condition. That was followed by life boat drills. Each soldier had a life preserver and a full Army back pack of equipment which made for a cumbersome task of climbing into life boats. You can be certain that the guys were taking this rehearsal very seriously. They know if they hear the command: "To the lifeboats"—it is not a drill!

The sailing of the USAT Edmund B Alexander moves steadily eastward. With the ocean being so smooth, not a single case of seasickness was observed. This ship appeared to be among the largest in the convoy. The scuttlebutt was that the top officers of the 75th Division—the Generals and staff— were on board so the conditions were top-flight.

As the troops awakened on an early November morning, they sensed that something was drastically different: the ship was not moving! As they rushed to the ship's railing, they saw a welcome sight! Just a few hundred yards beyond the dock was a small city nestled among the hilly terrain.

"Where are we? Do we get off here?" are a few of the many questions being shouted at the sailors. "This is the port of Swansea, Wales. Yes," responded one sailor, "you guys get off here!" So the sea journey of this unit of the 75th Infantry Division had come to an end. However it was only the first step to confront the raging conflict that lay ahead.

The debarking of the 291st Infantry Regiment began in earnest. The troops were trucked to a rolling countryside army camp consisting of British Nissen huts. As the troops dropped their duffel bags on the wooden floor of the huts, they eyes were drawn to those names that had been etched onto the supporting walls—names of previous occupants. It soon became very clear that many of those soldiers whose names they were reading had landed on the Normandy beaches just a few months past. This was a sobering occasion for these new troops.

Once on land, the 291st guys had a huge task ahead. In preparation for the sea voyage, all of their equipment, including the 105 mm guns of the Cannon Company, had been generously covered with "cosmoline" to prevent rusting from the salt water spray. The cannons had been chained to the desk during transport. Now they must spend hours removing this sticky rust preventive substance.

With the "cosmoline" removed, the equipment was completely rust free and ready for action. When and where those cannons would fire their first shots was in the thoughts of every soldier. Several retired to their assigned hut to compose a V-mail letter to their parents, wives, sweethearts and friends. They were aware that these letters would be censored by a regimental officer whose duty it was to make certain that no military secrets were revealed.

The camp near Swansea, Wales was situated on gentle rolling pasture land. The troops soon got out the softballs and bats and the footballs for some exercise and recreation. The troop carrier ship's deck was not expansive enough to permit these games. Allowing a ball to be dunked in the Atlantic was frowned upon.

The Cannon Company of the 291st Regiment did not bring their trucks from the States that tow the cannons. On the 3rd day in camp, the motor sergeant loaded up the truck drivers for a short trip to Cardiff, Wales. At this port the army had assembled a large "motor pool" of vehicles of all description. From this pool the Cannon Company drivers were each assigned a vehicle that was described as a "Jimmy" 6 x 6, a 2½ ton truck manufactured by General Motors, hence the "Jimmy" name. This type of vehicle had already established a reputation for reliability and dependability in North Africa and in the D-Day landings of last June.

This one truck driver was assigned an older model "Jimmy" that likely had been in the North African campaign. The odometer registered more than 5000 miles and looked a little "war weary." It was actually a civilian model with a steel cab that had been reconfigured for military use. The newer models had cloth cabs to save precious wartime metal. The other Cannon Company drivers had drawn this cloth cab model. The driver with the steel cab was quietly kidded about his "unlucky assignment" of an older truck.

This vehicle was Army # 436981 and Cannon Co. # CN 14. Rumors are bouncing through the camp. They heard that the German army was nearly defeated and that the war would be over by Christmas. Hitler was reported to be nearly out of planes, pilots, fuel and manpower. The Russian front had seriously depleted the German war effort plus the invasion of Western Europe has proceeded quite well. General Patton's armored tanks had made spectacular progress toward the German border.

These weary Allied troops and equipment had been on the front lines in combat since June and need a rest. The 75th Division was rumored to relieve those soldiers and take up those frontline positions as winter approaches. The crossing into Germany would likely be delayed until next spring due to the flooding of the border river. Again, this was the famous rumor mill at work in the army.

The *Stars and Stripes* army paper earlier reported that President Roosevelt had been reelected for a fourth term. Another item in the paper referred to an event that happened three years ago—Pearl Harbor Day on December 7, 1941. The Cannon Company drivers quietly shared what they were doing on this date in 1941. None were in service and two were still in high school. Another was the driver for the family livestock trucking business. Three were in college, as was the status of this truck driver.

The next day, December 8th, dawned with the news to prepare to leave the camp. The destination was not yet stated, but all indications were that the truck convoy would be driving across Wales and England for a port on the coast of the English Channel.

The rumors were correct. Two days later the 75th Infantry Division was assembled at Southampton, England. This extremely busy port was nearly overwhelmed by ships of all description. Landing Craft Infantry (LCI) and Landing Ship Tank (LST) were nudged up to the docks awaiting their next cargoes for that challenging "channel crossing." The Cannon Company truck drivers were instructed to line up their trucks on the dock facing the yawning jaws of an LST whose cavernous belly would transport their vehicles and equipment across the channel.

As they gazed across the English Channel, the men of the 75th silently pondered what awaited them when they debark on the shores of the continent of Europe in a few hours. One soldier opened his calendar to the date: December 10, 1944. He thumbed back to an earlier date: October 22, 1944— that is when he "Waved Goodbye to the Lady."

THREE ENEMIES: GERMANS, WEATHER, AND FEAR

Thomas R. Chambers
9th Armored Division, Trains Headquarters Company

Late in the afternoon of December 16 one of the truck drivers from Trains Headquarters Company of the 9th Armored Division, having just returned from Eupen, Holland stepped into our billet at 64 Rue de Mersch in Sauel, Luxembourg, and made the very quick announcement, "Something big is going on up north. There is shelling from artillery all over the place. I had to detour and go far west from my route to get back. I don't know what is going on but it must be something big."

That was my first knowledge of what has come to be known as the Battle of the Bulge. Little did I realize at the moment the great importance of what had been unleashed nor could I understand what the outcome would mean for the Allies and the American forces in particular.

I was not the only one who was in the dark, so was Maj. Gen. John W. Leonard, Commanding the 9th Armored Division which was strung out over a distance of nearly seventy miles from near the border of Holland in the north and down to near Luxembourg City in the south—in what was thought to be the quiet sector of the line and where various combat elements of the division were completing a period of combat indoctrination.

When the German offensive broke loose the majority of General Leonard's command was attached to some other division or some element of VIII Corps in a supporting role of some sort. General Leonard had to be the most frustrated Commander in Europe. For two and a half years he had organized, shaped and trained the officers and men of the 9th Armored only to find himself out of contact and unable to exercise any control over his division as a single entity. Thus he was confounded by events beyond his control at his headquarter in Mersch, Luxembourg.

Following a series of daily, even hourly, relocations my unit along with unidentified parts of 9th Armored Division Engineers, the 89" Cavalry Reconnaissance Squadron and various elements of support organization were positioned roughly from Arlon, and to the west along the axis of Etalle, St. Marie, Titigny and Florenville, all in Belgium. My unit was the Reconnaissance Platoon of Trains Headquarters Company of 9th Armored. Our equipment included an Armored car with a 37 mm gun and a single air cooled machine gun. We had four Peeps, the Armored term for a Jeep, and a weapons carrier that was used to haul ammunition and spare ordinance. This assemblage and crews came to rest in the Town of Etalle, where we were told that it would be our job to try to stem the German attack if it were to try to go toward Reims, the location of SHAEF Headquarters or on toward Paris.

We were part of an improvised defense that comprised three Task Forces. The first was identified as Task Force Halverson. I was told it was commanded by a Maj. Halverson of 9th Armored Engineers. It was on the Right flank of the three forces. The second was Task Force Fiore, so named for Lt. Col. Fiore, Commander of the 89th Cavalry Reconnaissance Squadron. It had its

Command Post in Sainte Marie and held the center position of the provision-al secondary line. The third Task Force, (whose names are now lost in the fog of time) was located in the village at Titingy, Belgium, of this hastily prepared but unused defense. The front covered by these three task forces amounted to something between eight and ten miles on the southern edge of the Bulge. It was master of strong points at cross roads or at some elevation with a clear view of a section of critical road bed.

It is believed that these three provisional Task Forces were under the com-mand of General John Leonard, who had established 9th Armored Division Headquarters at Etalle. Task Force Halverson was given the responsibility and the authority to snag every straggler or American soldier who was sepa-rated from his unit and came into the town of Etalle. Such individuals were impressed into the defense of various cross roads and strong points at strate-gic locations that could temporarily slow down a German column headed for Reims. By buying time in such an event, Corps and Army commands would have the opportunity to further strengthen the situation. All of this was the thinking before it was known that the Germans' objective was Antwerp. In the course of about two and a half days, Task Force Halverson had approxi-mately 700 troops in its command. The most important qualifications were the color of the uniform, the shape of the helmet and any kind of weapon that fired American ammunition.

On about the 21st or 22nd of December, 9th Armored Ordnance deliv-ered two cosmoline packed 105 mm howitzers to Etalle. It fell to the Recon Platoon to put these two pieces into firing order at once. Fortunately the sun was shining but the weather was as cold as the proverbial witch's tit. With a combination of gasoline, GI towels, bayonets and the cleaning brushes pro-vided with these guns, we did fast work and before night fall had them ready for inspection. The breeches would open without a hitch, we could elevate them easily to the fullest extent and traverse them smoothly. The bores of these two guns were as clean as could be, the sighting equipment was as clean as a whistle and aiming stakes were ready. Suddenly we were ready to become artillerymen.

But, who were going to be the cannoneers? The gunner in our Armored

Car had a fundamental understanding of a 37 mm gun, mostly with armor piercing ammunition. The others in the platoon knew about .30 caliber ball and .50 caliber ammunition, plus a smattering of .45 caliber for Thompson subs and Grease Guns. I knew about bore sighting from sniper school in the States. So, that was it. We decided that we would bore sight the guns at a tank at about 500 yards, fire, and pray. If we did not get the tank with the first shot, he would have the second shot and that would be that. Night fall came before we could put the pieces in position for firing. Someone announced that our chow truck had some hot "C"s so off we went for some supper. When we got back, much to our chagrin, the field pieces had disappeared.

A part of the regular duty of the Recon Platoon during its time as part of Task Force Halverson was the patrolling to the outposts around Etalle and at the same time ferrying "warm" men to replace those that had been on out-post duty and were so cold they could barely move. On one occasion, while picking up the cold men we found one who could not get out his hole. His feet were frozen.

Our platoon was fortunate to be billeted in the local one room school house, right in the middle of town. It was stucco and had double glass windows. Someone had put about two feet of straw on about half the tile floor. At the other end of the room there was a big pot belly stove about five feet tall. There was a pile of coal in an adjacent comer, so as far as Bulge billets were concerned, there was nothing to be asked for beyond this very comfortable situation.

Having finished the last regular outpost patrol for the afternoon the Recon Platoon was assembled in the school house soaking up the heat from the stove and chewing variously on "D" bars or fruit bars from "K" rations. For the moment, life was good. Then a runner burst into the school room and shouted. "Recon Platoon, Mount Up. Extra gasoline and extra Bazooka ammunition! Assemble at the CP at once. Every man with overcoats." With that the runner disappeared. In short order the platoon was assembled in the Company CP. At the moment a General Officer was inside. This was evidenced by the hooded Star Plate on the bumper of the automobile parked in front of the CP.

My platoon leader, Lt Vernon Chance, followed by Sgt. Angelo Rinaldi, my platoon sergeant, and Sergeant Bill Smith, my section leader, went into the CP with the remainder of the Platoon waiting outside with the vehicles in the last glimmers of daylight and in the miserable cold. The briefing seemed to take forever, maybe as much as thirty or forty minutes, but it was so cold miserably sitting in the wind and just waiting.

Sergeants Rinaldi and Smith came to the first vehicle and stopped while the members of all the crews gathered to learn the mission for tonight. Soon it was apparent that the General Officer inside had received a report that there were six Tiger Tanks patrolling in force approximately six miles to our northwest. Our mission was that of determining whether or not bridges across the Semois River were still passable and, if so, to determine if they had been mined by U.S. forces. Radio silence was to be maintained. We were to stay at the maximum intervals, so if in the event of a hostile encounter, the greater interval would improve the possibility of one or more vehicles being able to make it out to bring back the report of the findings relative to the bridges. If any German tanks are sighted, break off contact, determine the tanks location and return to the CP after we have accomplished the reconnaissance of the bridges.

With that instruction the patrol was off with the armored car in the lead. We very quickly climbed out of the valley of the Semois River and broke on to a plateau approximately 150 feet above the river. The high terrain was gently rolling agricultural land with big sweeping spreads of perhaps as much as fifty acres or more in the large fields. The full moon and the snow covered landscape made it possible to see 500 yards as clear as day, but we could see nothing in the shadows. The covering of loosely laid snow seemed to muffle the sound of our engines which suited our purpose perfectly. After about twenty minutes, traveling at perhaps ten miles an hour a barn came into view. Everything was clear where the moonlight struck and we could make out details of the building with ease. The barn was located at a ninety degree turn of the road and seemed to have a small plot of triangular shaped land right at the ninety degree bend in the road. This small piece of ground was in a shadow cast by the barn.

As we approached we were challenged from the dark shadow cast by the barn and we gave the expected countersign. When it became apparent that it was an American, our wide interval between vehicles went to hell. Everybody wanted to know what was going on. We soon learned it was a soldier from 9th Armored Engineers. He was manning a 57 mm anti-tank gun, but was not very happy with his fire power. He explained that earlier in the day when he had shot a German tank in the rear with his 57, all that happened was that the "Kraut wiggled his ass at me and kept on going." The engineer was not looking for a fight that night.

Our patrol continued on the plateau and after a bit the column slowed to about 5 miles an hour due to the extra chilling factor that came from driving with wind shields down. The snow-covered fields made a beautiful sight in the moonlight but that did nothing for us as we continued to patrol beyond the third and fourth hour, finally coming to the first of three bridges that we were to check. It was distinct relief to see that we were the first vehicles to make tracks over the bridge since the snow had fallen.

My preparation for the patrol included summer underwear, long Johns, OD uniform, wool knit sweater, field jacket and overcoat with a pair of over-shoes (my only pair while in the army) that I had picked up in an aid station about the second day of the battle. Add to that a wool scarf and gloves. It was as though the cold were made of needles that pierced my uniform and shot straight to the marrow of my bones.

Finally, I put on my rubber raincoat in the attempt to keep a little bit of warmth in my body. All the while I wiggled my toes to keep circulation up.

Driving away from the first bridge, I was suddenly filled with a grand upsurge of euphoria. It would begin in my abdomen and rise up through my chest and then into my head. I felt it was such a wonderful and beautiful world. Then I realized that something was happening that should not be happening and I would shake myself and say, "What's wrong with you man, it is not a wonderful world. You are out here looking for a bunch of German tanks. Wake yourself up and come to reality." Then I would beat myself with my fists in the attempt to make my blood flow faster.

The hallucinations continued for numerous episodes over the next hour or so. Each new episode became a bit more euphoric and considerably more difficult to suppress.

We returned to the CP at about 02:00 hours. To my happiness, the Platoon Sergeant and my Section Leader went to give the report of the patrol and sent the rest of us to the school house. Maybe six or eight soldiers were asleep on the straw and there was plenty of room for more. I wanted to warm up a bit before I hit the straw, so I proceeded to make myself a cup of hot chocolate. The water in my canteen was frozen hard. Fortunately there was water in a can near the stove, so I filled my canteen cup and emptied a pack of hot chocolate mix into the water and proceeded to heat it with the glowing bed of coals that shone out from the open door of the stove. The shortcoming to this procedure was that I was holding my cup with my right hand with my four fingers gripping the handle. I was so cold that I got a first degree burn on my fingers before I realized how hot the radiant heat from the coals really was. Nonetheless, the water did get warm and I had my hot chocolate. My fingers remained sore for several days.

A few hours later, the outpost patrols began again. By Christmas Day we had moved to another house and we found some Christmas tree decorations. Some enterprising soul went and got a tree and the festivities began. We secured a case of ten-in-one rations and we began to supplement with various "Cs" and "Ks." I discovered a butcher shop that had a showcase full of small steaks, about 4 or 5 ounces each and I bought all that I had money to pay for. I went to our new billet and showed my find and immediately raised enough money to get enough steaks for each of us to have two apiece.

It made for a great Christmas dinner. It was the only meal in my two and a half years in the army that I had a seated meal with our company officer.

One thing about being a PFC, a scout and machine gunner, in any military organization, is that one is not consulted very often about the grand plan. That was my case. I am not sure what took place in the other Tasks Forces. As a matter of fact I was unaware of the existence of the other two until I discovered them while doing some research in the National Archives at College Park, MD.

But I do recall that we left Task Force Halverson about January 6, 1945, when Division Headquarters and certain other units were moved to the south in France in the general vicinity of Metz. The division received new equipment and armaments and the ranks of the combat units were refilled first with officers and men who had been hospitalized and were returned to their units plus a big contingent of men that came though the Replacement Depot System.

In looking back, I have to thank God for having pulled me out of the 52nd Armored Infantry Battalion and for placing me in Trains Headquarters. The 52nd suffered casualties of killed, captured or wounded to the extent of 74% of its enlisted complement and 28% of its commissioned ranks, with those losses taking place in the relatively short period of the Battle of the Bulge.

AIR SUPPORT FOR THE BATTLE OF THE BULGE

Carl M. Christ
344th Bomb Group

[The following address was presented to the Long Island Chapter of the Veterans of the Battle of the Bulge on December 13, 2000, at West Point Military Academy.]

Air support by the B-26 Marauder medium bombers of the Ninth Air Force was reduced by the serious snow falls which carpeted most of Europe. Runways and taxi strips were constantly swept. Planes were often bogged down on the runways and hauled out by tractors. Wings accumulated snow, motors developed bugs from the cold and electrical systems in the planes "shorted out." The number of missions that could be flown were limited. Only eight missions could be flown in the month of December. An additional six missions were flown in January until the end of the Bulge.

Railway and road junctions were the main objects of attack assigned during the Ardennes Campaign to disrupt the enemy's lines of communication and cripple their lines of supply and reinforcements.

Dawn on 23 December brought improved conditions for flying. The Ninth Bomber Division gave the order for the mediums to take off. The bomber crews knew that their sorties were a matter of life or death to the beleaguered Allied troops on the ground.

With the sudden reopening of the Allied air campaign, and with so many bombers in the air, fighter resources were stretched. Mediums would have to brave the defenses alone. Some crews had never seen an enemy fighter in the air. Two days before Christmas many of them saw enough to last an entire combat tour.

One Marauder group, with an escort of fighter planes nearing its target at Euskirchen bridge, was devastated by the Luftwaffe. Thirty-seven Marauders were shot down that day and 182 planes sustained various categories of damage. In addition, three Thunderbolts were shot down. The day was the worst Marauder losses in the entire war.

When weather permitted, the Ninth Air Force blasted the German rail network. Luftwaffe attacks dwindled under the renewed onslaught from Allied fighters. Help from above—in more than one sense—soon enabled the Allied ground forces to gear up for a final push into Germany.

In the Ardennes campaign, the Ninth Air Force B-26 Marauder groups lost 49 planes, with a complement of six to eight men in each plane—approximately 316 airmen. Some were able to parachute to safety. Some managed to escape and evade capture. Others became prisoners of war.

On 25 January 1945 the last of the surviving German troops retreated to Germany. The supporting American forces from the Third and Ninth Armies went back to their previous battle positions, having accomplished their mission in eliminating the Bulge in the Ardennes sector. Allied air power played a major role in the German defeat as part of the air-ground offensive.

We are pleased to honor on this day, the 18 West Point graduates assigned to the 344th Marauder Group of the Ninth Air Force. Prior to D-Day, three of the 18 were to lose their lives in combat missions. Of the remaining 15, seven courageously led flights against the enemy during the Battle of the Bulge.

The 344th Bomb Group is very proud of one of West Point's finest—Major Lucius D. Clay, Jr., son of four-star General Lucius D. Clay, who flew and led flights during the Battle of the Bulge. He later became a four-star general himself, following in the footsteps of his father.

We are here today to honor and memorialize the gallant men who lost their lives in the air and on the ground in the greatest battle in American history. We also remember the men who returned to the United States and who have since passed away to join their fallen comrades in the Kingdom of Eternal Rest. May the memory of their courage and sacrifice live on forever.

YANKEE DIVISION DRIVE SAVED BASTOGNE
26TH RELIEVED - PRESSURE ON UNIT THAT BROKE SIEGE

Beresford N. Clark

26th Infantry Division, 328th Infantry Regiment, AT Company

With the 26th Division in Luxembourg: This is the first of three stories on the important part New England's Yankee Division played in stopping the recent German counter attack in Luxembourg.

This is a big story. It is the story of the big thing that was done by the men of the 26th Infantry Division. It is the story of how this division was called upon suddenly in a crisis and how it did the thing that could and may be written into the history of this war as the major reason why the German counter attack of December 18, 1944, met ultimate failure.

Was Blacked Out...

It is only now almost three weeks after the men of the YD flung themselves into that awful breach that the whole story can be told. For a while during the early stages of the operation the 26th was blacked out. It could not be identified in print.

Later that blackout was lifted. But the story could not be told because it was not a complete story. Yet now it is complete and there is not a gram of stale material in this late telling of it. For this big thing that the men of the 26th did among the snow-covered hills and angry gorges of Luxembourg is one of the few stories of truly magnificent achievement that have come out of this war.

Putting it "simply and without embellishment," they did this: They rushed 60 miles to the underside of the counter-attack east of Arlon, Belgium. They stopped the Germans in their sector, which was what they had been ordered to do at any cost, then they did a more magnificent job. They smashed the German attackers back into a retreat that saved the important Belgian City of Bastogne from capture by the enemy.

Probably no one can say what would have happened if Bastogne had fallen, but it would have been bad, very bad indeed. Bastogne is an important supply center and road net terminal. Inside the city was the valiant 101st Airborne Division, which was starting an epic defensive stand. The city's fall would have been a serious blow, perhaps even a disastrous blow to the Allies.

Meriwell Twist...

And it was the 26th Division called to the rescue in a veritable Frank Meriwell twist which saved Bastogne, for when the YD sent the Germans in its own sector reeling, enemy forces harassing the 4th Armored Division on the 26's left flank had to retreat to avoid being flanked. And thus the pressure on the 4th Armored was relieved, permitting its tanks to roll forward to the north and break the siege of Bastogne.

The YD did this big thing because it was fast and because it fought furiously and without letup. It left its area at dawn on December 20 and its first units drew up around Arlon that night. It attacked on December 22 and since that day it has pushed its assault day and night without cease. Up until today it has advanced 17 miles into the Jerry Midriff that is 17 miles as the crow flies. Actually the YD traveled many more miles than that on icy roads which wind around miniature peaks like the frosting on a birthday cake.

It seems a long time ago now to that night when the YD got that summons to move. The men of the 26th were resting a little that night, resting and relaxing in the building where the officers were billeted they had set up a little night spot dubbed the "Wolf's Den." Some Red Cross girls had come over. Among them was a round-faced, smiling girl named Mary Small from Cohasset and the officers were dancing and drinking mild wine. Even the big brass was there. Maj. Gen. Willard S. Paul, of Shrewsbury, the division commanding officer, and Col. Bernice A. McFadyen, the chief of staff sat at a corner table.

Wanted on the Phone...

About 10 o'clock an aide poked his head cautiously in the room, looked around and then walked over to the table where Gen. Paul and Col.

McFadyen sat and saluted smartly. The big brass grinned. "At ease, son," Gen. Paul told the aide. "Yes, sir, the chief is wanted on the phone, sir," the aide said as if saying one long word. Col. McFadyen excused himself, muttered something about "routine" and left. Gen. Paul turned back to the young lieutenant he had been chaffing about the latter's bashful attention toward a Red Cross girl.

A few minutes later Col. McFadyen, returned, marched softly to Gen. Paul's table, whispered something in the latter's ear. The general's mouth grew tight and he straightened up in his seat then both got their coats and helmets, apologized to the guests for having to leave and departed.

That was the night of December 18. The division was on 12-hour notice to move. Next day it received its marching orders merely that the 26th was moving north. A few hours later, the order was elaborated and the 26th was told that it would go into line on a seven mile front east of Arlon. Shortly after midnight on the morning of December 20 the cavalry reconnaissance troop moved out and the rest of the division followed in daylight.

The 26th Division arrived in its new sector late that afternoon, de-trucked and went into hidden bivouac in a stretch of beautiful fir trees. All the next day the men lay concealed in these woods. Equipment was cared for, weapons were cleaned, additional ammunition was issued and vehicles were given a final checkup. Every man was given an extra pair of socks. His other clothing was inspected. Line troops got three days' emergency rations. Next day before daylight the Yankee Division attacked.

THE MIGHTY 252ND ENGINEER COMBAT BATTALION: WE WERE THERE

Richard D. Curts
252nd Combat Engineers

In October, 1943 I was assigned to a newly-formed unit, the 252nd Combat Engineers, and sent to Camp Gruber, Oklahoma for basic training in a new cadre of non-commissioned and commissioned officers. We were shipped to England in August of 1944 where we went through some intensive training and then crossed the English Channel where we were dumped out in waist-deep water, crossed the beaches, and went up through St. Mere Eglise where so many soldiers had given their lives three months earlier during the invasion.

Being combat engineers we were trained in infantry as well. The front lines had moved north about 50 miles. We were assigned the task of removing personnel mines from hedge rows and fields so they could be used for staging areas for equipment. In the process of neutralizing the mine fields, our companies lost 13 men of which one of them was a very dear friend of mine.

After a week or so clearing mines, we were ordered to head north, following the front lines, repairing roads, building air fields, and other dirty jobs that engineers do in war time. We arrived in the Maastricht-Heerlen, Holland area in November 1944. We took over a saw mill and became engaged in felling trees and cutting them into lumber to build bridges. We were billeted in coal miners' barracks.

On or about December 12, 1944, I was assigned the task, as a squad sergeant, to take two heavy army trucks and travel south to a small village in the Ardennes. There we contacted a small lumber mill owner to make arrangements to bring back heavy timbers for some bridges that we were to repair. We arrived in this small village on the evening of December 13th. We were billeted in, as I remember, a kind of community hall for the night. We visited a little pub in the center of the village before retiring. While there, we were told that the German front lines, which were seemingly somewhat dormant at that time, were just a couple of miles deeper in the Ardennes. All during the night we could hear sporadic gun fire and we knew the Germans were close.

At the end of the day on December 14th, we had the two trucks loaded with the timber that was needed and, since it was getting late in the day, I decided to spend the night there and return to Maastricht the next morning.

Arriving safely back in Holland that evening we unloaded the lumber, not realizing that soon the place where we picked up the lumber and lodged on the 14th and 15th, would be overrun by the Germans on the 16th as they began their offensive to overthrow the allies.

It wasn't long after that, on January 5, 1945, the 252nd Engineer Combat Battalion was ordered to the front lines. We were placed under the 9th Army (British, I believe) and replaced an infantry division that was ordered elsewhere. For six days we sat in foxholes, on the banks of the Wurm River, protecting the north flank of the units engaging the Germans a few miles to the south. Although our losses were minimal with three dead and some frostbite casualties, we served our tour of the Ardennes well.

When the Allies finally broke out of the German offensive, the 252nd was drawn back to Holland to pack up and head north to the Rhine River. One of our main jobs there was to help the 1146th Engineers build the famous Rhine River Bridge, which was named in honor of President Franklin Roosevelt, who died just before the bridge was completed in April.

After 45 years, I decided to investigate why the 252nd never received any recognition or received the commendation ribbon with the battle star for their part in the Battle of the Bulge. In 1993 I contacted the Veterans Personnel Records Division, in St. Louis, to see if they had any records concerning the 252nd Engineers serving in the Ardennes encounter. Two years later, I received a letter from them, saying that they had no record of the 252nd Engineer Combat Battalion serving in the Battle of the Bulge, therefore, the unit received no credit for its part in it. (I have this letter on file and the unit was disbanded.) The sad ending to this story is that the unit had soldiers who lost their lives in the Ardennes encounter just the same as other units did and they got no credit. I believe this is a disservice to those who served their country in this battle. I personally knew a man who served in a Signal Corps during the event who sat in a plush hotel in Luxembourg and his unit got credit for the Ardennes.

The reason that I feel we never received any credit or recognition for service during this battle was the fact that we were attached and detached to so many armies and battalions that no one took the responsibility to see that the 252nd Engineer Combat Battalion did serve in the Ardennes Battle of the Bulge with honor. I still have a good memory and "We were there." I can remember it very vividly because I became a Christian while serving on the front lines.

FROM UTAH BEACH TO CZECHOSLOVAKIA

F. Keith Davis
16th Field Artillery

When the Allies planned the invasion of Hitler's Fortress Europe, they chose the Normandy Coast of France for their landing sites and they were code named, Sword, Juno, Gold, Omaha and Utah. The English, French, Canadians and others landed on Sword, Juno and Gold, and the Americans landed on Omaha and Utah beaches.

I went ashore on Utah Beach and the beach was secure and the fighting was a few miles inland. We were near the town of St. Mere Eglise. We fought in the hedgerows, towns and villages and fought our way to the huge Nazi Submarine Base at Brest, France. The Artillery fired on this base from the land, the Air Force bombed it from the air and the Navy fired on it from the sea. After much fire power the base surrendered.

I was in the 16th Field Artillery Observation Battalion. We were the eyes and ears of the Field Artillery. We fought our way through St. Lo, up to and through Paris and to the border of Germany. On Dec. 16, 1944, Nazi Field Marshall Von Rundstedt made a counter-attack on a 60 mile front in this area. He came through with the 5th Panzer Army, 6th Panzer Army and the 7th German Army. We were right in the center of this attack. I was in the area of St. Vith and Bastogne. They really clobbered us. Thousands of Americans and Germans were killed in this breakthrough (later known as the Battle of the Bulge).

It took Gen. George Patton two days to bring in the 101st and 82nd Airborne and the 26th Infantry Division to help reinforce our position. One Paratrooper asked me "where was the front line?" I told him he was standing on it. The Nazi's destroyed much Army material and killed many men. The German High Command sent an ultimatum to our Gen. McAuliffe at Bastogne and told him to either surrender or be annihilated. Gen. McAuliffe sent a reply with one word: "Nuts." The Germans did not know what to think of or understand the word "Nuts." This was American slang for "in no way will we surrender."

The weather was very cold and the fog was over the whole battlefield. The Nazis pushed us back from the German Border, back thru Belgium, Luxembourg and into France. The fog was so thick, we could not tell if an American Sherman tank or a German Tiger tank was coming toward us. Two weeks after the Bulge started, the fog began to lift and the sky was clear again. At this time the U.S. Air Force sent hundreds and hundreds of fighter planes over the front lines and they flew thousands of sorties, destroying supply lines, gun emplacements, infantry, tanks and everything they could see. At this time we began to hold our position and slowly, very slowly we began to advance again toward Germany. The Nazi SS Troops captured the 285th Field Artillery Observation Battalion. Our 16th. F.A.O.B. was to meet up with the 285th, regroup and form a new battalion. This never happened. The SS herded over 100 men of the 285th into a snowy field and machine gunned them down in cold blood. This was not war; this was murder. This was known as the Malmedy Massacre. On January 25, 1945 we were at the same position we were when the Bulge started on Dec. 16, 1944.

I was on an observation post in the city of Koblenz, Germany and ten Catholic Nuns came up to me and in perfect English asked me to tell them when the war would be over. How would I know?

I watched the Army Engineers build a pontoon bridge over the Rhine River. The river was fast, deep and over a mile wide. It was scary to watch our heavy Sherman tanks & heavy artillery guns being pulled by large Prime Movers and Army trucks loaded with supplies and soldiers cross this bridge. The bridge held and supplies and men continued to cross the Rhine River.

I was at the liberation of a Nazi Concentration Camp. The sights we saw were horrible and the smell was only a smell that can be made by torture and death.

We fought our way through Nuremberg and the smell was everywhere.

We zigzagged back and forth through Germany and Sudetenland and fought our way into Czechoslovakia. This is where we heard the war was over on May 8, 1945.

NO REGRETS

F. Keith Davis
16th Field Artillery Observation Battalion, Battery A

Our 16th Field Artillery Observation Battalion, Battery "A," was at Auw, Germany when the Battle of the Bulge began on December 16, 1944. We were pushed back to St. Vith and then to Bastogne and back and forth through Belgium and Luxembourg and the border of France.

After the fog lifted, the Air Force began to attack and the Germans were being pushed back toward Germany again. Near the end of the Bulge fighting, several of our "A" Battery ran upon a large, old stone barn which had been occupied by the Nazi troops the night before. There were American soldiers from several outfits in this barn.

We were talking to the man who owned this barn which had housed many dairy cows. The big barn was full of holes from artillery, tanks, and hand guns and his dairy cows were all killed and his farm house was in ruin.

The owner told us he was an American and had fought in World War I in this same area. He met this pretty Belgian girl, fell in love, and married her. After WW I they started their life in her home village and raised their family there and had a productive dairy farm.

We asked if he had any regrets that he did not return to the United States to live his life, rather than stay in Belgium with his new wife. He said that he was unhappy about the barn being damaged along with his house, and his cattle had been killed, but he did not regret making his choice of living a happy family life in Belgium.

The next morning we left this old broken barn and the farmer and headed for the front lines again.

WIRE CREW GETS A HAND

F. Keith Davis

16th Field Artillery Observation Battalion, Battery A

The 16th Field Artillery Observation Battalion, Battery "A," wire crew was usually with the Command Post and they would lay communication wires to the Observation Post where I spent most of the time. When they would lay the communication wires from the CP to the OP so we could communicate, they often would loop the wires around fence posts or anything sticking out of the snow for holding the wire in place. When they would come to a dead soldier they might wrap the wire around his protruding hand and go on down the road.

The artillery barrages and the tank duels would often break these wires and they would have to be spliced before the CP and OP could communicate.

One night the wires were broken and the wire crew had to go out in pitch dark to find the break and repair it. A new man was in the wire section and they had him lead the way to find the break. A common way to find a break in the dark was to run your hand along the wire until a break was found. This new man, while checking the wire and posts in the dark, grabbed the dead hand of a German soldier that the wire had been around.

Needless to say, he was shocked and more than a little scared! It was necessary to turn the lead over to a more seasoned man in the "Wire Crew."

RECURRING PAIN

Maurice Diamond

84th Infantry Division, 347th Infantry, Co I

Around Christmas we were rushed by truck to the Battle of the Bulge. We stopped over at Reims. The Red Cross had set up for coffee and doughnuts but told me I did not get any unless I paid. Since I had no money I thought I

was out of luck, but one buddy let me have a few coins. The coffee and doughnuts hit the spot.

We slept three to a tent overnight. I awoke with a terrible pain in my upper right side which I later believed to be a cramp. I went to the aid station
for help, but owing to the lateness, from inside the tent I heard, "Come back
in the morning." By morning much of the pain had subsided and I never did
go back to that aid station.

I was transferred to Company F a short time later and went to a different aid station for an explanation of my pain. On describing my symptoms
to the doctor, I heard him whisper to an associate, but loud enough for me
to hear, "I think he is faking it." I just shrugged and walked away. Company
F had lost many men in an encounter with a couple of Tiger tanks. I was told
the bazookas just bounced off the tanks with little effect. Now Company F
was part of a pincer movement from the south heading for Bastogne. As we
moved up a slope in Belgium, a sniper picked off a runner. We all dropped to
the snow-covered ground. A second runner was hit and we were ordered to
stay where we were.

As darkness fell nearly six hours later, we moved up and rejoined the
group. Another soldier and I dug a foxhole into the side of a steep slope that
night. Daylight came and with it, sniper fire. I started to stick my head out of
the foxhole to find that sniper, as I was getting tired of being shot at without
being able to fire back, but my companion insisted I keep my head down. My
foxhole companion and I suffered frost bite on our toes from being pinned
down and were sent back to rest for two weeks. One day of rest was all we got.
The second day we rejoined our outfit.

We were in a wooded area when Capt. Dahlke radioed HQ that a machine gun nest was directly ahead and he would wait for the flanks to take
it out. The colonel radioed back that the company should make the frontal attack on the machine gun nest. The radio stopped working. Shortly
afterward, a jeep arrived containing a driver and the colonel, followed by
a tank. As the colonel strode toward the captain, much shelling started.
The colonel ran back to the jeep, jumped in and rapidly departed, followed
by the tank. The shelling stopped. We never did make that frontal attack.

Sometime later, the captain that I learned to admire was killed by a German bazooka.

We were moving forward through a bare field when I heard a swishing sound. I raised my rifle to fall flat when I was hit by two mortar fragments in the right upper lumbar region, that same place I had suffered the excruciating pain some weeks before. The medic examined me, gave me sulfur and water and sent me to the aid station. There, my wound was cleaned and bandaged and I was told to guide an officer back to the front lines. There I rejoined my outfit.

34 DAYS IN BUZZ BOMB ALLEY

Alfred DiGiacomo
926th Signal Battalion Sep. TAG, 9th Tactical Air Command,
Ninth U.S. Army Air Force

Sgt Alfred DiGiacomo, a switchboard operator, has been working shifts on the Ninth Tactical Air Command telephone switchboard since the invasion of Normandy in June 1944.

The Ninth TAC fighter planes, under the command of General Elwood "Pete" Quesada, have been providing air support to the units of the U.S. First Army since the Normandy invasion.

I was assigned to the 926th Signal Battalion. The battalion provided communications for the 9th Tactical Air Command before and after the invasion of France.

After the breakout from Normandy in August, the battalion and the 9th TAC leapfrogged through France. Our advance was stalled and on October 2, 1944, we set up the Command Center for the 9th in Verviers, Belgium.

Starting in late October, we started to see buzz bombs flying overhead heading for Liege at the rate of one an hour. By December, the number of buzz bombs the Germans were sending over both day and night increased in intensity. They not only targeted Liege but the City of Antwerp was also targeted.

(The buzz bomb or V-I (Vengeance Weapon) was a small pilotless plane powered by a pulse jet. It was armed with a ton of explosives. It emitted a putting noise while in flight and was guided by a simple gyro mechanism which at a prearranged distance would cut off the fuel supply. The noise would stop and everyone waited breathlessly to hear how close it would hit.)

The following are excerpts from the diary I kept during my three years in the service.

December 16: Germans attack! On Saturday, 5:30 a.m. the Germans' counter attack began in the Ardennes. Winter weather hit us hard just as the offensive began; it turned bitter cold and several days later snowed heavily. Cloud cover limited visibility so our planes were grounded. This morning our Doctor Clugston and the ambulance driver were wounded when a shell from long-range artillery exploded near their ambulance near Spa.

December 17: Much confusion and rumors. Worked at midnight and at 1:30 in the morning of the 18th a phone call from Ninth Air Force G-2 to our G-2 reported that 90 Ju55s and 28 Ju88s were taking off from Germany to drop paratroopers in an area east of Aachen. All units were alerted.

At 0300, our radar picked up the planes; German paratroopers were dropped in three different locations. Most of them were soon captured.

We received a call from "Frontier Baker," a forward outpost of the 555th Signal Aircraft Warning Battalion that the Germans are getting so close that they have to close down and move. Some of our D Company radio and repeated outpost men had to fight their way out. I finished work at 8:00 a.m. and found that we are ordered to pack our bags and be ready to move.

A report came in saying the Germans had captured Malmedy, and are advancing toward Verviers. German planes have appeared overhead and buzz bomb activity seems to have increased. Today we counted 120 V-1s heading for Liege.

December 18: Infantrymen from the 29th Infantry rest camp in town have left to join their units. Units of the 99th Division are moving into town and the tanks of the 7th Armored Division drove through town going to the front. (The 7th Armored held the Germans at St. Vith for many days and six battalions of the 99th held off five German divisions for 36 hours and ruined the plans of 6th Panzer Army for a quick breakout.)

Administrative section of IX TAC is moving out. Operators Erickson, Unkelbach and others left for Charleroi to staff our back up facilities.

I worked from 4:00 to midnight and the switchboard was very busy for two pilots A1 Jaffee and Richard Cassaday from our 67th Tactical Reconnaissance Squadron, who in spite of the poor visibility located a German armored column near Stavelot and radioed their location. Four fighter groups from our 365th and 368th fighter groups attacked the column seven times until it was too dark: 32 tanks and 126 vehicles were destroyed.

We had an air raid warning around midnight but there was no attack. However, some long-range shell fire landed outside the town. The Germans continue their advance.

December 19: Heard that Dr. Clugston has died of his wounds. At 2:30, orders came through for us to evacuate. Packed our bags and bedrolls on trucks and pulled out at 3:30, traveling some 20 miles to Liege arriving at 6:30.

The road to Liege was congested so we did not arrive until late. The weather was near freezing; the rain was changing to snow. Just as we arrived at the school building that housed C Company, a buzz bomb cut out above us but landed elsewhere.

We had supper and bunked with C Company sleeping on the floor in the school gymnasium.

Liege is an important crossroad and the Germans are determined to knock out Liege. The air raid sirens sound several times a day, every day as German aircraft appear overhead trying to bomb the bridges and supply depots. But the worst is the sound of the buzz bombs that one hears day and night. They are coming over every 12 to 15 minutes. There is an occasional explosion from V-2s as well. It is all very nerve-racking and dangerous. As some infantrymen who were on rest leave said to me, "It is like a continuous artillery barrage."

December 20: We are sitting around waiting for orders and still living in the school gymnasium. Most of the operations men are here in Liege, some of A and D Company went to Roux (Charleroi) together with my barracks bag that contains all my clothing. Huntsman and McCrain have arrived from

Verviers having shut down the switchboard.

In the meantime our rear emergency system was put into operation. The backup communications in Charleroi provided the communications for the 9th TAC operations. We learned that shortly after we left Verviers our building was struck by long-range shell fire knocking out part of the wall.

We have no indication what is going on at the front lines. But we heard the Germans had massacred a large group of American prisoners in a field.

December 21: We were informed our switchboard van is being set up in a courtyard of a school, now occupied by 9th TAC headquarters which is now in Liege.

During the night a buzz bomb landed nearby and broke some windows in our bedroom (the gymnasium). We still have no idea as to what is going on except that Liege is under aerial attack by the Germans. (Little did we know that the enemy was just 20 miles south of us and that on December 22 a unit of the 2nd SS Panzer Division did try to proceed up Highway N15 to Liege but were turned away at Manhay.)

December 22: Liege is now off limits. We moved from the C Company billets to a boys' school across the street. We telephone operators are assigned to a classroom on the second floor of a three-story wing and have cots to sleep on. My bed is next to a partition wall. I was to work at midnight but the schedule was changed.

In addition to the buzz bombs, we had an air raid during the night with the air raid sirens sounding, flares from the bombers lighting up the ground, anti-aircraft fire, bombs exploding, the whole works. Some of it was pretty close to us.

December 23: Finally went back to work. I worked in the morning 8 to 4 in the switchboard van in the courtyard. It was a very busy day for today was the first day of reasonably good weather. IX TAC mounted 696 combat sorties and Allied fighter planes shot down 133 German fighters. However, we still have no information on what is happening just south of us where hundreds of our troops are engaged in desperate battles.

In the evening, we were told there was a rumor that the Germans were going to drop paratroopers into Liege that night. We grabbed our guns and went outside waiting for further news. At 9:00 p.m. the air raid alarm sounded and some German bombers came over. We watched the planes dropping flares to light up the targets. Anti-aircraft fire soon filled the sky. We could hear the bombs landing somewhere in the city, but there was still no sign of troop carriers or paratroopers.

During the day, 260 9th Air Force C-47s dropped needed supplies to the surrounded troops at Bastogne.

December 24: That night we had an air raid and then one time during the night we heard a buzz bomb stop overhead. We dove under our beds but it landed elsewhere. Rumors are that IX TAC may move again as Liege may soon be under attack.

December 25: Christmas Day: Worked from 0800 to 1600 and it was very busy. For on this day, the CCB 2nd Armored Division with the support of our fighter bombers, counter attacked the German Panzers and stopped them just two miles short of the Meuse River.

At our Christmas dinner held in the gymnasium, we had guests as well for we shared our meal with a group of children from town. Besides the buzz bombs, the German air force staged air raids all day long, including strafing the streets.

December 26: Worked in the morning and was on guard duty for two hours. We had a short air raid at night with the usual pyrotechnics, but our main concern was the buzz bomb that landed close by.

December 28: At 0225 in the morning, I awoke to the sound of a buzz bomb diving. A whistling sound that got louder and louder and then came the explosion. A buzz bomb had struck our building. When I realized it was diving, I covered my face with my blanket just before it struck but my hands were exposed. The windows blew out, walls collapsed. My bed was next to a partition, which had a blackboard. The blackboard fell on top of me and on top of the blackboard fell the plaster and brick infill from the stud wall. Flying glass cut my exposed hands, my bags and my blanket.

For a few moments there was dead silence, and then I heard someone crying for help from outside the building. I was able to crawl out from under the blackboard and in the dim moonlight make out there was plaster and broken glass everywhere. Some or part of the walls and ceiling was gone.

All the windows were blown out. Two large wooden ceiling beams straddled Jackson's and Fountain's beds.

I pulled out my trousers from under my head, where it was serving as a pillow and finally dug out my jacket and shoes. My right hand was bleeding badly so I wrapped it with a handkerchief. My left hand had some minor cuts. As I checked with the men, I found we all had received some wounds from the flying glass.

I went down the now rickety wooden staircase to the street with great difficulty. As I walked through the courtyard, I saw that the front wing and the kitchen was a mass of rubble. On reaching the street, I saw a number of men were digging in the debris. I could hear voices calling for help. The GI's were feverishly pulling away with their bare hands the bricks that covered the bodies.

I was limping from the weight of the blackboard as I walked across the street to C Company billets where I was able to bandage the cuts as best I could, as the medics were in the street busy treating many other injured men. There was snow on the ground and I was cold and shaking. I went to the gym, someone gave me some blankets, and I lay my sore body down, got warm, and went to sleep. The rest of the night was a haze. Late in the morning, we went back upstairs, carefully dug out, and collected our belongings in all the debris. Sgt. Hunt and was sorry to hear of his death and, of course the death of the other men as well. (And as happened to so many of us we never really had a chance to attend to the burial of our comrades.)

That afternoon I had dinner with C Company and as I had to work at 4:00 p.m., I left my belongings in the gym to be moved to my new billets in a school on the Boulevard de Avroy. I walked to work on the 9th TAC switchboards and at 4:00 in the afternoon operating with a bandaged hand, sore side and hip and still shaky and nervous. It was very busy as well.

In the afternoon, my belongings were moved to my new quarters that we are sharing with the 327th Fighter Control. After coming off duty at midnight, I went to the address of my new billets and went to my assigned classroom on the top floor. I found I was all alone.

Except for my bed and my belongings, the room and the rest of the floor was empty. It was kind of eerie in being the only one in the building. As there were no blackout curtains on the windows, I had a view of the events occurring outside. It was bad enough that I was still unnerved from the experience I had just gone through, but that night lying in my cot I could see the German bombers dropping flares that lit up the sky, the anti-aircraft fire and the exhaust of the buzz bombs flying by January and every so often, the explosions. I did not sleep well that night.

December 29: I discovered that the men had moved to the basement. I went to work at 8:00 a.m. with my hand still wrapped in a makeshift bandage. Our planes were flying again so we were very busy. Worked until 4:00 p.m. and after I finished work, I moved to the basement. I am living in a former coal bin with eight other men. The room is windowless, dark, damp, dirty and cold so we sleep with our clothes on. All of the men in the room are strangers to me. I felt all alone.

January 3, 10, 11, and 19: Buzz bombs stopped overhead but landed elsewhere. In several cases we switchboard operators were at work in the van when it stopped. Most of the unit moved back to Verviers on the 19th.

January 22: I packed up and arrived in Verviers around noon and went to work on the switchboard at midnight.

January 24: I worked from 4:00 p.m. to midnight and on January 25, I worked from midnight to 8:00 a.m.

January 22 to January 25: Ninth TAC flew some 1,500 sorties against the retreating German Army destroying hundreds of vehicles, tanks and armored vehicles. Our telephones were busy February 1: There are no more buzz bombs. The buzz bomb attack is over.

MY ARMY SERVICE

David Dixon
639th Antiarcraft Artillery Automatic Weapons Battalion

I was inducted into the U.S. Army on November 11, 1943. My military basic training was done at Fort Eustis, Virginia and Camp David, North Carolina.

From Camp Kilmer, New Jersey, we embarked by ship and after twelve days by sea, landed in Scotland. From there, we traveled by train to Aldermaston Court in England.

I was with the 639 AAA AW Battalion that crossed the English Channel to LeHarve, France. We were assigned to First Army attached to Vth Corps and the 99th Division. Our assignment at Bullinger, Belgium was to shoot buzz bombs. We knew war was getting rough on December 16, 1944 when the Battle of the Bulge had begun. I was a gunner on a half-track.

Our orders were to move. The front was so confused when we were ordered to withdraw, and if the machinery and equipment could not be moved, we destroyed it.

On the night of December 16, the 639 AW Battalion lost three 40mm guns, eleven M-51 half-tracks, and machine guns. When retreating that night, the German army was dropping paratroopers and flares that lit up the sky like daylight. The men that were manning the guns destroyed them and left on foot with only their rifles. We were, more or less, in No Man's Land in the Ardennes, Malmedy, Bastogne, St. Vith and other villages for about eleven days. The only food and ammunition we had was what other soldiers shared with us. We went without a bath the entire eleven days. The cold was very severe. It had sleeted and snowed and frozen about four inches or more with heavy fog. The foxholes had frozen, and we had to break the ice to enter them for protection and sleep, if possible, as we moved from place to place. We knew this was a very real war. Frozen bodies of German and U.S. troops were everywhere. On December 21 and 22, the 639th was attached to the First Infantry Division, who turned back Von Rundstedt's final attempt to reach Liege.

On December 25, a beautiful, clear day, the fog having lifted, the Air Force gave us some relief. The frozen bodies were stacked like wood on the backs of trucks. We received some turkey for Christmas and a lot of German 88 shells. Many of the soldiers who survived the Battle of the Bulge suffered severe frost bite. Because of my frost bitten feet, I spent ten days in a field hospital in Belgium. After December 25, we were called upon to plug holes wherever needed along the front line.

STRINGING WIRE IN THE DARK

Elmer M. Dixon
246th Combat Engineer Battalion, Co C

I don't remember Christmas, but I am sure we had something special, maybe pie or cake. But I do remember New Year's Eve. We had a midnight celebration that is still clear in my 77-year-old mind, so I thought I would write about this celebration which I am sure many besides myself will remember.

We were the 246th Combat Engineer Battalion in the Hurtgen Forest. We were fixing the road so that we could close it down in a hurry if the Germans decided to come through into Belgium. We mined little bridges over creeks and ditches, and we notched hundreds of trees alongside the road and wrapped them with plastic explosives so they would fall across the road if we blew them up. On the upper end of the road there was a little slope with a clearing on the top about 100 yards wide. In the woods on the far side of the clearing a German infantry division was dug in. Now this was freezing weather with about a foot of snow on the ground. Those that were there, living in those foxholes will long remember what a miserable holiday season they lived through. We engineers were lucky. After a day's work we went back to houses in a little village in Germany.

Anyway someone decided that we would go out after dark for a few nights and string barbed wire through the middle of the field because there was fear that the Germans were going to make a push and come across the open ground. We couldn't get our trucks closer than a mile from the area so we had to walk and carry our rolls of wire and steel stakes through the snow.

Sometimes we waited for hours in our trucks, waiting for clouds to cover the moon. In the moonlight the Germans would be able to see us out there, so it was a very scary situation. We were even worried about getting shot by American guards—the word was passed down the line that we were out there, but there was always the chance that someone didn't get the word, and American guards were supposed to shoot anything that moved in front of them

We did have one man shot by American guards. Sgt. Roy Page, of San Diego, California, was breaking trail in the snow for his crew of wire stringers when he ended up in front of a German machine gun. A quick burst from the gun and he flopped into a shallow shell hole unhurt. He could hear them talking, deciding if they got him or not. He knew if he got up and ran they would get him for sure, so he laid there without moving and soon it got light. Now he had three choices: get up and run and get shot; get up and surrender and probably get shot; or wait until night came again and start crawling in the snow until it seemed safe to stand up and walk. Unfortunately, we were not supposed to work that night, so when he got in sight of American guards he was shot. We heard later that he got shot in the shoulder and would be all right—if getting shot in the shoulder means you are all right. I have a feeling that many GIs, living in a frozen dirt hole in the snow after several weeks would be glad to trade their holes in the ground for a hole in the shoulder and a trip to a nice warm hospital.

The Germans knew we were out there stringing wire in the dark. One night several engineers were packing their rolls of wire through the snow and they came face-to-face with a German scouting patrol. They looked at each other and the engineers dropped their wire and took off, and the Germans took off in the opposite direction. Then one of the Germans stopped and shouted in big city American English, "Run you mother----ers." A vulgar expression popular among American teenagers at the time. This German had undoubtedly gone to school in America. Germans liked to have an ex-American along on scouting patrols, if they got challenged by an American guard he might be able to convince them they were not Germans. In a situation like that with the lines so close together none in the open after dark would have dared to fire a shot. Both sides would send up a flare and anyone in the middle would wish they were home.

Anyway, December 31st came along and we got the word, "It's going to be cloudy so we string wire tonight." We talked it over among ourselves, the 8th Infantry would be quiet when midnight came because they would know we were out there working, but the Germans would know it also and they might schedule some sort of celebration for us—not a happy celebration. So we decided when it got close to midnight to get close to a good hole. Anyway, at a quarter to midnight I had a good hole picked out and I stopped all open operations right there. At the stroke of midnight the Germans shot up two flares lighting up the whole area, twice as bright as day, then the mortars started coming in-exploding over the whole area. They were shooting all of their machine guns and I imagine every rifleman was warming up his rifle. I don't know how long it took those flares to hit the ground and die out but it seemed forever. When it got dark again, it got real quiet and I could hear the faint sound of singing coming from the German lines. It sounded like the German version of Auld Lang Syne. Now I don't think the Germans were expecting many casualties if any from their awesome fireworks display. I think they wanted to ring in the New Year with gusto, and also to let us know they were still there.

One party of five men led by Sgt. Dan House, of Holt, Michigan, discovered they had taken shelter in an abandoned German slit trench latrine. Fortunately, the bottom was frozen solid.

PUBLIC OPINION, MEDIA ENTERPRISE, AND THE REALITIES OF WARFARE – AN INCOMPATIBLE MIXTURE

Joseph C. Doherty
99th Infantry Division, 393rd Infantry Regiment, Company H

White House spokesperson, Tony Snow, told a CNN interviewer Sunday, June 18 (2006), that "if somebody had taken a poll in the Battle of the Bulge I dare say people would have said 'Wow, my goodness, what are we doing here.' But you cannot conduct a war based on polls."

Unfortunately for Snow, somebody did conduct a poll at the time of the Bulge when some 750,000 U.S., British and German troops were engaged in a mortal struggle in eastern Belgium and Luxembourg. (December 16, 1944, to January 31, 1945).

The Washington Post Federal Page writer, Al Kamen, reported that

George Gallup polled a sampling of the American people at the time. He found that in spite of the carnage an overwhelming percentage of people interviewed continued to support the war on Hitler, and opposed any compromise (Post, June 23, 2006).

However, as usual with polls then and now, generalized and volatile public opinion reflects only part, and not the most important part, of the historical reality.

The poll results at the time of the Battle of the Bulge would surely have been more nuanced and negative if the media covering World War II had been as multi-faceted, uncensored, free-wheeling, and eager for leaks by insiders as it is now.

Certainly there were plenty of negative happenings and major failures on the Allied side, not to mention high-level disputes crying out for exposure, if exposure had been the order of the day as it is now with our Iraq experience.

To call the roll of only the most egregious and unreported or glanced-over aspects of the Battle of the Bulge:

In November and early December 1944, the Wehrmacht was able to bring a half million troops, thousands of artillery pieces and rocket-throwing tubes, more than a thousand armored fighting vehicles, and twelve hundred aircraft up to or near the American front line at its most vulnerable place, the Ardennes Region.

Yet American corps, army, and army group commanders whose troops were most at risk due to the German buildup made virtually no preparations for what this mighty enemy force may have been planning. Nor did General Eisenhower's headquarters at SHAEF.

The American Army suffered eighty thousand battle casualties in six weeks of bitter fighting. Not a few of the casualties were rear-area soldiers hastily dispatched to the front and men from replacement depots with very little training in infantry warfare.

The U.S. Army was plainly unprepared for a major battle on the Western Front during the coldest, most punishing winter weather in 50 years. The soldiers' OD (olive drab) uniforms made obvious targets against the snowy fields and woods and were inadequate to protect them from the cold. The cuffed boots most of them wore sucked up icy water at every seam. This resulted in tens of thousands of men who had to be evacuated due to immersion foot and frozen feet.

Some of the most important weapons used by American troops in the Bulge fighting were inferior to those of their German foes: high velocity anti-tank guns, anti-tank weapons operated by individual soldiers, machine guns, armored fighting vehicles, for example.

The crisis of men and arms of the American side in the early days of the German counterattack gave General Eisenhower's two principal allies, General Charles deGaulle, commander of the 1st French Army, and Field Marshal Bernard Law Montgomery, commander of the British 21st Army Group, many opportunities to assert themselves, which they did.

DeGaulle threatened to remove his army from the Allied coalition if Eisenhower did not rescind an order to shorten the American lines in the Strasbourg area in order to obtain reinforcements to fight in the Bulge.

Montgomery used the crisis to push hard once again that a single commander be put in charge of all Allied forces in combat, from the North Sea to the Swiss border. The Field Marshall's opportunism infuriated Ike. So much so, that he told his staff he planned to message the Allied Joint Command to choose: "Monty or me." Ike's staff talked him out of it.

Monty wasn't through. He called a press conference as the Battle of the Bulge was winding down to announce that he and his British Army had turned the tide and saved their American allies. General Omar Bradley, U.S. 12th Army Group Commander, and the generals commanding his three armies were outraged. They urged Ike to fire his incorrigible British subordinate. (And wouldn't that have been a media sensation in Great Britain.)

Both Winston Churchill and Eisenhower appealed in secret to Stalin to step up his plans for a winter offensive in the East to relieve pressure on the U.S. forces fighting in the Bulge. As might be expected, Stalin took maximum propaganda advantage of his Allies' pleas, which he didn't keep secret. Stalin would claim thereafter that the Red Army, though not prepared, speeded up its offensive and thereby "saved" their American allies from a crushing defeat.

In Washington, Secretary of War Henry Stimson, was shocked and unnerved by the dramatic early success of a foe believed was on the verge of surrender. He met with General George C. Marshall. U.S. Army Chief of Staff, to ascertain how bad the damage and what now should be done.

At the time of the meeting Wehrmacht troops had torn a wedge in the American lines sixty miles deep and sixty-four miles wide at the base, destroyed one infantry division, come close to destroying two more, and chewed up American armored units in the breakthrough area. American rear guard actions and repositions were going on all across the battlefield.

Marshall was optimistic about stopping the German counteroffensive. But he was not unrealistic about the new conditions that might result. He told Stimson it might be necessary to go to the American people to obtain their approval of an expanded mobilization and a more cautious strategy that could prolong the war. Marshall added he didn't believe this would be necessary in the end, however.

A few reporters of major newspapers sounded a pessimistic note after so many months of writing and broadcasting upbeat stories and predictions of an imminent German collapse.

Hanson W. Baldwin, chief military analyst of The New York Times, wrote that if Liege, Belgium on the Meuse River was taken by the Germans two U.S. armies would need to pull back and the great Port of Antwerp, Belgium, would be endangered. Drew Middleton, another Timesman that people paid attention to, wrote, "[The German] offensive has lost its local character. It now affects... the whole character of the war in the West."

In general, however, censored U.S. media was content to file and broadcast stories of heroic American soldier conduct on the Bulge battlefield and rewrite Army press releases on the general situation (bad, but getting better).

None of the media efforts at the time even began to cover what General Bradley described in a memoir written long after as, "The high-level political and strategic battles (that) violently shook, and very nearly shattered, the Allied High Command."

Tony Snow made a mistake not looking up George Gallup's post-Battle of the Bulge polling before his off-the-cuff remarks. His larger mistake was not drawing the logical and important big lesson of the Battle of the Bulge happenings, their coverage by the U.S. media at the time, and its influence on public opinion.

Error, surprise, failure, lack of sufficient forces, ineffective weapons, and lots more are a constant in warfare, intrinsic to the actions of commanders and the experiences of their men (and now women).

If a freewheeling and uncensored media make these the only reality for our side hereafter, America better find a safe, terrorless, death-and-injury-proof way of fighting its wars, large and small. Or renounce war altogether, if it can.

THERMOPYLAE IN THE ARDENNES

Joseph C. Doherty
99th Infantry Division, 393rd Infantry Regiment, Company H

How six battalions of the 99th Infantry Division held off five Wehrmacht Divisions for 36 hours and ruined the plans of 6th Panzer Armee for a quick breakout in Hitler's Ardennes counteroffensive of December 1944.

The 99th Division moved to the Western Front in mid-November 1944. The sector assigned fronted Germany's fortified West Wall. It extended from the picturesque little town of Monschau on the headwaters of the Roer River, all the way south to the Losheim Gap, Germany's historic route for breaking into Belgium and France.

The distance covered by the 99th's front line was 23 miles–as the crow flies. But soldiers and their machines are not crows. Given the lay of the land in this eastern Ardennes region, the many obstacles on the ground, and time of the year with winter coming on, a 23 mile-long line can't even begin to suggest the actual amount of front line the 99th's three infantry regiments would be defending.

The high hills, trackless forests, marshes, and farmers' fields, and the few villages connected by poor roads or none at all were more suitable for guerilla warfare than for warfare between mechanized armies.

Nonetheless, Adolph Hitler, the absolute ruler of Germany and his armies, thought otherwise. He personally selected the sector occupied by the 99th for his favorite army, the newly created 6th Panzer Armee. It was heavy with Panzers and would have a tough time with the terrain.

Sixth Panzer Armee's 1st Panzer Korps with its attached 67th Infanterie Korps was the most formidable aggregation of armed might in the Wehrmacht's Ardennes counteroffensive of December 1944.

It brought to the front—and that front, mind you, was mostly in the area occupied by the 99th—the following power:

Two SS Panzer Divisions, each with 20,000 men and boys and 200 tanks and other armored fighting vehicles.

One Panzergrenadier Division, well-armed with mobile, armored assault guns.

One Luftwaffe ground division of infantry—paratroopers they were called, but weren't—poorly trained and led but large in numbers and determination.

Four infantry divisions—called Volksgrenadiers.

A battalion of Tiger tanks. All of this power on the ground supported by 1,000 artillery and Werfer (rocket throwing) tubes.

The sector in eastern Belgium held by the 99th was the gateway for the infantry and armor of 1st SS Panzer Korps' right wing to reach their first objective, the Meuse River near Liege, Belgium. They were not about to let a little enemy infantry division new to the front hold them up one single hour after they struck.

Six 99th Division battalions were particular targets for this Aggression of power. They occupied respectively:

A village south of Monschau called Hofen.

A vital—for the Germans—logging road through Uic woods to two little towns, the Twin Towns we'll called them, because they were pretty much joined together, they were located half way between the 99th's front in the woods and the Elsenborn Heights.

And the most critical of all in the plans of 1st SS Panzer Corps, the Losheimergraben Crossroads, where two major highways came together at a custom post on what had been the German-Belgium border.

Lieutenant Colonel McClemand Butler's 3rd Battalion, 395th Infantry, occupied Hofen. The 38th Cavalry Recon Squadron was in Monschau and the village close by west of it.

Following an enormous artillery and rocket barrage that brought down many houses in Hofen and set Butler's command post afire, two battalions of the 326th Volksgrenadiers came marching in files in the glow of searchlights.

Their objective was to get through Butler's front line and into Hofen. The wave of marchers was beaten off by the mortars, machine gunners, and riflemen of the 3rd Battalion. And a couple of anti-tank gun crews on the line helped also, as did 99th artillery fire. A regiment of the 326th suffered awful casualties.

Over the next two days the 326th would try again and again to breach Butler's line. A hundred or so VG did get through the storm of the 3rd Battalion's fire to capture a few buildings in the town. They were routed out.

The story was much the same on Butler's left flank, a mile or so west of Monschau. The cavalry had lots of automatic weapons. It was reinforced by a platoon of big, mobile tank destroyers and artillery. After several sharp and costly assaults on the cavalry by the 326th Volksgrenadiers, they gave up. In three days of beating at Butler's men and the cavalry, the Germans had taken 1,500 casualties, Butler's unit, scarcely 50.

A Luftwaffe drop of a few hundred paratroops in the marshes a few miles west of Monschau was a fiasco. The brave Germans who managed to reach the ground safely were hunted down or lost in the wilderness.

Eight miles to the southeast, deep in what I called the Todeswald, the woods of death, was a logging road, muddy, gravel-covered. It went from the vital International Highway just east of the 99th front line, to the Twin Towns.

Two companies of Lieutenant Colonel Jack Allen's 3rd Battalion, 393rd Infantry, were emplaced on the left of the road. The other on the right.

On the right flank, the rifle companies of Major Matt Legler's 1st Battalion were spread around the snowy forest floor in foxholes and dugouts.

In the dark before dawn, the same horrendous artillery and Werfer attack came down on the two battalions as at Hofen.

When the fire lifted, the searchlights came on. Two battalions of the 277th Volksgrenadiers came running and screaming. 99th Division artillery hurt them badly, but they kept coming. Within an hour, two companies of the Allen-Leglar defensive front were overwhelmed.

There now followed two days of close-in battling in the dense woods north and south of the logging road. Rifle and automatic fire was everywhere as small groups of opposing fighters dodged among the trees and had it out Indian style. Mortar and artillery shells on both sides kept exploding in the trees, also.

Both battalions received small reinforcements. Allen's company of riflemen; Leglar's a scratched-together platoon of 393rd headquarters men.

By nightfall December 16, Allen and his officers had been able to pull together enough survivors to form a perimeter around his command post. It was three miles west of what had been their front line when this all started.

Leglar, too, was trying to build a fall back defensive hedgehog based on his command post. But another battalion of 277 Volksgrenadiers had come into the forest. Having already lost the equivalent of four platoons of riflemen, dead, wounded, and prisoners captured, his 1st Battalion was in bad trouble.

The bad trouble got worse for both battalions that night (December 16-17). The commander of 1st SS Panzer Korps ordered a regiment of Panzergrenadiers (12th SS Panzer Division) riding troop carriers into the melee. He was frustrated. The attack by 277 VG on the 99th Division had not made the breakthrough he expected. His Volksgrenadiers were still stuck in the forest among the troops of the two American battalions.

Late December 16 Allen received a radio message from the 393rd regimental commander, Lieutenant Colonel Jean Scott: Prepare to attack the enemy after daylight. Restore your lines, i.e., drive the Volksgrenadiers and Panzergrenadiers back to where they started.

Allen did as he was told. Even though his officers had to lean on their cold, tired, and hungry men to make them go. Everyone considered it a doomed effort. It was. Dogged, courageous, the company making the attack was broken apart by the Germans.

Shortly after noon December 17, even Scott knew the game was up. He ordered Allen and Leglar to break off contact with the enemy and get their soldiers out of the woods to an area behind a battalion of the 2nd Division, 23rd Regiment. It had been sent in as reinforcements early that day.

Five miles south was the Losheimergraben Crossroads. The 394th Infantry units there had formed a kind of triangle covering the good, paved roads and by-roads that were of first priority to 1st Panzer Korps. I called it the Fatal Triangle.

These roads, which passed through the triangle, formed the gateway to the upper part of the Losheim Gap, Germany's historic route of invasion.

Lieutenant Colonel Robert Douglas' 1st Battalion, 394th Infantry, occupied one point of the triangle, the Losheimergraben customs post and the buildings supporting it, plus the fields and forests nearby.

Major Norman Moore's 3rd Battalion, minus one rifle company, occupied a railway station and the area around it a mile or so west of the crossroads. The second point.

Lieutenant Lyle Bouck's 25-man intelligence and recon platoon was positioned inside the Losheim Gap on a hill a mile south of Moore. The third point of the triangle.

Everywhere in the triangle space, the predawn shelling and rocketing by the guns and Werfer of 6th Panzer Armee were more intense than at any of the other target areas along the front line of the 99th.

When the crashing and slashing, and storm of metal ceased, the 12th Volksgrenadier Division struck hard at Douglas and Moore's battalions. A third enemy division, 3rd Parachute, was also on the scene. Its vanguard marched confidently past Bouck's men well hidden on a hill nearby.

The Fusiliers (light infantry) of 12th Volksgrenadier came marching up the railroad track into Moore's 3rd Battalion space. They got in a fire fight with his infantry and command post soldiers, retreated, only to come back in force several times thereafter. Each time the Fusiliers were sent off licking their wounds.

Almost from the first moment after the shelling ceased and the 12th Volksgrenadiers' attacked, Douglas' soldiers at and around the crossroads in the buildings and in foxholes and bunkers dug out of the earth were in a fight for their lives.

A regiment of 12th VG sent combat teams straight at Douglas' company in the woods east of the crossroads. The attackers were hurt by their own artillery rounds falling short. Yet they were still able to break up Douglas' company; kill, wound, and capture about half of its soldiers; and send the rest running back to the crossroads.

Another company around Douglas' headquarters and the crossroads buildings was hit in the flank and pushed closer to the buildings. The Germans had more armored assault guns than the defenders had anti-tank guns. An 81mm mortar section of 1st Battalion's weapons company raised its tubes to a near 85 degree angle to drop its bombs on enemy soldiers about to overrun them.

Moore's battalion around the railway station, already shorthanded and suffering battle losses too, was ordered by regiment to send a company to reinforce Douglas. They took up positions on a hill overlooking the action.

By early morning December 17—it happened to be a Sunday—Douglas' principal fighters were holed up in the buildings around the crossroads. They had turned them into little fortresses. They were surrounded, had retreated to the basements, and were firing at the Germans from the windows.

The commander of the besieging Volksgrenadier regiment put an end to it. He made plain that the buildings would be blown up with Douglas' men in them if they didn't surrender. They did.

Bouck's little platoon on the hill was soon discovered by the paratroops. The only message he received by radio from regiment was "Hold at all costs." Hold at all costs against a battalion of paratroops, 25 against 600.

The 600 were inept and poorly led. Bouck and his men held them off from dawn to dusk December 16. But the sheer weight of the attackers, plus a few Uteroffiziers who finally got some smarts, won out Bouck and his surviving men were taken prisoner.

On the left flank of all this action, the 2nd Battalion of the 394th was located deep in the forest. They had orders from regiment to hurry south to help in the Losheimergraben battle. In fact, they had no orders at all. Even though one of their companies was east of the International Highway.

And the battalion was in a fight of its own. Several, in fact, when Fusiliers of the 277th Volksgrenadier, supported by assault guns, struck at leading companies along the highway. Artillery fire, controlled by the forward observers using the 99th Division artillery radio net, drove the attackers off, finally.

The 99th Division command radio net was delivering mixed messages about the situation. And the battalion's commander had fallen apart. Captain Ben Legare and other HQ officers had to take over.

The mass withdrawal of the three battered 99th battalions from the wood west of the International Highway and the two at the Fatal Triangle around Losheimergraben, began in the afternoon of December 17. This was close to 40 hours after the 1st SS Panzer Korps' divisions attacked them before dawn December 16. Officers of these tired and wounded units had little information from higher commands as to what was expected of them, and what their eventual destination would be.

For the five battalions, now down to maybe 3,000 in total numbers, give or take, a dangerous new struggle was about to begin.

Their journey over the five or so miles of snow-covered fields, and icy, muddy roads and trails was a nightmare of confusion, loss, and mistake. All of which would cost more lives.

Cold, wet, hungry they all were. Few officers in the exodus knew they were supposed to be heading toward the Elsenborn Heights. This was, and is, a high plateau, about eight miles from north to south. It was six miles west of what had been the 393rd Infantry's front line on December 16. The long, flat ridge line at the top was perfect for defense, but if the ridge should be overrun, both Spa, Belgium, headquarters of US 1st Army, and Eupen, Belgium, headquarters of Fifth Corps, would be in mortal danger.

Officers of the Fifth Corps HQ and the 99th and 2nd Divisions were working obsessively to build an impregnable final fallback line in depth covering the heights of Elsenborn.

No small part of the defense would be a huge aggregation of artillery and mortar tubes: 16 battalions of artillery of four US divisions; 394th, even battalions of Corps artillery including large-bore howitzers and guns; the cannon companies of 12 infantry regiments; a 4.5-inch chemical mortar battalion; the 81mm mortars of 36 infantry battalions.

As the soldiers of the 99th Division and the 2nd Division 23rd Regiment withdrew from the area east of the Twin Towns and the Losheimergraben Crossroads triangle, their Volksgrenadier enemies did not stay behind.

Soldiers of the 277th and 12th Volksgrenadier and 3rd Parachute Divisions kept pressing the 99th and 2nd Division battalions hard. These included two of the 393rd Infantry, three of the 394th, and two of the 23rd Infantry. (The latter's 1st Battalion had come up late to reinforce the 394th, fought a short, sharp fight, and was also moving west before the German tide.)

In some places, the Germans had advanced to strong points they hurriedly put in place in front of the withdrawing American battalions. Vicious and costly little fire fights followed as the 99th soldiers stumbled on these strong points by mistake or pushed to get around them.

Uncounted numbers of vehicles were in the withdrawal, adding to the impediments the walking soldiers encountered: gun carriages, trucks of all sizes, ambulances and improvised ambulances trying to get the badly wounded out, big artillery trains of trucks and guns.

The murderous enemy guns and Werfer had not gone silent. Shells and rockets kept crashing down at random on the masses of men moving over the fields and woods, and friendly artillery fire of 99th and 2nd Division didn't always stay friendly.

On the left (south) of this boiling cauldron of moving struggle and strife, not a mile away was another 1st SS Panzer Korps power rolling west: Kampfgruppe Peiper of Malmedy Massacre fame, a 15-mile long Anaconda of SS infantry and armor.

Peiper and his troops had already lapped up and made prisoners of the mixed groups of 99th Division and other American troops at the 99th rest camp along the way. His men murdered at least 20 of the scores of American troops they captured. The hugely powerful force was now on its way to take a 2nd and 99th service and supply center at the base of the Elsenborn Ridge.

Peiper would make another haul there of prisoners and of American fuel, food, and cigarettes.

One group of major actions have been left out until now.

On December 13 after daylight, two regimental combat teams of Major General Walter Robertson's 2nd Division, and the 395th RCT of the 99th, Colonel Alexander MacKenzie commanding, started to besiege the pillboxes of Germany's West Wall. These guarded a crossing of two forest roads sur-rounded by woods, five miles northeast of the Twin Towns.

A big force of some 9,000 men, backed by many guns, was brought in for the operation. Combat Command B, of 9th Armored Division, waited south of the Elsenborn Ridge to move forward once the infantry had pushed through the pillboxes.

After three days and nights of awful combat for the American side flesh vs. barbed wire, machine gun bullets, exploding enemy mortar and artillery shells, and concrete walls, gains were made but at great cost to two of the combat teams, 9th and 395th.

About noon December 17, four days after the start of the operation. General Robertson ordered it halted in place. Bad things were happening on the flanks. The three combat teams were in imminent danger of being encircled.

Also, they were needed to defend the Twin Towns. 99th and 2nd Division Headquarters and other troops there were facing a full-scale attack by 12th SS Panzer's grenadiers and armor.

Robertson believed the two little adjoining Belgium farm towns had to be held long enough for the Elsenborn Heights barrier line to be completed before the 12th SS Panzer Division and the grenadiers of 277th VG got mov-ing against it.

The 2nd Division commander now took on a heavy burden: bringing his 38th and 9th regimental combat teams south over a hilly, graveled road through the snow covered forest. All the while 6th Panzer Armee artillery and Werfer had the road under fire. And the 277 Volksgrenadier Division was also pressing the 395th RCT from the northeast.

He ordered MacKenzie to keep his men in the woods to serve as a flank guard for the 2nd Division soldiers moving south.

The 2nd Division commander was double handicapped in preparing for the defense of the Twin Towns by two decisions made at Lieutenant General Courtney Hodges' US Army headquarters.

1. On December 16 the combat command of 9th Armored Division was taken away as Robenson's support and sent south toward St. Vith, Belgium, then under serious attack. He thereby lost a powerful force that was needed for the defense of both the Twin Towns and the Elsenborn Heights,

2. And Hodges did not want to give up the operation to break through the West Wall. He refused to allow Robertson to clear the forest until the morning of December 17. This forced the 2nd Division to lose precious hours needed to race south to the Twin Towns, and prepare a defense against the onslaught of 12th SS Panzer Division.

Now it would be touch-and-go whether the tactics to be employed would be made inoperable by the speed and power of the onrushing Panzer division.

Two days of dangerous and destructive combat followed. Twelfth SS Panzer Division commanders sent wave after wave of armor and Panzergrenadiers at Robertson's men defending the two towns.

An unknown number of 99th infantry, medics, and artillery forward observers also mixed in the battle, as did a battalion each of tanks and mobile tank destroyers.

It turned out to be one of the most memorable tank-infantry battles of the war on the American side in WWII:

Thousands of infantry, more than a hundred armored fighting vehicles on each side, artillery and rocket fires of both friend and foe adding to the conflagrations and carnage, night and day, up and down the narrow streets of the two little towns.

By the night of December 19-20, Robertson's valiants had forced 12th SS Panzer Division to change plans. They started to move out of the Twin Towns—or what was left of them—so try to keep their advance to the distant Meuse River near Liege on schedule. 12th SS Panzer would go south to the Loshimergraben Crossroads, then roll west to the Meuse—or so 1st SS Panzer Korps hoped.

However, the two-day delay and upset of this schedule gave officers of US V Corps' four infantry divisions—1st, 2nd, 9th, and 99th—just about enough time to build an impregnable barrier line on the crest of the Elsenborn high plateau. And this spelled more disaster for 12th SS Panzer when one of its Kampfgruppe attacked the 1st Division on December 21.

However, 6th Panzer Korps wasn't done with the 99th Division just yet. No sooner had Robertson's 38th Regiment evacuated the Twin Towns to move to the Elsenborn barrier line than the 3rd Panzergrenadier moved in. They used the towns as a base to mount a series of attacks directly at the 99th's positions still being built up on the heights. After three days of taking heavy losses, 3rd Panzergrenadier stood down. The tired and sorely tried 99th soldiers still showed enough gut power to fight off the Panzergrenadiers. And the masses of howitzers and guns supporting them laid on brutal punishment.

By the end of December, 1st SS Panzer Korps would have pulled all of its four armored and one armored infantry divisions out of the Elsenborn area.

The depleted Volksgrenadier divisions of 67 Korps remained to mount hopeless attacks directly at the 99th's positions still being built up on the heights.

Now loaded with replacement, all the 99th infantry had to put up with from December 20, 1944, until the end of January, 1945, was bitter cold, blankets of snow, sleeping in icy foxholes, dodging sporadic enemy shelling and mortaring, and patrolling into enemy positions, which always resulted in wounds and death from mines, potato mashers (hand grenades), and small arms fire.

And this is not to mention three days after Christmas, when the German 67 Korps, now running the order of battle in front of the Elsenborn barrier line, sent its newly arrived 246 VG straight at the front line of the 394th and 393rd Regiments. The Germans were scattered by the massed fires of the artillery and mortars. The same fate overcame the 246th Infantry and that of the now badly injured 12th VG when these two attacked the 2nd and 1st US Infantry Divisions on the right flank of the barrier line simultaneous with the action against the 99th.

Thus ended aggressive enemy action to overcome the American barrier line on the Elsenborn Heights.

But not the killing and dying when the four US infantry divisions started the long road back in mid-January. They now became attackers. The diehard Germans made them pay dearly for every forested hill, field, and village the Americans recaptured in late January and February.

From the first of December until the end of January, 534 soldiers of the 99th and attached units were killed in action. The 99th and attached units suffered 1,700 dead and wounded between December 15, 1944, and January 15. 1945, when the fighting I described was raging. And a thousand more were taken prisoner and marched off to the miserable Stalags of Germany.

By far most of the dead and wounded were from the five battalions who fought in the woods east of the Twin Towns and at the Fatal Triangle based on the Losheimergraben Crossroads. The stalwarts of the 3rd Battalion, 395th Regiment, at Hofen lost some 40 to death and wounds. Ninety-ninth units supporting the infantry-artillery, combat engineers serving as infantry, military police, medics, and signalmen, etc. also took hits. Enemy counter battery fire extracted a heavy toll of the 99th artillery, as did service with the front line infantry of their forward observers.

The 99th men paid in blood on December 16–17, 1944 to buy time:

Time for officers of the V Corps and the 2nd and 99th Divisions to put together the fallback barrier line on the Elsenborn Heights.

Time for General Robertson to get his three regimental combat teams south and west from the penetrations they had made in the forests north of the Twin Towns; put them in a blocking position in and around the towns; and engage in the horrendous infantry armor battle that stopped a Kampfgruppe of 12th SS Panzer Division and the 277th Volksgrenadier Division from pushing west to and over the Elsenborn Ridge.

Time for Brigadier General Cliff Andrus, CO of 1st Infantry Division, to mobilize his men and guns to beat back repeated attempts of another 12th SS Kampfgruppe to go round the southern flank of the heights and keep moving west.

The delays and obstacles caused by the stubborn fight of the 99th's infantry all of the first day after the 1st SS Panzer Korps attacked December 16 and most of the second day, made it possible for 2nd and 1st Infantry Divisions to stop 1st SS Panzer Korps' planned march over the Elsenborn Heights and on to the Meuse River near Liege, Belgium.

The plan of 6th Panzer Armee, of the Wehrmacht high command of Hitler himself was for 1st and 12th SS Panzer Divisions to move swiftly in parallel along five designated Rollbahnen, Panzer routes west to the Meuse. Three of these Rollbahnen were in the sector assigned to the 12th SS. Elsenborn Heights cleared of American forces was necessary to the success of the Panzer mission.

After a day's delay, 1st SS Panzer Division's Kampfgruppe Peiper did break for the west; the two Kampfgruppe of 12th SS Panzer did not. A tactical setback that ruined 6th Panzer Armee's Hitler-given mission of Schwerpunkting the Ardennes Counteroffensive. The late, renowned military historian and veteran of the 23rd Infantry Regiment in the Battle of the Bulge, Charles D. MacDonald, gave deserved credit to the soldiers of the 1st and 2nd Infantry Divisions for the crucial role they played in the Elsenborn Ridge battle. He also wrote of the 99th Division:

"The Germans had expected to penetrate the 99th Division's line and commit their armor soon after daylight on the first day. Despite some disarray in command at the division level, the fighting men of the 99th had denied that expectation by many hours." (A Time for Trumpets, page 410)

The soldiers of the 1st, 2nd, 9th, and 99th Divisions in the battles made it possible for the Elsenborn Heights barrier line to be made impregnable and hold to the last paid a terrible price.

And the 99th Division infantry paid the highest price of all.

Between December 15 and January 16, the four divisions participating in what historians now call The Battle of the Elsenborn Heights, which went on for just about that much of time, suffered a total of 4,028 dead and wounded. Forty-two percent of these were in the 99th.

Before dawn the soldiers of the 99th were hit by a devastating artillery and rocket barrage from a thousand tube and Werfer. Their battalions holding Hofen, in the woods, at the Fatal Triangle were attacked by overwhelming numbers of enemy, outnumbering them three and four to one. The up-front fighters lost contact with leaders and each other. Reinforcements were late in coming. The 99th's fighters were not well served by higher commands far from the front and confused as to what was happening there. Land lines rearward had been torn up by the huge pre-dawn artillery barrage. There was a pervasive belief at higher echelons that the Germans had no power remaining except for feeble local spoiling attacks that had to be put down quickly.

The only discernible orders that the CO's of the 99th battalions in the eye of the storm received were to stand fast, if they received any orders at all.

Their men did, to their triumph and sorrow.

Triumph that they stood fast against an overwhelming enemy force of infantry and armor.

Sorry that so many of their friends—from the training camps, the classrooms, and the foxhole line—lay dead, wounded or were missing.

THE TAKING OF DOCHAMPS, SAMREE AND BERISMENIL

Donald A. Edwards
84th Infantry Division, 335th Infantry Regiment, 2nd Battalion, Co E

An issue of *The Bulge Bugle* contained an article about the 2nd Armored Division and their activities in the Bulge from January 9, 1945 to January 14, 1945. The article dealt with the capture of Samree which the author described as a battle similar to that of St. Lo. Several years ago, I published a book entitled *A Private's Diary*, which covered my activities during World War II as a member of Company C, 335th Infantry Regiment, 84th Infantry Division.

One must first acknowledge that the Second Armored—"Hell on Wheels"—Division participated in numerous battles where their outstanding achievements were noted. However, the actual facts were not stated for this particular area in this article.

The actual situation must be reviewed. After the German advance in the Ardennes had been stopped, the U.S. Army commenced its counter-offensive on Wednesday, January 3rd. An area on the north side of the Bulge from

Hotton to Manhay, then south to include LaRoche and Houffalize, was designated as the joint operational zone of the 84th Infantry Division and the Second Armored Division. The 2nd Battalion of the 335th Regiment was assigned the road running from Amonines through Dochamps, Samree and Berismenil along with a unit from the Second Armored. To the left of this narrow highway ran the Aisne River which was open and flowing rapidly. It never froze.

On January 3, units of the 75th Infantry Division captured Amonines. The next day, the 2nd (White) Battalion took over their positions. On January 4, the attack started to capture Dochamps.

The attack by Company E stalled just outside Amonines. The reason was that the Germans had erected a road block of logs that completely blocked the highway. On the highway were three tanks from the Second Armored Division. An enemy machine gun covered the approaches. The next day Company G was ordered to proceed to the adjacent woods and flank the barricade. A flanking attack to the left was not feasible due to the flowing Aisne River. The flanking attack was successful. Company E had suffered one dead and 13 wounded.

January 6 brought a renewal of the attack by the Second Battalion. Every company proceeded into the woods on the right side. We had been informed that the armored men had dismantled the barricade. They had proceeded forward and met another roadblock.

As the Second Battalion proceeded through the ankle-deep snow, we heard periodic shelling from the German mortars and artillery. Shortly after 1400, the enemy found the correct range. Tree bursts from their mortars rained down. After fifteen minutes, the shelling ceased. About 150 yards from me were two artillery spotters from the Second Armored, a lieutenant and a sergeant. The sergeant had been hit in the right thigh. He was bleeding profusely, George Teets and I rushed over to give aid. The lieutenant knelt over the wounded man but did nothing. He was shell shocked. We pushed him away. Two bandages were applied. A third bandage was taken from the stunned lieutenant. He was told to wait for the medics. We later learned that the radio operator lived. The lieutenant was transferred to the rear. As we returned to the advance, Teets remarked, "Those guns from the armored are going to be able to help us." No new artillery observers were sent.

The next roadblock halted the Second Battalion's attack. I was ordered along with Teets and Jim Rochester to go back to a small hamlet to secure a building for the Advanced Command Post. In the hamlet, most of the buildings were occupied by personnel from the Second Armored. The following is from page 315 of my book.

"In one of the occupied houses," I inquired. "When did you men arrive here?"

"Oh, we came in this afternoon," replied a lanky blond.

"Did your outfit take this place?"

"Yea, the Krauts must have seen us coming and vamoosed."

"Any other outfit help you?"

"Some infantry outfit is assisting us, I think."

My face must have turned beet red when I replied. "Soldier. I know you're from a very famous outfit, but your tanks can't do anything without us dough-boys from the infantry. In these woods and on the highway, all the Germans have to do is erect a log roadblock. They had one yesterday and your tanks couldn't move. They have another one about 800 yards up the road. My company and some others are trying to get around them now. If you don't believe me, walk up that road. Get in front of that lead tank; Jerry will let you know its presence with some machine gun fire. Unless our battalion gets around it, you'll stay here until hell freezes."

"Sorry fella, you must have had a rough day."

"It could have been rougher but some guys are out there bleeding so we can get your damned tanks through that road."

On Sunday, January 7, the attack continued. The enemy had vacated the barricade. The advance by the Second Battalion finally captured Dochamps about 0100 on the 8th. The road into the village was completely icy. The tanks could secure no traction. On the afternoon of January, an episode occurred at Company E. From page 326, I quote;

"At 1600, the daily edition of the Army newspaper (*Stars and Stripes*) came. I immediately woke John Crable to relate to him what the paper stated. As he read the article, he kept shaking his head.

"It's just not true. The Second Armored Division had nothing to do with the capture of this place."

Credit for the capture of Dochamps had been given to the Second Armored Division. When I delivered the papers to Company E, the officers and enlisted men were about to explode. Someone said to me, "Edwards, you brought the wrong paper today."

On January 9, the attack resumed. I, again, quote from page 326:

"Early in the morning, the Third Battalion came through Dochamps. They started an attack on the next village, Samree. Several of us watched the start. We saw the Second Armored go into action. The attack went across an open field. Here the armored vehicles could maneuver."

On January 10, we could still hear firing around Samree. One GI remarked, "I sure hope Blue (Third) Battalion got more support from the armored than we did."

Although the capture of Samree was accomplished by the doughboys of the Third Battalion, credit in the *Stars and Stripes* was given to the Second Armored.

Inquiry was made about the number of German prisoners taken. The reply was, "Not a single Kraut was captured either in Dochamps or Samree." Everyone realized that the enemy knew how to resist and when to retreat was in good order.

Berismenil was captured by the Second Battalion in the early hours of January 14. The White Battalion had successfully flanked the town. The roadblocks on the main road had prevented any assistance from the armored. The big surprise in Berismenil was that about 50 Wehrmacht soldantens had not retreated with the main group and had to be flushed from the cellars.

Thus, out of the four villages on this narrow icy road in the Ardennes, the infantry alone had captured three. The armored has assisted in the capture of one, namely, Samree.

REMEMBERING THE CALL TO THE BULGE

Phillip S. Edwards
17th Airborne Division, Division Headquarters

I was assigned duties at Chilbolton Air Base to help coordinate the arrangements for following flights of our personnel. However, the weather
got socked in real bad, and it was impossible to fly across the channel. We
waited at Chilbolton on Christmas Eve, and then Christmas Day arrived. We
sang a few carols and listened to Major Glenn Miller's Army Air Force Band
play "American Patrol," "Londonderry Air," "Serenade in Blue," "A String of
Pearls," "In the Mood," "Anvil Chorus," and other songs, over the BBC.

Conversations with Air Force personnel included talk of what to do,
and what not to do, in various actual combat situations, which made us realize clearly that we were about to engage the enemy face-to-face. Late on
Christmas Eve, we heard the tragic news that, despite the bad weather, Glenn
Miller had taken off in a small plane for France, but had not arrived there and
was presumed lost in the channel.

We also listened anxiously to reports from Belgium where the Battle of
the Bulge was being waged, and we knew that the 101st Airborne Division was
already surrounded at Bastogne. This was the reason for General Ridgway's
urgent night call, and for our urgent need to be on the continent to help
stave off the German breakthrough in the Ardennes. The 82nd and the 101st
Airborne Divisions had been in areas in northern France, resting and re-
equipping after the Holland airborne landings in September, and had been
rushed to critical areas (Werbomont and Bastogne) Belgium.

Finally the bad weather over the channel cleared, and the remainder of the
17th Airborne troops were flown over, landed at air strips in northern France,
and in our case, transported in trucks in Mourmelon-le-Grand, where the
101st Airborne troops had been before they were rushed to Bastogne.

I was temporarily assigned to the skeletal force of 101st personnel who
were still at Mourmelon. My first duty was to help their Military Government
Section accomplish some liaison activity with the local citizens. I soon found

myself, along with a few other Americans, trying to convince these citizens that we were indeed Americans and not German Airborne troops dressed like Americans. This was an example of the havoc that the Germans were creating behind the American lines by doing just that.

It was extremely cold, and the snow was deep, as the area experienced the worst winter in 50 years. It was emotionally difficult to know that within a matter of days, or even hours, the 17th Airborne would be committed to combat. General Maxwell Taylor, Commander of the 82nd Airborne Division, later said that the 17th Airborne Division, committed on January 5, 1945, went into battle under the most difficult conditions, for a baptism of fire, he had ever seen (see page 430, *The Bitter Woods*).

ONE SMALL CORNER

John W. Fague
21st Armored Infantry Battalion, Company B

The beginning of our part in the Battle of the Bulge was the 29th of December 1944 near the town of Neufchateau, Belgium [France]. Our column of tanks and half-tracks as Combat Command Be had been rolling north all day, where to and what for I had no idea. The day was cold and windy. There was a layer of snow blanketing the ground; here and there it had drifted. We met many supply trucks on the road headed for the rear—their mission was accomplished. I was particularly aware of the ambulances that we met, red lights flashing, passing to the rear. They were evacuating the wounded and this meant there must be fighting ahead. Finally we passed artillery with their muzzles pointed skyward. The guns would cough and spit and belch their flames and then relax. First we passed the big boys, the Long Toms, 240 mm and 155 mm howitzers, and then closer to the front the standard army 105 mm pieces which backed up the line. From this I realized that our time had come, the moment of truth had arrived.

Late in the afternoon my company pulled off the road to the left. It was on a hill, which made an ideal place to bivouac. The first thing I noticed was the wreckage of an airplane and two lifeless forms on the snow that resembled bodies. The sight of dead bodies was something new to a nineteen-year-old boy from Shippensburg, Pennsylvania. I was anxious and curious to have a closer look at them. When I inspected the first body in the snow, I knew I should not have looked. It was the body of a German fighter pilot. His face was frozen and gray in color—it had a horrible far away stare. He had been lying there 36 hours or more and was frozen stiff. His fingers were gray and rigid. His legs were broken and doubled up under him. G.I.s had already looted the corpse. Someone had taken his fleece-lined air corps boots and he lay in his stocking feet. The pockets of his uniform had been pulled out and the contents removed. I noticed the stump of a finger. It has been cut off to get the ring he wore.

That was enough. I had seen more than I wanted to. I walked away with a hollow sickening feeling in my stomach. It was chow time but I didn't have much of an appetite anymore.

This was my first encounter with death. It left a vivid impression on my young mind. All during that sleepless night I could see the face of that flyer before me. In the days that followed I rubbed elbows with death many times. I saw my friends die and the strangeness of the phenomenon of death became blurred.

As had become instinctive with us, the company set up an all around defense and prepared to bed down for the night. We set up our machine gun outposts and dug slit trenches in the event of an air or artillery attack. Other elements before us had dug foxholes and gun positions on this slope so that we had few holes to dig.

Fortunately there was a straw stack in our area around which we made our beds. I pulled some straw off the stack and laid my bedroll on it. I got some more straw to put over me. That night was bright with a moon illuminating the snow. While I took my turn as outpost guard, a German reconnaissance plane swooped low over our position. The second time it came down some of our units arched machine gun tracer bullets in the direction of the sound but with no effect. During the night our artillery kept up its harassing fire on the enemy positions. They were firing on the enemy rear and shell bursts would illuminate the sky. The firing was spasmodic during the night but the tempo increased toward morning.

Early in the morning my platoon leader, Lt. Roy C. Stringfellow, came back from a meeting with the company commander, Capt. Elmore F. Fabrick, and brought information of the attack we were to make the next day. I was lying awake in my bedroll and heard him give the details of the attack to the platoon sergeants and the squad sergeants. One instruction of the lieutenant I could not forget: "There will be enemy artillery fire and plenty of it. The Germans always advance their fire, so keep the men moving."

At 4:30 a.m., I rolled up my bedroll and took off for the kitchen truck. After eating a hurried breakfast I came back to my half-track and got things ready to move out in the attack. Our company was to follow Baker Company of the 22nd Tank Battalion. The tanks were to pass our area at 6 a.m. For some unknown reason the tanks passed too early. Capt. Fabrick signaled for our platoon to take off down the road after the tanks. We hastily threw our equipment of the half-track and took off down the road. There had been some delay after the last tank had passed and so our platoon lost contact with the tank column. At the first intersection Lt. Stringfellow asked the battalion commander, Col. James R. Hoffman, who was standing there, the direction the tanks had taken. The colonel directed us down the wrong road.

Our half-track was now in the lead heading an independent attack. I noticed a few tanks peeking out from behind some buildings as we went by. And these I soon learned were our advance outposts. The next thing I knew we were out in no man's land [land between opposing forces] and all hell was breaking loose. The Krauts [nickname for the Germans] were preparing to make an attack of their own and their artillery was preparing the way. When the lieutenant realized we were on the wrong road, he brought our little column to a halt. There we sat on the road while he was attempting to establish contact by radio with the rest of our column. It was just beginning to get light, that gray sort of dawn. The German shells were exploding only a short distance away, and I could hear the shrapnel whining through the air. A farmhouse was smoldering in ruins beside our vehicle. It gave me a very terrifying feeling to sit there in that vehicle and hear those shells land. I knew that at any moment one might hit our vehicle or burst in the trees overhead. This was my first experience with the thought that I might die or be horribly wounded. Even though I was scared I tried to make a few jokes out of it but the boys were in no mood for my humor. We all sat huddled together in the half-track trying to make ourselves as small as possible and trying to keep our heads down below the quarter-inch armor plate that formed the sides of the track.

In the meantime Lt. Stringfellow had gone back on foot to the last crossroads and discovered that we should have turned left there. He came back to our vehicle and got our column turned around and started back. Once we moved back I felt better. As long as we were moving or doing something I had no time to be afraid, but when we stopped I felt helpless.

The lines through which we were passing were held by another division. They were very worried and concerned when they saw our vehicles withdraw. I saw a line of infantrymen bearing the insignia of the red keystone withdrawing across the railroad tracks. I later learned that they were my own Pennsylvania 28th Division which had been gallantly trying to hold their line against the German onslaught. They had been holding on, I learned, ever since the attack began. Groups of these infantrymen were straggling down the road beside our vehicle. They looked tired and weary, as if they didn't care anymore. Their rifles were slung over their shoulders and a dark growth of beard was on their faces.

The sight of these withdrawing men filled me with fear. I expected to see German infantry coming across those tracks. The fighting was coming closer and I wanted to be prepared. I put a cartridge in the chamber of my rifle, and kneeling on the seat I was ready to fire on any Germans that came over the rise formed by the railroad tracks.

When we reached the crossroads again, the situation was in general confusion. Vehicles were trying to go all ways at once. Several officers were trying to direct traffic and restore order from chaos. The tension was increased by the sound of shells crashing in the trees on each side of the road. We drove up a hill and found our tanks deployed in battle formation at the crest of the ridge. My vehicle stopped at the top of the hill and then moved on about 20 yards. I heard an explosion behind us and saw that a mortar shell had hit the second squad vehicle behind us when it pulled into our old position. The vehicle was disabled and three men wounded. These were our first casualties so far as I knew at the time. They carried the wounded to a pit that the Germans had evacuated just before we came over the hill. I later learned that several shells had hit the crossroads after we got through. One shell had made a direct hit on the third platoon half-track, killing three and sounding several others.

My position in the platoon was that of runner for Lt. Stringfellow. I followed him around like a dog following its master. The object of this was to keep one shell from injuring more than one or two men. It was here I received my first lesson in German camouflage. In a comer of a haystack the Germans had neatly concealed a machine gun. They had dug out a corner of the stack and placed strands of straw in the fence. You could walk right up to the gun and not notice it. I was so intent on following the lieutenant that I didn't notice it as we walked by. He pointed it out to me. The Germans who had occupied this position had left only a few minutes before. They had left the machine gun, ammunition, rifles and personal equipment lying around. I remember that we were all "booby trap" conscious from the lectures we had received on the subject. Leonard Dricks got a long strand of fence wire and hooked it on the gun. He backed off ten yards and jerked. Much to my surprise it wasn't "booby trapped" in spite of all the lectures to the contrary.

We waited on the hill for a short time until the arrival of Capt. Fabrick. He had taken the other part of the company, which was not with us, and gone down into the little town of Jodenville. He came back all smiles telling about the nice little fight they had down there in the town.

Very soon the battalion commander arrived and there was a conference among the officers. It was decided that we would attack cross-country. Our objective was a wooded area on a distant hill. The tanks led the attack. I remember seeing the light tanks scooting across the snow, bucking and tugging and kicking up clouds of snow. The tanks were attacking in a skirmish line and our infantry half-tracks followed in dispersed formation at a distance of 100 yards. I remember as we dashed down the hill seeing several of our General Sherman tanks burning in the plain below. Our tanks were no match for the German low silhouette Tiger tanks with their "88" cannons. The tanks that were leading were already on the crest of the slope facing the woods that concealed the enemy guns. The engagement was on. Our tanks were blasting away and receiving fire. We pulled up beside our tanks and dismounted. We formed a skirmish line of infantry across the hill. It was easy to see that our tanks were taking a beating. All along the line tanks were beginning to bum. The German anti-tank guns and "88" pieces were well dug in and camouflaged. We had failed to register preliminary artillery fire on the enemy position. Our artillery only now was beginning to land a few shells into the woods. As we lay in the snow, Lt. Stringfellow gave the command to fix bayonets. I think every man in the platoon had a little of the hysterical feeling of fear which will grip a new soldier. The enemy must be close or why the order to fix bayonets. I expected to see a wave of German infantry come charging over the slight rise in front of us. All the time a few shells were coming in on us. A piece of shrapnel hit the half-track. Our tanks were firing and being fired at. At the time, the privates were ignorant of the plan of attack. We did not know what we were to do. I had only the faintest idea that the enemy fire was coming from the woods ahead. I saw some of our shells land in those woods, which were about 500 yards in front. I blame our officers for not acquainting us with the situation.

I later learned we were to assault the woods with the tanks in support. The lieutenant must have decided that we were too far from our objective to make a direct foot assault, so he gave the order to mount up. This order didn't take any coaxing. We all piled into vehicles. With all the equipment in the track it didn't seem as if there was enough room. Several of the boys in their haste sprawled across the knees of us who were sitting. We were gripped with a fear that at any time one of those German anti-tank shells, which were knocking out the tanks, would hit our vehicle.

It now became apparent that some of our tanks were pulling back, trying to take shelter behind the crest of the hill and screen themselves from the murderous fire. Our lieutenant yelled to the tank major in the tank next to our track and asked him why the tanks were withdrawing. The major didn't seem to know Lt. Stringfellow gave another order to dismount and withdraw. Then began a mad scramble down into the draw from which we had just come. The drivers brought up the vehicles just as soon as they could turn them around. We attempted to form a temporary defense line along a fencer-ow, but when the vehicles came by we mounted up and returned to the town of Jodenville from where we had just come.

At Jodenville the tanks were dispersed in a field behind the town and the men found what cover they could. This was the end of our action for the first day.

THE QUIET SECTOR OF THE ARDENNES

Frank Fancher
32nd Cavalry Squadron

Troop A 32nd squadron, being in reserve in this so-called quiet sector of the Ardennes, was planning on a lot of rest, a little Schnapps drinking and some hell-raising. Instead, all hell broke loose all around us and we caught the brunt of German Field Marshal Von Rundstedt's counter offensive mounted by three German Armies in a tremendous two-pronged attack. One was to-ward Bastogne and the other toward St. Vith, our area. The bloody Battle of the Bulge was on. Massive artillery barrages preceded the attack. Poor intelli-gence on the part of our higher Commanders resulted in not having seen the tremendous German build up. Our lines were spread thin with only a group or regiment holding where a division or more should have been. This poor intelligence resulted in the following account by Eugene Murphy ("A" Troop Communications Sergeant):

Along with much confusion, in general along the front, these and other factors resulted in our capture by a spearheading tank element of the First S.S. Panzer Division of the Sixth German Army (the same outfit involved in the Malmedy Massacre). We were captured forward of St. Vith, Belgium early in the morning of December 17, 1944, in the small village of Honsfeld on the German-Belgium border.

It was later said that the valiant defense work of the 14th Cavalry Group, commanded by the spit and polish West Pointer, Col. Mark Devine, slowed down the powerful armored Nazi spearhead during the early hours of the counter offensive. The Germans were driving to capture the important road center of St. Vith and this threw the Germans off schedule, thus gaining time for our forces to regroup.

The day preceding our capture, December 16, 1944, about 7:00 a.m., 1st Lt Robert Reppa (Panama Canal Zone Commander of "A'" Troop of the 32nd) assembled the troop in full battle gear and told us "C" Troop of the 18th was in trouble. Five enemy tanks were raising hell with them and they were being forced to withdraw from Krewinkel to Manderfeld. We were ordered to move up and give support. Moving up, our armored column twice was under heavy artillery fire, once in the village of Ander and another time in a wooded sector. We buttoned up and came through without any casualties.

On arriving at Manderfeld, we set up a defensive position on a hill to the west overlooking the town. More important than anything else, our squadron and group HQ was located in this town and we had to get them somewhere that it would be safer. It was almost dark after seeing Col. Devine and his staff, escorted by an armored car and three Jeeps, on their way to his new command post in Poteau. I understand that they ran head on into a German tank. A German sentry, standing close to the armored car, yelled "Hah!'" But an American officer, riding escort in the commander's position, shoved his 45 in the sentry's face and emptied the entire clip. The gunner in the armored car opened up with the 50 and 30 caliber machine guns and the light from the tracers illuminated between fifteen and twenty German tanks lined up along the road. The armored car and Jeeps were able to get their lights on and turn around and get away with only one anti-tank shell whistling harmlessly overhead.

Remaining in Manderfeld, as the afternoon wore on, the situation around us worsened. The 18th got information back to Group, and Col. Devine's Executive Officer called General Jones at his 106th Division Command Post at St. Vith. (We were now attached to the 106th Division). In the meantime, Lt. Reppa, in a defensive position above Manderfeld, ordered Platoon Sgt. Fancher to take the first platoon and do combat patrol to the north, east and south of Manderfeld to keep the roads open between Lt. Ferrens' unit and Manderfeld. This he managed to do. A little later, "C" troop was ordered to pull back through Sgt. Fancher's first platoon and the rest of "A" troop, and then Sgt. Fancher was ordered to bring up the rear and join the rest of A troop.

They reported to him that Germans were passing southwest of the 14th's position and moving toward the Our River, and if he wasn't allowed to withdraw at once, they would be cut off from the rear. Permission was given and soon the 18th was evacuating Manderfeld covered by the guns of "A" Troop of the 32nd. We of "A" Troop were last to leave town. In departing, we could hear the lumbering of German tanks approaching the east end of town. Our troop then moved northwest parallel with our lines. In the gathering darkness, artillery duels were taking place all along the line with 30 caliber and 50 caliber tracers, buzz bombs and screaming meemies. It put Fourth of July celebrations to shame.

After several miles, we came to the village of Holzheim. Here we set up in a defensive position, as an anti-buzz bomb battery was pulling out. Later a young lieutenant of one of the outfits pulling by told us me "Krauts" had cut the road to Schonberg. They would be here any minute and if we were smart, we would follow them out north to Honsfeld. Lt. Reppa told him he didn't have orders from Squadron to withdraw, so we remained uneasily in the village. The villagers became cool and almost hostile as they began to clear their homes of signs of American occupation. Someone said, "Next they will be hanging out German flags." After about two hours without hearing from Squadron, Lt. Reppa, without order or regrets, moved "A" Troop out of this unfriendly town. He prayed we would get to Honsfeld before the Krauts. It seems that about this time the Germans were as confused with the situation as the Americans and for the moment, we were unknowingly safe.

In Honsfeld, we found the town being used by the 349th Regiment of the

99th Division as a Rest Center. Here we found the officers and men placidly taking their rest and recreation. Yes! They had heard there was some trouble up front, but the situation was now in hand. Lt. Reppa tried to impress a captain of the 99th in charge of the Rest Center that the situation was everything but in hand. The captain was not impressed and informed the lieutenant, "The good word here was to relax." Lt. Reppa ordered us in Headquarters Platoon to set up the troop command post in one of the houses and to keep trying to make radio contact with Squadron. The "Krauts" were jamming the American frequencies, making radio contact next to impossible. Lt Reppa then had Sgt. Creel and his 1st Platoon establish a road block at the east end of town. He then ordered Sgt. Pat O'Brien (Springfield, Illinois) and his dirty 3rd Platoon to set up a perimeter defense of the area.

On returning, Lt. Reppa was still uneasy and the 99th Division captain was amused by his nervousness. Lt. Reppa demanded to know, "Where the hell is everyone, and how come I'm all alone?" The captain explained by calling his regimental headquarters and connecting the lieutenant with a Regimental staff officer. Lt. Reppa tried to explain to the officer the situation. In turn, he informed Lt. Reppa, "You have nothing to worry about. You are well behind the front lines and since you will come under my command at daybreak, I want you to prepare to make contact with the enemy."

"At daybreak," muttered Lt. Reppa to himself, "The Krauts will be here making their own contact!" The officer wanted to know what he had said. Lt. Reppa told him, "Nothing, sir," and bid him good night! Later a captain and his driver came into our command post, both hit with shrapnel, looking for medics. The captain was not badly hit but his driver was hit in the face and his complete lower jaw was missing. He was still walking, so the medics sat him down and shot him full of morphine, then took him, still standing, to a field hospital. I understood that later, this hospital, along with our two medics, was also captured. So under the circumstances, this fellow's chances were at best, real bad.

Once during the night, a full colonel with an anti-aircraft outfit of the 99th Division with his heavy equipment, pulled back by us. He told Lt. Reppa that if he was smart, he would pull our unit out behind his. His orders were to withdraw and reform on a line a few miles back. Lt. Reppa told him that we had to await orders from Squadron. Later that night, we finally made radio contact with Squadron and received orders to move south-west at daybreak, so we awaited the dawn!

About four a.m., American vehicles, trucks, armored cars, artillery pieces, anti-aircraft units and half-tracks bumper to bumper, were still coming into and passing on through Honsfeld. As it turned out, not far behind this creeping column was German Obersturmbannfuhrer S.S. Lt. Col. Peiper and his spear-heading tank unit of the 1st S.S. Panzer Division.

107TH EVACUATION HOSPITAL

William R. "Woody" Ford
107th Evacuation Hospital

The 107th Evacuation Hospital arrived at Clervaux, Luxembourg, on October 1, 1944, after completing a 700-mile journey from the Crozan Peninsula following the capture of the German garrison at Brest, France.

Our hospital site was on a wind-swept hillside about three miles from the town and twelve miles northeast of Bastogne. Our hospital staff was comprised of 40 doctors, 40 nurses and 205 enlisted personnel. It was a 400-bed tent set-up.

In early December we had evacuated all our patients, pending a move to a new location at Caserne, near Aachen, Germany. Our advance party returned, unable to locate a suitable hospital site. We expected to remain at Clervaux until a decision could be made. Rumor had it there would be no action until spring time.

Suddenly everything changed! At 2230 hour on December 16th, warning orders were received for movement. Equipment and supplies were hastily loaded on trucks. The distant sound of shell fire was getting louder by the hour.

The following morning reports came in about street fighting in Clervaux. We vacated the area promptly and set up our hospital in a palatial hunting lodge located between Libramont and Libin, Belgium. It was owned by Baron

Coppee, and was named Chateau de Roumont. Pre-op and Shock took over the entrance and ballroom. Surgery, the banquet hall. Corridors and even stairways were full of cots. By midnight we were functioning. Stragglers were streaming in with horrible tales. German paratroopers in American uniforms were creating havoc. The Nazis were taking no prisoners. Individual soldiers reported having seen members of their squad annihilated. Wounded were pouring in from all sectors of the front. The confusion was great and necessarily required immediate level-headed decisions by our Commanding Officer Col. Henry Daine.

Since the chain of medical evacuation was greatly disrupted, many of the wounded were in dire need of extremely serious medical surgery. During an 80-hour period 388 delicate and/or complicated operations were performed. Men worked 12 hours at their usual assignment and then continued to assist as litter-bearers for hours more. Officers, even nurses, carried litters. No one slept if they could help in some way. The mess personnel fed more than 1,500 people at each meal. The spirit was magnificent. On December 21st we were alerted that German patrols were closing in. Orders were issued to evacuate all patients and immediately move to a new location. Three hundred patients were speedily loaded on ambulances and trucks and transported to the next echelon. Another 100 accompanied us to our next station, St. Joseph's School in Karlsburg, Belgium. We arrived in the early afternoon of the 21st. About 150 additional patients were soon admitted. Then, shortly after our personnel had completed sorting equipment and properly stocking ward boxes, blankets and surgery boxes, we were ordered to move again because of enemy activity in the area. All 250 of our patients were evacuated, and our unit withdrew to Sedan, France where we occupied the Ecole de Textile de Nord (Textile School). Our personnel were quartered at the College Turenne. Patients were waiting when we opened at 1000 hours on December 24th. After the siege of Bastogne was lifted about 1,200 total patients were brought into the hospital, many suffering from combat exhaustion. Many others required xrays to locate stray bits of metal previously undetected. In a 24-hour period 245 patients were xrayed, most requiring two, and some six or eight exposures. On January 17th, 1945 we

closed station at Sedan with a total of 3,771 patients as our part in three
set-ups during the Bulge.

LIEGE TO VIELSALM

Frank Fancher
32nd Cav Recon Sq, Troop A

We went on to Liege, where we got replacements of men and equipment and
started back to the south around Andler. It is hard to put a time and location
frame to this. While I was there, I received my Battlefield Commission for action in Luxemburg. I had not had time to pick it up previously because I had
been moving too fast for it to catch up with me. On the pull back, we crossed
the Salm River into Vielsalm, and I thought, for a short time, that the Bulge
was over for me.

Vielsalm was in our hands and there were still nurses and Red Cross girls
in town. They helped cook, etc., so I thought we were safe. It was not long before I found out how very, very wrong I was. Several German tank divisions
had crossed the Salm River several miles both above and below Vielsalm and
were attempting to encircle the town. Once again, we were caught between
a rock and a hard place. I still had my seven men and the same replacement
first lieutenant and also my half-track.

The job of the Americans in the town and surrounding area was to prevent the Germans from completing the circle. For the present, my group had
not received any assignment. It just so happened, that sitting outside a nearby
house, was a tank that no one seemed interested in. I said to my men, "Guys,
I'm sick and tired of fighting tanks with carbines. I'm going to borrow that
tank." And with that, I told my driver to check it out. He wasted no time in-
forming me that he didn't know how to drive a tank. Sgt. Pat O'Brian (from
Springfield) was still with me, so I said, "Pat, you are the tank commander.
Get a crew and I will drive."

I jumped in and told my driver to follow us in the half-track. I took off down the street, and not being reed to the tank, I took off the steps of the houses on both sides of the street for a couple of blocks. I turned on the radio and received a call from an infantry unit that needed tank support, so off we went. I said, "Pat, have you got plenty of ammunition ready?" About this time, we came up to the rear of the American unit. They had some light German armor that was giving them problems, as they only had light weapons.

Immediately following my orders to Pat to fire when ready, I heard the angry response from Pat, "This damn @#*@ gun won't traverse. It will only go up and down!" I told him to put the gun on target and that I would move the tank to the right or left. On my execution of this maneuver, Pat said, "That's it. Hold it. Hot damn, that's right on. Now pull right. I'll make a sweep with my machine gun." Again came the exclamation, "Right on," and "Mad Dog, we had better get the hell out of here before we run into some heavy German armor."

We now knew why the tank had been sitting there and not being used. During this small battle, my half-track had cut loose with their 50 caliber gun and completely destroyed the whole enemy unit, so we came out smelling like a rose. We took the tank back and parked it where we found it. I'll bet the people living along that street still wonder what happened to their steps.

While we were playing with our tank, headquarters had started to evacuate all the non-military people like the Red Cross girls and nurses, along with non-combat troops. In the meantime, I managed to find an ammunition dump and replenished our ammo for our carbines and 50 caliber machine guns and also picked up a few grenades and 30 caliber light machine guns with ammunition. We also filled our canteens and were issued one K-ration per man.

Now we were attached to a tank unit as a security for their tanks. Again, as we pulled out, we ended up as rear guard to keep the enemy from hitting us in the rear. As far as could tell, we got everyone out and were now headed for Liege, Belgium, where we hoped we would be able to get more replacements of men and equipment. I think Liege was about forty miles away, so we're talking about possibly two travel days because of the fighting we would encounter along the way. One thing that did disturb me was that our back door would be left open because Montgomery (British) had pulled the 82nd Airborne back on a line to Vaux-Chavanne. I said it before and I will say it again, in my opinion, if they had sent the British Army home, the war would have ended six months sooner.

As we moved from Vielsalm on toward Liege, we moved through the 82nd Airborne's main line of defense and we were now pretty much on our own. As it was getting on toward evening, we began to look for a good place to spend the night. We pulled off into woods and found that it was already occupied with one of our tank outfits that had set up a defensive position. I asked their commanding officer if we could spend the night and he said okay, but he could sure use some ground security as his tanks were in the woods and just across an open field.

VON DER HEYDTE'S PARATROOPERS

Arnold C. Franco
9th U. S. Air Force, 3rd Radio Squadron Mobile, Detachment B

The 3rd RSM was a secret signals intelligence unit tasked with intercepting and deciphering German Air Force communications. The job of Det. B was to listen to German fighter pilots communicating with each other and their controllers by radio telephone. Once the Luftwaffe was "picked up" on the radio our direction finders would get a fix on their location, direction and speed. That done, 9th Air Force fighter controllers would be notified by phone and scramble our fighters to intercept. Since November, 1944, Detachment B had been stationed in the Town of Jalhay, Belgium, just near the Eupen-Malmedy road. Its camouflaged D/F van was situated some six miles away at Baraque Michel (right off the Malmedy road).

At 6:00 a.m. on December 17, Sgt. Bob Siefert, of Bennet, Nebraska, drove the D/F relief crew in his jeep to Baraque Michel. On the way they noticed several parachutes in the woods off the road. When he pulled up to our van the guard whispered to him, nervously, that he had seen soldiers skulking around in the woods and he suspected they might be Germans. (We later learned that the majority of Von der Heydte's Fallschirmjagers who were able to land in one piece headed for their rallying point which was between Jalhay and Baraque Michel.) Siefert sped back to Jalhay where he reported his findings to the CO, Major Ted Silverstein. The major was greatly alarmed, thinking that the Germans were actually out to capture our outfit. Because of all the information we had gathered since D-Day, and the occupation of the Eiffel Tower when Paris was liberated, we would be a juicy plum. Silverstein immediately called 9th Tac in Verviers.

They were so confused by the situation they could offer him no guidance. By the end of the day, with enemy air action in the area getting more intense, he finally gave orders to pack up. "B" moved some 20 miles north to join their sister detachment "D" located at the Chateau de la Commanderie in Fouron St. Pierre (now Saint Pieters Voeren) at the point where the Belgian, Dutch, and German borders met. When they arrived late at night, they found the boys in "D" in the midst of a firefight. There had been intense air combat during the night, with searchlights sweeping the sky and machine guns rattling. A guard had spotted a parachute descending in the glare and everyone started firing their weapons into the woods across the castle moat. It was the following morning that a patrol discovered the parachute attached to a slightly wounded German fighter pilot. Since most of the men in Det "D" spoke fluent German, he was thoroughly interrogated before being turned over to an MP detachment.

In early January, once the threat of a breakthrough was truly over, Det B returned to the Jalhay area and resumed operations.

A FRIGID MEMORY

Frank Freese
84th Infantry Division, 333rd Infantry Regiment, Co F

It is 8 February 1994 and I sit here in Madison, Wisconsin, looking out of my window watching the wind-blown snow go by horizontally. The temperature outside is 2 degrees and the wind chill must be down between 30 and 40 degrees below zero.

On an evening exactly like this nearly 50 years go (12 January 1945), I was trying to dig a foxhole in ground that seemed to turn into flint below me faster than I could chip it out with my little G1 shovel. An hour earlier, F and G Companies of the 333rd Infantry Regiment (84th Division) had finally driven into the little village of Les Tailles, Belgium, after being held off and repelled by the German defenders since before noon. Before getting into town, F Company, with only about 70 men at the start, had had eight men killed and 31 wounded and as I futilely pounding away at the stone hard earth with frozen fingers, I almost envied the wounded if not the dead. As we entered town we had passed a large German machine gunner who had been severely wounded by an artillery tree burst and pleaded for help that we could not stop to give him. With the feeble remnant of my high school German, I told him that I would send a doctor back if I saw one, but even as I said it I knew that was not going to happen. Any medical person- nel who showed up would be kept busy with our own wounded. The Kraut may have killed or wounded many of our men and I should have hated him but I didn't. The thought of lying wounded and alone in that frozen land seemed too terrible. Every time the Wisconsin winter deals us a night like this one, my thoughts go back to the Ardennes, to that frozen foxhole and to the wounded German. I can't help but wonder whether he survived that horrible night. I hope so, but I doubt it.

MY STORY

Gilbert Gardner
253rd Armored Field Artillery Bn.

It was March, 1945. I was a forward observer in the 253rd Armored Field Artillery Battalion that served in the E.T.O. supporting the 4th and 6th Armored Division plus the 26th and 80th Infantry, and last but not least, the 28th Armored Cavalry. While supporting the cavalry we left our tank behind and traveled in a jeep. We pulled into a small German town, Butzbach, and our jeep stopped in front of a two-story house.

Being the ranking non-commissioned officer, I walked up the driveway to check things out. About halfway up the driveway, I heard German voices. Staying in the shadows, I walked to the back of the house and spotted four German soldiers standing outside one of the buildings. I said to myself, "What am I going to do now?" I didn't want to kill them unless I had to, so I gave a short burst over their heads with my Thompson submachine gun.

I then ran across the driveway and got down on my knees. They shouted, "Comrade!" and more soldiers came out of the building and lined up in military formation. Finally one said, "Das is allies." I said, "Comen ze here," and marched them down the driveway to my crew waiting in the jeep. I asked my crew to check these guys out while I checked the house. After knocking on the side door, an elderly white-haired woman came to the door.

I walked into a dark room and told her that I needed a light so that I could see. She understood and lit a candle. I checked the rooms downstairs and all was clear, then I motioned upstairs. There were three rooms, two rooms were empty but the third door was closed. I asked her to open it and she said, "Nein." Again I asked her to open the door and she again replied, "Nein." I then raised my voice and demanded that she open the door. She saw that I was relentless and proceeded to open the door. When I walked into the room I noticed a chair with a uniform folded neatly on it and a male asleep in the bed. I woke him up; he got out of bed and walked to the end of the bed and turned left towards the chair for his pants... or his gun!

The odds were 50-50 that he was going for the pants or the gun but I preferred the better odds, so I diverted his direction and ran him downstairs, barefooted and in his long-johns. Our night ended with a collection of 41 prisoners, 13 pistols, Lugers and P38s.

A DAY I WILL NEVER FORGET

James W. Gardner
106th Infantry Division, 422 Infantry, 2nd Battalion,
Headquarters Company

One has several dates, or days, that are unforgettable, but almost in every case one day must stand out.

The night of December 18th, 1944, three days into the Battle of the Bulge, I was trying to get some rest. I was under a fir tree in the Ardennes forest on the Schnee Eifel Ridge in Germany. Fir trees offered good protection from the wind because their boughs come all the way down to the ground. The snow could not penetrate the boughs, therefore it was a good place to get some rest. Rest was almost unheard of during the German break-through. We were surrounded by the Germans with no hope of help getting to us. We needed rest desperately because the next day we were going to try to break through the German encirclement.

On the morning of the 19th of December I awakened to the sound of artillery, or 88s from tanks. The shells were trimming the fir trees around us. I had to uncover myself from the fir tree boughs, or limbs. The Germans were zeroed in on us. I was lucky not to get hit by this first barrage of shells.

Our leader thought it would be better for us to cross an open area to the ridge on the other side. This open area reminded me of a stubble field after wheat had been cut. Of course, there was snow covering most of the weeds, or stubble. We went across the open area, a small group at a time. Each group was drawing fire. Many soldiers were hit. We could see black puffs of smoke when each shell would hit. It then came our time to go. We advanced in a diamond formation, well spread out.

It was here that my thoughts wandered back home. Would I come out of this? Why should human beings have to fight each other? Aren't there other ways to solve our problems? Of course, the answer is, "No. Sometimes there does not seem to be any other way." Freedom is something special, so special that it must not be taken for granted. We must sacrifice once in a while in order to keep it. As we moved across the open area we were pinned down several times. The bullets were spat splatting all around. I don't see how I got across without a scratch, but I did.

After reaching the ridge on the other side of the open field, we were instructed to dig in. We were back in the woods, or at the edge of the woods. This was a bad place to be because of the tree bursts (shells hitting the trees). When a shell hits in a tree the shrapnel will rain down, as well as up. One can be in a foxhole and still receive a hit from the shrapnel. The bursts were coming closer and closer. I dived beside a log. I had my right side protected by the log, but my back and left side were open. I caught a tree burst. The tree was about 15 feet from me. The concussion was terrible. My helmet flew off, my gun left me, and when I got my senses back I had to look to see how badly I was hit. If you are not hit in a vital spot, you are numb; the pain comes later.

Before I could get organized again, I was looking into the barrel of a German Luger. Our leader had sent someone with a white flag, and surrendered us to the Germans. Our cause was hopeless, he thought. My eyes met the German's eyes, and he looked about as scared as I imagine I looked. He motioned for me to get up. I did not know if I could get up. I knew I had been hit in the leg just above the ankle, and also in the left hand, and I was stinging on my posterior. I forced myself up and with a limp and a hop I started down the hill toward another experience when I will never forget—one that I would not take a million dollars for, but would not want to have again.

MY LUCKY FOUR LEAF CLOVER

James W. Gardner
106th Infantry Division, 422 Infantry, 2nd Battalion,
Headquarters Company

I was wounded and captured the evening of the 19th of December, 1944. Several days later, on the 24th of December, I found myself in a barn-like structure awaiting my turn to go into a little room where a German medic, or doctor, was. I had a wound just above my ankle; my left hand was hit with shrapnel; I also had stinging in my left rear. A piece of steel had gone through my billfold, cutting my four leaf clover in two. I had been carrying it for good luck! This happened during the Battle of the Bulge.

There were both German and American wounded in this barn-like structure. I assume it was meant to be a field hospital. I watched Germans and Americans come and go from a smaller room. Many of them looked worse after they came out than when they went in. When it came my turn I did not much want to go in, but the German guard poked me with his rifle, so I thought he meant business. I went hopping into the room. I saw two people next to a table. I don't know whether they were doctors, or just medics, but they gave me an order to get up on the table. Thoughts ran through my mind like, "Will I still have two legs if I get out of this, or will I be leaving them here?"

They ordered me to lie down on the table; I did, but I sat up immediately to see what they were going to do. They pushed me back down again, and I sat up again. I decided I was going to kick them with my good leg if they tried anything funny. One of them hit me across the nose with a medical instrument. Thank God, it was the blunt side of the instrument that hit me. I decided I was the loser, so I laid back and cocked my head so I could watch. They immediately opened up my wounds with a sharp instrument to allow them to bleed, and then wrapped my leg and hand with paper bandages. They did not put any medication on my wounds. They then ordered me out into the bigger room again. I hopped out on my good leg and took my place on the floor.

In a few hours I was ordered to hop outside and was then put in the back of a truck with several other wounded. We did not know where we were going, but we were headed somewhere. Several times the truck stopped. The driver and his partner would dive for the ditch as our planes strafed us. We were not allowed to take cover. This happened a few times, but we lucked out. We thought we saw Red Cross trucks headed toward the front with supplies. Our truck did not have a red cross on it. We finally came to a railroad yard; here we were placed in a boxcar that had wooden bunks in it. I suppose this was a "hospital train." At one end of the car above the door was a big picture of Hitler. Our guard, or medic, was older than the average. He looked both ways before he pointed to the picture and said, "Him no good, him no good." There were Germans in the car behind us, so the guard was careful when he said this about Hitler.

I remember even though we were all wounded, we sang Christmas songs since it was Christmas Eve. I couldn't help wondering what my family was doing at home. I doubt that they were enjoying the Christmas of 1944 any more than I was. I spent Christmas Day in the boxcar and then we were at Stalag G for a few days.

After having our paper bandages changed (no medication), we were loaded into boxcars for a six-day stop-and-go trip to Stalag 2A north of Berlin. I consider myself darned lucky to be alive today.

BROTHERS IN DIFFERENT TANKS

Albert Gaydos
4th Armored Division, 66th Armored Field Artillery, Headquarters Battery

Our field artillery battalion had three forward observer Sherman tanks. One or two were always selected to go along with whichever tank battalion was leading in an attack. I had a brother in the #1 tank and I was in #3 Tank. He had been attending an officer's meeting and got the information that my tank was to go along with the light tank Co. D-35th Tank Bn. leading Combat Command A going north on the Arlon Highway to Bastogne, Belgium... this was December 21, 1944.

My brother advised that as soon as the light tank company made contact with the enemy, the medium Sherman tanks would come up with infantry and artillery. We pulled out of Arlon at dusk and were met by a M.P. Colonel who told us to get off the road, go along a pine woods to join a platoon of light Stuart tanks of D Co. 35th Tank Bn. Our officer talked to the tank platoon officer and they both came back to my tank, closed the hatches, turned on the dome light and discussed our mission. We were to drive on to Bastogne and when we had made contact with the enemy, we were to radio our position.

We gassed up at 11 p.m., no one slept; German two engine planes were buzzing us in our open field. We pulled out the next morning at 5 A.M. during a heavy snowstorm. Shortly thereafter, coming into a village, a group of infantrymen told us that they had seen a German patrol at 4 a.m. At 8 a.m. it was daylight and we were ready to cross a bridge about a quarter of a mile away when it was blown up in front of us. It was still snowing as we continued on a road through a thick pine forest. As we were about to exit from the woods, out walked two Germans with rifles and hands in the air... deserters? It was slow going because of German paratrooper action all around us. On the 24th, it was dark, and we could now see the village of Warnach about a mile away.

Over my tank radio, I was able to hear everything that was going on. When the light tank platoon with the infantry rifle platoon went into Warnach and were quickly overcome, this was the conversation Col. Oden had with Capt. Ridley of D Co's tanks. Col. Oden said, "Take your light tanks and go into that town and see what's in it."

Capt. Ridley replied, "I am too light...how about we send in some of our big stuff?"

Col. Oden said, "I don't give a damn, we have to get to Bastogne!"

I can remember hearing that two tanks were hit right away...the firing, the silence and then new conversation. Col. Oden said, "Put someone from the infantry on the microphone...son, what is your rank?"

"I'm a private." a voice replied.

"Consider yourself a Sergeant...how about you taking a patrol into that town?"

Followed by Col. Oden saying, "Forward Observer, I want you to fire into Warnach as I am sending in a patrol...make it easier for them!"

Our F.O. officer, "Five volleys, O.K.?"

Col. Oden, "Fine, eighteen guns, each gun five rounds!"

The patrol went in when we lifted our fire. The Germans put out during the volley and came back in after the patrol came back. Col. Oden asked the newly made Sergeant, "What did you find, son?"

"We saw no Krauts, but did retake one of our own 6x6 trucks with two Krauts in it... but no others."

We drew fire all night and the next day Sherman tanks and infantry went in, and finally took possession of the town after a hectic and bloody confrontation, coming out with lots of German prisoners.

We were still with D Co.'s light tanks. In the afternoon we were joined by the rest of their company's tanks and remained in an open field. Suddenly ten German paratroopers stood up from a tree line about fifty feet away. They were loaded with our American cigarettes, gum, G.I. shoes, and our olive drab shirts under their jackets. While a tank officer was searching them, one of the tank men jumped out with his Tommy gun and told the officer to move away as he was going to kill them all! In the distance we could see a lot of German tanks coming toward us. Just then our P-47 planes came over and had a field day. Finally, we moved forward with the tanks and infantry across open ground through a pine wood forest and took up positions on the other side of the woods in an open field. While standing in the turret, I heard two explosions and learned that two gasoline trucks coming to gas us up had hit mines on the road.

The next morning, Germans were seen on the highway about a mile from us. We were now left with some infantry in half-tracks, our Forward Observer tank and what was left of light tank Company D... about five miles from our objective... Bastogne.

25 DAYS IN THE BULGE

Albert Gaydos
4th Armored Division, 66th Armored Field Artillery, Headquarters Battery

When daylight came, Col. Olden did send into Warnach medium tanks (35th Tank Battalion) with what was left the 51st. This day was the morning of 24th of December. The mediums went in, took the village, killed 135 Krauts, killed and wounded many prisoners. We lost 68 officers and men. It was declared an error to use tanks for night action.

We stayed in our position, just on the edge of Warnach. We watched the mediums coming out of the village herding large numbers of Kraut prisoners. Our radio went dead. We waited for radio maintenance. They came up from the rear, fixed our problem and that was the last time I saw my brother alive. His tank was repaired and he was rejoining his unit. He waved, giving me the "V" sign, that he was OK. It was December 24 at 2:00 p.m. and we got orders to move up about 1/2 mile from Warnach to join the rest of the light tanks of the 35th. There were maybe 10 tanks left. In this position about 50 feet to our right, out of a thin tree line, up stood 10 Kraut paratroopers, hands up. They were there all along and we didn't see them. They came forward and Capt. Ridley searched each one. They had on, underneath their jackets, our OD shirts, our new shoes, cigarettes and gum. Ridley was throwing them to me standing in the turret. He punched every one of them in the face as he took American stuff from them. One light tank member got out of his tank with his Tommy gun. He told the captain to get out of the way, he wanted to kill them. He was wounded early in the war and had just come back from England to duty in the Bulge.

We could see in the distance, across open, flat ground, Kraut tanks coming our way. Just then, a squadron of P-47s appeared asking ground liaison for targets. Soon they went into action against those tanks; what was left we could not see.

About 4:00 p.m., we moved up across an open field, stayed off the road and went through pine woods. We took up positions for the night (Christmas Eve) on the other side of these woods. The mediums also took up positions a little to our left. My brother Paul's tank, FO #1, was with them. The moon was full and I could see them.

We pulled straws in our crew as to who would pull guard first. Lt. Romig would not join the other officers as we had done. He took his sleeping bag and went into the woods where the infantry dug in to sleep. I was standing first watch in the turret when I heard an explosion, a big fireball explosion. Capt. Ridley came to our tank and told me that it was two 6x6 trucks loaded with gas, to gas us up. He said that nobody told them not to use that road, that they should've come through the woods like we did. They had hit mines. My time on guard was over; sleep came over me. I was cold and laid on the 75mm ammo and fell asleep. Soon after, we drew artillery, heavy stuff, landing close to the tank. Lt. Romig left his bag, got into the turret. I heard him tell Lefty to turn the engine over and get ready to move, at the same time nudging me to wake up. As the barrage was lifted, he went back into the woods. The rest of the night was quiet.

Christmas Day was quiet and the lieutenant came over to us and he wanted me to see the staff sergeant that was lying near him and had his throat cut. Some Krauts got in there during the artillery firing. We spent the day in position. The officers were planning our next move—5 miles from Bastogne. The 35th was still to our left. Rumors were Patton and new people were in the area but we did not see him.

That evening, we were waiting for gas trucks and German twin-engine planes buzzed us. We lost our white paint so we moved onto blackened shell holes. They kept coming back and forth. We had to move fast as the gas trucks came; they went through our circle position hollering out and asking how many cans did we need. They also brought us our Christmas dinner which was one piece of cold turkey, a Hershey bar, apple and a cigar. We gassed up, stayed up the rest of the night, and enjoyed our goodies. That was the end of Christmas Day.

On the 26th we moved up to engage Krauts close by in the woods about 100 feet away. We all fired into those woods but did not go in to see.

All of a sudden a P-47 came over us. It was a P-47 that was captured by the Germans and flown by a German pilot. We were surprised when he dropped a 500 pound bomb 50 feet from us into the pine woods. He buzzed us again. Col. Olden on the radio, "If that son-of-a-bitch comes back, fire at him!"

Our Headquarters Battery was in position behind us a few miles. We watched him drop another bomb on their position, killing two men and wounding four. At that time we (FO #3) didn't know it was Headquarters Battery—our people. We then moved along a highway. We engaged a large group in the ditch along the road. They quietly lay there a good while, near us. We killed 19 and captured the rest, including a blonde woman. The last thing I saw was one of our men running behind her towards the rear.

That afternoon, our planes were strafing Kraut positions ahead of us and large groups of B-17s all day. We watched 3 groups of C-47 planes coming in on our left, a couple of 100 feet from us, dropping supplies. Some of it was picked up by German units. I counted eleven planes shot down by these same units, another group of C-47s came in. We are still five miles from Bastogne. There were still many Kraut troops to our left, and in front of us where the supplies hit the ground. Night came and the Krauts moved up even closer. It was December 27th, the day my brother, Paul, was killed. We made a move against them. My brother's tank company (35th) and we moved up along the highway. They had crossed to the right side of the road and we stayed with the light tanks on the left. Soon we made contact. We lost some men and captured a lot as they gave up easily. There were some very young and some old men mixed in.

While searching the prisoners, we heard a lot of firing in the vicinity of the 35th mediums. On the radio, there was a desperate call for medics and ambulances. My brother and I had a habit (in all attacks) to talk on the radio when he saw smoke near us as we moved up. We heard (over the radio) this plea for help and I felt something was wrong in FO #1 tank. I called my brother's tank. Hyde, his gunner, answered. I asked, "Who is it (hurt)? He answered, "Hyde, it's King (his driver). Al, it's King."

They were pinned down by Kraut mortar fire. Each tank carried infantry on the backs of tanks. They jumped off only to be cut down. My brother's lieutenant, Lt. Mitchell, got out of the tank, laid on the ground with what was left of the infantry, unable to observe the location of mortars.

The firing stopped. My brother, King, the driver, and Hyde, the gunner, got out of their tank and joined another tank crew to scan (on the ground) a tree line edge. They wanted to see if they could locate the mortar positions, so my brother could fire our artillery that were in position most of the time.

These are the words of Bill Hyde: "We all stood together looking at those woods. I turned to go back to our tank. When the Krauts opened fire again, one round landed on them. I went back to see if I could help. They were all dead (6 men) except King, who lived." (We heard later from the hospital that he had 27 pieces of shrapnel in his chest.)

In the meantime, I heard all of this over the radio on the 27th at 3:30 p.m. We moved the prisoners out of our way. Near dark, we received a call from Col. Olden to go to that position to relieve FO #1. They needed an observer... us. Our officer, Romig, commented, "Sir, I don't know if it's proper but I have a brother of Sgt. Paul Gaydos, who was killed in our tank."

Olden again, "I don't give a damn, we have to get to Bastogne."

It was dark now and we moved to that position. The moon was full and I picked out his tank easily. I climbed up and called down his turret. "Paul, Paul, Paul!"

Hyde answered, "Paul isn't here."

I asked, "Where is he?"

Hyde answered, "Paul's dead."

I asked where he was laying and he got out and pointed out the direction.

Lt. Mitchell still was with the infantry. At least 14 tanks deployed in that moonlight. It was cold and quiet now, no firing. I walked in the snow to where the men were hit. No one was there, just blood in the snow. I found Paul's tank helmet. They were picked up and taken to the rear. I looked around some more and thought I was in the wrong place. I saw many dead that weren't picked up. This lasted a good many hours before I finally went back to our tank, filled with grief, and the war went on. This all happened near the nearest village on the map of Sanlez, Belgium.

The next morning at break of daylight I again went looking for my brother's body. I found the first aid station that was near the Arlon-Bastogne highway. I lifted many blankets, still hoping I could see him. The graves registration officer in charge asked me who I was looking for. I told him my brother. He asked for his name. He remembered the name when he was picked up the night before. He said he was taken to the next town near Martelange. I do not remember the name. The officer told me to get into the next ambulance that was going there with the dead and wounded.

I found him still lying on a stretcher on the hood of a jeep. A month later,

I was notified by graves registration where he was buried and instructions how to get there, to visit his grave with permission from our CO. He was buried in a large cemetery nearby the Villages of Fallex and Grand Falley. His remains were brought back in 1949 to rest in our family plot.

From that position, we moved up again toward Bastogne. It was cold with lots of snow and the temperature was zero to below. We took up position January 1st near a small lake with enemy tanks in the area. We are together now, light tanks with the mediums. We drew much artillery while there. We got a call over the radio that Krauts were in the area wearing our uniforms, driving our captured vehicles. We were told to make sure you identified the person beside you. Kraut artillery landed mostly on the lake on the ice. When it stopped I was talking to some of our infantry about how bad things were up ahead—P-47s strafing the woods.

About 50 feet to our left, I saw a group of about 20, digging in. Me and my driver, Lefty, walked over there. I asked them, "What outfit?" and "Why are you digging here?" One answered, and I can't remember what he said but we felt something was wrong about those American uniforms and rifles that they had. We walked back the 50 feet to our tank and looked back to that direction and they were gone while our backs were turned.

The next day we moved up a mile or so off the road to our right, to take on German tanks (about two miles from Bastogne). We made contact and the Germans were still strong. We were joined by a company of the 704th tank destroyers with their high-powered 76s. In our position, we could not see the German tanks. It was January 2nd. Conversation on radio, 35th tank commander to Col. Olden, "We just killed a few Kraut tanks. We got a couple of more."

"Olden... What is your rank?"

He answered, "First Lt."

"Olden... Consider yourself a captain as of now."

It was January 3rd after this tank battle. The weather was without new snow, very cold and we were not able to get warm. Our feet were cold. We got new socks with our rations; Eisenhower's orders—change every day. Keep one set in bosom, next to skin. Tankers: while inside, pound your knees with fists almost steady to keep circulation in feet. Many men were sent to the rear with black, frozen feet.

P-47s and a large group of B-17s were overhead daily, helping us. Kraut action slowed in our area early in January. We, FO #3 observers, pulled out and were sent a few miles on secondary roads which I thought was a CCB sector. We stayed with a large group, bumper to bumper, in columns day and night.

Then as FOs the next day, we were ordered by radio to report to tank company of the 35th back where we were to Arlon- Bastogne highway. They were lined up on the road, 14 tanks, engines idling. Our officer to tank commander: Our orders were to go to Bastogne one mile away, up ahead Krauts laying 4.5 mortar fire right on the middle of the road. We have to go through that fire. We buttoned up, being that our officer Romig didn't have tank experience. I told our driver, Lefty, "Make sure you were in fifth gear, when we get to that area, we, the Sherman tanks never had enough speed."

We moved out while the rest of the tankers watched. We made it and shortly entered Bastogne. Maybe it was around the 7th or 8th. As we entered, one of our half-tracks was hit in front of us, burning, but we kept going farther into the city. The men of the 82nd and 101st greeted us with a wave and a smile; the place was demolished.

We stopped and got out to stretch our legs and spotted one of our own men from the wire section in a jeep, Bill Bacon. I said, "How in the hell did you get here?" He said he didn't know. He looked real worn out and said he just followed our tanks markings. While we were talking, our crew stayed in the tank and all hell broke loose. German artillery was coming in from four sides. Bill and I ran into a bombed-out building, laid down against a wall. It seemed like they kept it up for two hours. We thought this was our end, the first time in the war that I felt like I was in hell. After the fire was lifted, we moved into a house nearby to rest for the night.

At midnight everyone was dead tired, sleeping. A runner found us with a message to go to the area of the Village of Magaret. Our officer Romig was an expert at map reading. We followed the overlay the runner gave us. We pulled out cold and tired at 4:00 a.m., January 9th, after three or four miles north along another road.

We stopped at daylight and joined up with the 35th mediums again. We had the high ground and we could see enemy vehicles down in the valley. We fired many missions, accurately. The tankers were very pleased. In front of us there were nine 10th Armored tanks knocked out. We could not figure out why they were in a straight line together. In our training, we were taught to move in a scattered position. When it got dark we received new orders, to go back to Bastogne and to go south to the position of 30 December. I rode the small fender near the driver's hatch to help the driver see. They stayed off the road and traveled across open fields for fear of mines.

When we stopped, it was after midnight. We were five tired and frozen men but had a bottle of wine. Lt. Romig gave an order to open the bottle. We had saved it for after a tough day.

On January 10th we found out that all of our division (4th Armored) was pulling out of Bastogne. The next day we traveled those cold, slippery roads south until we reached Luxembourg. We then took up positions on the outskirts near the Our River, because of strong German activity on the other side and to help the units that were there.

So ends the story and events of five light tank crews, 25 men, and of five men in a Sherman medium tank crew, who were artillery forward observers, who fought in the Battle of the Bulge for 25 days. This lasted from December 17, 1944, to January 10, 1945. Those involved were: Lt. Romig, officer; Sgt Albert Gaydos, loader; Norman Thomas, gunner; Joe Kurimsky (Lefty), driver; and Charles Cable, bow gunner.

ANTWERP X - A COMBINED DEFENSE

Cecil D. Gilliam

788th Anti-Aircraft Artillery Automatic Weapons Battalion, Battery A

There were over 22,000 men and officers, British, Polish and American, who served in "Antwerp X." History will record many outstanding feats and accomplishments in this war, but none will overshadow the heroic defense of the Port of Antwerp against flying bombs by 22,000 of the world's finest anti-aircraft artillery men.

Organized quickly and secretly, this huge command was dubbed "Antwerp X" and placed under Brigadier General Armstrong as the attack on Antwerp started late in October 1944. Then for 154 days and nights without letup and with ever increasing fury, the "battle of the buzz-bomb" was fought on the cold wet flats of Northern Belgium and Southern Holland.

Bald facts and figures will never convey the full story of endless hours in freezing gun pits, the sweat and strain of endless "digging in," the constant roar of firing guns, the deeper and deathly roar of V-1s in flight, and the burning eyes from constantly seeking after that last small margin of error.

But facts and history do tell of a clear cut victory over Hitler's vaunted Vengeance Weapon Number One. In the words of Major General Revell-Smith, 21st Army Group: "This is a great victory; perhaps not heralded or understood by the world at large in the same way as they would appreciate a victory by other arms. The victories of other arms have territorial gains to show. You have not, but nevertheless this does not make it less important than any other form of major military success on the final outcome of the war."

In a letter to the members of Antwerp X, their commander, Brig. Gen. Clare H. Armstrong, wrote the following;

[Excerpt] "I should like to take this opportunity to personally commend every officer and man who took part in this long and grueling campaign. Only through your steadfast devotion to duty, your unflinching determination and your utter disregard for self while facing hardship and danger, was this unparalleled anti-aircraft record made possible. I defy contradiction when I say the men of Antwerp X were and are the 'best damn gunners' in the world."

You are now scattered far and wide... the team is broken up... but to each of you, British, Polish and American, I want to extend my sincerest thanks for a job well done and wish you the best of luck in all future tasks.

MIKE

Clarence "Code" Gomberg
343rd Medical Battalion

Somewhere towards the end of the month of April 1945 and the liberation of Buchenwald Concentration Camp near the town of Weimar, Germany the 7S Hospital Train pulled into a rail siding not far from the deserted camp. A small boy approached the train; I was standing at an open door and the boy put his hands out and said, "shwine-fresser." I answered, "I nix farshadet."

He raised his hands and repeated the words again and I answered in English that I didn't understand. He walked closer towards me and answered in English that he was begging for our garbage to use as food. He told me that he was a twelve-year-old Polish Jew and his name was Mike. He lost his family in Auschwitz.

I got permission from our company commander to bring Mike aboard the train. We adopted him. He became our orderly and interpreter. I took him into Paris and for a couple of chocolate bars and a cake of soap, had a uniform cut down to fit him. September 1945 the train unit was disbanded and we were transferred to the 239" General Hospital, a section outside of Paris, Petain. Mike worked with me and a civilian helper in food rations and supplies. February 1946, I received orders to be sent home. We took Mike to Paris and left him with the French Jewish Welfare Board. He thought that he had relatives in Indiana. I never knew his last name and I don't know if he ever got to the United States.

MY MILITARY SERVICE

Clarence "Code" Gomberg
343rd Medical Battalion

I was inducted into the United States Army, February 10, 1943. Received basic training at Fort George Meade, Maryland (Infantry). Transferred to Camp

Lee, Virginia (Quartermaster), Station Compliments, Section One. Unit was transferred to Camp Ellis, Illinois and the Seventy-Eighth Hospital Train was activated on September 21, 1943. On November 11 the unit departed Camp Ellis by rail for Camp Edwards, Massachusetts. Here the unit was attached to the 3116th Service Command Unit for training. On December 1st were alerted for movement to a staging area. On December 8 moved to the staging area at Fort Devens for further processing at Camp Miles Standish until December 18, then moved by rail to Boston POE. Boarded the ship "USAT Marine Robin." Two days out of Boston Harbor we sustained two submarine attacks. One ship in our convoy was hit.

Trip across the Atlantic was completed on December 27 and the unit disembarked at Swansea, Wales then traveled by rail through London to Camp Crookston, Glasgow, Scotland. Attached to the 28th Division, 3116th Service Command Unit, 3rd Army, 343rd Medical Battalion. Completed forming up unit and received all equipment for the train. On May 13, 1944 received orders to depart Camp Crookston and moved to a holding camp in Southampton. On June 12 embarked on the Hospital Ship, "HMS Duke of Lancaster" and arrived in Cherbourg, France. Worked our way down toward Paris as Combat Medics. Arriving in Paris the unit was attached to the 343rd Medical Battalion. On July 20 the unit began operating U.S. Army Hospital Train No. 5. (Hospital Train 78) From this date until February 1945 traveled approximately 24,000 miles and 10,000 patients were evacuated either from first aid stations, field hospitals or general hospitals to ports in the Corn Z. On February 25 while advancing toward forward installations in the vicinity of Evreux, France, enemy aircraft strafed the train. Several cars were derailed and several personnel members were injured. The unit was awarded the Battle Participation Award, German Campaign.

On May 5, 1945 during a routine run to Frankfurt am Maine the unit was dispatched to a siding behind the I.G. Farber Ammunition Plant to await ambulances to transport wounded for evacuation. Two ambulances unloaded eight (8) litters with patients wrapped in blankets. Aboard the train, (ward car No. 6) the patients removed their blankets revealing their identities.

These eight were German officers and we were to transport them to Reims, France, "the little red schoolhouse" for the surrender of the war in Europe. The surrender was signed on May the 7th at 0241 hours. On May 27 Hospital Train No. 5 was removed from operations. Approximately half of the unit was placed on Hospital Train No. 76. The balance of the unit was placed on DS with the 239 General Hospital, a medical installation in the Seine section of Paris.

While in operation, the unit "Blazed a Trail of Glory" through France, Belgium, Netherlands, Luxembourg and Germany, traveling approximately 63,000 miles and evacuating over 20,000 patients. From the date of activation to the deactivation of the unit, not a single Court-Martial, AWOL or case of VD marred its perfect record.

On February 10, 1946 I was transferred to Camp Herbert Tarrington, LaHavre, France to be deported back to the states for discharge. Departed LaHavre on March 19 aboard the Liberty ship "USAT Texarkana" and disembarked at Fort Dix, New Jersey and was discharged from active duty on March 27, 1946. (3 years, one month, seventeen days).

A HINT OF DEUTSCH

Jack Graber
75th Infantry Division, 219st Regiment, Co I, 3rd Platoon

We had relieved elements of the 424th Infantry at Manhay and took up defensive positions. I inhabited the cellar of a bombed out farmhouse with three others. We received heavy shelling while we were there.

At one point I started up the basement stairs to the main level when we took a direct hit, knocking me backwards down the basement stairs. Unbeknown to ourselves, a 1st lieutenant artillery observer who attempted to take cover in the ruins of the farmhouse was killed in the blast.

A few days later while at the same location, a message was received that there was an American jeep ambushed, with its five occupants killed and their 82nd Airborne uniforms and dog tags taken.

That same night while on guard with another squad member named Janik, we heard the eerie sound of a vehicle moving down the road. I remember that night was pitch black when the jeep approached, headlights out, of course. When the jeep was right in front of the farmhouse, I yelled, "Halt!" They stopped immediately and, because it was so dark, they were looking all over. I didn't think they could see us when I asked for the password. After a pause one hollered "We forgot, but we're looking for Item Company, 82nd Airborne." After noticing his slight German accent I immediately demanded that they throw out their weapons. When they complied, I was sure they were not GIs. They were taken to Company Headquarters and l never heard any more about this incident.

On. January 5th. 1945, the company withdrew at 2300 hours from Manhay after attacking forces had advanced beyond our town. While in Manhay, we had four killed and five wounded. The German soldiers we captured at Manhay during the first few days of January could very well be the same Germans that ambushed Corporal Robert Mangers.

MY TOTAL FRUSTRATION AND MAYBE YOURS TOO

Philip Howard Gray
78th Infantry Division, 303rd Engineer Battalion, Company A

[Philip attached several documents to illustrate the matters he is concerned about; however, because of length, they are not attached.]

Hoping that I would be coming to the 60th anniversary of the Remagen Bridgehead, a German friend called the Mayor of Remagen, who e-mailed me information on the 78th Division Association. After joining, and getting into the spirit of reminiscence, I dug out my box of WWII memorabilia and began reviewing things that had once puzzled me but had been all but forgotten during 30 years in academia, where I seldom met anybody who knew first-hand what war was like.

Among the puzzles was a sheet of printed paper headed by the cachet "Battle Honors." What the hell was it? It had been sent to me just as I was nearing discharge. Going on the internet and querying 78th veterans from my company, I finally established that it was a presidential unit citation. I also found that only a few of the veterans I contacted had a firm idea that it was the highest unit award offered by the military.

I also revisited two irritations. First, that my discharge papers failed to give me credit for the Ardennes Campaign and, second, that my transfer-al from the infantry replacement center had cost me the Combat Infantry Badge. Up until the moment I looked at my discharge papers in June 1946, I'd assumed I was entitled to wear three stars on my EAME ribbon. Since the discharge was already written up, I took it and quietly faded back into civilian life again. Now, though, the irritation had resurfaced.

I've asked for a copy of my service papers, although the likely reality is that I've provided the government with more papers than it will likely pro-vide me.

My discharge shows the source of my irritation. The fact that the clerk gave the date of my departure as 18 Jan 45 and the date of my arrival as 18 Jan 45 demonstrates the lack of skill on the part of said clerk. Only Dr. Who's "TARDIS" and the Concorde airliner could provide such departure and arrival on the same date, the former machine science-fiction and the latter far in the future. Besides both dates being wrong, is the additional possibility that the clerk erred in not listing an Ardennes Campaign for me by failing to follow General Orders No. 114 (a summary of which is posted on VBOB's website), namely, "Battle participation credit for the campaign Rhineland will not be accorded during this period for operations in the area defined above." That I actually was in the "area defined above" is tacit in the fact that I was a member of the 78th Division which basically had not moved much within the area defined. That I was there "during this period for operations in the area defined above" can be shown by these additional documents (which I'm probably lucky to have retained all these years):

Document C: Individual Clothing and Equipment Record. This was handed to me as I was about to leave Germany as the lucky winner of a "recuperation furlough" lottery. I was told to keep it until somebody asked me for it. Nobody ever asked for it. It shows that in a period beginning on January 11. 1945, I was issued supplies by H&S 303 Eng, this okayed by Andrew F. McGuane, 2nd Lt., Inf, 78th Division. I have no record to prove it, but shortly before this I had been issued a .45 sidearm (my MOS was heavy machine gun, infantry) in Aachen, but that sidearm was surrendered when I was shifted to the combat engineers.

Document D: Immunization Register. Probably another document I was to pass to whomever asked for it but nobody did. This shows that on 16 Jan 45 I had a typhus shot by WJG with a booster a week later.

Document E: Order for Re-assignment. Up until the end of my "recuperation furlough" I was obviously carried on the rolls of the 303rd Engineers and probably would have been sent back to my unit had I been on leave say to Paris or somewhere near. Since I was only a few months away from discharge time, it made sense to reassign me Stateside. Accordingly, I became part of the First Service Command at Ft. Devens, helping soldiers being discharged to receive their clothing and unit patches. Note that WAC Adjust Margaret Smith (later a senator from Maine) said that I had been 12 months in my unit service. Since the army does not "round up," this means that my service records showed that I had joined Co A, 303rd Engr Bn on or before 21 January 1945.

Since I may never be able to get enough of my service records to appeal through appropriate government channels the evident errors made by the clerk typing up my discharge papers, I am endeavoring an alternative way to feel better about the whole matter by applying for membership in your organization with the frameable Battle of the Bulge certificate.

THE BATTLE OF THE BULGE:
THE TRUE NORTH SHOULDER AND HOW IT UPSET
HITLER'S SCHEDULE[1]

Philip Howard Gray
78th Infantry Division, 303rd Engineer Battalion, Company A

A few months ago, a man who had been knighted by two countries intro-
duced himself to my wife and me. He was the president of the Veterans of
the Battle of the Bulge. The occasion was the gathering of several hundred
survivors of the largest land campaign that warfare has ever seen, technically
called the Ardennes-Alsace campaign. En effet, it had more than 600,000
American soldiers directly involved with another 400,000 as support. Some
50,000 GIs were battle casualties, many more were victims of winter weather,
accidents and diseases, and another 20,000 were captured. My certificate of
the veterans organization of this battle is bordered with the shoulder insignia of the major American units involved in the defeat of Hitler's last bold
gamble: three armies, six corps, ten armored divisions and 23 infantry divisions. The hundreds of smaller units involved fell under the command of one
or another of the larger units depicted.

At the time of the attack, however, these units were scattered throughout Europe, only a half-dozen divisions were actually on First Army's combat line, and these few were either green and untested, or badly battered
from the mistakes of the autumn campaign. For his bold stroke, Hitler had
amassed 200,000 men in 13 infantry and 7 Panzer divisions with almost
1,000 tanks, and in reserve behind this force was another almost as large.
The striking force was partitioned into two Panzer Armies to form the
spearhead of the attack with two infantry armies supporting the Panzer
flanks. The Panzer armies were to use their infantry divisions to force open
a route for the strike across the Meuse River with a swift capture of the seaport of Antwerp to follow[2]. It's what happened to these German infantry
divisions that form the raison d'etre for the present reanalysis of an often
told story.

Bad Intelligence or Distracted IQ?

Allied intelligence failed to see any significance in reports of unusual activity behind German lines, deeming the reported activities as normal defensive preparation of moving armor into position where it could be shifted north or south to meet whatever attack the Americans were sure to launch[3]. Such is the roundelay that the historians of this battle, many of them military officers of middle rank with their careers still ahead of them, have voiced for the past half century. American military historians glissade around an interpretation of our intelligence failure. Other historians, perhaps because they have less career involvement in the matter, are more forthright.

The first note that's off-key in the American accounts involves the verified substantial reports of huge tank movements to the Schnee Eifel (which lacked road nets to more armor either north or south). The second off-key note is the modem warfare adage that armor's major responsibility is attack, not defense. The truth is the Allied command up to and including SHAEF had plenty of information that the Germans had spent weeks moving material into position for an attack that had nowhere to go except west into the Ardennes.

Since the German and Japanese codes had both been broken, the Allied command knew the Japanese ambassador was reporting home that Hitler had a plan to launch a counter-attack as soon as bad weather began, with the main objective of capturing Antwerp. Although Hitler had imposed radio and landline silence about the armies he was moving into position, code-breaker Ultra nonetheless was picking up relevant Reichsbahn and Luftwaffe communications which soon established that each time a troop or transport train was to move across the Rhine the German army command asked for fighter cover. British historian Charles Whiting's *Last Assault: The Battle of the Bulge Reassessed* adds information I've not found in any history of an American. Well before Hitler launched his bold move, Number 100 Group of the Royal Air Force had acquired sixty B-17 Flying Fortresses. Some of these planes were modified to fly at night, not as bombers, but as intelligence gatherers. As well as having jamming equipment, their bomb bays held the newest version of British radar, the H2S scanner. Despite the bad weather, the spy planes were able to look down and observe the large amount of vehicles being moved to, and assembled behind, the Schnee Eifel. This activity was reported to the American 67th Tactical Reconnaissance Group, which relayed the information to Hodges' First Army.

Of the Battle of the Bulge histories I've assembled, Hugh M. Cole's 1965 *The Ardennes: Battle of the Bulge* does mention the Eifel flights of 67th Tactical, noting that SHAEF intelligence dismissed the troop movements as part of the "procession" which had been judged to be defense transitions in preparation. The substantial vehicle traffic via the Reichsbahn, especially Tiger tanks, seen by the 100 Group radar scanners and reported to 67th Tactical is not mentioned in this official U.S. Army history, nor have I found it mentioned in any other American history bearing even slightly on the Battle of the Bulge.

Other critics may interpret this failure of intelligence, which was superb in its gathering, as a failure of analysis. However, my interpretation will be psychological, befitting my profession. To me, the problem with the Allied command was they had what German psychology labels an Eingstellung, that is, a mindset so stubbornly emplaced in the brain that simple things like facts can't modify it. Our commanders were Eingestellt that the Germans were beaten and must soon surrender, a form of mass hypnosis, as it were, among the starred generals that extended from Eisenhower to Bradley and on to Hodges and Patton and from there to mid-level intelligence assemblers, who were quite willing to second guess reports from the soldiers on the line.

The Ghost Front

The German offensive failed, but at heavy cost to both sides. Media attention was always focused on the first half of the battle when the Americans lost more than 4,000 men killed in action. The most savage fighting in the Battle of the Bulge, however, was in the second half when we suffered more than 6,000 men killed in action. German casualties were even greater. Combat losses to the British, Canadian and French armies were miniscule. This contrast in battle casualties was noted by Winston Churchill as in the order of a hundred to one. To correct the great statesman, it was closer to a thousand American casualties for one British casualty! It was to be the largest land battle ever fought, and it was between Americans and Germans.

Actually, neither Germans nor Americans wanted it that way. The Allies wanted peace and quiet along what came to be known as the "Ghost Front," which stretched nearly a hundred miles from the Aachen salient, down along the Siegfried Line to the Luxembourg frontier. As noted, the allied command expected the war to virtually be over by now; but approaching the middle of December 1944 the enemy still showed force. The ETO Quartermaster Command had the same mindset, with the result that it had declined efforts to convert its summer uniform supply to warmer clothing, incorrectly believing the latter would not be needed. Field Marshal Montgomery's error in not securing the land approaches to the Antwerp supply port was a major reason for the poor supply train to the Hurtgen-Ardennes front. As a result, it would take the Allies some time yet to provision their troops for the eventual assault into the Ruhr, the industrial heartland of Germany.

These were errors affecting supply. Other errors had affected manpower.

The decision of First Army's General Hodges to drive through the Hurtgen Forest, where American supremacy in tank and air force could not be utilized, had almost destroyed the 1st, 2nd, 4th, 9th, and 28th Infantry Divisions which gave the Germans exactly what they needed; time to recoup from their mauling cross France. This story of disastrous generalship is well delineated in Edward G. Miller's *A Dark and Bloody Ground*. It was primarily the lack of good supply lines delaying the assault over the Roer-Rhine plain desired by Field Marshall Montgomery for the glory of his British and Canadian armies (and himself). Fortunately so, for it wasn't until late November that Allied command finally realized that if Montgomery had ventured onto the Roer-Rhine plain in force, he could have been washed out to sea by the German release of the more than 20 billion gallons of water locked up behind a chain of dams on the Roer River. A description of these dams, and how they were discovered, is thoroughly explained by Frank A. Camm in *The Flash* (newsletter of the 78th Infantry Division), April 2006, p. 92ff.

Quiet ghosts are good ghosts, so the American command hoped the Ghost Front would remain so, while it resupplied and recuperated, and figured out what to do about the Roer River dams. At this point, two ambitious schemes conflicted.

On the American side, the somewhat rested 2nd Infantry Division was moved up from its quiet position on the Schnee Eifel to attach toward the upper and smaller dams, while the new and wholly green 78th Infantry Division was to fight through the fortified Siegfried Line to capture the lower and largest of the Roer dams. These two divisions, one trying to recover from its brutal mauling in the Hurtgen Forest, and the other with no combat experience whatever, were probably all that General Bradley could spare from the stretched front of his 12th Army Group.

On the German side, Hitler had planned what turned out to be the greatest counter attack in the history of warfare, the planning beginning almost as soon as he realized that Germany could not hold France. On the eastern front, the Soviet army had exhausted his supply pipeline and needed to rest and resupply. Hitler's scheme, built on his bizarre but accurate insight into the frayed relations among the Allies, was to marshal the last of his capabilities to launch a massive attack across the Ardennes plateau. The goal to capture Antwerp would deprive the Americans of their seaport for food and ammunition while splitting their armies from the British and Canadian armies to the north, thus perhaps yielding a separate truce. Such would permit the Germans to concentrate their strength against the Soviets. Hitler managed to stage virtually all his attacking units a few miles behind the apparently quiet Ghost Front, not moving them to forward positions until just before the attack upon which he was staking the survival of the Third Reich. The irony is that this strategy almost succeeded.

Order of Battle

There are three arguable reasons why it didn't. First, Eisenhower was able to make significant military decisions days earlier than Hitler believed possible. Second, the American soldiers stood their ground and fought doggedly, even when separated into small units, whereas Hitler was certain they would cut and run when confronted with the force of two Panzer armies suddenly in front of their thin front lines.

Military historians concentrate on these two reasons for Hitler's failure. Flushing out their accounts of military movements are anecdotes of individuals remembering what their part of the battle had seemed like, while at the other end of the command chart the top officers were portrayed in favorable light, with special accolades to General Patton for his role in lifting the siege of Bastogne. *In his Battle of the Bulge Then and Now*, French historian Jean Paul Pallud has diminished Patton's glory by explaining: "Bastogne was not a prime objective for 'Wacht am Rhine' but an important road centre to be taken on the way, as is clearly shown by the fact that when the 2 Panzer Division could have easily taken the town on December 18 it was ordered to by-pass it, pushing on westward." Nonetheless, Bastogne was a talking point for a media that wasn't otherwise very favorable to the conduct of the American soldier and his officers. Relevant to today's scene is Eisenhower's quip that if all he knew about the early days of the battle was what he got from the media, he'd deem the war lost—evidently some things about warfare and the media don't change much.

The third reason why the Hitler strategy failed is not mentioned in any of the several dozen histories of the Battle of the Bulge that I've managed to accumulate, including the official Army history by Hugh M. Cole. Nor did the Germans in retrospect seem aware of the significance of the 78th Infantry Division's Kesternich salient as indicated in *Hitler's Ardennes Offensive: the German View of the Battle of the Bulge* edited by Dupuy et al. When I mentioned to 78th historian Stanley Polny my discomfort over the omission of the 78th from most of these histories, he sent me a copy of the relevant portion of the Command and General Staff College report concerning the German winter offensive. I quote part of this, both to demonstrate its emendations to the official history by Cole, and to set the stage for how the two ambitious schemes mentioned earlier conflicted: "The Sixth Panzer Army was to have nine divisions, four of these armor, to penetrate the US V Corps and make its dash for the Meuse. These were organized into three corps, I and II SS Panzer Divisions, the 12th and 277th Volks Grenadier Divisions, and the 3rd Parachute Division. The II SS Panzer Corps had the 2d and 9th SS Panzer Divisions and the LXVII Infantry Corps had the 246th and 326th Volks Grenadier Divisions. The I SS Panzer Corps was to make the initial penetrations in the south, and the LXVII Corps, in the north. The II SS Panzer Corps was to follow the I SS Panzer Corps.

"The German attacks began before dawn... with a long and heavy artillery preparation. Within 10 minutes after the end of the preparation, German infantry moved forward to breach V Corps defenses. In the north, LXVII Corps attacked north and south of Monshau against the 38th Cav Sqdn and one battalion of the 99th Inf Div. LXVII Corps did not, however, have both of the divisions with which it was supposed to overwhelm these few defenders. The unexpected V Corps attack by the 78th Inf Div had prevented the 246th Volks Grenadier Division from being shifted south for the attack, and the 2nd Inf Div attack held a pan of the 326th Volks Grenadier Division at Wahlerscheid. This left the LXVII Corps barely four battalions with which to make the penetration and then try to set a shoulder for the breakthrough from Mutzenich to Eupen as planned. The V Corps units further frustrated these plans by having extremely well prepared defense positions from which they halted the German assault with much hard fighting."

This analysis is the best I've seen. It still has errors, however, particularly in the Order of Battle.

The Sixth Panzer Army had eleven divisions rather than nine. Staff College missed the 3rd Panzergrenadier Division (Denkerk), which was part of LXVII (67th) Corps. The Staff College analysis also missed the 272nd Volksgrenadier Division (Kosmalla), which was part of the LXVII Infantry Corps, according to the organization chart given on page 40 by Jean Paul Pallud in his hard-to-acquire *Battle of the Bulge Then and Now*, but is assigned (I think erroneously) to I SS Panzer Corps by Danny S. Parker whose Order of Battle is favored by Charles B. MacDonald in his highly popular *A Time for Trumpets*. Regardless of Corps assignment, however, the 272nd was part of General Dietrich's Sixth Panzer Army, the hammer to Hitler's anvil.

The True North Shoulder

In summary, Hitler had his massed units open with an artillery barrage all along the Ghost Front, starting at 5:30 a.m. and continuing until 7:00 a.m. on the morning of 16 December 1944. This was Hitler's timetable, which Allied Command accepted as the beginning of the Battle of the Bulge. Militarily, the argument can be made that the Battle of the Bulge actually started three days earlier when, at 6:00 a.m. on the morning of 13 December 1944, the 78th Infantry Division launched its attack toward Kestemich for the largest of the Roer River dams. I believe the consequence of the 78th Division attack was militarily important far beyond what small notice of the 78th Division's operation in the Monschau Corridor can be found in the extant histories.

With the exception of Miller's *A Dark and Bloody Ground*, which covers the 78th at Kestemich while missing the connection to the Sixth Panzer Army, the military histories drop the 78th from sight as soon as it is mentioned, its accomplishments merged into that of the 2nd Infantry Division so far as the Battle of the Bulge is concerned. In these histories, the 78th and its upset at Kestemich of Fieldmarshall Model's elaborate planning might never have existed. Even the best of these histories fail to encompass what I've just quoted from the report of the Command and General Staff College. None of them are aware that a substantial part of the infantry components of Dietrich's Sixth Panzer Army passed through the Battle lines of the 78th Division, although *Hitler's Last Gamble* by Trevor Depuy et al notes that the 272nd VGD was unable to participate in the attack as planned because of involvement with the 78th Division at Kestemich and Simmerath. The later notice seems to be the closest the historians have come to solving a puzzle they never saw in the first place.

On this salient point, while Lightning: *The History of the 78th Infantry Division* is a helpful reference for background, a meaningful review of the Battle of Kestemich must be based on the declassified After Action Reports for December 1944 and January 1945 of the 78th Infantry Division.

Although the official Army history by Cole does refer to After Action reports of some units, it is a serious factoid that none of the histories of the Battle of the Bulge I have inspected ever mention the After Action reports of the 78th Infantry Division, for it is from these declassified reports that we get a fuller indication of how important the assault of the 78th toward Kestemich really was.

If the American command regarded Kestemich as a stepping stone to the Roer River Dams, the German command regarded it as something else. The few historians who pay attention seem agreed that the Germans fought so hard for Kestemich because it was on a supply route for material. And there, I think, is the analytical error. Kestemich was a supply hub, all right, but not for logistical supplies. It was instead a transit point for infantry divisional components heading south from Duren railroad transportation center to join the LXVII Corps as Dietrich secretly staged his Sixth Panzer Army behind the Ghost Front. These historians pay so little attention to Duren as an important transportation center that the only time it is mentioned as more than a point on a geographical quadrant defining the Hurtgen Forest is when *Hitler's Last Gamble* by Depuy et al noted that "Hitler had decreed that the Duren bridgehead was crucial to the success of the Ardennes offensive" (p 18).

The military historians ignore the role of Kestemich maybe because, like John S. D. Eisenhower in his *The Bitter Woods*, they note that since some captured German troops came though Furst Germund the tacit inference must be they transitioned directly south from a transshipment area near Cologne. Only if one has actually been in that area, as I have, will it be obvious that Model would not have sent whole divisions across the Cologne-Vlatten plain to be readily spotted, but would instead have routed them secretively through the forests and ravines beyond the Kestemich road hub. We can deduce the route by noting that the 326th VBD was encountered by the 78th near Kestemich and by the 2nd near Forests Wahlerscheid (the village itself no longer exists).

A totally new division to the ETO, the 78th spent the early part of December moving into position south of the Ninth Army under Gen. Courtney Hodges' First Army. Its virgin operational mission was to secure the last and largest dam on the Roer River. Per Field Order #1, the 78th was to crack the Siegfried Line, capture the Towns of Rossesbroich, Bickerath, Simmerath, and Kestemich. Then it was to swing behind the Siegfried Line and secure the Towns of Konzen, Ingenbroich and Eicherscheid. The Division was then to turn north, capture Strauch and Steckenborn, then capture the significant small City of Schmidt. From there it was to take over the largest of the Roer dams (bearing the almost impossible name of Schwammenauel, which I never remember hearing announced aloud!).

As an aside, if the German sector had been thinly protected, Field Order

#1 might have been a reasonable goal. However, this Siegfried Line sector was anything but empty of German soldiers, as the After Action Reports show.

In a linked operation, the 2nd Infantry Division was to attack toward the upper of the Roer dams. However, the attack by this battered and still recuperating unit stalled, and after seeing what danger it faced from the German assault after December 16 along the route of Hitler's Plan A, V Corps moved it out of harm's way to a better defense on the Hohe Venn, along with what could be salvaged to the infantry and armored divisions engaged. This movement, now regarded as brilliant, involved many rear guard battles famous in the context of the larger battle, although its success would have been unlikely had not Montgomery, now in command of the northern forces and maintaining a capable liaison known as the Phantoms, overruled the battlefield command by ordering the tactical withdrawal. Of this command decision, *Hitler's Last Gamble* says: "American historians are often reluctant to give Monty the credit that he deserves. It is clear in retrospect that in this instance the British field marshal was absolutely right, and his decision saved the equivalent of two American divisions from disaster" (p 158). All this left the 78th Division in its lonely position of hanging on to the salient into German soil obtained with its drive through the Siegfried Line; it could not be extracted; it could not be rescued; it was on its own.

Sixth Panzer Army's Mission Divisions

At this point let's look at the 78th Division's "Narrative of Operations" in its December 1944 AAR. First, the division was not up to strength by some three thousand combatants, its 311st Regiment having been detached and put in support of the 8th Division to help XIX Corp to the north. Jump-off hour was for 0600 December 13 when the green division faced the Siegfried Line proper, in this area highly organized and fortified. The fortifications consisted of the dragon's teeth (huge cement blocks that tanks could not get over without bridging), strung wire, interconnected pill boxes with bunkers and firing trenches, and some mine fields (for which I could find no archival photos, although my mental picture of them still seems vivid sixty plus years later).

The 78th soon found that within the division zone were elements of two Volksgrenadier divisions, the 272nd and the 277th. This much the Lightning history tells us, but tells no more and doesn't explain why. We can find more vital information in the "enemy order of battle" section of the divisional After Action Reports. The regiments of the 272nd VGD were 982,980 and the 981 and their locations in the area were ascertained, meaning this was not part of an infantry division at rest, but a full division at that particular location for a purpose—my guess is that when Field marshal Model heard of the 78th attack he diverted the nearest transitioning division to block the advance toward Kestemich. If this surmise is correct, it isn't noted as such in any of the histories of the Battle of the Bulge I have examined.

After the onset of the 78th attack, elements of the 277th Volksgrenadier Division were also encountered. On December 16, prisoners of war were captured from several battalions of the 326th VGD. This division was nearly reformed and had arrived in the sector from Duren. After a brief interaction with the 78th, the 326th sideslipped south. On the same day, elements of the 89th VGD were encountered. Information was then obtained that the 277th VGD had also sideslipped south. The last actual contact with 272nd VGD was made about 20 December. On 21 December, a regiment of the 246 VGD appeared at the front of the 78th before following the 326 on the southern transition. Note this date was almost a week after the unit was supposed to be placed as the vanguard for Dietrich's Sixth Panzer Army! The 78th interrogators ascertained that the 272 had been constituted near Berlin, mainly of air force, navy and men older than normal draft age; near 277 had been formed near Munich with personnel similar to 272; the 246 had been formed near Prague with personnel including convalescents and defense workers; the 326 was formed in Hungary and had been in the 78th vicinity for only a short while before moving. Although the fitness levels of the personnel were under par, all were well armed, often with automatic weapons.

What the 78th G-2 didn't know was that these German divisions were on their way to join Dietrich's Sixth Panzer Army. The 272 was to join Dietrich's LXVII Infantry Corps. The 277 was meant for the I SS Panzer Corps, which spun off the four thousand men and a hundred tanks for Kampfgruppe Peiper. The 326 and the 246 were slotted to LXVII to be used to clear the way for Peiper's strike force. The absence of these units, because of the attacks by the 78th and 2nd Divisions toward the Roer dams, obliged Peiper to force his own opening, causing him delays which he never could ameliorate. There was an intelligence report that the 12 SS Panzer Division had moved from in front of the Ninth Army, ending up as part of Dietrich's I SS Panzer Corps, somehow eluding the attention of the 78th.

The After Action Reports of the 78th Division for the month of December show it had taken prisoners from these German units: (a) 272 Volksgrenadier Division (en transit to LXVII Corps). (b) 277 Volksgrenadier Division (en transit to I SS Corps). (c) 326 Volksgrenadier Division (en transit to LXVII Corps). (d) 426 Volksgrenadier Division (en transit to LXVII Corps). (e) CT von der Heydte (overshot airborne to Hohe Venn). (f) 89 Volksgrenadier Division (not seen in any major battles—apparently one of the "phantom" divisions created by Jodel to meet Hitler's demands since Cole says it "amounted to the strength of a single rifle battalion."

Verily, the 78th Division, assigned a simple operation—simple to Hodges' planners, that is—found itself astride one of Model's transportation hubs, probably the most important one possible considering that these units were to be used as the battering ram to break a hole in V Corps Elsenborn defenses through which the Panzer elements could drive their way to the Meuse, with Joachim Peiper's strike force in the lead. This could easily have been done with the aid of the infantry divisions that could not be brought into timely play because these German divisions were delayed by an unanticipated blockage in the true north shoulder of the Battle of the Bulge caused by the 78th Infantry Division's disruptive battle at the Kestemich hub.

The exigencies of this action by the 78th Division can be seen in a summary of the casualties engendered. The AAR for December reports daily medical statistics under the headings (no unit designations) for battle casualties, trench foot, combat exhaustion and common respiratory. For 12 Dec these are: 13 battle casualties/15 trench foot/0 combat exhaustion/4 common respiratory. For 13 Dec: 238/8/6/1. For 14 Dec: 198/36/5/1. For 15 Dec: 173/208/30/3. For 16 Dec: 132/105/19/2. For 17 Dec: 91/54/12/4. For 18 Dec: 87/34/4/4. For 19 Dec: 46/21/4/3. The battle casualties are tapering off as the 78th grinds to a defensive position and the focus of combat shifts to the south. However, in this week the division suffered nearly a thousand battle casualties. For the whole month of December this statistic was 1235. Total battle casualties in January were only slightly less—938. For January, however, I'm able to calculate the portion of battle casualties for several organic (no attached armored) units of the division that might be of interest. These figures are as follows with Units/Strength, Casualties/Percentage of Casualties to Unit Strength: (a) 78th Division Overall/11/408/938/8.2%; (b) Infantry/7,099/890/12.0%; (c) 303 Engineers/560/26/4.4%; (d) 303 Medics/435/3/0.06%. As an aside, I note that other units had negligible battle casualties. Two statistics, which I may never have another occasion to use, are interesting. The battle casualties for the engineers are nearly half that of the infantry, a factoid evidently ignored when a badge for combat engineers was denied by army brass. Combat medics did have influence enough to be granted a badge, for courage and dedication, surely, but not for the risk of life that Ken Burns alluded to when he co-wrote in *The War: An Intimate History 1941–1945* that "medics suffered proportionally higher casualties than riflemen." In the months I was on the front line I never saw a medic or a medical vehicle deliberately targeted, so Burns has put before the public a myth the public will easily embrace—one often sees medics in movies, but who ever saw a combat engineer in a movie? And what are combat engineers anyway?

Thus, in summary, Dietrich's plan to use five infantry divisions to secure the northern flank of Sixth Panzer Army for his quick thrust to the Meuse had a major problem: four of these five divisions had been interdicted in their transit south by the 78th Infantry Division with at least some delay, and surely some crippling readiness.

With this knowledge of how much of the strength of Dietrich's Sixth Panzer Army was passing through the Kestemich area, we can understand why the Germans so bitterly fought the intrusion of the 78th Infantry Division. General Hodges of First Army and General Gerow of V Corp couldn't have done more to interfere with Hitler's plans if they had known exactly what they were doing. A good point to remember, though, is that if the untested, green 78th Division hadn't put up such a strong fight, then Dietrich and his Kampfgruppe Peiper could have gotten a lot closer to

Hitler's ambitious goals.

Foot Notes:

(1) Invited lecture given at the 100th anniversary meeting of the Wyoming Sons of the American Revolution. (2) This is a quick summary of forces involved. Three slightly different lists of forces, called Order of Battle, may be found in the Pallud, MacDonald, and Depuy et al books I've cited, with some more recent information given inter alia in the brochure written by Roger Cirillo for the U.S. Army Center of Military History as part of its campaigns of WWII series. (3) The touted legend is that American intelligence was so blissfully aware of what was about to happen it gave their one worrying officer a pass to Paris to cure him of his fantasy that the Germans were up to something big. Regardless of veracity, that story formed the opening motif of the movie "Battle of the Bulge," which Eisenhower judged to be the worst war movie he'd ever seen. Privately, I think "The Bridge at Remagen" was even worse—at least "Bulge" had Robert Shaw doing a sterling impression of Joachim Peiper.

KEEP THE ROAD FROM ARLON TO BASTOGNE OPEN

Bob Hagel
35th Division, 320th Infantry Regiment, L Company

The 35th Division was part of Patton's 3rd Army and was en route to Luxembourg to fight in what was later to be known as the "Bulge."

We departed Metz early on the morning of December 26 by truck and traveled all day in the rain and cold until sometime after dark when we were finally able to bed down in an old barn. We were awakened in the early morning by an artillery barrage (our own) and after a hasty breakfast we departed for the front line passing through several badly shelled towns, one of which was Bigonville, Luxembourg. That was the last time we had a warm meal or slept in anything other than a foxhole for the next ten days. The weather turned colder and it started to snow. L Company was held in reserve the first day but then moved up into the line. The 35th Division's job was to keep the road from Arlon to Bastogne open so the 3rd Army and supplies could continue to flow north. We found out later that we were facing the infamous 1st SS Panzer Division and their orders were to cut the supply road no matter what the cost.

We probably didn't move more than a mile or so in the next ten days. Every day was almost the same. Around 2:00 p.m. we would attack the enemy position, push them out with small arms and mortar fire, dig in, fight off counter attacks, care for and carry back our wounded and bring up supplies. We were fighting in heavy pine forests and mountainous terrain with no roads. Everything had to be moved either by carrying it or pulling it on sleds that we had found in towns along the way.

At night the temperature would drop to near or below zero degrees. The only food we had was "K" rations that we tried to warm over the burning cardboard boxes during the day. We wore every piece of clothing we could find. Many men had their feet frozen because of the shortage of galoshes or winter boots. Our blankets froze and looked like plywood. When you would climb out of your foxhole in the mornings you would find two to six inches of snow.

To make matters worse, there was a lot of confusion. At times we would lose contact with our sister companies on our flanks. Several times we were told we were surrounded, which made it tough trying to get our wounded back and our supplies up to us. Another thing that had to add to the confusion was the number of new replacements in "L" Company. I believe the figure had to be about 30 percent when we moved into the lines. I'm sure the veterans worried about us as much as the enemy. Needless to say, it wasn't easy. I was told later after the war ended that "L" Company lost over 100 men, either killed or wounded, from December 27, 1944, until they were pulled out of the line on January 8, 1945.

Because of the forest and terrain, we were fortunate that we had very little contact with enemy tanks and not much in the way of heavy artillery. We had very little support from our own artillery probably because of the confusion I mentioned earlier and the fact that we were within 50 yards of the enemy most of the time. We could hear them talk and dig their holes when it got quiet at night and could even hear their wounded moaning.

Even though I had never fired a bazooka in basic training because of a bad right eye, I was told to carry one after the former bazooka man was killed. I then became attached to the light machine gun section where my duties were, as mentioned before, helping carry the wounded back and going for supplies. My rifleman buddies accused me of being "rear echelon."

The busiest people at this time were the medics. There was not a lot of heavy fighting but it was constant, and there were casualties every day. You can imagine that if we lost over 100 men in two weeks that the medics had to be overworked. That, plus not being able to get a vehicle within a mile of the front line didn't help. Granted there were some wounded with minor injuries and able to walk back themselves but when a man was seriously wounded a medic had to help get him back to the aid station and then return to help another.

On January 6, I had been talking to the machine gun crew and then returned to my foxhole about 20 feet in the rear. Five minutes later a shot was fired, hitting the gunner in the head and killing him. We immediately got back in our holes and started digging them deeper. A few minutes later I was shot through the shoulder and chest by the same sniper, was knocked down and passed out. When I regained consciousness a while later, I was told by those in the hole with me that they were unable to get me out because one of the two medics that had come up to get me was shot through the red cross on his helmet and killed. Another man had been shot through the neck. He eventually recovered.

It was an hour later before the Company Commander came up with the second medic and some help to get me out of the hole, on to the stretcher and carried back to safety. I was taken by sled, jeep and ambulance to the aid station and field hospital where I was operated on. Eventually I ended up in England for treatment and rehabilitation.

I was the lucky one. I had the million dollar wound which got me out of the fighting but didn't cripple or disable me. I'll never forget the medic or the machine gunner even though I never knew their names. I also felt sorry for the ones that never got touched but had to fight on for months not knowing if and when it would happen. They were the heroes.

A CHRISTMAS I WILL NEVER FORGET

Donald Hahn
28th Infantry Division, 112th Infantry Regiment

Prior to the start of the Battle of the Bulge we were in a holding position next to the Seigfried line. We were there for a couple weeks because intelligence figured the war would be over by Christmas. On the morning of the 16th a company of Germans attacked us and after a firefight they gave up.

Over on the next hill German tanks were in a clearing but they couldn't get to us because there was a river between us. They were shelling the hell out of us and we were surrounded for two days. On the second night we fought our way out and left our wounded and dead behind. From then on it was hold, fight and retreat. The night before Christmas we ended up in a pine forest; no snow yet but everything was very cold and we had nothing to eat for couple of days.

The next day, Christmas, we retook a Belgian town and stayed in some of the houses. There was an infantry unit nearby but all they could spare in food was turkey and pineapple. The next few days were fight and retreat. One night they moved us into the edge of this large town. It was awful cold and some stayed on guard while the rest of us went into a house where there was a fire. Again we had no food for a couple days. A Belgian woman came down into the room and motioned to us if we were hungry so she bought potatoes and carrots; we helped her and she made a stew for us.

The next morning they relieved us and we dug in on a hill overlooking the town. The 7th Armored Division was moving out and we wondered what was going on. We could see in the distance German tanks coming but as soon as the last 7th Armored Division tanks went over they blew the bridge. That was the first day of sunshine and American planes came out so we could watch the dog fights, it was quite a sight.

That was the only time we had armored artillery make a direct hit on a foxhole; nothing left of the poor soldier. After a few days we started to take back some ground. We went over a river, which was frozen and all day long we fought in a snowstorm and suffered lots of wounded.

I don't remember the name of the town but the Germans had killed all the people in their houses. We stayed one night and the next night they brought in a regiment of the 106th Infantry Division.

We left there after spending the night and in the morning trucks were waiting for us to load up. They drove all day and night until the morning and were back in France. We boarded box cars and they shipped us to the Vosges Mountains.

A NIGHT IN THE POTATO BIN

James A. "Bob" Hammons
825th Tank Destroyer Battalion, Company A

In December, 1944, we were singing Bing Crosby's "I'll Be Home for Christmas," thinking the war was just about over. But December 16th it was a different tune as we were moving under cover of darkness over mountainous terrain to plug a hole in the line at Stavelot, Belgium. We arrived there at 0400 hours and suddenly, hearing tanks being revved up on the other side of the hill, Lt. Jack Doherty, our platoon commander, ordered two units to proceed across a bridge, up a hill to investigate. Sgt. Armstrong's unit was first up the hill and we followed, with Sgt. Jonas Whaley in charge. We paused momentarily to check a soldier in a jeep that had been shot but he was dead and we continued up the hill.

In just a few minutes as we reached the top, a flare went up from a trip wire and the Germans opened up with fire power. Our own troops back across the river began to shoot and we were caught in the cross-fire. We tried to retreat but the Germans had pulled a tank or an 88 in a curve and began to shoot, hitting Sgt. Armstrong's unit, setting it on fire. We were behind them and trapped so we had to leave our unit for cover, I was handed a 30 caliber M.G. from the pedestal mount and four of us took shelter inside a tin shed. Momentarily, the German infantry came in droves and we ran into a house and upstairs by a window. The only weapons we had were the machine gun and a carbine with the barrel filled with mud. Naturally, we had to hold our fire as we were out-numbered by the Germans. We watched as they used a burp gun to kill Sgt. Armstrong and part of his crew, trying to get out of the burning unit.

Realizing there was nothing we could do, we retreated to the basement where there was a potato bin and got inside. Later a German soldier came down and took a position just outside the open potato bin, and we waited for him to toss in a hand grenade or shoot us with his burp gun but evidently they wanted to interrogate us. All day long we waited while our own outfit, the 825th Tank Destroyer Battalion, knocked out several Tiger tanks and one Royal. Lt. Doherty's jeep was hit at that time and he and his driver Earl Shugart were blown out, but Lt. Doherty continued to direct fire against the oncoming German Army.

In the evening at about 2000 hours, after it had gotten dark, the German soldier went upstairs to eat, I guess, and we took advantage of his absence to escape. We ran down a hill, silhouetted by a burning building, when the Germans opened up with machine gun fire. We managed to get to the river as three mortar rounds landed on the other side of the cold, swift river we tried to cross. We crawled several miles to a dam and skimmed across, finally making it to the 119th Regiment of the 30th Infantry Division where we were shot at but were quickly identified as GI's and were taken in and given warm clothing and "Ks."

Next morning the four of us-Willie Banes, Leonard Walsh, Ike Eichorn and myself were taking two German prisoners back to the C.P. when we met Lt. Doherty and Sgt. Wes Lowe looking for us. We were so elated when we saw them, we let the prisoners go, jumped into the jeep and were taken to Malmedy where we were attacked the next morning by the Germans at a road block using captured American vehicles. There were no prisoners taken because we had already heard about the massacre of Americans just outside of Malmedy toward Stavelot.

While in Malmedy we were bombed three days straight by our own planes whose pilots were told the Germans held Malmedy, but they didn't.

Fortunately, we escaped with only vehicles destroyed and no loss of life, but much shaken by that experience.

GROUND AIRCRAFT OBSERVERS

Arthur G. Holmes, Jr.
565th Anti-aircraft Artillery (AW) Battalion, 38th AAA Group

I would in comparison uncloak one small unit, not well known, with parallel functions in the WWII, U.S. Third Army. Perhaps there were other units of which I am not aware—"The Forward Observers of the Anti-Aircraft Artillery." I and others as follows held the MOS of #518 designated as "Ground Aircraft Observers." In today's army we have been replaced by radar.

Allow me to state at once, although the two operations should seem similar, there was a distinct difference. The Field Artillery FO had the responsibility of placing destructive force onto an opposing force with accuracy immediately. We, on the other hand, were required to identify enemy aircraft, plot their course by compass points, their altitude and numbers and report same in a timely manner. Friendly aircraft were identified by using a coded phrase preceding the same vital information. Our position was pre-designated on a grid map, as our reports were received and the aircraft were plotted and relayed to the proper AAA, units and destructive force was thus applied.

The proper weapons to best accomplish destruction of each target were greatly determined by the altitude at which the aircraft were flying. The 90mm batteries consisting of four weapons and attached M51 mounts were assigned the higher flying targets. The automatic weapons batteries were made of up to eight 40mm cannons on a wheeled carriage towed by a 2-1/2 ton truck and eight M51 units. An M51 was four caliber .50 machine guns mounted two over and under on each side of an electrically operated swivel mount, all on a special trailer pulled by a 2-1/2 ton truck. These weapons covered medium and low flying aircraft.

Our "Out Post" so designated, consisted of three enlisted personnel, a corporal was responsible for our actions. We were assigned to one of four gun batteries. Ours was Battery B of the 565th AAA AW Battalion, Third United States Army. We were recognized by assigned call numbers. Another OP was also assigned to B Battery and two each to the other three lettered batteries A, C, and D.

We arrived in Luxembourg on the 21st of December, 1944. B Battery was assigned the protection of an emergency/fighter field, now the Luxembourg International Airport. I believe that C Battery provided the defense of the towers of Radio Luxembourg. The two remaining batteries and Headquarters were set up in Luxembourg City with other AAA units to protect the 12th Army Group Headquarters, General Omar Bradley, commanding.

That was our MO until the Third Army Headquarters-General George Patton, commanding, moved into Luxembourg City nearing the conclusion of the Battle of the Bulge. The eight OP's of our battalion were then assigned positions forming a ring around the city some 40 to 50 miles out, to provide early warning for protection of the two headquarters. Later, as the fighting progressed into Germany, we then changed from static positions to being highly mobile.

Our equipment in Europe consisted of one Willy's Jeep, one trailer equipped with ribs and cover and a pole antenna attached to the side, one radio receiver with associated gasoline motor powered generator, and remote controls on cable, plus personnel gear and firearms and necessary supplies.

From then on, we were each day assigned map location coordinates, usually a position on high ground. In many instances we were joined by or shared or were in close proximity to field artillery forward observers. On some of the more ambitious assignments we were not able to reach precise site, for we were advised by the infantry and/or tank units that the locations were still in enemy territory. The three of us hop-scotched northwest from Luxembourg, across Germany to a location just west of Weimar and beyond the Buchenwald Concentration Compound. Then southwest into Austria to a position overlooking where the Danube and Iser Rivers joined.

HOME IS WHERE THE YANKS MAKE IT

Billie E. Houseman
561st Field Artillery Battalion, B Battery

We, the 561st Field Artillery Battalion, arrived in the Ardennes on October 4, 1944, from reducing the submarine pens at Brest, France. We were told this was the ghost front, nothing ever happens here! We went into positions behind the 106th Infantry Division to give longer range fire support.

Our weapon was the 155mm long rifle, better known as the Long Tom. Since the weather was getting increasingly colder and we did not know how long we would be in these positions, we started to build huts. Since some of the Ardennes was part of a forestation project, many of the trees were in a straight line and thus you could pick how big you wanted to make your hut: 10'x10', 10'x20' and so forth.

The huts came in many shapes and sizes, based on the ingenuity and material available to the builder. They ranged anywhere from a square hole in the ground with a pup tent over the top to a more elaborate hut built from cut trees, to several doors, removed from houses, and nailed together to form a box with tarpaulin for a roof. Pine branches were used for camouflage on the roofs and sides. These did not have to be replaced as the extreme cold kept them green.

I, personally, was sleeping on the front seat of our kitchen tank. The weather was getting colder each day. Cpl T/5 Arthur Turner, our cook from Chattanooga, Tennessee, had started a hut 10'x10'. He asked me to help him finish it and said it would be big enough for both of us. We acquired rough, sawed lumber from under the Germans' noses and built the hut from these boards. They were about 12"x1"—different lengths, and they still had the bark on the outer edges. You had to handle them carefully, otherwise you got some nasty splinters. These boards were nailed into the tree trunk. Because nails were so scarce, only one nail was allowed at the end of each board. Turner had already liberated (never stole) a small stove, a window with six small panes, and a door. We made hinges out of leather belting. Turner kept his canvas cot from our days in England and I built a cot from tree branches. This I covered with cardboard.

Some of the fellows came up with an ingenious way of making a roof, since our powder charges came in a heavy cardboard to be 8" in diameter by about 4" in length, the cannoneers split them down the entire length on one side, then scored them on the opposite side. When you flattened them you had two semicircular pieces. Since they were impregnated with pitch (to keep the powder dry) they did not leak. They overlapped them to simulate a Spanish tiled roof. We also lined the inside of our hut with flattened cardboard from cartons that our canned goods came in. This made good insulation.

One of the men from our 5th section (the fellows that did a terrific job keeping us supplied with projectiles and powder charges) came through a small town that had a hardware store. He liberated 5 or 6 railroad type lanterns and sold them to the highest bidder. Turner bought one (I have no idea how much he paid). But we built a shelf for it. Our dehydrated potatoes, carrots, red beets, etc., were packed in a moisture-proof material that was paper on one side and aluminum foil on the other with a pitch substance in the middle. We put the foil side behind the lantern. Just as we were getting things cozy, Hitler had other ideas and, as everybody knows, all hell broke loose on the morning of December 16, 1944.

Just before dark, one of our L-4 cubs got airborne and reported that the Germans were in our huts, and had fires going in our stoves.

THREE SHORT STORIES ABOUT THE BULGE

Billie E. Houseman
561st Field Artillery Battalion, B Battery

The First occurred as we were withdrawing from the enemy south east of St. Vith. We the 561st F. A. Bn. had just come through the village of Vecmont. As we were leading, I could see many trees up ahead with blocks of TNT wrapped around one side of the tree on both sides of the road. Up ahead was a sergeant standing in the back of a 3/4 ton truck, a sheet of paper in his hand, and his other hand on a detonator box. He was pumping his arm up and down, the signal to hurry up. I am sure he had a list of outfits that would be coming down that road. I am sure glad he did not push that plunger prematurely to fell those trees, or we would have been trapped. Apparently we were the last outfit to pass him, because shortly thereafter we heard a series of explosions.

The Second episode occurred also while fleeing the onrushing Panzers. Since the ground was frozen and covered with snow, any field would do, as we could not dig the guns in. We would pull off the road, lob a few shells back in the direction we had come from, then load up and go down the road another 2 or 3 miles and repeat the same thing. At one point it was reported the enemy was only a mile or so behind us. On or about December 20, 1944 we pulled off the road and our Captain Victor Woodling, (Baker Battery Commander) came running down the middle of the road yelling to the truck drivers to remove all their excess gas cans and get ready to torch their trucks. He also told us if we had any pictures in our wallets of loved ones back home to get ready to destroy them. He no more than told us that when we heard tank tracks clanking. The sound was coming from a nearby patch of woods. We all thought this was it—that we had done bought the farm. The man above was surly with us this day, as it turned out to be an American T. D. outfit, with a young Lt. standing up in the open turret. He yelled to Capt. Woodling, "What outfit are you, and did you come down that road?" Pointing to his right, Capt. Woodling said yes. The Lt. said, "Get your people loaded up and get down the road as fast as you can." The truck drivers threw their gas cans into the back of the trucks, and we all mounted up, and really took off. To this day I've wondered how those T. D.s made out meeting the enemy head on.

The Third episode occurred two days later. Around midnight I was riding in the back of our kitchen truck, when our convoy came to a halt. Out of the woods came two American officers, a Captain and a Lieutenant. They asked our one cook, T/5 Arthur R. Turner of Chattanooga, TN, what outfit we were, where we had come from, and where we were headed. Only the

Capt. spoke. I said to Turner out the side of my mouth, "He's asking a lot of questions." Turner being from the south said, "Beats the shit out of me, Captain," and at the same time our convoy started to move again. Two days later we found out Germans were running around in American uniforms. I thought something was wrong, as our officers never wore their shiny rank on their uniforms on account of sunlight bouncing off the metal. Officers always were preferred targets for snipers!

MEMORIES

Billie E. Houseman
561st Field Artillery Battalion, B Battery

We, the 561st Field Artillery Battalion, arrived at our first firing position near Schonberg, Belgium, on October 4, 1944, after helping to destroy the submarine pens at Brest in France.

Our weapon was the 155mm (Long Tom) rifle. We were Corps Artillery, and our prime objective was to take out warehouses, ammunition dumps, road junctions, etc., and to beef up the Divisional Artillery to our immediate front.

On or about November 20, 1944, my battery, Baker, set up 3,000 yards out in front of our other two batteries, Able and Charlie. As you all know, all hell broke loose in the early morning hours of December 16, 1944.

To our front was the 106th Infantry Division which only days before had replaced the 2nd Infantry Division (Indian Head). 150mm German shells began landing in our area by 10:30 a.m. that morning. We had built log cabins, or huts to protect ourselves from the increasing cold. We stole rough-sawed lumber from under the Germans' noses and nailed it to the trees, clapboard fashion. Since nails were in short supply, we allowed only one nail to each end of the board. We used flattened cardboard boxes to insulate the walls.

With the uncertainty of the 106th, we were ordered to pull back. C Battery dug in on a hilltop to cover our withdrawal. Three of their guns had to be destroyed to prevent capture. By 1:30 p.m. on the 16th, we pulled back through St. Vith, Bastogne, Houffalize, and Arlon finally stopping at Neufchateau. All of this occurred over a period of several days.

We, along with several other artillery units including AAA joined in with the 26th Division, 80th Division and the 83rd Division with Colonel Creighton Abrams leading a combat regiment of the 4th Armored Division. It would be February 4, 1945 before we returned anywhere near our original positions. There were still several more months of hard fighting ahead.

Those booming 155s took us across five countries, earned us five bronze campaign stars in 303 days of continuous combat, while expending 54,991 rounds of high explosive shells.

SPEARHEAD TO BASTOGNE

Albin F. Irzyk
4th Armored Division

A veteran of the Battle of the Bulge tells the story of the 4th Armored Division's drive to relieve the encircled town.

Just before dark on the day after Christmas 1944, elements of Third Army Commander Lieutenant General George S. Patton Jr.'s 4th Armored Division, attacking from the south, succeeded in making contact with the beleaguered Americans at Bastogne. The encircled 101st Airborne Division had occupied that critically vital Belgian town for several days, categorically refusing German demands for surrender.

The dramatic linkup of the two forces broke the siege of Bastogne and was one of the great turning points in the Battle of the Bulge. This legendary event has often been described in histories of World War II, but there is a fascinating little known subplot to the story.

It took the 4th Armored Division five days of bitter, costly fighting to break the ring of German units encircling the 101st, but only six days before the linkup elements of that same division had actually been in Bastogne, on the day it was being surrounded. In fact, during that earlier movement into the town, those forced had come within one kilometer of the same spot to which they would return six days later, after heavy fighting. How could this have happened?

To understand this enigma, we must go back to December 8, 1944, the day the 4th Armored Division was pulled back from heavy fighting after reaching the Maginot Line, at a point a little more than nine miles from the German border. It was time for refitting and rest so that the division would be better prepared to cross the border and continue its assault to the east. The move to the rest area was not only welcome and richly deserved but necessary. The men of the division were exhausted after incessant fighting during the heavy, record-breaking November rains. The weather, the enemy and the gummy mud combined to make conditions deplorable and had taken a serious toll on the men and their tracked vehicles. Such extended breaks in the fighting were rare and spirits were high.

At the time, I was serving with Combat Command B (CCB) of the 4th Armored Division, commanded by Brig. Gen. Holmes E. Dager, and its 8th Tank Battalion, which I commanded as a young major. During the division's rest period my command post was in Domnom-lès-Dieuze, a tiny, wet, muddy and depressing French village about 40 miles northeast of Nancy. Almost immediately, the town became littered with tank parts and equipment of all types. Not knowing how long we would be there, the men wasted no time in pursuing their tasks.

On the fourth day the troops were excited and energized by the visit of the Third Army commander, General Patton, who swooped in for a quick stop. He arrived at high speed in his Jeep, with a wide, crooked grin and all his stars blazing. He was jolly, animated and interested in how we were doing. After jumping out of his jeep, he worked his way along the entire length of the small town. He stopped at every vehicle, talked with every cluster of soldiers and had something to say to each—a question, a word of encouragement or appreciation, a compliment, a wise-crack, a good-natured dig. He was a master at this kind of rapprochement. His visits were brief, and he kept moving. But in 30 minutes or so, he had worked his magic—he had touched virtually every man in that battalion.

We soon learned that the 8th Tank Battalion was the only battalion in the division that he visited. Although the troops had no inkling of the momentous events that lay just ahead, Patton was apparently aware that an attack might be in the offing. After visiting the three other divisions of the XII Corps that day, he wrote in his diary that he had decided to put the 6th Armored Division and the 26th Infantry Division into the III Corps because if "the enemy attacks the VIII Corps of the First Army, as is probable, I can still use the III Corps to help."

December 18 is a day I will always remember as the most confusing day of the entire war. Early that morning I was told to attend a meeting at division headquarters, but before I left for the meeting it was called off. The previous day I had been told that a move was imminent and to have my troops ready to move on short notice.

At 10:45 a.m. on the 18th, CCB was placed on a one-hour alert. I continued with my preparations for the move the next day to the east, as well as the subsequent attack into Germany, by sending parties forward to obtain billets for the battalion to occupy at the end of the march to the border.

At 5 p.m. the one-hour alert was canceled. Shortly afterward, I also received word that the move to the east the next day was off. I recalled my billeting parties. With no order for the next day, the men settled in for the night after the evening meal.

Then, suddenly, at 11 p.m. the 8th was ordered by CCB to be prepared to move at once. That directive was quickly followed up with instructions to cross the initial point, or IP (as yet to be designated), at 12:50 a.m. and then move in a totally different direction-north! We would be moving to the III Corps zone (wherever that was) to assist in stopping a strong German counterattack in that sector.

The radical change in mission, the confusion that had preceded it, the lack of information, the uncertainty, the hasty departure in the pitch dark and the highly unusual timing of the move—50 minutes after midnight—all combined to indicate we were involved in something serious. A cloud of apprehension hovered over the entire battalion.

As ordered, the 8th Tank Battalion moved at 12:50 a.m. on December 19. We had no information about the situation up ahead or about the enemy. CCB's orders were to move to an area in the vicinity of Longwy, France, many miles to the north. The 4th Armored Division, previously attached to the XII Corps, was now assigned to the III Corps.

Combat Command B, with its 8th Tank Battalion out front, led the advance of the division. Combat Command A (CCA) would be the next to move out, nine hours behind CCB and along the same route. Thus, the 8th led the odyssey north into the cold, black night, reinforced with the half-tracks of the 10th Armored infantry Battalion. At the head of the 8th was my tank, making it the lead element of the Third Army in its advance to the north.

Amazingly the combat command had but one map, and that was with General Dager.

During our rapid movements across France that summer and autumn, we occasionally had to rely on Michelin road maps for direction. But to be completely without maps was a new experience.

Once the column was on the road, we rolled mile after mile into the unknown. I was guided and directed by General Dager in a variety of ways. He radioed instructions from his jeep, his staff relayed radio messages, he sometimes rode alongside to shout directions at me in my turret, and at tricky intersections he dismounted and pointed the way.

The hours and miles passed, and Longwy loomed closer. The end was in sight. But then our spirits were dashed. As we reached Longwy, we were waved on, and we rolled through the city without slackening our pace. Our tank guns were still pointed to the north, and now, for the first time in the war, we were in Belgium. We passed through Arlon and changed direction to the northwest, still with no reduction of speed.

We began our journey in darkness and were to end it in darkness, as night came upon us again. A difficult situation became considerably more difficult, since we now had to travel under blackout conditions, and our progress would be greatly slowed. On top of that we had absolutely no idea of what lay ahead, and we were expecting to be fired on by the enemy at any moment.

As we neared the town of Vaux-les-Rosieres, we were at last told to stop for the night.

Combat Command B moved into that location, which was west of the road. I selected a spot about two kilometers east of the road for our bivouac area (I would later learn that it was near a town named Nives). By the time we settled in, it was 11 p.m.

Except for brief halts, and one longer one to refuel, we had been on the move increasingly for more than 22 hours, half of one night, all day and half of another night under blackout conditions. Remarkably, we had traveled 161 miles over roads that were sometimes bad—without maps and without confusion.

The fact that we arrived was a tribute to both our men and vehicles and spoke volumes for the work we had accomplished during the recent rest period. Most important, there had been no enemy contact.

That night none of us realized that we were the vanguard of what would later be called the greatest mass movement of men in the shortest period of time in the history of warfare. Patton's troops had been poised to attack the Saar to the east. Forced to abandon that plan, he ordered the major part of his Third Army to make a gigantic 90-degree wheeling movement and then drive north at full speed. Involved in the spectacular maneuver were thousands of men and vehicles operating in damnable weather, often over icy roads.

Once we reached the bivouac area there was still no rest for many of us. Many of the men were exhausted, but as soon as we reached our position we sent forward some strong patrols of light tanks and armored infantry to detect any enemy movement from the north.

Early the next morning December 20, I was, figuratively speaking, hit by a thunderbolt. General Dager called me on his radio and, without any preliminaries, ordered me to send a task force into Bastogne. I was stunned. I protested vehemently, reminding him that the situation up ahead was unclear, terribly confused, and that this was no time for a piecemeal commitment of my forces. To my great surprise, Dager agreed with me. He said that he had just made the same arguments in a tug of war with Maj. Gen. Troy H.

Middleton of the VIII Corps. Middleton had ordered him to take all of CCB into Bastogne, and he had hotly resisted, insisting that Middleton wait until Maj. Gen. Hugh J. Gaffey arrived with the rest of the 4th Armored Division. Middleton finally agreed not to commit the entire combat command, but only after Dager conceded that he would send a task force instead. As ordered, I formed the task force. It consisted of A Company, 8th Tank Battalion; C Company, 10th Armored Infantry Battalion; and C Battery, 22nd Armored Field Artillery Battalion. I placed Captain Bert P. Ezell, my battalion executive officer, in charge of the task force. His force would henceforth be known as "Task Force Ezell." Ezell's mission was to report to Brig. Gen. Anthony C. McAuliffe, commander of the 101st Airborne Division, learn about the situation in Bastogne, receive instructions and render support if so ordered.

This task force moved northeast on the Neufchateau-Bastogne road and reached Bastogne without seeing any enemy troops. Upon entering the city, Ezell was told to report for instructions not to McAuliffe, but to Colonel William Roberts, commander of Combat Command B of the 10th Armored Division.

Shortly after Ezell radioed me that he was in Bastogne and had made contact with our troops, I was astonished to receive an order from divisional headquarters to recall the task force to Nives at once. I immediately called Ezell, whose radio operator told me that he was out talking to a colonel. I shouted, "Get him!" I reached him not a moment too soon, for at that very instant Ezell had been receiving instructions for deployment from Colonel Roberts. When I told him to return, Ezell was dumbfounded. As was to be expected, he had a difficult time convincing Roberts that he had to leave with his force just after arriving in Bastogne. A short time later, just after noon, a delighted and vastly relieved task force was on the road again.

Seven hours after it set out for Bastogne, Ezell's task force returned to our bivouac area with many more vehicles than it had when it pulled out. The men were beside themselves, chatting and shouting excitedly. They had seen some strange sights—so strange that they had a difficult time explaining it all to the rest of us.

As the task force moved away from Bastogne, they had encountered an

American 2-1/2 ton truck in a ditch on the right side of the road. The truck was barely damaged and its driver was still sitting behind the wheel. But the top of his head had been blown off above the eyes, apparently by an armor-piercing round.

Moving a little farther down the road beyond the ditched truck, the troops noticed tank tracks running across the asphalt pavement. They were much wider tracks than could be made by American tanks and must have been made by German Panther or Tiger tanks.

The task force then came upon another strange sight—about two battalions of U.S. artillery stopped along the road. The equipment seemed to be in good shape, but there was no sign of any troops. Some of the vehicles were still idling. It was not clear whether the artillery units had been attacked and their positions overrun, or if they had been spooked by the sight of German tanks crossing the road just to the north of them and had abandoned their guns and vehicles. Given the evidence they had seen so far, it appeared that a strong German force had moved rapidly west and cut across the Neufchateau-Bastogne road while Ezell was moving toward Bastogne. Perhaps the lead German elements had been moving so quickly that following forces had not yet caught up with the vanguard. Ezell's units had apparently managed to slip through a gap in the enemy echelons driving west. The task force hauled back as much of the abandoned artillery equipment as they could handle and encountered no resistance on the way back to the bivouac area.

As December 20 passed, events continued to move swiftly. At 2 p.m., CCB was reassigned to III Corps with the rest of the division. The 8th Tank Battalion was ordered to retrace its steps of the previous night and move southwest to Neufchateau, then southeast to Leglise. We arrived in the vicinity of Leglise after dark on the 20th. Shortly afterward, I was surprised to learn that the rest of the division had remained in the vicinity of Arlon, and none of its units had made any attempt to close up on CCB. Only later did we learn why CCB had gone where it did and when it did.

On the 21st, I received my orders from General Dager at CCB headquarters for the attack that would take place the following day. I was also informed that during the previous night and early that morning very strong

German forces had driven west and flanked the City of Bastogne on the north and south. The two forces had met west of the city and completely encircled Bastogne. Trapped in the city was the 101st Airborne Division, to which were attached elements of the 9th and 10th Armored Divisions.

This was shocking news, but Task Force Ezell had provided ample clues that the Germans had been on the move the previous day. What really was disturbing was the realization that the encirclement had been taking place while Ezell's group had been in Bastogne, and it had continued with unabated fury after the 8th Tank Battalion and CCB had left the area.

I could not help but think about what could have happened. If he had not been recalled by divisional headquarters Ezell and his men might have been trapped in Bastogne along with Colonel Roberts' combat command of the 10th Armored. And what if General Dager had not won the day in his tussle with General Middleton? All the 4th Armored's CCB—if we had moved into Bastogne as General Middleton had originally ordered—might well be stuck in the besieged city.

We moved out of Leglise at 4:30 the next morning—the 22nd—so as to arrive at the starting point at 6. The 8th Tank Battalion and the rest of CCB were part of the 4th Armored Division's attacking force, coordinated with the 80th and 26th Infantry Divisions of III Corps. The 4th Armored was on the left flank.

We began our slow, difficult return to Bastogne. The following day at Chaumont, the 8th Tank Battalion was on the receiving end of one of the most powerful tank-led counterattacks of the war, temporarily slowing its advance to Bastogne and inflicting heavy casualties. Ironically, the battle at Chaumout was fought just four kilometers east of the quiet bivouac area we had occupied at Nives just three days earlier.

It took five days of bitter fighting to relieve the 101st in Bastogne, but by December 28 the area had been cleared of the enemy, and all of our positions had been consolidated. When Captain Ezell walked into the 8th Tank Battalion command post in Assenois, he was just one kilometer southeast of where his task force had been eight days earlier as it rolled into Bastogne.

Those of us who participated in this confusing operation, as well as historians who have analyzed the Battle of the Bulge in the years following World War II, could not help but note the ironies and incongruities surrounding the battle.

A number of questions have been raised about our mission:

Why did CCB, whose original destination was the vicinity of Longwy, continue on alone until it reached a position in VIII Corps sector, only nine kilometers from Bastogne?

Why did General Middleton of VIII(sic) Corps seem to exert "ownership" of CCB?

Why did the rest of the 4th Armored Division not close up behind CCB instead of leaving CCB near Bastogne while the rest of the division assembled well to the rear, in the Arlon area?

If General Dager had not protested dividing his command, what might have happened to CCB if it had rolled into Bastogne as ordered, on the day when the enemy was very much on the move?

After moving into Bastogne, why was Task Force Ezell immediately and summarily recalled, especially considering that General Middleton had argued strongly for its presence there?

After the elements of Task Force Ezell had returned to their parent units, why was all of CCB relieved from assignment to VIII Corps and withdrawn—back to the rear—less than a day after arriving in the forward position?

Should commanders at higher levels have exploited Task Force Ezell's rapid progress to Bastogne once they knew the unit had entered the town without a fight and returned? And should General Middleton have been allowed to hold onto CCB and use it to try to keep the Neufchateau-Bastogne highway open, possibly preventing the encirclement of Bastogne?

Once CCB had moved into it bivouac at Vaux-les-Rosieres, should the rest of the 4th Armored Division have capitalized on the situation, moving up to attack from the bivouac location only a short distance from Bastogne rather than consolidating for the attack farther south and then fighting its way north along the difficult forest axis from Arlon to the encircled city?

Among those who have answered Yes to the last two questions is Charles B. MacDonald, who stated in his book *A Time for Trumpets*, "If Middleton had been allowed to hold CCB and with it keep open the Neufchateau/Bastogne highway, Bastogne probably never would have surrounded. Even if the Germans had cut the Neufchateau/Bastogne highway, the Fourth Armored Division might have capitalized on the location of CCB and attacked from Vaux-les-Rosieres instead of from Arlon. Which would have spared many officers and men of the Fourth Armored Division a great deal of misery and, in some cases, death." The following additional information about the events leading up to the battle of Bastogne provides answers to some of these nagging questions.

On December 18, Lt. Gen. Omar N. Bradley, commander of all U.S. ground forces, called off Patton's planned offensive into the Saar. Without hesitation, Patton told Bradley that he would concentrate the 4th Armored Division in the vicinity of Longwy, pull the 80th Infantry Division out of the line and get in 26th Infantry Division moving in 24 hours. Much later that same day he issued the order that got CCB moving just after midnight.

Patton met with his staff at 8 the next morning, December 19, as CCB was already well on its way to Longwy. His plan, he told his staff, was to strike north and hit the underbelly of the German penetration where it would hurt. During the next hour, Patton and his staff planned, in outline, three distinct operations. Arrangements were made for a simple code to indicate via a brief telephone call, which operation would be implemented.

Later that same day, Patton met at Verdun with Supreme Allied Commander General Eisenhower and a distinguished gathering of senior commanders that some have called perhaps the most historically significant conference of the 1944–45 campaign. All agreed there should be a counterattack at the earliest possible moment. Patton told the group that he could be ready to attack with three divisions of the III Corps on December 22. A stronger force, he said, would take several more days to assemble and would forfeit surprise. The group was astonished at his rapid response to the situation and was more than satisfied with his proposal. It should be emphasized that at this meeting Patton pledged a three-division counterattack with the entire 4th Armored Division as the key division in the corps. He was completely unaware CCB was then on its way toward Bastogne.

Given the situation, it is absolutely inconceivable that CCB should have been sent on its merry way all the way to the outskirts of Bastogne and told to report to the VIII Corps. It turned out that General Bradley was responsible for that trip. Whatever the rationale for its mission may have been, the motivation for this decision is difficult to comprehend.

In his memoir *War As I Knew It*, General Patton wrote: "The next morning I arrived at Bradley's headquarters in Luxembourg and found that he had, without notifying me, detached Combat Command 'B' [General Dager] of the 4th Armored Division from Arlon to a position southwest of Bastogne. Since the Combat Command had not been engaged, I withdrew it to Arlon [not Arlon but Leglise]."

Historian Martin Blumenson, in the second volume of *The Patton Papers* quoted from General Patton's diary entry of the same day, December 20; "In the morning I drove to Luxembourg, arriving at 0900. Bradley had halted the 80th Division at Luxembourg and had also engaged one combat command of the 4th Armored Division in the vicinity east of Bastogne [not east but southeast] without letting me know but I said nothing." General Middleton still must have been anxious to send CCB into Bastogne behind Task Force Ezell and surely requested permission to do so. Elements of his corps were already scattered and his armor was especially fragmented. Middleton wanted to avoid more of the same. General Gaffey must have wanted his combat command returned. With a major attack coming up in just two days he needed his division at full strengthen, and it would have been severely handicapped without CCB. General Milliken also knew that the key to his III Corps three-division attack was having the 4th Armored at full strength. He surely must have supported Gaffey's argument to have his CCB returned.

As events later developed, CCB shouldered an extremely heavy share of the 4th Armored's fight at Bastogne. The combat command acted as the powerful left ITank, not only of the division, but also of the III Corps all the way to the encircled city. In retrospect, General Dager's resistance to committing CCB to Bastogne earlier surely saved the unit. If he had not protested, fragile craft were lost en route, the remaining 33 arrived at the landing zone with their cargo relatively intact.

Supreme Allied Commander Dwight D. Eisenhower later claimed that the resupply drops had ensured victory at Bastogne.

77TH EVAC HOSPITAL IN THE BULGE

Andre Jamar
77th Evacuation Hospital

On December 16th the Battle of the Bulge began. During the day the robot bombs came over in increasing numbers until late in the afternoon there were actually ten within sight at the same time. That evening during the show there was an air raid alert and bombs were dropped on the town. Early the following morning two patients were brought in and through them news of the offensive was learned. The first patient stated he had been fighting a German paratrooper. A few minutes later a lieutenant was admitted and said he had been shot by a German paratrooper.

Germany's general staff had realized that the war of attrition at the Siegfried Line had no future for them but Field Marshal von Rundstedt had a plan and two Panzer armies to carry it out. This was to break through the lightly held southern part of the First Army front and push to Liege and then on to Brussels and Antwerp on the north and toward Namur on the south breaking through between Monschau and Trier. The first phase of the offensive ended December 22.

During the Battle of the Bulge, the personnel of the hospital worked harder than at any time. In addition to the large number of patients admitted the hospital was harassed continually by the bombing, strafing, shelling, and the V-weapons which landed all about.

During the afternoon of December 17 the fog and clouds cleared for a while and dog-fights were seen over the hospital. The robot bombs came over at 5 minute intervals with scarcely a pause during day or night. In the afternoon the patients began coming in and their stories were repeatedly that of retreat, positions overrun, confusions, huge losses of men and material, temporary stand and then further withdrawal. There was no "strategic with-drawal." As far as these men were concerned, the powerful German forces were more than they could cope with and they had been forced to pull out.

Some of the operating personnel began working eighteen hours daily and by this means the backlog was overcome. Being in almost the exact center of the northern flank of the Bulge, the 77th was receiving nearly all the ca-sualties from the northern flank. Once again there was a constant stream of patients to the operating room as the eight operating tables and two fracture tables were kept occupied night and day.

December 18 was a repetition of the previous day and night.

Verviers had become an important road junction, a bottleneck through which thousands of American and British troops were being funneled into the northern flank. The Germans were quick to appreciate this fact. From the maps it was obvious that there must be a large volume of traffic through Verviers if the central part of the northern shoulder of the Bulge was to be re-inforced rapidly. Such a target was too valuable to miss and the enemy wasted little time in carrying out the expected attacks. On the night of December 19 the enemy planes came over and dropped flares which lit up the entire town as though it were day. This was perhaps the heaviest raid which the towns experienced during the entire Battle of Bulge.

During this particular night one of the patients was being questioned concerning the manner in which he was injured and the story which he told later appeared in the papers under the heading: The Malmedy Massacre. He had been captured early that day along with about 140 American soldiers. They had been herded into an open field and when it was night several enemy tanks lined up along the road bordering the field. The men were forced into a tightly packed group and suddenly the machine guns from all the tanks began firing on them. The night was soon filled with moans of the dying but still the intermittent chatter of the machine guns contin-ued. Finally these stopped and the officers and men of the German troops walked among the group of fallen men. If one of the prisoners moved or groaned he was summarily shot through the head. The patient had been only slightly wounded and although desperately frightened he lay quietly and made no sound. One of the men came close to him but passed on after a quick inspection. The patient dared not move and scarcely breathed for fear he would be discovered.

After an interminable time the tanks finally turned off their lights and went on down the road. Only a few men were left to guard the mass of bodies. As it was now completely dark the patient finally moved slowly to the edge of the group and then into the woods where he at last stood up. He was soon joined by two others who could walk and they set out for their own lines through the darkness. After what seemed like hours they came upon the American troops and were soon back to the relative safety of the hospital. Later on it was possible to identify the German unit which had carried out this horrible affair.

December 20 brought more patients, more buzz-bombs and more work. December 21, 22 and 23 were more of the same. A continuous stream of patients during the afternoon and night, gradually lessening early in the morning and regaining momentum again during the afternoon, was sufficient to keep all of the hospital personnel fully occupied.

On December 24 the sun was out bright and clear for the first time since the start of the Battle of the Ardennes. The Allied air forces were ready for such a break in the weather and that day there were hundreds of planes in the air. Dog fights took place over Verviers and a great number of German planes were shot down.

It was at this time that the hospital received a number of enemy patients who were dressed in GI clothing. They had been dropped by parachute behind the Allied lines and only after several days were the military police successful in capturing them.

Christmas Day, 1944 will probably be forever the most unpleasant Christmas in the lifetime of thousands of soldiers. The personnel and patients of the 77th were no exception.

On December 30 the first good news began to trickle through. The Allied troops had gained the initiative and the Bulge was beginning to shrink. Even with such good news, the work of caring for the wounded went on day and night.

Then the final order came through stating that the 77th was to move out.

BATTLE OF THE BULGE

Morphis A. Jamiel

7th Armored Division, 38th Armored Infantry Battalion, Company B

We had just finished fighting the Krauts (Germans) in northern Germany and expected a rest period. Our hopes were shattered when an officers' meeting was called and we were informed that our outfit had a secret mission to perform. All they could tell us was to expect a long journey.

Everyone was tired and cold but we managed to crawl into our half-tracks and try to get some sleep. It was so cold outside and the inside of the steel half-track felt like a refrigerator car. The men huddled together in order to keep warm. No one got much sleep due to the cramped space.

We traveled all that night and the next day without any rest period. The following night we arrived at a small town in Belgium, which they called St. Vith. It didn't hold much interest to us at that time. Another officers' meeting was called and we were told of the German's expected drive. We were also informed that our mission was to hold the high ground east of St. Vith at all costs and to prevent the Krauts from taking the town.

It was approximately eleven o'clock in the evening when the men finally assembled and were ready to move on foot. It was bitter cold and the men stomped their feet and rubbed their hands in an attempt to warm them. A reconnaissance patrol returned and guided our company up one of the main roads leading into St. Vith.

We walked approximately one and one-half miles to a road junction. This was to be the company's left boundary. My platoon was assigned the mission of holding the road junction. The rest of the company deployed to our right along the road running perpendicular to the road we advanced on. There were dense woods on both sides of the road, which restricted our visibility to the width of the road which was approximately ten feet. If the Krauts attacked, they would come within ten feet of our position before we would see them.

The men were instructed to dig two-man foxholes so that one could sleep while the other stood guard. The ground was frozen which caused some difficulty in breaking the top layer. The difficulty increased when the men encountered tree roots and large rocks. The tired men finally gave up in disgust. This proved fatal later on. The hard ground, cold weather and the nature of the situation prevented the men from getting much sleep.

The next morning things were quiet so I ordered the men to dig their foxholes deeper and to place some logs overhead to protect them from artillery fire. Whenever artillery rounds fall in woods, they hit the top of trees and explode causing the shrapnel to fly down into the foxholes with deadly effect. Four medium tanks were assigned to support the defense of the road junction.

About three o'clock in the afternoon, the Germans launched a small attack to feel out our positions. We drove them off but they succeeded in discovering that some of the foxholes were not dug deep enough to form a strong defense.

The following morning the Krauts heavily shelled our area and the men with shallow foxholes and no overhead cover paid dearly for their lack of preparation. About two o'clock in the afternoon, the Krauts attacked the center of our company with two tanks and a company of infantry. There was plenty of shooting but we couldn't see the Germans because of the dense wooded area. Finally the tension was broken when the Germans appeared firing direct fire into our troops. The noise was terrific and the explosions deadly. One of our tank destroyers, which maneuvered into position, knocked out one of the German tanks. The German infantry then appeared out of the woods ten feet from us. The dopes walked straight up and started to cross the road. We destroyed them all. After the attack, we checked the bodies and determined them to be paratroopers. Their canteens were empty but emitted a strange odor. They may have been drugged or intoxicated which explained their foolish action.

During the following two days, the Krauts shelled our position with harassing fire. Several cases of trench foot and frost bites developed, which seriously reduced our number. Our defense line was now thinly held. During the hours of darkness, German vehicles could be heard assembling for a possible attack. Often German voices could be heard in the woods to our front but appeared to be a safe distance away.

During the fifth day, the Krauts threw an unusual amount of artillery on our position and on the town of St. Vith. Our ammunition and ration dumps were destroyed. We did not receive any food or ammunition that day. Just at darkness, the Germans began their mighty offensive, which was opposed by a group of hungry, tired and cold men who determined to hold their ground.

It seemed like all hell broke loose. Our nerves were shattered by this time. We fired wildly into the darkness toward the road. The Krauts were yelling in German, which sounded like a million men. They were firing all types of weapons in our direction. The familiar sounds of burp guns, machine pistols, 42 machine guns and carbines were heard.

My runner, sent to contact the unit on our left flank, returned with the information that they had pulled out. About this time the Krauts broke through the center of our defense and were behind my platoon. It was dark and no one knew who the other person was. From that point on it was every man for himself. The troops ran in all direction under the cover of darkness. The mental strain the troops were subjected to and the fear of death had shown its effect. Some of the men escaped while others were captured. At this time the German tanks could be heard slowly moving down the road toward St. Vith. It was pitch black. Our gallant tankers sent to defend the road junction, fired toward the noise of the German tanks. They missed and as a result gave away their positions.

The Krauts immediately fired flares, which lit up the entire countryside. Our tanks stood out in the light and became easy targets for the German tanks. In less than two minutes, our tanks were in flames. As the tank crews emerged through the hatches, they were met with machine gun fire from the Germans. They fell back into their tanks and were cremated. A few of us ran into an abandoned house behind our lines. Our house stay was cut short when a German tank fired two rounds of high explosives into the house. Only three plaster-covered men emerged from the ruins and went streaking cross-country out of St. Vith.

Three days later, we heard a German news flash stating that our outfit had been completely destroyed. Little did the Germans know that we were back licking our wounds and regaining our strength. In less than a month, we were back in action and succeeding in driving the Krauts out of St. Vith and regain our former positions.

CHRISTMAS NIGHT, DECEMBER 1944

George Karambelas
84th Infantry Division, 333rd Infantry Regiment, A Company

The blinding flash and the deafening explosion were followed by screams. The medic, who a minute before was kneeling over me to give first aid, groaned and slumped on me.

"I'll help you," I said, but he was already dead. And this is the way it is when riflemen are sent to fight tanks.

It was Christmas night, December 25, 1944 when the allied armies in Europe began a desperate and costly struggle, since known as the Battle of the Bulge. Snow that Christmas was not one of nature's beautiful decorations but an enemy just as deadly as the German machine guns and tanks. Some of the events that took place on the night of the 25th are only hazy recollections; others are still very vivid and will never be forgotten. Some of these events are responsible for saving my life while others may be viewed as premonitions of the impending tragedy. Every year at this time I find myself reflecting on these events and I wonder!

Christmas was uneventful except for the bright sun and clear sky which permitted our Air Force to become operative after a prolonged period of inactivity due to bad weather. The elation felt at seeing thousands of planes on their way to bomb the German Panzers was short-lived because I knew that there was still a long, long road to travel before sanity would return to the world.

"All right you guys, pack up; we're going for a nice little walk," barked the platoon sergeant. We crawled out of our foxholes, a few miles from Marche, and after marching, waiting and freezing for what seemed an eon, we stopped at last in the courtyard of a large farmhouse. Orders, we were told, had not come through as expected and we would have to sit. A nearby barn, filled with hay, provided a perfect haven and as I crawled into the hay to warm my freezing feet, I thought how wonderful it would be if orders were delayed until morning and I could spend a whole night in luxurious comfort. The heavy guns roaring in the distance seemed very far away and the whole war seemed to detach itself from my little world. At the moment, the only thing that mattered was that I was under shelter and among my friends.

John Shaw, a close friend who always took meticulous care of his overshoes, said to me, "What kind of situation do you think we're in, anyway?"

"I don't know."

"Hazard a guess."

"I can't even do that. I've got a sense of foreboding, that's all."

With the customary abruptness, orders were passed around to assemble in the courtyard. There were moans and groans from everyone; our little haven was about to crumble. In the courtyard, I remember thinking that this would probably be just another "hurry-up and wait" affair because we were totally unfamiliar with the terrain and it would be suicidal to send troops on a night mission without adequate briefing. I was sure that a night mission was out of the question, and worse, we would maneuver for position for the rest of the night. We were told briefly that German paratroopers (about one company) had occupied a strategic hill but since we would attack with an entire battalion, it would simply be a matter of policing-up just like we did in camp. (In camp, soldiers were formed into a rank and went along picking up trash; this was known as policing the area or simply police-up.) I said to John Shaw, "If anybody has the notion of ordering us to attack now, he's crazy."

No answer.

"John, didn't you hear me?"

"I heard you."

"Then why the hell don't you say something?"

"I will, when I get my overshoes stashed away in a good, safe place."

We had been ordered to remove our packs, overcoats and overshoes.

Soon, we started marching toward a hill silhouetted against the sky. I wasn't particularly frightened but I kept wondering if we would find only a company of German paratroopers. I remember seeing a truck pulling an anti-tank gun up the hill, skidding and going into a ditch. The sight of the antitank gun didn't register at that moment but I have thought since about it a great deal and wonder if someone knew that anti-tank guns and plenty of them, were the main thing needed for that mission.

During the march to the top of the hill I kept stumbling for no apparent reason; I even dropped my rifle and was afraid that the bore might be plugged up. Shortly thereafter, I dropped one of my grenades and going through a few strands of barbed wire, I became entangled and nearly lost my helmet. When I look back on the stumbling, dropping of things and the barbed wire, I feel sure that they were warnings. I had never before dropped my rifle. At the time, however, I was more concerned with cleaning it and catching up with my platoon.

Someone was firing tracers behind us. "Shaw! Do you see those Roman candles?"

"I see them."

"And you aren't nervous in the service, buddy?"

"It's only grazing fire, quit worrying."

The hill was very quiet and I remembered the scout in the Indian movies saying, "Yeah, it's too quiet." One platoon attacked the Chateau of Verdenne on the hill but very little firing ensued and we were told that the castle was taken and not to worry about it anymore. We were then lined up and told to proceed through a designated section of the woods firing and screaming in order to demoralize the Germans. The woods consisted of a few large trees and many smaller ones fairly close together. There was a wide path or road on our left flank and we were told to stay away from it but to guide on it. I was about ten yards from the road blazing away from the hip and screaming like mad. Someone was firing from my left and a little to my rear but too close for my comfort. "Hey, burr head," I yelled, "do me a favor and point that pea-shooter at the Krauts instead of me."

"Sorry, George, I'll get up on the line with you."

It was my platoon leader.

All of a sudden the Germans began to return our fire; their machine guns appeared to span the entire width of the woods. I didn't feel particularly concerned about the machine gun fire and I don't think anyone else did. After all, German small arms fire had always been dealt with before; it was their artillery we feared. I don't think anyone in my immediate area was wounded but we began to crawl and continued to fire. The screaming was far less enthusiastic and soon no one screamed. I reached a small clearing in the woods near the road. The lieutenant came up and asked me if I could see anything. I said no but I thought I had spotted a machine gun nest and would try to hit it with a rifle grenade.

As I edged toward the road, the machine gun opened up again for a few seconds and the lieutenant cautioned me not to get too close to the road. In order to fire at the position I had picked out, I had to get on one knee to clear some trees. I fired the grenade, saw it hit and felt certain that I had knocked out the German machine gun. As I turned to crawl back, I felt something crash into my left thigh. It felt as though someone had struck me with a baseball bat. The blow knocked me backwards but I managed to crawl away from the road without much difficulty. I felt only surprise and amazement that I had been hit; after the initial pain, I felt only a mild burning sensation.

The lieutenant came up and asked me where I was hit.

"In my thigh."

"Medic!" he called.

The medic crawled up and said to me, "I'll check it to make sure an artery hasn't been severed."

I was flat on my back with my feet toward the Germans; this position (feet toward the enemy) saved my life. The medic kneeled beside me, examined the wound and said it wasn't bad; no broken bones. He told me to take my sulfa tablets, while he applied a dressing. (The medic had come to our company just a few days before and I didn't even know his name.)

As he started to leave I felt an explosion which seemed to be right at my feet and felt a sharp pain on my right foot. I heard the medic groan and he fell over me. I tried to help him but he was already dead. The shrapnel from the German tank almost cut him in half. Then I heard screams from all around. Several of the men were hit and some were calling for a medic while others were just crying. I remember two in particular, one who spoke English with an accent kept saying "I die, I die," and the other was screaming about a wound in his back and that he couldn't move. I started to crawl toward the voices when another explosion, practically at the same place as the first one, knocked me unconscious.

I don't know how long I was out but when I came to I thought I was dead. What had been pitch dark before was now fairly bright, with fires burning in some places and flares going off. My first thought was that I was in hell. Slowly I regained my senses but when I started to move I knew that my legs had been shattered. I tried to sit up just as another shell came in and I fell flat again. This time I was very frightened because a small fragment hit me above the eye and the blood impaired my vision; I thought I was blind. When I wiped the blood away I could see and turned to examine my legs. My right foot felt as though it was held on hot coals.

I reached down to feel it—I suppose to make sure that at least it was there—when I heard a voice to my right rear saying, "George really got it that time; I think he's dead."

I turned my head and said, "Hell, I'm not dead; where is everybody?"

"Orders have come through to withdraw. Somebody must have admitted that we can't fight tanks with rifles."

Time had lost all meaning and I had no idea how long this whole thing had taken. I tried to get up, hoping against hope that somehow I could walk but soon resigned myself to the fact that I would not get out of the woods under my own power. I crawled over to the other men; there were at least five whom I had known very well.

I asked, "How badly are all of you guys hurt?" They seemed to have their legs shattered so completely that the slightest movement was impossible.

Then I asked the question that combatants have been asking since the first two tribes of primitive men clashed.

"Why hasn't help been sent to take out the wounded?"

Someone answered, "That's what I'm up here for, but now I'm hit and can't even help myself."

He was sure that no one would venture into the woods. Earlier, most of the wounded had been taken out, but now nobody would return.

"We can't stay here," I said, "the Germans might come though at any minute and finish us off. Nobody is returning their fire."

All agreed but there didn't seem to be much point to try to do anything. I searched around with my hands hoping to find a rifle. All the weapons had suddenly disappeared; the only thing I had was a grenade in my pocket.

After trying to think of something to do or something to say I also joined the mood of the little group which seemed to be if help doesn't come, we're lost, because there's nothing we can do by ourselves. From the German lines, machine guns sprayed the area periodically but not even close to us.

Finally one soldier spoke up and said, "If anyone thinks he can crawl, he'd better start, because the Krauts will be here in no time."

"I can crawl," I said, "but I don't know how far, and I don't want to become separated from the rest of you. I haven't any idea how far back the others have withdrawn. I'll try it with somebody else."

Compared to the others I was in fairly good shape and I would have to try to get back and send help. The next few minutes were the most heart rending moments I have ever known. I am sure that all the wounded doubted that I would ever get back and knew that even if I did, help for them would not arrive in time. They gave me messages for wives, sweethearts and families (two of the men had babies which they had never seen) and last farewells to their loved ones which made me break down. (I may add that all of the wounded died but I did not contact any of their families.) After reassuring them that I would have help back in no time, I started crawling away from them. It soon became apparent to me that I would never get through the woods but would have to risk the road. I crawled to the edge of the road, was unable to see any sign of a human being, no gunfire of any sort and decided to crawl as fast as I could. The next period of time is very hazy. I am almost sure that I got up and walked a few steps but I can't be positive. In the meantime, the Germans had started firing again and

I remember watching their tracers overhead. Nothing seemed to matter, however, except finding friendly troops because I knew that before too long I would pass out and freeze to death. At last I arrived at the point where we entered the woods some hours before. I was very tired by this time and crawled into a ditch to rest for a little while. I don't remember how long I was there but when I tried to crawl again, I knew that I had reached the end. I heard someone walking toward me on the road and became very frightened because I was certain that they were Germans and that they would see me and finish me off.

I took a grenade from my pocket, pulled the pin, and called out, "What company are you guys from?"

"A Company, 3rd platoon," one of them said in a surprised voice.

I replaced the pin. "Help me get to the first aid station. And then get word to headquarters that there are still wounded in the woods; and tell them to be quick about it."

But self-preservation comes to the fore at such times and the soldiers probably felt that I would be too much of a burden to them. They suggested I be carried to a nearby shack and they would hurry back to get help. I pleaded, threatened, cursed and did everything I could think of to persuade them to take me with them. At last they made a seat with a jacket and their rifles and carried me to the first aid station. I remember passing out several times on the way and I know what a burden I was to these two soldiers. Needless to say, they saved my life and I am very grateful. The aid station was set up near some trenches in which stretchers had been placed. I was lowered into one of them, covered with a blanket, asked where I was hit and given first aid, which consisted mainly of applying a dressing over any spot that was wounded. It was impossible to cut away clothing and boots for proper care.

Daylight came and with it a jeep. I remember being lifted out of the trench and placed on the hood of the jeep. A very kind voice asked if I was cold and gave me another blanket. In fifteen minutes or so I was in a building, placed on a table and attended to by an army medical officer. I don't remember what he told me but I felt very reassured. He gave me an injection, the pain ceased and I felt pretty good. He gave me a tin of hot coffee and a tube to drink through and then I saw what remained of my company. They asked about friends, I asked if help had been sent for the others, nothing really made any sense.

Shortly thereafter I was placed in an ambulance with some of my friends, and was told that we were going to a hospital.

Before long I began having terrific pains and asked the attendant to please give me something. He did and I remember falling asleep with two of my friends looking at me. I woke up in a hospital ward, looked for my friends, but they had been taken elsewhere. Soon I was transported to Paris and began the long route through the hospitals to my eventual discharge from the army. To this date, I have seen only two of the men in my company but wherever they are and whatever they are doing, may God bless them all; they were the greatest.

THE BULGE WAS A VIOLENT AND COLD BATTLE

Chuck Katlic
99th Infantry Division, 394th Infantry Regiment, Company F

It all began at 0500 hours. Chuck Katlic recalls being on watch 65 years ago today: December 16, 1944 in the Ardennes. One of 70,000 men in four and a half divisions, covering a 70-mile front. Katlic looked out across the Siegfried line from his log fortified snow-covered foxhole. The quiet was shattered by German artillery and mortars, as the enemy opened up on the 99th division.

The Battle of the Bulge had begun.

The weather was cloudy and cold and artillery landed in our area all day and night. Company F was awake and on the alert when it started, but thank God we had covered our foxholes with logs.

Katlic believes that the logs were the only thing that saved him and his buddies from being ripped to shreds by shrapnel and wood shards from trees blasted to smithereens. Some men who are caught out of their foxholes were wounded or killed, he said.

Artillery continued to hit their positions on December 17 as German and American planes went at one another overhead. Eventually the German artillery ceased. The 2nd Battalion was surrounded by Germans and separated from their regiment. We received orders to withdraw. We withdrew, leaving a covering force to an assembly point near Hunmgen, Belgium. No artillery fell December 18 and the evidence of the past two days' barrage was concealed under a blanket of new snow. The temperature dropped to near 5 degrees and circumstances grew dire as we were low on ammo and food. The Germans were closing in for the kill. We moved along a draw but the mortar rounds started landing in the draw. So the company moved into the woods where we were temporally held up for a couple of hours. The company was given the orders to fix bayonets. Company F and the rest of the battalion moved toward Merrigan, Belgium. At about 1500 hours a German burp gun opened up on our column and pinned us down. Heavy weapons were called for.

The Americans attacked in German positions and met stiff resistance. Our company commander was given command of the battalion. Lt. Goodner led the battalion through the draw to the town of Elsenborn, believed to be in Allied control. But the battalion fell under intense artillery and small arms fire. We were wet and cold and hungry. He said the 2nd Battalion was given up as lost in action.

Rumors of the battalion's demise were premature. We reached the outskirts of Elsenborn and the men of Company F slept in a barn until about 1000. Hot chow was served around noon (hot pancakes and syrup, a feast). It was our first hot meal in days.

The company moved to Elsenborn Ridge to take the high ground. We dug foxholes and set our defenses. Our meals would be cold C rations until our kitchen was set up in Elsenborn. We improved our positions and sent out patrols. On Christmas day we were served a cold turkey dinner.

They stayed there for a while and Katlic celebrated his 21st birthday on January 8, 1945 in a foxhole on the Elsenborn Ridge.

"It was the coldest day of my life," he said. The 99th division held the northern shoulder preventing the Germans from expanding the bulge. Katlic described the 99th action as decisive. The 99th spent the month of January defending the north shoulder of the bulge, he said. After many attempts the Germans could not break through and they eventually withdrew to a defensive position.

Wet cold weather met Katlic and the rest of the men who climbed from their foxholes at 1 a.m. on January 31, 1945 to answer the long-awaited call to attack. Our company left the area at 0300 hours and starting moving toward our objective. Snow was waist deep and rain had made a slushy surface on top of it. That delayed their departure. By 0600 hours company had advanced only about 700 yards.

No enemy resistance was initially met. The Company F commander led the way and with covering fire from light machine guns and 60 mm mortars, the men moved forward into enemy installations. We were moving due north through the enemy's outpost reaching our objective, when light resistance was met. Swinging the company due east we drove the Germans from our objective and into the dense woods. That's where we were held up by intense automatic and sniper fire, which inflicted heavy casualties on our infantry and medics. The company was pinned down in four feet of snow for the remainder of the night.

Artillery was called in to eliminate the enemy fire and shells landed within 50 yards of the Americans' position. We spent a miserable night laying in the snow wet, cold, hungry, sleepy, and tired. Eight of our men were killed and many who were wounded did not make it through the night. He and his brothers in arms regrouped and advanced back to the lines where they had been on December 16.

The next day we began to push the Germans back to the Rhine River and into Germany. It was the end of the Battle of the Bulge. In those six weeks Americans suffered 90,000 casualties including 19,000 killed in action. It was the largest land battle ever fought by the U.S. Army.

CHRISTMAS EVE PRESENT

Frank Kaye
8th Air Force

Flying bombing missions 23,000 feet over the Bulge was somewhat different than fighting the war hip-deep in snow on the ground. Nevertheless, it was on Christmas Eve and again on Christmas Day while flying over the Ardennes, better known as "The Battle of the Bulge" that I was feeling sorry for myself, thinking of all the festivities I would normally be celebrating back home on this the most festive of all holidays. Not thinking at the moment that I was about to be part of the greatest battle ever, so fiercely fought by the U.S. in the greatest war ever fought, as it was later described by Gen. Dwight D. Eisenhower and Prime Minister Winston Churchill. The surprise German counter attack began on December 16th, creating a huge bulge in the allied front line, giving the ensuing battle its name.

Due to inclement weather and fog that blanketed most of the continent, there was a lull on all flying activities, giving the Germans an advantage on their ground operations. However, the weather finally cleared and we were able to deliver our Christmas present to the Nazis on Christmas Eve by a combined aerial armada of more than 2000 Consolidated B-24 & Boeing B-17 heavy bombers, escorted by over 900 P-51 Mustangs, P-47 Thunderbolts & P-38 Lightning fighters. This mission is presently inscribed on the historic plaque erected in front of the old National Guard Building on Bull Street, Savannah, GA., where the Eight Air Force was born in 1942, now the home for The American Legion Post #135.

This mission, the first of its kind to utilize such a mass force of bombers on a single raid, was designed to pound the hell out of all communication lines supplying and reinforcing the German armies, thus stalling their counteroffensive drive.

The December 24th mission took off for Germany in the dusky early morning. The first bombers were approaching their German targets as the tail of the large column were still taking off from our bases in England. Never before has anyone seen such a mass formation of aircraft assembled in the sky at any one time. During the three-day weekend of flying, the Eighth Air Force knocked out 218 enemy planes while we lost 38 heavy bombers and 40 fighter planes. Ironically, this was our crew's 24th and 25th mission on this the 24th and 25th day of December.

These missions were always outstanding in my mind, yet, they are not the most memorable ones. We were told midweek that there would be no missions scheduled for the coming New Year day and many of us made some plans. Well there was one hell of a New Year's Eve party going on at the NCO club when about 3 A.M. there was an abrupt halt to all activities with a special announcement. The band was silenced and the voice came loud and clear. Due to the extreme reversal of condition at the Bulge, there will be a special mission this morning.

There was no time for rest or sleep. After a fast good bye to your dancing partner there was a quick change into flight gear and a grumbling trip to the briefing room. Griping could be heard throughout the base. However, after the briefing, tensions were somewhat eased when we learned that due to the extreme conditions on the ground, created by the surprise German counter-offensive, compounded by heavy snow, bitter cold, and a lack of supplies all adding to the troop's misery. Moral support was desperately needed.

This put a different light on the situation and the angry mood was quickly changed. Upon leaving the room, we were like a bunch of college kids returning to the second half of a close football game. Gung Ho for Victory, ready for whatever.

Anxious to get going to raise some hell, I recall our nose gunner who in the process of checking his nose turret guns, accidentally fired a short burst from his twin fifties across the flight line, almost hitting the Engineering Officer who was sitting in his shack a couple hundred yards away. Scared half to death, he tried for days to find the culprit who cut loose that burst and I'll bet he is still talking about it today.

It was customary for Catholic crewmen to receive Holy Communion before leaving the briefing room but there was no time this day. Father Beck, the Catholic Chaplain from Ohio rolled from plane to plane looking for

Catholics. He knew his crews real well, so when he pulled up to C-Charlie, our B-24, he shouted "come get it, Polack." I being the only Polish Catholic on the crew received mine under the wing. Before he drove off, I asked where he got the Jeep he was driving as I never saw him on anything but a bicycle? He grinned, saying God left it for him at the Chapel. Can you picture a Catholic Priest swiping Jeeps? Later, before take-off, our waist gunner, Travis West, a wisecracker from Texas, jokingly asked what it was I had for breakfast.

Knowing that food supplies were scarce on the ground, we made a slight change from our regular routine in preparing for this mission. In addition to the bombs, we loaded up with extra crates of K-Rations, in the event we were downed. K- Rations was a heavily sealed wax container about the size of a Cracker Jack box that contained some chewing gum, hard candy, sticks of cheese, a couple of bouillon cubes and a few cigarettes. Not exactly Christmas turkey but sure nice to have around when nothing else is available. The alternative plan was to jettison most of it, if we had a successful mission, hoping they got to the right people. Which we ultimately did.

Breezing through another seven missions after this memorable New Year's Day, we returned back to the States where I had the occasion to meet up with Hank Altyn, a good family friend with a pitching arm destined for the big show, if not interrupted by the war. We often played catch together and I had no idea Hank was one of the guys hip deep in snow that cold January. He spoke of finding some of the K-Rations we tossed overboard. He talked about the tremendous boost in morale to all of the troops after seeing thousands of American bombers overhead, at a time when things were looking so bleak. At the time having no idea that I was up there tossing them out, nor I knowing he was below. Hank's recollection made my war worthwhile. It was a regular routine for crews returning from a mission to excitedly describe the actions encountered on that particular mission, to the crews who were not flying that day. However, after a few hours and maybe a few beers, the stories became so boring, that the common response was: Yea, Yea, tell it to your grandkids. The following day, the situation would be reversed. Now, it is reality. And for some, we are telling it to our great grandkids. And some are actually listening.

512TH FIELD ARTILLERY BATTALION

Eugene C. Kazanecki
512th Field Artillery Battalion

[Excerpts] I just received the second publication of *The Bulge Bugle* and after reading some of the letters and articles I noticed that most only mention one or two outfits that were involved.

I was a gunner corporal on the 105 mm Howitzer, 512th Field Artillery Battalion XII Corps, under Lieutenant General George S. Patton, Jr. We were on the line for 19 months with only one day off. I have been checking the VFW News for 54 years for any reunions or a mention of my outfit without finding any.

I never spoke of my experiences in the service until my youngest son found a manuscript in the basement. He sat there and read the entire story of my outfit. I hadn't seen the manuscript in 53 years. I have no idea who the writer is or where I got it. It mentions every outfit in the Third Army that we fought with side-by-side and supported. It also mentions the names of all those killed or injured and how it happened. After reading it, my son said, "Dad, I did not realize what you had to go through."

The manuscript is so old and brittle that I had to be careful how I turned the pages. It was then that I decided to retype every page and included maps and pictures and made a copy for each of my three children. The cover page reads, "I decided to put this journal together to let you, my children and grandchildren, know what my army life was like when I was 18, 19, and 20 years old, which are the best years of a young man's life. I thank the Lord for letting me come home in one piece with the exception of some bumps and bruises, frozen hands and feet, and a hornet's stinger in my eye while those around me never made it."

[We have extracted from Mr. Kazanecki's papers that portion which leads up to and immediately follows the Battle of the Bulge—as that is our area of concentration in this newsletter.]

[Excerpts from Foreword] The 512th had quite a career. It was known and respected by some of the most famous outfits in all the armies. In 265 days in combat it fired over 87,000 rounds and had one day off the line in the entire period. It had been commended by the Army Commander, General George S. Patton, Jr., and by other high officers under whom it served, received more high decorations for valor, a DSC, several Croix de Guerres, and Silver Star Medals, than many an infant regiment in combat. ...The 512th had no history previous June 25, 1943. It will probably cease to be at the end of 19?? and those who hope for a peaceful world hereafter will join hoping that it will never again be called into existence.

[Excerpts from text] In November another river had to be crossed... the Seille. The 512th pounded out another path for 80th Division—over 700 rounds were delivered to the enemy between 0500 and 0615 on November 8th. The guns of the 512th thundered... and the heavens thundered in echo. Down came the rain... torrents... flooding the entire area... and it was a miserable night spent in crossing the Seille River. But in all the rain and mud, the artillerymen moved forward... into the Saar Basin.

On the 6th of December orders came through that the 512th would be relieved of their position...and would move to the rear to fire a demonstration of the new POSIT Fuze for the 12th Corps. Morale might have bounced for the battalion... what with the chance to get out of the line even for a little while... a welcome rest. But joy disappeared as quickly as it had come. On the 7th... just one day later... they were ordered back into the line... to support the 35th Division's push against the Saar River line. The first goal was Saareguemines... and the resistance was tough all the way. Mile by mile...it became more and more difficult to crack the German wall of defense. There were heavy counterattacks, and heavy counter artillery fire...a position would be selected for the coming guns... but before it could be used... it was very often destroyed. And the rain continued... the 512th was mud-bound more often than not, but in all of this morbid state... the artillery men managed to squeeze off at least 700 rounds a day... contributing in no little manner to the softening of the 35th Division advance toward the Saar.

Rain turned to sleet... and mud to snow. For the 512th Field Artillery was moving north now. It was the 19th of December and the night was spent marching... without rest... for there was no time for rest. The Third Army was now fighting time. Came the dawn... and the 512th was once again in support of their old running mate... the 80th Division. This time in the bitter battle of the Ardennes. Staggering in the snow to hips... casualty lists mounting not from the mere sting of bullets... it was the cold. Frozen feet and hands claimed the finest soldiers as victims... more Purple Hearts. The advance proceeded... through snow covered and shell wrecked Belgium...on to the junction of the Our and Sauer Rivers. There facing the 80th Division and the 512th Field Artillery was one of the densest portions of the Siegfried Line. Von Rundstedt's Bulge had burst like a bubble. All the ground taken in the German offensive was now wrested from the enemy and the Third Army was now ready to strike into Germany. On the 19th of February, 1945, the 512th crossed the Our river near Bollendorf... the frontier was pierced.

THE AROMA WAS GREAT - CHRISTMAS 1944

Lester R. King
643rd Tank Destroyer Battalion, Company A

At Christmas time in 1944 every member of the U.S. Armed Forces was promised a traditional Christmas dinner: roast turkey and southern baked ham, candied sweet potatoes, mashed potatoes, corn bread stuffing with giblet gravy, a fresh veggie tray, corn and peas and green beans, along with fresh, hot-out-of-the-oven dinner rolls, pumpkin and mince meat pies.

1 was a member of "A" Company, 643rd Tank Destroyer Battalion. At the time, we were equipped with M5 Towed 5 in anti-tank guns. On Christmas Eve we were selected to stand rear-guard for the retreating GIs through Manhay, Belgium.

The incoming German artillery and mortar fire was constant. All we could do was helplessly watch as the advancing enemy infantry, supported by armor, flanked us on both sides of Highway N-15.

Finally, at about midnight, we received orders to save our own skins. We hooked the gun to the half-track, forced our way into the line of retreating vehicles and headed north through the burning town of Manhay.

We had already pulled as many fleeing foot soldiers into our track as it would hold.

By now, the Germans landsmen were in force on our flanks. The scene was much like an old-time western movie where the Indians are on both sides of the stagecoach with all of the Cowboys and Indians shooting at each other.

We managed to escape the town without casualties and positioned the run for the night north of the village.

Christmas Day was spent guarding one of the hundreds of single lane bridges located in the area, with one-half of a K-ration breakfast as the only meal for each man.

On the day after Christmas the surviving members of the company were divided among the remaining guns. We found a few replacements and received our new assignment.

The next day we were ordered to dig-in our gun on a bluff overlooking a wooded valley occupied by the enemy to prevent their tanks from advancing any further.

The never-ending artillery and small arms fire was devastating and casualties were heavy among our supporting infantry men.

The following day, December 28th, the "incoming" slowed considerably and our Christmas dinner finally arrived. Late, but never the less, a very welcome sight. The mess truck was parked and the cooks began preparing the long anticipated meal.

The smell, no, the magnificent fragrance of the cooking food was phenomenal. Every man's juices began to flow uncontrollably as the ice cold air was filled with it.

The eager men queued up at the portable serving table when suddenly the gates of Hell opened! "SPANG-SPANG-SPANG!" The area was completely bracketed with artillery fire!

The startled men hit the ground trying to make themselves invisible. The cooks gathered their gear, threw everything haphazardly into the bed of the truck and flew down the road with pots and pans banging and clanging like a runaway chuck wagon in an old Tex Ritter movie.

They had made the almost always fatal mistake of parking on a hilltop.

We never did get our Christmas dinner, nor did we ever see the mess truck again until we were waiting for the boat to take us home.

THE GHOST OF A SOLDIER

Lester R. King
643rd Tank Destroyer Battalion, Company A

Visualize if you will the ghost of a GI somewhere in Belgium on Christmas Eve of 1944 as he clutches his M-1 rifle with frostbitten fingers. He stands with frozen feet knee-deep in the snow, weak from lack of food, fatally wounded by constant enemy artillery and heartbroken from the eternity away from his loved ones.

He is sickened by the death and carnage of war.

He looks at us through lifeless eyes, inflamed with anger and disgust.

He tells us through clenched teeth: "I died for your birthright bestowed by your forefathers in the Constitution and now you allow school boards to graduate your children too illiterate to comprehend its meaning.

"I fought in the freezing hell of the Ardennes for your freedom to vote and you stay home because the line is too long or the weather is bad.

"I left my family alone and heart-broken to guarantee your freedom of speech and you remain silent on controversial issues because you're afraid to offend.

"I orphaned my children to ensure you a government of the people, by the people, and for the people and now you have allowed it to steal your democracy from you.

"It is I, the soldier, not the president who tolerates your freedom to choose your soul-mate.

"It is I, the soldier, not your Congressman, who grants you freedom of expression.

"It is I, the soldier, not the Attorney General who demands that your protection granted by the Bill of Rights be honored.

"It is I, the soldier, not the priest or rabbi who provides your right to worship whomever, however you wish.

"It is I, the soldier, not the political activist, who allows you the right to demonstrate.

"And it is I, the soldier, who follows the flag, who fights for the flag and whose dead body is embraced by the flag, who permits the protester to burn the beloved flag.

"And it is, for damn sure, just about time you did something about it!"

OH, MY ACHING HEAD

Mike Klemick
7th Armored Division, 87th Reconnaissance SP

I just can't help but tell my story of my experience with the dentist in the field shortly after the Bulge. I had a toothache that was second to none. The only remedy was to see a dentist. This I dreaded, because some of the stories I heard about our field dental equipment.

I believe we were still in Belgium but I don't remember exactly where in Belgium. I was driven by a medic in a jeep to a field hospital. This place was kind of a holding pen, a temporary aid station that was recently set up to treat frost bite and trench foot.

Every time the medic looked at me he did so with a kind of "army style" grin. This guy knew something that I didn't...why the sneaky grin? I did realize why a short while later.

After reaching the hospital tent, we were greeted by a little, skinny nurse. She was blond and beautiful. She also gave me that "Boy, are you in for it" look. I knew I was dirty, but so was everyone else there.

The nurse escorted me to a corner of the tent where the dentist had his crude equipment set up. She pointed me to a folding chair and told me to sit down. Now I was really scared. Sitting in the dentist chair was a staff sergeant. He was cleanly shaven but otherwise dirty. Oh! How well I remember this day. He was soaked with sweat, and his face was the color gray. The guy was in great pain and my toothache was no longer. I was ready to leave. I knew now why all the grinning.

Behind the dentist chair was a corporal sitting on a stool-like chair peddling what looked like the bottom part of a Singer sewing machine. The type like my mom had. The dentist was a captain, short and stocky and his white coat hung down to his ankles. The doc kept repeating "faster, corporal."

The sergeant was done, now it was my turn. I remember the sergeant looking at me and just shaking his head. The nurse helped me to the dentist chair. Kind of a bucket seat with a head rest, a metal one at that, covered with a towel. This is what I remember anyway.

Next step the nurse placed a towel across my chest and shoulders. She asked when I had my last bath. I believe my answer was "It's been a while." It had been a while, believe me. That much I truly remember.

"Open wide, soldier," were the next words I heard. This I remember quite well. The probing began, after which the needle, that really hurt. Now the ever-present sweating began. It was only a few minutes when the side of my face became numb. I had one cavity. Was I ever glad. His next words were, "Full speed ahead, corporal." That I'll never forget. I don't recall the corporal ever speaking a single word.

To my surprise I didn't feel anything. The nurse held a small rubberlike suction tube and used it to drain my mouth from time to time. She asked me how I felt. I mumbled, "How much longer?" At least that's what I think in my mind today.

While I tried hard to relax, the Doc and his nurse began mixing a batch of filling. This I remember quite clearly as the color of this was gray, not white. Regardless of the color, that stuff lasted over a year until I saw my dentist back home.

When I told my dentist back home as to the type equipment used by the military in the field, he couldn't believe it and said that's what they used during the First World War. Nevertheless it was quite an experience. Just another I'll never forget.

The contraption the corporal was peddling supplied the power needed to a gear box that turned the cable through a flexible kind of tube to the drill the dentist held. All this was done by belts. One thing I remember is that there wasn't any sound like a drill in today's modern equipment.

Would like to mention that I received a letter from my friend Charles Whiting recently, telling me that there's not much left to see of the Bulge battle any more as they are now filling in the foxholes. Get your stories in, fellows, as we're fading at the fast rate of about a thousand each day. Not much time left.

A GOOD START PROVIDED

Ben Klimkowsky
9th Armored Division, 89th Cavalry Reconnaissance Squadron, Troop "C"

It has been written many times that the 9th was called the "Ghost Division" by the Germans because our units had been encountered at all points in the combat of the Bulge. As a result of the splitting of the Division into many areas we were a small task force with three Armored vehicles assigned to attack the town of Neufchateau from the high ground above the town.

The attack started and we could see the German vehicles moving around and then the attack was called off. In the process an armored scout car bogged down and Vernon Fehr, the driver, refused to leave and remained attempting to free the vehicle. He was wounded by shrapnel and later recovered by the 11th Armored Division.

In the meantime, we withdrew with heavy woods to our left into which Sgt. Fred Chartier fired with the ring mounted 50 cal. machine gun. Once reaching the high ground overlooking the town, we stopped, took positions and observed the 8 shells hitting in the field. Shrapnel hit the back of the armored car where I was heating my feet by the exhaust pipe. It just missed hitting me chest high by about 6 inches and I still have that piece of shrapnel.

Shortly afterwards we saw an armored column coming up the road and when it stopped by us it was the 11th Armored coming into the combat zone for the first time. Their tanks had the canvas covers on their guns and no ammunition loaded. Sgt. Fred Chartier spoke to the Major and told him the situation. We then helped position their equipment. Fred Carter was to be commended by the Major and he later received a battlefield commission. I'm not sure that it was the result of this action although I think it was.

When the 11th Armored jumped off to attack Neufchateau, we later understood that they did real good and we felt that the few of us helped to get them off to a good start.

VIEW OF THE BULGE BY AN AIR OBSERVER

Jack H. Kruse
770th Field Artillery Battalion (SEP), Headquarters & Headquarters Battery

Following the end of the month-long campaign at Brest, France, our battalion, as a VII Corps support unit, motor-marched across France to Belgium. We took up positions south of St. Vith in the vicinity of Oudler, Belgium, with headquarters in the village. This was just west of the Our River. I was billeted with a local farm family, who by the way I visited about 10 years later while being on Occupation Duty in Germany.

Weeks of flying as an air observer in an L-4 aircraft through October, November, and early December yielded a limited number of fire missions. A very quiet sector patrolling our Our River and Schnee Eifel range sector from Echternach in the south to St. Vith in the North across the 2nd and 28th Division fronts. Around 12 December, about the time the 106th Division was replacing the 28th Division, we happened to fly too close to the West bank of the Our and took several rounds in our aircraft. (Several of which came within inches of bore-sighting me in the rear seat.) Fortunately, we made it back to our airstrip intact. About two days later, while taking off on a mission, our aircraft stalled out and we crashed in an open airfield in about 3 to 4 feet of snow. The pilot, Lt. Davis, was severely injured and eventually evacuated back to the States to end his part in the war. My injuries were minor rib and cartilage bruises. Capt. Wolfe, our battalion surgeon, taped me up and grounded me for several days.

We were awakened on the morning of 16 December by intense shelling from across the Our River. Oudler Village was in defoliate so the rounds were landing beyond us in our service battery area. Colonel Burnett, our battalion CO, sent me, taped as I was, to the air strip, where we began flying missions to attempt to assess the situation and fire some missions where possible. We had to fly low level due to bad weather, but were able to spot long columns of German units on our side of the Our River. Then we got one of those once-in-a-lifetime breaks. SPs, troop carriers and flak wagons were passing by a checkpoint where our battalion had registered previously. So many of our ground forces were shifting positions that it was difficult to get a fire mission set up. Finally, a response from fire direction center set up a mission of approximately a battalion of 3 rounds along the target area. Much fire, smoke and explosions indicated that the mission caused a lot of damage to the German column. However, smoke screens then obscured the column and flak wagons began intensive fire in our direction thereby driving us away from the area. There was nothing left to do except return to the airstrip for refueling and new orders.

Since the FA units, along with many others, were withdrawing westward and out of position, the FA Group to which our battalion was attached directed all aircraft to assemble in a rear area. The air sections vehicles and personnel joined them there. The plan was to have the aircraft leap-frog to fields in a south-westerly direction. The air sections were to follow as well as possible. I was directed to form a column of the group, battalions, and 106th Division air sections and link up with our aircraft "somewhere" along the way. Considering the fact that we had no communication connection with the air units or any other ground units, we moved on, guessing the best way to avoid the German advance.

The first night we stopped in Marche to regroup, determine our route northwest and rest. However, our rest was short lived when an engineer unit roused out all units to cross the nearby river before the bridge was blown. A long motor march ended sometime later with our arrival in Namur, Belgium. There we found billets and parking for the column and replenishment of our depleted stock of C-rations.

Through contact with an MP battalion in Namur, we learned that our aircraft were located in Sedan, France. We started a night motor march south, but within a few miles were strafed by a German night-fighter, fortunately with no casualties. Returning to Namur, we waited until daylight and again started toward Sedan, a march of several days. Finally, without further incidents, we made it to Sedan on Christmas Day and rejoined our respective command units. Next began our battalion move north and west pushing the German armies back into Germany. We fired some missions, and at one point, observed U.S. troop units moving toward relief of Bastogne. Further on during an observation flight in the vicinity of Prum, I spotted several SP guns and a rank on a ridge. They appeared to be setting up firing positions. (Now comes the "second" of those once-in-a-lifetime breaks.) Just below, on a crossroads near the German armor, was a checkpoint used by our battalion to register the guns. I set up a fire mission and was given a battalion 2 or 3 rounds. The result for the Germans was disastrous! When the smoke cleared all SPs and the tank were destroyed and mostly on fire! An artillery man's dream come true!

We continued on westward in support of different units, but finally, due to a shortage of 4.5 ammo, we were removed from combat and carried out a new mission of "peaceful capturing" of by-passed towns, posting the "Eisenhower Bans" (removal of all guns, cameras, personal weapons, establishing curfews, etc.) later to be followed in by civil affairs units. We did liberate a small concentration camp and was the first U.S. unit into Stalag VII A at Moosburg, Germany. At the war's end, we were guarding SS prisoners in the Dachau Concentration Camp! My contribution to the Battle of the Bulge was 138 combat firing missions.

Note: The 770th Field Artillery Battalion (SEP) was one of several activated and equipped with 4.5 inch guns, tractor drawn, with separate loading ammo. Extreme range of these guns were around 24,000 yards, which made them ideal for long-range interdiction missions. These units were almost identical with 155 Howitzer battalions except for different gun tubes, ammo, and utilization.

MY MEMORIES OF THE BATTLE OF THE BULGE

William E. Leopold
75th Infantry Division, 291st Infantry Regiment, Company C

I joined the Army from the small town of Mauch Chunk, PA. I went to Camp Breckenridge, KY and joined the 75th Division and then went overseas with the Division on October 15, 1944. I was a PFC in the 291st Inf. Regt., Co. C, 1st Bn. I was a Rifleman and 1st Scout in the squad.

My memories of the Battle of the Ardennes are about the same as any other man who served there. The awful cold, deep snows, being wet and hungry most of the time. I remember the brightness of the moon, the reflections on the snow, the marching fire going through the thick forest, taking one village after another, the heavy artillery and the mortar fire.

On January 22, the 1st Bn., 291st Inf. Regt. launched an offensive against the village of Maldingen about noon and we ran into heavy artillery, mortar and tank fire as we went up the hill and crossed open fields. The town was located on a small hill. It was about 5 p.m. and it started to get dark. We finally got into town and took one house after another as well as some prisoners out of the church; then things quieted down for a while. We started to clean out the rest of the village. I went around the corner and stayed close to the side of the house, when someone yelled, "There's a tank in between the houses."

I was twenty feet from the tank when I saw about six inches of the gun barrel. We told a bazooka man to work his way behind the tank and knock it out. We moved out again and advanced about ten feet when they opened fire on us with rifle fire and automatic weapons. Six of us were hit; some of us badly. I lay there and saw tracers going in all directions. I started to burn and someone threw snow on me to put out the fire!

They pulled us into a barn and the medic feverishly worked on us. We lay there all night.

The next day we were tied on a jeep and taken by ambulance from one hospital to another. When they took off my boots, my toes were black with gangrene and I had a bad case of trench foot with machine gun wounds in the stomach, hip and leg. I was seriously wounded and went to Paris, to England, and then back to the United States where I was hospitalized for a year.

I was in the New York Harbor on May 5th—V-E Day.

This is one of many experiences during the awful days in the Ardennes.

SUDDENLY, I WAS NO SPECTATOR

Harold Lindstrom
75th Infantry Division, 289th Infantry Regiment, Company F

About 10:00 p.m., Christmas Eve, we were marching across a long gentle, treeless hill in front of Grand-Manil. I will call it a slope. I was the 60 mm mortar assistant gunner in the 4th Platoon. I think it was the entire F Company marching single file on a narrow road. We knew we were getting close to combat as during the day we had met jeeps with wounded and had passed an area where another 289th Company had met a column of German tanks. By the looks of things many must have been killed or wounded. There were jeeps on the road that had been crushed to a flat metal scrap pile from being run over by the tanks, there were burning trucks in a clump of trees alongside the road, and much equipment laying around such as helmets, rifles, canteens, and what not.

Until now we had not been fired upon—I didn't think we would be this time. The night was beautiful. A bright moon glistened off the white clean snow. I was very tired so just kind of shuffled along behind the guy ahead of me. Surprisingly, I wasn't frightened by what I saw. There were many burning buildings in the small Village of Grand-Manil about 1/2 mile ahead and down the slope. What's more, there was fighting going on down there! I heard the rapid fire of German machine guns in the village. Their tracer streaks went out toward an area on our side of the village but further down the slope. Slower firing American machine guns were firing back. Their tracer streaks went into the village. The whole thing fascinated me. I seemed to be a ringside spectator. I learned later the Americans were K Company, 289th, who had taken the village and then were driven out by a German counter attack.

Suddenly, my unrealistic thinking that I was a spectator was shattered. A machine gun on a German tank fired at us! I heard the sharp crack of the gun being fired directly at me and saw tracers streak across the road just ahead of me. Instantly, I awoke from my dull dream world and looked for cover. There was no ditch or protection by the road. I spotted a slight terrace-like surface to my right and up the slope slightly ahead of me. There was a fence next to the road but I went through it as though it didn't exist. I hit the ground on top of the terrace just as the Germans fired again. They swept the area from right to left with a long burst. They seemed to know approximately where we were but I do not think could make out individuals. I was very much afraid. I had never been so frightened before or have never been since. I was sure they could see me dressed in dark clothes lying on the gleaming white snow. The German bullets plowed into the ground ahead of me, spattering pieces of frozen dirt on me. Some were very close. I found a bullet hole in my shovel carrier flap the next day! One of the burst hit the 60 mm mortar baseplate in front of Ralph Logan's head (the mortar gunner). When they hit the baseplate the bullets made a ringing sound, made orange and red sparks, whistled and made tracer streaks as they flew over him. Someone squirmed and moaned to my left indicating he had been hit. I froze in fright and didn't move a muscle. I decided to move though. I was laying on top of my ammunition pack which positioned me above ground surface. If I had my say I would be lying under the ground! We laid there some time. I began feeling cold as the snow under me began to melt and come through.

Finally, our platoon sergeant, Laverne Ives, said, "Men, we can't lie here all night and wait to get hit. Immediately after a burst sweeps by you, start crawling up the slope toward that clump of trees." Boy! That was comforting to receive some directions. Up to now, I just laid there not knowing what to do. I waited for that next machine gun sweep. They hadn't fired for a while. I heard the tank engine start, run a little and then stop. Someone yelled something in German and laughed.

I don't understand German. I hoped they wouldn't decide to drive up the slope and crush us. I decided to start crawling up the slope. I was afraid to make a broad side target as I turned around to crawl up so crawled backward. It was pretty difficult. My belt and equipment would catch on the ground under me. My coat wanted to slide over my head. When far enough up the slope I turned around and crawled faster head first. Farther up the slope I got up and ran the rest of the way. When near the trees I was stopped by one of us. He asked for the password. I was so frightened I couldn't remember it at first but finally did about when I heard him cock his rifle.

He told me the guys were in the woods. I was surprised to see so many. I thought I was the only one out. Only two men in our platoon had been hit. Many of us were to be hit later.

I think of that night during every Christmas Eve since.

DETOUR

Leonard Loiacono
5th Infantry Division, 50th Field Artillery Battalion, A Battery

After a long delay in Metz, we moved toward Germany which included the Saar River, Karlsbrunn, Saarlantem and the Siegfried Line. We were about to try to cross the Saar River when the Germans started their offensive in Luxembourg and Belgium.

The division was making good progress through the Siegfried Line on the 21st of December when told to move north to Luxembourg. We moved 100 miles in 22 hours through rain and snow. In Luxembourg the column had stopped briefly when a civilian came up to us. He was excited when he saw the red diamond. He told us he fought with the 5th Division in World War One. He married a local girl and never went back to the United States.

On Christmas Day we were on line and firing. It was overcast but off to the horizon the clouds opened up and the sun shone. American planes were bombing and strafing. We were on high ground and could see all of this. It was still overcast in our area but we just kept firing the Howitzers as fast as we could load them. Also in this position, we saw a buzz bomb launched in the German sector. We fought until January 25, 1945 to close off the Germans retreating the Battle of the Bulge. We then headed east to Germany.

16 DECEMBER 1944

Samuel Lombardo

99th Infantry Division, 394th Infantry Regiment, 3rd Battalion, Company I

This is just an example of how little information we had on the 16th of December about the strength and disposition of the German army. It was normal for a division to have one regiment in reserve. Our high command thought that the German army was almost through; then we would declare victory by Christmas of that year.

Instead of a regiment our 99th Division assigned just one company and that was my Company I of the 394th Regiment. I was a first lieutenant and platoon leader of the second platoon with additional duties of executive officer. At about 1000 hours on the morning of the 16th of December we received a call from headquarters that the headquarters of the 393rd Regiment had lost communications with Lt. Colonel Allen the CO of 3rd Battalion.

We were assigned the mission to go to the front from Elsenborn and re-establish contact with Colonel Allen. Since I specialized in map reading, my CO, Captain J. J. Morris directed me to lead our company I to Colonel Allen's position and to stop on the way at the 393rd headquarters and receive our final orders. After walking 4 or 5 kilometers we stopped at the 393rd head-quarters, which was in an old house along the roadside.

Captain Maurice sent me in to receive our orders while he remained with the company along the roadside. I entered and saluted, identified myself and listened to my orders. I still remember like it was yesterday. The S3 informed me that they had lost contact with Colonel Allen. They thought that a patrol in force maybe 50 or 60 German soldiers had come through and cut the telephone lines. Our mission was to contact Colonel Allen and have the telephone lines repaired. I saluted and began leaving and before I reached the door, he called me back and told me that I should have a secondary order that was to restore the MLR.

At that moment it didn't seem like something monumental. Little did they know that there were two Panzer divisions and one Volksgren.

REMEMBERING ANOTHER ENEMY: COLD WEATHER

Reuel Long
90th Infantry Division, 357th Infantry Regiment, 2nd Battalion, Co E

Although the information we had received about the Battle of the Bulge from articles in the *Stars and Stripes* was old and sketchy nevertheless the situation must have required help from our division, as we headed north in trucks on January 6, 1945. We were always kept in the dark by our company command-ers as to where we were headed next, except the immediate objective of a hill, town or stream as we departed Monneren, Alsace-Lorraine, France.

We kept track of any major towns or cities that we passed through, however, and when we reached the City of Luxembourg, we knew we were nearing the fighting and reasoned why we had been pulled back from our foothold across the Saar River in December. This must be something big, and as we continued north after spending all night in the truck sitting up in what was below-zero weather, we started to see our ambulances coming back from the front. I recalled seeing a road sign point directions to the Town of Wiltz and of St. Vith, which I later learned had been flattened by a battle in which the 7th Armored Division had heroically held up the German advance for a time to enable American defensive positions to form farther back in Belgium, back in December.

Our division was evidently going to strike the enemy on the left flank of their salient into the American positions. I remember our trucks moving up the road with a steady stream of ambulances moving down the other side as we could now hear the noise of battle near the front. It was here that General Patton later wrote that during that afternoon he drove through the 90th who stood up and cheered as he passed. These men did this in spite of spending a great many hours in trucks at 6 degrees below zero and in spite of all the wounded coming down the other side of the road.

I didn't see the general, but feel certain this is the place he wrote about, figuring he passed through the 90th ahead or behind our particular truck. We stayed the night in a farm house that had just been liberated by other American forces that we would soon be relieving. The warm accommodations were welcome after two bitter cold days in the truck.

The father of this family in Luxembourg brought out an all-wave table model radio that he had kept hidden from the Germans, and our squad gathered around it to listen to BBC and other broadcasts, including Nazi propaganda broadcasts in English. Somehow I ended up sleeping on the living room rug instead of in the hall, which was a big treat. Actually, we grew to become thankful for just little things, like a clean drink of water, or warm water to shave in.

The next day we had a festive celebration dinner of chicken (procured by our squads' backyard "recon" crew) and dumplings. The farmer, his wife and 15 year-old-daughter ate with us. He spoke little English, but we enjoyed sharing his jubilation of liberation. It was a fine dinner all around and made us feel very satisfied. We stayed again through the night and moved out the next morning. I had gotten rid of the bazooka, but found a different responsibility with my new mobility, that of taking turns being the "point" man for the squad. When in the lead, you had to be very alert for any movement or sounds up ahead, but with the ground now completely covered with a white blanket of snow, it was easier to detect the enemy. We still just had our leather boots and our feet were cold all of the time. Foxholes were harder to dig, and even though strapped to our sides, the water in our canteens would always be frozen by morning. We were getting three square "K" ration meals per day though and used the cartons to make a fire to melt our water.

After digging our two man foxhole at night, and spreading down our raincoats on the ground, each having one blanket, we placed one doubled under us and one doubled over us for what warmth we could get for one hour of sleep. At daybreak, a normal day would include, since we were already dressed, of thawing our water and eating our "K" ration breakfast. Our latrine was a slit-trench, and we had soap and ice-cold water for our hands. We now had wool gloves with leather palms, and stocking-cap style helmet liners which would pull over our ears.

Following breakfast our squad leaders would receive instructions about our objectives for our platoon leader, a 2nd lieutenant. We made certain our little cardboard fires were out and then folded up our blankets in our little combat packs, attached our shovels to our belts, shoulder-strapped our rifles and got ready to move out. If there was no enemy fire, leaning up against a tree lent support to the various paraphernalia that you had to carry. The M-1 weighed 9 pounds, extra ammunition, two grenades, canteen, pack, shovel, bayonet and helmet must have weighed at least 20 pounds, making it almost easier to walk and get all those things on a synchronous motion than to try to stand still in one place.

Then we reminded whoever's turn it was to be point or scout, and upon command we moved out, almost always in single file with about 15 feet between squad members, as an average distance, which varied according to terrain, enemy location, etc. Advancing through woods, up a road or through an open field was always a cautious affair, looking to see what might be in the next group of trees, over a small rise or behind a hedgerow, particularly troublesome because they were usually built partially of stone, with a thick hedge on top to obscure your vision. The Germans were to use the hedgerows to good advantage as we were soon to learn in the Battle of the Bulge. Advancing up a hill was also a grueling ordeal, moving cautiously or quickly as the conditions dictate.

The mental stress was more tiring than the physical strain though (I thought). And even though you didn't find enemy for hours or sometimes a full day, several "breaks" a day besides lunch were necessary and welcome, unless of course, the enemy was encountered or an incoming shelling attack was experienced. All the "break" had to be was a drink of water, an extra "K" ration dog biscuit, a cigarette for some, where possible, or a stick of gum to provide a few minutes away from the concentration of advancing.

Often times there was a few extra minutes for lunch, other times on the move it was eaten later in the afternoon, sometimes on the move, and other times, of necessity, skipped entirely. The Battle of the Bulge was fought largely in overcast weather and there was about an average of 8" loose snow on the ground, depending on the area, and the temperature probably averaged about 20 degrees overall, although usually not windy.

When dusk arrived, we would try to stake our foxholes in a defensive perimeter to the front in case of counterattack, unless we planned a night attack. There were times when we would have our foxhole well started, or even completed, when we would be ordered to change our positions to be on the line with other units. Sometimes this change came after dark, making another hole more difficult to dig, as you couldn't see the rocks, or even worse obstruction, roots, while digging. We usually ate our supper ration as a reward after the hole was completed. We felt more protected then, and one of us could relax at a time to partake of food.

There wasn't much of a ritual to get ready for bed—no clothes to change, no shaving or even taking off the helmet. I usually tried to brush my teeth and then tucked the breakfast "K" ration under my armpit before retiring for an hour, to keep it thawed for breakfast. Our feet were becoming almost as big a concern now as the enemy and during this period of time we started losing men we couldn't afford to spare to frostbite, trench feet, and frozen feet.

We weren't getting our usual dry change of socks every few days, and it didn't help to bare your wet foot in below-freezing weather. So most of us tried to keep wiggling our toes while on night guard duty, or during periods that we weren't marching during the day. But we all soon became run down and tired due to the strain of combat and being outside in the cold for an extended period so that many just gave up the additional effort to take care of their feet.

This, then, comprised what was a representative day of the foot soldier during the Battle of the Bulge except for the various experiences in combat, which we were very soon to encounter.

CLERVAUX, LUXENBOURG

Frank A. LoVuolo
28th Infantry Division, 107th Field Artillery Battalion, B Battery

In the immense forested area of eastern Belgium and Luxembourg, known as the Ardennes, the Village of Clervaux, Luxembourg served as a rest camp for soldiers of the 28th Division who were rotated there for three-day stays. There they enjoyed the luxury of hot showers, comfortable beds, good chow, clean clothing, recreation and entertainment. For me it was a respite from regular duty with Battery "B" located in Diekirch, Lux. I believe I arrived at Clervaux on Dec. 15, 1944, accompanied by a Sgt. Truman Foster. We were billeted in a huge villa that I learned 45 years later to be the Villa Priim on the Rue Brooch just off the main road leading to Wiltz, Lux.

On Dec. 16, I was on guard duty at the end of the villa driveway when at 5:30 a.m. the German attack began. The artillery barrage and exploding shells became so intense that I could hear shell fragments strike the pavement and nearby buildings. I was forced to race for the protection of the villa but as I did, tracer bullets buzzed my head and I scrambled into a ditch along the drive. Whether the machine gun fire was meant for me or the villa itself, I didn't stop to ask.

Crawling, running, crawling, I finally reached the villa front door. After entering, the door was quickly slammed shut behind me. No one knew at that time what all the German activity really meant. We were completely out of communication with everyone, and as the German artillery concentration on Clervaux and on the vicinity of the villa increased, the entire complement of personnel sought refuge in the villa cellar. Here we stayed until late morning of the same day. At that point in time we heard the clanging and creaking sound of armor coming down the Wiltz road and through the worst. We learned that the armor was American when an officer from the lead tank entered the villa. He told us that there were fragmented reports that the Germans had mounted a major offensive and that they had broken through our lines in several places. He advised us to get out of Clervaux as quickly and as best we could and to avoid encirclement. Those were the last semblance of orders I was to receive until I rejoined my unit. Without hesitation and without packing any of our belongings, everyone filed out the villa by way of a side door and onto a side hill behind the villa with the Wiltz road above and to the left, and the Clerve River below and to the right. The monastery on the heights to the right served as a guide and gave us some sense of direction.

Sgt. Foster and I had left the villa armed only with 30 caliber carbines (peashooters), and each with one clip of ammunition. In a fire-fight the ammo would have lasted less than a minute. I felt just a little more secure; I had the added luxury of a trench knife which I promptly lost in the brush as we made our way along the side hill. We came under severe artillery fire and it was then that Sgt. Foster and I became separated. I never saw him again, and I never knew his fate until September 14, 1989, when I found his name listed among the G.I. dead. He sleeps with his comrades at the Henri Chappelle American Military Cemetery in Belgium.

History tells us that the only Americans remaining in Clervaux at that time were the dead and the captured. For them the war was over. Those of us who successfully made our way out of Clervaux eventually became part of an ever-growing stream of Americans moving west. There was mass confusion and I was a part of it. I decided that as long as I was on my own and under no direct orders, I would strive for three objectives: #1 stay alive, #2 avoid capture, and #3 find my artillery unit (in that order). I was to succeed in all three.

To the best of my recollection and after what seemed like an eternity of foraging for food, sleeping in barns, sprinting across open fields, and hiding in deep woods, my odyssey finally came to an end when I made contact with my outfit around Christmas time, 1944. My artillery battery was in position and in action near the Belgian village of Neufchateau. Once again I was a part of something; it was good to be home. The fighting continued, and if the good Lord's grand scheme had dictated that I not survive it, then at least I would have died among people I knew, and with people who knew me.

REMEMBER OUR FALLEN COMRADES EVERY DAY

John F. Magill
17th Airborne Division, 466th Parachute Field Artillery
Battalion, Headquarters

The initial psychological adjustment to front-line combat duty was a ponderous thing. Such an adjustment demanded more than mere training and "esprit de corps." It drew on every bit of reserve and stability that a man possessed. The first twenty-four hours were the critical ones.

First came the unique stench of war. I couldn't describe it, except that it included the smell of burned-out buildings and bodies. Then came the sight of dead horses and cattle, grotesque in their rigid state; next came the sprawled, inert forms of the German dead—still somehow somewhat impersonal. Finally, moving ever closer to the shell fire, I encountered the first American dead. The impact of the olive-drab garbed soldiers struck home. I couldn't seem to avoid the open, unseeing eyes of the young American boys who had not been picked up by the burial detail yet. This was not death as I had remembered it where the dead were respected. This was the raw, devastating by-product of war, with no reverence and no respect.

1 lost my radio operator and an F.O. officer (within the first twenty-four

hours) to the psychological trauma and their inability to cope. What troubled me more than a little was the realization that both of these men seemed to be towers of strength while in training.

For me, it wasn't the coveted wings or shining boots that served as a mainstay; it seemed more a combination of things, some conscious and some subconscious. The conscious aspect told me the horrible task ahead was necessary; it told me the world, Marge, Dad, and Mom were not safe with Nazi ideology; it told me that exhibited fear is contagious, that I owed it to my buddies not to show this gnawing feeling in the pit of my stomach. The subconscious aspect seemed to be a supporting, bolstering thing. For want of a better way to describe it, I sensed it as things like believe and faith.

As we honor our fallen comrades, let us highly resolve that we will always love and serve our country but that we will always seek alternatives (all alternatives) before we send our bravest and our finest into deadly, insane combat. Going to war must become our last resort. Keeping the peace must be a mission of the world not a single nation. Honor the hundreds that have paid it all in Iraq and Afghanistan and the thousands who have been maimed in mind and body by resolving on this day that we will seek peace always, keeping war as a last resort.

The above excerpt is from my late daughter's book, A Soldier's Psalm. The haunting statement below was issued by Otto von Bismarck in 1970.

"Anyone who has looked into the glazed eyes of a soldier dying on the battlefield will think hard before starting a war."

FALL DAY IN PARIS, 1945

John P. Malloy
75th Infantry Division, 291st Headquarters Company

I waited on the Gare de l'Est Station platform. The train to Reims would leave momentarily. I stayed at the far end, worried about M.P.'s. I had been AWOL, absent without leave, for two weeks. As soon as I boarded that train I would be safe. There was constant confusion due to troop redeployment. I would just slip back into the crowd at Camp Boston; no one would know I had been gone. The war had ended in August.

Thank God, Harry Truman had them drop the atomic bomb. That was one of the greatest things that had ever happened to men in the U.S. military. Like most infantrymen I had expected to die on the beaches of Japan. Millions of Americans were headed home. The redeployment camps shifted into high gear, shipping everyone back to the States. Tens of thousands arrived and departed these camps weekly. This huge shuffle of men and units made for massive confusion and clerical errors.

My combat unit, my wartime family, had been deactivated months earlier. We were transferred from one paper unit to another as the army was contracted. We had no duties. You sat in a tent among hundreds of other tents. Some days the weather was clear. More often, as the fall progressed, it was dreary, overcast and depressing. You could sleep all day. You could read, play cards; go to the PX—whatever you chose to do. It was a boring, uneventful life. Due to the constant shuffle of men from one unit to another you knew no one, you had no friends. It could drive you crazy. You waited in limbo. You were in a time warp.

Rather than going stir crazy in camp I had spent recent weeks partaking the joys of Paris. Three-day passes were plentiful. After a while though going back and forth became a nuisance. Why not just stay in Paris? I had nothing else to do but sit in a tent and wait. But how to do it? The answer: liberate a blank pad of passes and write my own liberty passes. Everything was so screwed up, who would ever know?

As a result I had a wonderful time in recent weeks. Paris sun-lit cafes were full. The company was great, the French girls exciting and accommodating. There was lots of wine and cognac. Money was available through the black market. As the song goes: "Summer time, life is easy and the days are long." What more could a twenty-two-year-old want? Don't worry about tomorrow. Live for today.

Now I had to get back to camp. I knew I was stretching my luck. Once there I would be okay. My immediate danger was Military Police on the lookout for AWOLs. The train's engine whistled. It was time to go. I hurried to board. Two M.P.s appeared—I hadn't spotted them. "Soldier, let's see your papers". I gave them the pass I had forged a couple of days earlier.

"This says you were due back in Camp Boston at noon today. It's two PM now. You're kind of late aren't you Malloy?" "I'm on my way on that train. I'll be in camp by four. There won't be a problem." The other MP said to his partner, "He's absent without leave by his own admission." The first MP, "I think you better come along with us. We're going to check you out."

I got in their jeep. We traveled a couple of miles and arrived in front of an old, forbidding looking, fortress-like, building. It must have been two hundred years old. We went inside. They stood me in front of a tall desk. An older bespectacled GI looked down at me. "What have you got him for?" "AWOL by his own admission." "Book him." "OK Sarge." They took me to another area. "Empty your pockets of everything you got on you." They searched me. They took my billfold, my watch, my barracks bag and some other things. They sealed them in a package. I signed it. "Take off your shoe-strings." "Why?" "Shut your mouth and do as you are told."

They walked me down a long, dark passageway, the high walls cold and dank. A cell door was opened. They shoved me in. The gate to freedom clanged shut behind me. I entered my cage. There were nine other prisoners. I spotted the spare bunk and climbed into it. What happens now? Here I am-how do I keep it together? All I had were the clothes on my back and the small bag the MPs had confiscated. A Pfc. in the infantry didn't have much or need much. Uncle Sam took care of him.

The cell was a bleak, barren space. There were eight double bunks. The ceiling was high, the single window barred. There was a sink and toilet stool in the corner-no walls or door. You had to do your job in full view. Three light bulbs, hung from the ceiling, provided light.

We were in a holding tank. The Military Police gathered those violating military law and held them here until transferred back to their unit. Their company commander would confer punishment-from minor detention, to a major court martial with prison time. It was clear the key to getting out of this place was to make your unit aware you were held here. Most men would leave in less than a week.

My problem was I had three new company commanders who had come and gone. No one in command at Camp Boston knew me. The turnover among all personnel was constant. No one knew anyone. When men arrived, some shipped out immediately; all had to wait until their number came up. My hope now was that someone at Camp Boston would know me and get me transferred back there. I didn't know who that person might be. Nothing happened for two days. On the third day a guard shouted through the door. "Malloy, front and center." A guard walked me to an office. A GI clerk sat at his desk. "Sit down. I want you to tell me what outfit you really belong to. We couldn't find you in Camp Boston. And don't lie to me. It will only make it worse."

I explained I had been transferred in name only to different outfits. That was normal procedure. Soldiers with too few points for discharge were transferred on paper to a new unit. I had given up trying to keep track of all that. I told him, "With all the confusion in Camp Boston the best bet would be to try to track me through my former combat outfit, the 291st Regiment." I could tell he thought I was lying. Back to my cell, this time for days. Three weeks crawled by and still no word. I felt a terrible isolation. Depression swallowed me. As time passed I fell into the black abyss of despair. Now I understood why they took my shoestrings, they wanted to prevent an attempt at suicide.

As the days passed, I went to the window and pushed my hand out as far as I could-at least part of me was outside this hellhole. Still no word. I lost track of time. I gave up hope. I would rather die than live like this. I heard a bird one day. Oh to be a bird. One day: "Malloy, front and center!" They took me back to the clerk. I signed for my personal effects. They gave me my bag. They told me nothing. "Get in the jeep." We drove east for two hours. The M.P.s ignored me. What now? There it was-Camp Boston-home. The M.P.s turned me over to the company clerk. He signed a receipt for his prisoner.

A Captain I had never seen appeared. He looked at me. "So you are Malloy, the guy who has been AWOL for more than a month. You and your buddies have cost me more trouble than you will ever know. I have had my ass chewed out because of the likes of you. I'm going to make an example of you. It will put the fear of God into anyone else who thinks like you." The Captain called out, "Sergeant Eisenberg come out here." My God, it was my old First Sergeant from the 291st. All at once I saw hope.

"This is one of that AWOL crowd. See this bum is put under guard. I'll deal with him when I return from Paris next week." "Yes Sir," Eisenberg said. Eisenberg didn't acknowledge me. I kept my mouth shut. A guard took me to my tent. I knew no one. I sat on my cot. It felt good. Now what? Several hours later a corporal appeared. "I'll take over," he told the guard. "Grab your gear, Malloy, all of it." He had a jeep. We drove for an hour.

We arrived at Camp Baltimore. We went to Company Headquarters and found the First Sergeant. "Sergeant I'm delivering this fellow from Camp Boston. Eisenberg said he had talked with you about him." "OK, I'll sign for him. Welcome to your new outfit, Malloy. Eisenberg and I are old buddies. He gave me a good report on you." The Corporal turned to leave. "Malloy keep your mouth shut. Eisenberg said to tell you good luck. He also told me to tell you to walk the straight and narrow from now on."

Army officers give commands but the Army is run by the noncoms. I was free and clear—Hallelujah! After all these years, I still have a special place in my heart for Eisenberg. I still can feel cold fear in my bones when I recall that desolate old French prison. I've walked the straight and narrow for more than sixty-five years. I learned recently Eisenberg, like so many of my comrades, had died. Time marches on.

WORLD WAR II STORY

Kenneth Mar
2nd Infantry Division, 23rd Infantry Regiment, Company C

I was drafted during my second year of high school at the age of 18 years old. My military experience began at Camp Roberts near San Luis Obispo, California for seventeen weeks of infantry training in 1944, just in time for the Normandy Invasion. After two weeks of preparation and training in

Southern England near Bath, I landed on Omaha Beach fourteen days after D-day and was put on a train to Brittany, France. This is where I joined the Second Infantry Division as a replacement combat soldier.

I experienced my first combat duty for the liberation of Brest, France. As soon as we finished clearing out the remaining enemy troops in Brittany and after the liberation of Paris, the Second Infantry Division was redeployed to the Siegfried line at the border of Belgium and Germany to await orders to invade Germany. I was taken ill and ended up in the hospital before a German counter-attack for the Battle of the Bulge. No sooner had I recuperated from approximately four days in a hospital in Belgium, I was hastily ordered back to my company to stem the tide of the German attack at the border.

After two days of trudging through the snow in freezing temperatures, we finally reached our objective with tank support by flushing the Germans out of the forest. I was dead tired and fell asleep in the captured German bunker oblivious of the enemy counter-attack in the morning. I was awakened by my buddy to join the other four soldiers to hold off a company the size of 100–200 attacking Germans. At that time, I realized we were out-numbered and deserted by our company with no alternative but to surrender as POWs (prisoners of war). I and three other fellow soldiers remained in the custody of the Germans as POWs for two months, until the end of the war, May of 1945. Our liberation occurred when our captors deserted us and we roamed free in the local town where we scavenged for food in empty homes.

LONG FORGOTTEN PHOTO SURFACES

Hal Mayforth
4th Armored Division, 25th Cavalry

During the winter of 1943 the 4th Armored Division was on maneuvers in the Mojave Desert in California. It was being prepared, the situation warranted, to join the fighting and North Africa.

During the first two weeks of May 1943 Columbia Pictures in the nearby

Salton Sea area was filming *Sahara*. The producers approached the Army brass and had received permission to use some of its men as extras. From the 14,500 men in the 4th, then a heavy division B Troop of the 25th Cavalry Reconnaissance Squadron, Mechanized was lucky enough to be selected for this role.

When it arrived on the set, it was issued authentic uniforms, helmets, Mauser rifles and miscellaneous other gear. It was to portray the Wehrmacht assaulting an adobe fort in which a downed American Flyer, a.k.a. Humphrey Bogart, was manning a machine gun. As the plot thickened he had moved down the entire attacking force.

The presence of B Troop provided Columbia Pictures with a low over-head production. Their major investment for their use of extras was reflected in the kegs of beer they provided at the end of every day's rushes.

The uniqueness of being attired in German uniforms prompted several to have their photographs taken as a memento. One such person was Sergeant Salvadore Scalzo from Beacon, New York. When his photo was developed he put it in his wallet where it was completely forgotten.

As this yarn continues, the date advances to late December 1944 and then the scene changes to the Saar Basin in western France. Patton had committed the 4th Armored Division to where the Battle of the Bulge was raging. Whereas B Troop usually rode point for Combat Command B, its role was now revised. Because the forced march to the vicinity of Bastogne covered 162 miles, the order was for slower moving tanks to lead, followed by vehicles based on their potential speed. This was designed to negate an accordion effect on the column.

The only map used for this march was reputed to be one of the Michelin vintage. That was in the possession of General Dager, the CO of Combat Command B. He and only a few others knew where we were going, even why. Dager was like a shepherd herding his flock of sheep. If he wasn't in radio communication with the lead tank commanders he was riding his jeep up and down the column talking with them personally.

As the miles rolled on, and then since ignorance prevailed, rumors were rampant. At one point during the first night order was given to remove the canvas covers of the headlights and to turn them on. This was an occurrence that had never happened before, even in stateside training. Because the Luftwaffe had long been absent, the gamble accelerated the column to its destination.

The unusual aspect of this extended march was that all vehicles survived the grueling marathon.

That is with the exception of an M-8 armored car belonging to B Troop of the 25th cavalry.

When that vehicle became disabled the maintenance half-track riding shotgun dropped off a mechanic to solve a problem. It probably was no more than points having closed up in the distributor but because there was a copious bar in town they milked it for all it was worth. A day later they decided it was time to move on but they didn't have the vaguest idea of their outfit's destination.

They came upon several command posts busily being disassembled for a move to greater safety. The commanders were uncertain of the disposition of their own men to say nothing about the 25th Cavalry. Later on when they were still trying to find their outfit a Lieutenant leapt out of a ditch to confront them. "You're here because I radioed for a tank. There's a German one in yonder woods. Go get 'em!" In reply Sergeant Scalzo, the armored corps commander, replied, "Sir, all I have on my turret is a 37 mm cannon. Its high explosive rounds would bounce off that Kraut tank like ping pong balls. I've never disobeyed a direct order in my life but if we were to go down there we'd never come back and my outfit would never know what happened to us." With that the Sergeant ordered his driver to make a change in direction and off they went on another tangent.

Suddenly, this lone armored car with four GI-clad individuals was apprehended by an MP roadblock. In the wake of Colonel Otto Skorzeny's ruse of infiltrating our lines with English-speaking Germans in captured American disguise, the MPs believe they had bagged a real coup. Their search began with everyone having to empty their wallets. Everything seemingly was running smoothly went out from Scalzo's wallet popped a photo of him resplendent in his German uniform; his long forgotten souvenir from the set of *Sahara*. Such an explanation when given was not acceptable. When Salvo insisted his hometown was Beacon, New York the MPs figured it was more like Stuttgart, Germany.

At last the MP questioning of Scalzo turned to baseball. They apparently reasoned no true German would be privy to the American national pastime. Bingo! This was his forte. To all their challenges he had the correct answers. This appeased the MPs and they were released after being informed where their loosest 25th Calvary was located.

Scalzo's photo was last seen totally shredded, littering the Belgian countryside.

TASK FORCE IZELL

Hal Mayforth
4th Armored Division, 25th Cavalry

At Verdon, France, the severity of the Battle of the Bulge was first discussed among top brass at SHAEF's headquarters. In regard to Bastogne, the energetic Gen. George Patton boasted, "I'll make a meeting engagement in three days, and I'll give you a six divisional attack in six days." This evoked laughter.

Said Ike, "It can't be done."

Patton retorted, "It can be, and I'll prove it." As it developed, his time table was not too far wrong.

Trapped in Bastogne were one Combat Command of both the 9th and 10th Armored Divisions, an Afro-American Artillery unit, and the 101st Airborne Infantry Division. The 101st had been held in reserve in France, and, rather than jumping, they had been trucked into Bastogne. They had been ill-equipped without adequate winter clothing, and limited in personal ammunition. At first, it was decided to withdraw these troops, but then that decision was nullified when it was realized that Bastogne was the hub of roads used by the Germans in their offensive.

The 4th Armored Division of Patton's 3rd Army began its forced march to the Bastogne area at midnight of Dec. 19th. Although few knew where we were going and why, we reached our destination 100 miles and 46 hours later. By that time, we had come under the command of Lt. Gen. Middleton of the VII Corps. He had ordered the CO of the newly arrived CCB, Gen. Daggart, to send a task force into Bastogne. Daggart immediately saw the fallacy of such an order, but in spite of his objection, he was outranked.

Capt. Bert P. Izell, Executive Officer of the 8th Tank Battalion, was selected to head the task force. With him was A company of the 8th Tank Battalion, "C" of the 10th Armored Infantry, and "C" Battery of the 22nd Armored Field Artillery Battalion. They arrived unscathed and unchallenged on their trek to Bastogne.

Shortly after arriving, Capt. Izell reported to Col. William Roberts, commander of the 10th Armored Division CCB. As ordered, he was to receive additional instructions from him. Meanwhile, there was an urgent radio message for Izell. When told he was with Roberts, it said, "Go get him immediately." The task force had been ordered back to rejoin their organizations. Gen. Hugh Gaffey, CO of the 4th Armored, having been belatedly informed of the task force, wanted them back at once so that the division might be solidified.

Again, the homeward trip avoided any direct enemy contact, but they were exposed to many strange phenomena. Along the way they detected tank tracks extending from the fields on either side of, and in the road. From the width of these, it clearly established they were German. Not too far distant, they found an American 6X6 off the road and into a ditch. The driver was still behind the wheel minus his head, which appeared severed by a high velocity shell.

Several miles later, they apprehended a road block, a congestion of field artillery pieces with some of their prime mover still running. There wasn't a soul to be found. Its personnel had either panicked and fled, or had been taken prisoners by the Germans. The task force retrieved much of these, and returned to their lines with more than when they started.

An aftermath of this episode, months later, when some 101st parachutists spotted the 4th Armored patch on our apparel, their admonishment would be, "So, you're one of those S.O.B.s who deserted us at Bastogne." This so dominated their thinking that they completely over-looked the fact they were eventually liberated by the wearers of that same patch.

THE WERETH 11 - REMEMBERING THE INVISIBLE SOLDIERS OF THE BATTLE OF THE BULGE

John E. McAuliffe
87th Infantry Division, 347th Infantry Regiment, M Company

Few realize that a decisive factor in the defense of Bastogne, during the Battle of the Bulge, rested in the artillery support of the surrounded town. One of the heavy (155mm) artillery units was the segregated 969th Field Artillery Battalion joined by a few howitzers and survivors of the segregated 333rd Field Artillery Battalion. For their actions the 969th FAB received the Presidential Unit Citation, the highest award a military unit can receive. In spite of this meritorious service, participation by black GIs in the Battle of the Bulge, or for that matter in WWII, is not well known or recognized.

Everyone knows of the Tuskegee Airmen and some know of the 761st Tank Battalion and the Red Ball Express. However, the majority of the black GIs in World War II, 260,000 in the European Theatre of Operations, were not forgotten to history—they were simply never acknowledged. They were the "invisible" soldiers of World War II. They include eleven young artillery-men of the 333rd Field Artillery Battalion who were murdered by the SS, after surrendering during the Battle of the Bulge.

The 333rd Field Artillery Battalion was a 155mm howitzer unit that had been in action since coming ashore at Utah Beach on June 29, 1944. Typical of most segregated units in World War II, it had white officers and black en-listed men. At the time of the Battle of the Bulge, the unit was located in the vicinity of St. Vith, Belgium. Specifically it was northeast of Schonberg and west of the Our River in support of the Army VII Corps and especially the 106th Infantry Division.

On December 16th, German artillery began shelling the Schonberg area.

With reports of rapid German infantry and armored progress, the 333rd FAB was ordered to displace further west but to leave C Battery and Service Battery in position to support the 14th Cavalry and the 106th Division. By the morning of December 17th, these two positions were rapidly overrun by the advancing German troops and armor. While many personnel tried to escape through Schonberg, eleven men of the Service Battery went overland in a northwest direction in the hopes of reaching American lines. At about 3:00 p.m., they approached the first house in the nine-house hamlet of Wereth, Belgium, owned by Mathius Langer.

The men were cold, hungry, and exhausted after walking cross-country through the deep snow. They had two rifles between them. The family welcomed them and gave them food. But this small part of Belgium did not necessarily welcome Americans as "Liberators." This area had been part of Germany before the First World War and many of its citizens still saw themselves as Germans and not Belgians. The people spoke German but had been forced to become Belgian citizens when their land was given to Belgium as part of the WWI repatriations. Unlike the rest of Belgium, many people in this area welcomed the Nazis in 1940 and again in 1944, because of their strong ties to Germany. Mathius Langer was not one of these. At the time he took the black Americans in he was hiding two Belgian deserters from the German Army and had sent a draft-aged son into hiding so the Nazis could not conscript him. A family friend was also at the house when the Americans appeared. Unfortunately, unknown to the Langers, she was a Nazi sympathizer.

About an hour later, a German patrol of the 1st SS Division, belonging to Kampfgruppe Hansen, arrived in Wereth. It is believed the Nazi sympathizer informed the SS that there were Americans at the Langer house. When the SS troops approached the house the eleven Americans surrendered quickly, without resistance. The Americans were made to sit on the road, in the cold, until dark. The Germans then marched them down the road. Gunfire was heard during the night. In the morning, villagers saw the bodies of the men in a ditch. Because they were afraid that the Germans might return, they did not touch the dead soldiers. The snow covered the bodies and they remained entombed in the snow until mid-February when villagers directed a U.S. Army Grave Registration unit to the site. The official report noted that the men had been brutalized, with broken legs, bayonet wounds to the head, and fingers cut off. Prior to their removal an army photographer took photographs of the bodies to document the brutality of the massacre.

An investigation was immediately begun with a "secret" classification. Testimonies were taken of the Graves Registration officers, the army photographer, the Langers and the woman who had been present when the soldiers arrived. She testified that she told the SS the Americans had left! The case was then forwarded to a War Crimes Investigation unit. However, the investigation showed that no positive identification of the murderers could be found (i.e., no unit patches, vehicle numbers, etc.), only that they were from the 1st SS Panzer Division. By 1948 the "secret" classification was canceled and the paperwork filed away. The murder of the Wereth 11 was seemingly forgotten and unavenged!

Seven of the men were buried in the American Cemetery at Henri-Chapelle, Belgium, and the other four were returned to their families for burial after the war ended. The Wereth 11 remained unknown, it seemed, to all but their families until 1994.

Herman Langer, the son of Mathius Langer, who had given the men food and shelter, erected a small cross, with the names of the dead, in a corner of the pasture where they were murdered, as a private gesture from the Langer family. But the memorial and the tiny hamlet of Wereth remained basically obscure. In a tiny hamlet with no school or shops there were no signs on the roadway s to indicate the memorial, and it was not listed in any guides or maps to the Battle of the Bulge battlefield. Even people looking for it had trouble finding it in the small German speaking community.

In 2001 three Belgian citizens embarked on the task of creating a fitting memorial to these men and additionally to honor all black GIs of WWII. With the help of an American physician in Mobile, Alabama, whose father had fought and was captured in the Battle of the Bulge, a grassroots publicity and fundraising endeavor was begun, and has had modest success. There are now road signs indicating the location of the memorial, and the Belgian

Tourist Bureau listed it in the 60th Anniversary "Battle of the Bulge" brochures. Three families of the murdered men have been located, including one U.S. grave site.

WHERE ARE WE?

John E. McAuliffe
87th Infantry Division, 347th Infantry Regiment, M Company

I arrived in France as a replacement without an overcoat (stolen), blanket (misplaced), or helmet (??). I was an ill-equipped soldier expected to fill in the gap in the battle line. Fortunately, I was refitted at the replacement depot and ready to join my new outfit with M Company, 347th Infantry.

After being briefed by the commanding officer, Capt. Green "Big Jake" Keltner in a barn, the platoon sergeant took four of us out into the snow-filled woods and told Sergeant Joe Kelly of the first mortar section to select two men. He said, "I'll take Manley and McAuliffe," and then pointed to the ground and said, "OK, there's your hole." Luckily we were spared the task of digging that one as the ground was brick hard. My first night of standing guard was a cold one and lonely as I stood under the snow laden firs and was told to be on the alert for German patrols with dogs. We were along the Sauer River.

A couple of nights later we moved up into a log hut with a make-shift stove probably built by the Germans earlier. This was better than sleeping on the ground. It didn't last, though, as the division soon made a mass move to the St. Vith area by truck convoy to relieve the 17th A/B Division beyond Wattermal, Belgium. The names of these towns and units were unknown to me at the time and it was only years later upon reading the division history that I was able to put the pieces together. Being in the 81mm mortars, we did not always see the enemy and upon asking what we were shooting at on one occasion, the sergeant growled, "Never mind that, Mac, just attend to your job." Likewise I envied our platoon leader, Lt. Ray Erickson, because he carried maps of the immediate area and I was always curious as to our position and that of the enemy and just what our location was. But like so many things in the army, we weren't supposed to know everything but just take care of our job at hand.

As we boarded the trucks for the trip to the St. Vith area, I purposely sat on the rear, hoping to catch a good look at the countryside. I didn't realize the others were vying for seats behind the cab to be more out of the cold and perhaps for protection. A slightly built, fair skinned lad placed his Dopp kit containing his razor and some personal belongings under my seat by my feet and entrusted them to my care. Did I look that confident and secure?

The convoy moved out and we stopped for nothing. Being on the tailgate, I was the one who emptied the urine from the steel helmets that were passed down. Along the way I saw many wrecked vehicles, disabled tanks and strewn equipment; the ravages of the initial German breakthrough. Houses were bombed out and gutted and the countryside was a very bleak sight and covered by a deep snow. We passed through a little town and two hours later I saw the same scene again. The driver lost the convoy and we were riding in circles. After eighteen hours of cold trucking, we got to our destination only to find the kitchen closed and we had no supper. Tired from the long trip, I completely forgot about the Dopp kit and that kid gave me hell for not minding it. Why he didn't choose to hold on to it himself, I'll never know. It was like he lost his only possession. I never saw him after that. As we walked along the road among some displaced villagers, I tried my high school French on them. It was bad and didn't work anyway because they were Belgians.

That night our platoon slept in a small country catholic church. The pews had all been removed and the men spread out on the floor with their gear. I was a religious person and having attended strict catholic schools, my first impression was that we were desecrating the sanctity of the church. But those notions were quickly dispelled by the graveness of our situation and my mind turned to prayer. I remember ascending the three steps to the altar where the relics are kept, on which the sacred chalice and host are placed during mass. I put my hand over the spot and prayed for our protection and then found a place to lie down on the floor.

The next day was typically cold and bleak and we were out on the road again. We came to a bend in the road where five G.I.s lay dead off to the side, one body propped against a wall. It was then the shells started to come in, bursting all around us. Black soot settled on us and the acrid smoke filled our nostrils.

It was like that spot was a chosen target for the German 88s. I was scared; the invoking of God's name came easy. We pressed onward and again were hit up the road a bit. I slipped and fell three times on the icy roads under my heavy equipment. No one helped me up, all were hustling towards the protection of a group of houses up ahead in the evening darkness. We took comfort in the seclusion afforded by that small compound of houses. In looking for our platoon OP, I ran smack into the muzzle end of an M-1 pointed from a darkened doorway. I was challenged; I was lost and I returned to my squad room. Those guys in the OP never did get their evening rations.

Up near Manderfeld we came to the edge of the forest and a lieutenant was sending the men out across a clearing at spaced intervals. As I came up to him he looked me over and said, "That's too much!" meaning too much to be carrying. Besides my regular gear, I was carrying 42 pounds of HE-light mortar bombs. I said nothing, and he said, "O.K. Go now." About 100 yards out, several rounds of 88 shells burst near me and I fell face down in knee deep snow. The shelling was scary enough but my next concern was getting myself up from under the weight I was carrying and from the deep snow. I weighed only 154 pounds and all the gear and ammo must have come close to 80 pounds.

On the other side of the clearing in the forest the shelling started pouring in again. This time it was the devastating tree bursts and the shrapnel was scattering every which way. A fellow named Huber from Baltimore and I took cover under a fallen fir tree. When we came out there was a guy sitting on the log holding his blown-up knee. I looked around for help and hollered, "Where is everyone?" Someone yelled, "They're down in the bunker." I asked, "What bunker?" Behind a camouflaged mound I found the stairs leading down inside. This was in the West Wall, near Ormont.

The squad slept in the bunker that night. It had been evacuated by the

Germans. It was a relief to remove my boots and galoshes for the first time in weeks. When morning came I was asked to go on detail to guard an ammo stockpile. Sgt. Kelly yelled, "Alright, Mac, what's holding you up?" I was taking forever to put my boots and galoshes back on over my aching and numbed feet. They really never thawed out until the beginning of March when we had our first hot shower in two months. That winter I wore long woolen underwear and two sets of olive drabs and a sweater and field jacket with a scarf and overcoat, with two pairs of woolen socks under my combat boots and galoshes. I had no feeling in my toes for two months, but the two guys who wore the shoepacks were evacuated with frostbitten feet. We never saw them after that.

CHRISTMAS SERVICES, ARMED TO THE TEETH

George E. McAvoy
9th Armored Division, 149th Armored Signal Company

Our division was on the line spread out the full length of the Luxembourg border with Germany when the attack began. The three combat commands were assigned in different areas covering close to one hundred miles. Our company was to supply communications between these combat commands and headquarters and as a result our company was also spread out over this whole area.

On December 24th we were ordered to withdraw and regroup at a town called Fratin, Belgium. I was one of the lucky ones who arrived during daylight and we were taken in by a farmer and his family on the edge of the small town. The ones arriving after dark had to find whatever shelter they could and bed down there, mainly in sheds and barns.

This town had been freed from the Nazis just a few months before and for the first time in five years they were planning a gala Christmas Eve midnight service. The Germans had forbidden these services over the past five years. When we withdrew into the community the CO forbid any activity at night which included the midnight mass. Apparently the parish priest was very persuasive as he finally received approval to hold the mass but with the warning that the guards would shoot at any light showing. When we heard that there was going to be a midnight service we decided that we would like to go. All those that were not on duty—there were no atheists that night—attended the service. We all figured that the Good Lord had been good to us so far and it wouldn't hurt to ask Him for a little more help.

Imagine attending a Christmas Eve service armed to the teeth. Combat dress and equipment was never made to fit into a church pew. It was very embarrassing in a lot of ways. We had to find some place to put our rifles and carbines, mainly laying them on the floor under the pews and occasionally one would slip on the hardwood and crash to the floor. Nobody seemed to notice. We also took off our helmets and placed them on the floor under the pews and the people sitting in front would occasionally bring their feet back under the pew and kick the helmet so that it would spin along the wooden floor. It was the noisiest service I ever attended but the sense of comfort, well-being and safety was amazing. The church was jammed and all of us took the seats in the back of the church.

We noticed that the young boys up in the choir stall were giggling and laughing and seemed like kids anywhere. The service was in French and a memorable one. The church was a good size and there wasn't an open seat in the place. It was a very devout service and everyone in that congregation was well aware of what was just a few miles away.

When the service ended we left the church and a Junkers 88, flying just above the housetops, went over us with the right engine on fire. It was a full moon and the plane passed the moon and we had a clear sight of the two pilots in the blister fighting to get control of that aircraft. We did not hear it crash.

The following morning, Christmas Day, we found out why the choir boys were giggling and laughing. One of our crews, arriving after dark, had found the church door open and the men had gone into the church, thrown their bedrolls down around the altar, and had gone to sleep. The priest, when he arrived, saw the men and figured that he would not disturb them since they were probably exhausted. These six men were asleep around the altar when the service began.

The men were relating their feelings about all of this and it was a riot. One fellow said that he heard the organ and immediately thought, "I've bought it!" He pulled the zipper down on his bedroll and there were the choir boys all giggling and laughing. All of them agreed that it was the longest service that they had ever slept through.

Of the four Christmas days spent in the service this was by far the most memorable.

179TH FIELD ARTILLERY BATTALION

James M. McCabe
179th Field Artillery Battalion, Battery B

The 179th FA Bn landed on Utah Beach, Normandy, France on 13 August 1944 as part of General George S. Patton's Third Army and attached to Fourth Armored Division. Our first brush with the enemy came the following night. We had our first fire mission on 22 August 1944 at dusk. Our artillery battalion stayed at Boisie-Rot, France from 22-24 August. In a short time we destroyed fourteen artillery pieces, a horse drawn train and several hundred Germans. In this position the 179th had three men killed. I looked in a burned out German tank and observed one of the tank crew that had burned and about all that was left was his intestines still in place looking like link smoked sausage.

The 179th FA Bn was assigned the task of holding outpost at Fresnes-en-Saulnois, France from 19-24 September 1944. Under dense fog a German tank was firing down on us from the hill above. Our artillery started firing point blank at the tank. The climax came on the fifth day when it was determined that Germans were preparing a strong counter attack. I manned an outpost several hundred yards from the Battery with my machine gun in place and dug a two man foxhole. My partner and I sat back to back to observe both directions. It was raining steadily and there were two of our men with bazookas about fifty feet away. About mid-afternoon you could hear tanks beginning to rumble. It was overcast and still raining. Tanks were on our right moving toward our outfit. I was continually praying to my God for help. There were several tanks in that group. The clouds began to part. In a little while, a squadron of P-47 fighter planes was circling overhead waiting for a clearing. It wasn't long before they started diving on moving tanks with machine guns firing and well-aimed bombs stopped the German tank movement. One of the planes didn't come out of the dive and exploded on contact with the ground. While this was taking place, there was much smoke and explosions. The 179th FA finished the task. The 35th Infantry Division relieved the 179th before nightfall. The 179th was recommended for the Presidential Citation for defense of this critical spot. The 179th had two men killed.

The 179th went in a holding position at Athienville, France from 28 September to 1 November 1944. On a quiet Sunday afternoon in mid-October, I was writing a letter home. I was sitting in a vehicle that my machine gun was pedestal mounted on. "B" Battery commanding officer was strolling around the battery area and stopped and was talking with me. At this time we heard the chatter of machine gun fire and roar of planes. I manned my machine gun and told the battery commander to get in my foxhole. The battery commander was larger than I and had difficulty squeezing in my foxhole. Scanning the sky, I saw German ME-109 fighter plane coming my way at tree top level to my left. I started firing just before the plane crossed in front of me. My tracers showed that the plane was being riddled by machine gun fire and started a nose dive. The plane crashed landed about 300 feet to my right, exploding on impact with the ground. The battery commander was pleased with the results that Sunday. Five ME-109 fighter planes were attacking our area and five planes were shot down. On the first day of November 1944 the 179th FA left Athienville, France, going toward Germany.

On the afternoon of 19 December, the 179th FA left position Maginot Line at Rimling, France where our batteries were firing across the German border. We were unaware at the time that we were headed for the Battle of the

Bulge in Belgium and Luxembourg. During the period of 11-17 December, the 179th FA Bn was called upon twice to furnish five percent of its table of organization strength for infantry replacements. In addition to my machine gun duties and because of the ammunition section manpower shortage, I was called on to assist the ammo section with unloading, stockpiling and delivery of 97 pound projectiles plus powder charges to the battery gun section. During the Bastogne mission, the 179th FA Bn was firing over 1,000 rounds of 97 pound projectiles in a 24 hour time frame. The temperature got down in the range of 13 degrees below zero and mostly in the zero range while supporting the 4th Armored Division during the Bastogne mission. The snow was deep and we used quarter pound TNT charges to break the crust of the ground in order to dig foxholes. My shoes cracked where they bent and hurt my feet. I cut strips from a wool blanket and wrapped my feet and stuffed them in my oversized rubber boots. My blood soaked woolen underwear would freeze to my backside and with any movement, I could feel and hear the cracking.

I was evacuated on 31 December 1944 by the battalion medic. Arriving at the hospital in Luxembourg City, I was put in a bathtub and warm water was continuously poured on my backside and the underwear was cut off a little bit at a time until it was all removed. I was then sent to a convalescent hospital in Nancy, France. When I was finally healed and I was released from the hospital back to duty, I returned to my outfit. I have many more memories of the Battle of the Bulge and the 179th FA Bn travel across Europe from Normandy to Czechoslovakia, with Luxembourg, Belgium, Germany and Austria in between that I could ever put on paper!

The end of January, the Bulge was no more and the 179th went in the holding position from 1-24 February 1945 at Siebenater (Bockholz), Luxembourg near the German border. "B" Battery moved in this large field that was covered with snow that was pretty deep and had small raised up mounds scattered around the field. Since we were in a holding position the kitchen truck setup and began serving us hot meals. After a few weeks, the rains came and the snow melted. The small mounds scattered in the field turned out to be dead German soldiers. On 24 February 1945 we moved out of this area and went into Germany supporting the 4th Armored Division.

In Germany around March 1945 while stopped on a road in the countryside for a period of time, an enemy soldier (sniper) began firing on our column from a field. I kept looking and preparing to fire my 50 caliber machine gun but couldn't see him. Firing continued at intervals and one of the artillery gun crew called out that he saw the sniper rise up and shoot. He instructed me to watch his small caliber tracer that he was going to fire. I watched the location of the tracer, which appeared to be near some small bushes located near what looked like a drainage ditch. After a few minutes I saw the sniper rise up to fire again. At this time I fired a good many shots because of the distance between the sniper and myself. After firing, I didn't see the sniper again. In a few minutes I saw our half-truck going in the direction of where I had fired with the executive officer and several non-coms. They got out of the vehicle and were standing in a group looking down watching the sniper die. They got back in the vehicle and went back to the front area of the column. The incident was never mentioned, even though many of the battery had seen what happened. About 30 or 40 years later, I asked one of the non-coms (who later became first sergeant) who was in the half-truck checking on what I was shooting at, if I had dreamed that incident. His reply to my question was, "That incident was no dream. I have waited all of these years for you to ask me about it." He said, "The German soldier that I had shot was nearly cut in two and he had the SS tattoo showing that he was one of Hitler's elite troopers." He also said that the German soldier had a P-38 pistol that was hit with one of my shots.

On 1 April 1945, Easter Sunday, in a small town or village near Frankfurt, Germany, our battery had pulled out on the road from the field, where we had bivouac the night before. While waiting for the Battalion to move out, I had my K-ration breakfast. Our vehicle was one of the last in the column. The rest of the Battery and Battalion were stretched out through the town. There was a small low fenced-in apple orchard next to the road and a barn with an open hayloft facing the road. I had a nature call and stepped over the fence thinking I was out of sight. At this time, what sounded like a German burp gun (rapid fire) started shooting and dirt was flying all over me. I looked up toward the barn and the open hayloft and saw some German soldiers around what seemed to be a jammed burp gun because it was not firing anymore. I jumped the low fence, climbed on my vehicle and started firing my 50 caliber machine gun. In a very short time the bam and hayloft were in flames. There was no activity seen in the hayloft. About the same time, snipers throughout the town started firing on our column which had started March order. Machine guns throughout the column started firing on the snipers as we went through the town. That night we were a distance from the town that we had left and you could still see the red glow of fire in the sky.

In Germany around April 1945, we were going up a hill and it had been raining. Dead German soldiers had fallen all along the edge of the road, probably from machine fire from our tanks or fighter planes. I was manning my machine gun mounted on the tractor pulling our 155mm howitzer. Vehicles in front of us had made a rut, sliding a little bit sideways; one of the dead German soldier's heads was right beside the rut. The large tires on our 155mm howitzer were sliding in line with the soldier's head. I couldn't look at what I thought would happen. I didn't look back. The sight of our sliding howitzer will always be in my memory. On our drive through Germany about March and April, we came upon and near several fenced in barrack type buildings housing prisoners of war soldiers, labor camps and others. I remember this British POW running up to me with a big hug. He was so happy to see us! Reaching in his pocket, he came out with a large brass nut (about the size of a quarter) with brass buttons soldered on each side, probably from his overcoat. I asked the POW what it was and he showed me it was a cigarette lighter he made while a POW. With tears in his eyes he handed it to me and said, "I want you to have it." That cigarette lighter was prized by me for many years and was misplaced several years ago. I hope that it will show up eventually.

I went into one of the labor camps occupied by laborers from countries Germany had invaded, I assumed. They worked and harvested the farms and also did factory work. All of them we saw were very happy to see us. The first thing that they asked for was cigarettes. We were able to give them some. One of them wanted us to see the barracks or someone in there. We couldn't understand what he was saying and he motioned for us to follow him. A couple of us followed behind him and went in this long barrack. Inside were two rows of double bunks with some of them occupied. The smell was like nothing I ever encountered. By this time we bade them good-bye but couldn't get out before receiving many hugs.

Our column was stopped along the road in one of the small towns. Off to the side of the road was a mound of dirt and a small homemade cross marking a grave. Walking along the road going in the opposite direction from us were two men with sticks to assist them in walking. They hobbled up to our vehicles, pointing to their mouths, indicating they wanted food. Both men were nothing but skin and bones. They were given food and the look on their faces said it all as they walked away in their striped clothes. It seems like many of the fenced in barrack type camps were located in East Germany. When you would see these men in striped clothes, it would mean that they were out of one of the camps. Usually the guards in these camps would leave just ahead of the advancing allies. Some of the camps were probably more humane than others. But, the one with that human waste smell in close quarters will stay in my memory. I was told about one and saw the pictures of skin and bones with heads attached and stacked like cords of wood, hardly recognized as humans, waiting to be tossed in a furnace. That had to be the worst. At the end on VE day, 8 May 1945, the 179th FA Bn was near Zechovice, Czechoslovakia (7-10 May). There was dancing in the streets by the Czechs and we were all very happy.

We moved back to Germany as military government forces (10 May–1 June, 1945). We ended up in Bogen, Germany located on the Danube River, 1 June 1945. We set up road blocks on all roads coming from the east, and we detained German soldiers who were fleeing the Russians. After searching them, they were moved to the fenced in compound with barracks located near Bogen. "B" Battery was housed in a former two-story courthouse in Bogen. After a couple of weeks the Germans stopped coming and the compound was full. My buddy, Joe, and I were picked along with others to pull guard duty in the convoy transporting the German prisoners to a destination unknown. One morning before daylight, a large number trucks, jeeps and men assembled at the prisoner compound to start loading prisoners. The German prisoners must have sensed where they were going. At the start of the loading, one of the prisoners dashed around to the dark side of the truck and disappeared in the darkness and couldn't be found. The convoy was loaded without any other mishaps. Jeeps with two men were scattered throughout the convoy. Dawn was breaking as we headed toward Austria. The convoy was going a pretty good speed when one of the prisoners jumped off the truck. The convoy couldn't stop. Our jeep was near the end of the convoy. Every few hours the convoy would stop for periods of time, I assume for directions and nature stops. On one of the stops, we were in the mountains on a narrow road with a cabin close by. Someone came out and one of the prisoners asked if they had water.

They answered, "Yes." After consultation, six were allowed to go inside the cabin; we could see the front and back with no problem. After a little while, March order was passed through the column to be ready for movement in a few minutes. We called to the prisoners that we were ready to go. They came out but I counted only five getting in the truck. I called to my buddy, Joe, who was close by the cabin. He went inside and lifted a spread on the bed that was hanging to the floor and called to come out. The prisoner came right out and climbed into the truck. In a few minutes the convoy started moving out.

We traveled a few more hours and came to a fairly big town. I think we were still in Austria near Czechoslovakia border and in the Russian zone. The convoy pulled over and stopped while still in the town. While stopped several civilians were talking to the German prisoners on the truck. They left in a short time and then an elderly couple appeared. The lady was crying as she held one of the prisoner's hands. They stayed a long time holding hands and crying. I think it was one of the prisoner's parents. After being in this location close to an hour, the convoy moved out. Traveling several miles (I believe we were led by Russians) and we came to a barbed wire fenced in compound. The Russians were taking charge of the prisoners as we unloaded them. Several of the prisoners tossed watches to the GI's standing by the vehicles. I guess they preferred the

Americans over the Russians. After all of the prisoners were unloaded, we followed the Russian vehicles a short distance to the buildings (I believe it was a Catholic convent.) By this time it was night. Armed Russian soldiers appeared along with nuns with rings of keys (I think it was two nuns.) In my memory I picture a two story building with a long wide hall and rooms on each side. We probably had about 30 men including guards and drivers. There was a sort of a line following behind the Russians and the nuns. The rooms appeared to be locked. You could hear frightened children crying. There were women and children who had probably taken refuge at the convent. If the rooms were empty two men would drop off and the line would be shortened. If the room was occupied, the Russian soldier would motion them to leave. If the door was difficult to open, he would point his gun at the lock and make the nun that much more nervous, indicating that he would open it with the gun. Finally, our turn came. Our room was occupied by a mother and several children, who had started crying when the soldier motioned for them to get out. In a few minutes the mother and children came out carrying their few belongings. The Russian soldier motioned for Joe and me to go in. The soldier and the nun continued down the hall with the GIs that were left. Joe and I were standing in the doorway looking at that mother in the hall trying to comfort those crying children. Joe looking at me and said, "Mac, we can't do this." I was thinking the same thing before he said a word. We walked over to that mother and children and motioned for them to go back in the room. The look on their faces was truly that of deep appreciation. The mother and children returned to their room and the crying had just about stopped as they closed the door. Later on I heard a shot and have always wondered if that was a room the nuns couldn't get unlocked. We spread our sleeping bags out in the hall and went to bed with our shoes off and our clothes on.

After eating our K-rations breakfast, we returned to Bogen, Germany and continued our Army of Occupation. After a few months, we received orders to travel to Marseille, France, to board the ship to the Pacific. While waiting for the trip to Marseille, the war in the Pacific ended. Our orders were not changed, so we still went to Marseille to await our turn for travel to the states. After arriving in Marseille, Joe and I had duty at the Officers Club which was okay. After a month or two, I was sent to the Riviera on the Mediterranean at Nice, France. I had duty at the Motor Pool driving a jeep to check service stations gas consumption. I had a private room with meal service in a large hotel which was great. After a couple of months, I received a call from the Battery and went by train back to Marseille. We boarded the Liberty ship back to the states. We landed at Newport News, VA after nineteen days at sea. Then we headed to Fort Bragg for discharge.

At wars end, the 179th Field Artillery Battalion final report showed the following:

8,996 rounds of 155mm Howitzer projectiles were used against the enemy

2,350 tons weight of this ammunition

266 days of continuous combat

Over 1,000 prisoners captured.

For its World War II service, the 179th Field Artillery was awarded combat participation credit for five campaigns: Normandy, Northern France, Rhineland, Ardennes-Alsace, and Central Europe. It was also awarded the French Croix de Guerre with Palm for action at the Moselle River.

CLOSE CALL IN BASTOGNE

Robert T. McConnell
770th Field Artillery Battalion

We went into Bastogne with Patton's 4th Armored Division. Patton was in the second tank. We had to fight our way in. Tanks were firing on both sides of the road.

I had six 50 caliber machine guns on my trucks. We were firing on both sides of the road at anything that moved. That's the way we went into Bastogne with Patton's tanks.

After we set up our guns and started firing, Ole Sarge and I had to carry ammo around to the other side of Bastogne. The colonel was over there lay-ing in on some buildings. We unloaded ammo and started back to our outfit.

Sarge was driving and traffic was heavy. Shells were coming in all around us. The traffic came to a standstill. I told Ole Sarge to get up on the wide side-walk. We were moving pretty good and I yelled, "Hold it." We almost ran over Patton. He was there trying to get MPs out of basement doors to direct traffic because shells were hitting a lot of vehicles.

We had to stop to keep from running over Patton. He said, "These are the only two SOBs who know where they are going." We made it back to the outfit alright and after the war was over, we both got back home.

A MEDIC'S MEMOIR

Marge Flados
From notes written by Henry McCracken,
99th Infantry Division, 395th Infantry Regiment

The memories had remained sharp and well defined in my mind over the ex-panse of 52 years. But as I trampled the battle sites on a 1997 visit to Belgium, where I once served as a young medic, the memories flooded back in all their gory, glorious detail. I wanted to record it as I remembered it.

I was a Medic in the 99th Infantry Division, 395th Regiment, before, dur-ing and after the Battle of the Bulge. Prior to our withdrawal to Elsenborn Ridge the Headquarters Aid Station of the 395th was in Rocherath and af-ter the Battle of the Bulge began, the Aid Station received its share of shells pointed in our direction on the 16th, 17th and 18th. We had set up in a house on the outskirts of the town and by the 18th of December, we were receiving many casualties and some DOA, as well. That evening, an attempt to move the bodies back to the Graves Registration area on litter jeeps was unsuc-cessful, so we returned to our station and placed them alongside our station house in neat rows.

We had a roomful of injured men and we attempted to make them as comfortable as possible by giving injections of morphine to control their pain. Later during the night, a lieutenant from the 2nd Infantry Division stopped by with his patrol and he asked why the injured had not been evacuated. I told him that the ambulance drivers had reported that all the access roads were blocked toward the west. He then instructed us to load up all the injured and that he would try to get them through to medical units behind our lines. We did as instructed, but I never knew whether they made it or not.

The next morning we received orders to move out, and we loaded our vehicles with equipment and supplies and headed toward the 395th Headquarters Company. When we were about a mile from our destination, the road was heavily shelled and many of us opted to follow the vehicles to the Headquarters area on foot. By this time it was late afternoon and the shells kept coming. While walking along this rural road I heard a shell coming in and I hit the ground. It landed nearby, took two skips along the ground, came to a stop and never exploded.

By the time we got to the Headquarters area, the trucks were already in convoy so we hopped on the nearest vehicle and headed cross-country. The ride was pleasant but short, because the trucks began to bog down and it was necessary to jump off and resume walking. No one knew our destination; we just walked in the direction we were told to go. Having not arrived at our destination by dark, it was necessary to find a place to spend the night. We came upon a dug-out about 12' X 12' and 3' deep, covered with logs and tin. It looked great to us at the time and a group of us shared the protection it provided for the remainder of the night. The shrapnel and dirt hitting our overhead cover during the night didn't keep us from sleeping and feeling grateful for our safe haven. The next morning a GI was brave enough to poke his head out to assess the situation, and detecting no immediate danger, we all left our dugout and began walking once again. We came upon a U.S. Army truck that had some C rations on board that the drivers were willing to share. They were frozen solid but we ate them as if they were good.

As we approached a village, we saw a 6 x 6 truck approaching with a Red Cross flag flying from the front bumper. It turned out to be our Headquarters medic truck out looking for me. Interestingly, I was MIA for a period of one night. That's okay; I needed the rest!

Elsenborn

The truck driver took me to a house where our aid station was located at an intersection of the road from Elsenborn to Butgenbach. No sooner had we settled in when we were told that German tanks were coming up the road from Butgenbach to Elsenborn. The house had a small fruit cellar with a window facing the road. Someone had left a bazooka and some shells in the aid station and Walter Pawlaski (from Minneapolis, Minnesota) and I decided to go to the cellar and from the vantage point that the window provided, fire the bazooka shells at the tanks when they approached. Medics were not allowed to carry weapons and we were a little short on expertise in the use of the bazooka, but we felt inclined to take some action in the face of oncoming tanks. We were greatly relieved to learn later that the tanks were stopped before they could proceed to our location. An officer came down into the cellar and asked what we were trying to do and we explained our plan to him. He may or may not have been amused at our bravado, but he told us that if we had fired the bazooka in those close quarters, the concussion could have done a lot of damage... to us! So much for stopping a German Panzer column in its tracks!

Shelling continued to be heavy and it was suggested to our CO, Capt. James Fyvie (from Manistique, Michigan), that we were in a very vulnerable location and that the Germans were zeroing in on our intersection with great accuracy. He said he would look for a better location for us and promptly left. On his return, he informed us he had found a likely place for the Aid Station in a very sturdily built school house a short distance away and we lost no time in packing everything up once again and moving into the new location.

The school building was located at the edge of the town of Elsenborn and there was nothing between us and the German lines. It resembled a fort and was well built with thick, stone walls. And a lucky move it was, for two days later a shell made a direct hit on the house we had formerly occupied.

The school house was surrounded by a sea of mud when we arrived, but it did indeed look sturdy. It had a concrete floor in the basement and we slept there because it provided us the best protection. Since the front entrance faced the German lines, we used the side door of the building.

As we settled in, the weather worsened, became colder and snow fell intermittently. We used two rooms in the building; the first room nearest the side entrance was our medical room and the second room was our overflow room which contained a pot belly stove with a smoke pipe sticking out the window. Whenever possible, the GIs would come in out of the cold to warm up at our little stove and snatch a little sack time. Rags were placed over all the windows to maintain blackout conditions.

One night I smelled smoke and to my surprise saw that some GI had stoked up the fire, making the stove pipe red hot, setting the rags over the windows on fire. Guys were sleeping on the floor all around. There was very little water so after getting the guys out of the room we beat out the flames with whatever we could grab. In a room where we were not allowed to smoke a cigarette in order to keep any light from showing, we had flames shooting out the window! This was not lost on the Germans, because we took a few shells as a result of this breach of our blackout protocol.

We had many casualties coming in from Elsenborn Ridge, many with frozen feet. Replacements were in short supply during this time so we did not evacuate the injured as readily as previously. If a GI could use a weapon, he was not sent back for further treatment but expected to join his outfit as soon as possible.

On the 24th of December, Joe Maner and I were going back to Malmedy for medical supplies and water. En route we were strafed by a German fighter plane at an intersection and our jeep was hit and totally demolished. The water cans were shot full of holes and an M.P. was hit in the shoulder as he was directing traffic at the intersection. I went back to take care of him. After he was bandaged and cared for, and afoot once again, we set out toward our Aid Station. As I slogged along, my right foot felt squishy, and I looked down to discover I had a flesh wound in the lower calf and blood was running into my boot.

After hearing out story back at the Aid Station, Capt. Fyvie decided I should be evacuated for treatment of my wound. My thought was that he was a doctor and could take care of me where I was. Later on when pieces of the bullet began coming out of my leg, he again wanted to send me back to a medical field hospital. I refused for a second time. Later, I received a Bronze Star for providing care for the injured MP before attending to my own wound. Truth be known, at the time, I had not yet discovered I was wounded! As the war progressed, all combat medics were awarded the Bronze Star. I have two.

Trips continued to be made back and forth to Malmedy for supplies and it was my job to supply all four of our 395th aid stations, the 1st, 2nd, 3rd Battalions and Headquarters. There was an ample supply of plasma for transfusion, however, it is supposed to be transfused at body temperature. This was impossible. The plasma came packaged in a kit with needles, lines and in powder form. The powder had to be dissolved in a bottle of saline solution before it was administered intravenously. Nothing stayed warm in Elsenborn and it was a challenge to try to warm the plasma. We tried to keep the plasma warm by placing the bottles in a pan of water that sat on a little gasoline burner. The bottles stayed there until we went out in the field, then we carried the saline bottles in our arm pits to maintain their warmth.

After transfusing one GI with several liters of cold plasma, he looked a hopeless case. We placed a blanket over him because we thought he was dead. After a time we saw movement under the blanket and we hurriedly transfused him again, loaded him in an ambulance and sent him back for further treatment. Working near the front lines, we sent the wounded back as soon as possible and seldom ever knew whether they recovered. I have wondered about that one.

While we were at Elsenborn we received our first shipment of penicillin. It came to us as a powder that had to be reconstituted with normal saline. Previous to this time sulpha was the only drug we had to fight infections. Shortly after Capt. Fyvie had been promoted to major he became very ill and was running a high fever. He decided to try the new medicine on himself right then and there. It worked like the miracle drug that it was. It made believers out of all of us.

The weather worsened and the army issued us Weasels, a more suitable vehicle with tank-like tracks for maneuvering in the snow. We promptly set about white-washing them in the hope of becoming invisible to the Germans when we were out and about.

Our 395th Headquarters kitchen was set up about a block from the school building so we had to make trips to chow. On Christmas Day it was turkey and trimmings for all. Due to the heavy shelling, we did not go in groups, but singly or in pairs. There was a jeep sitting about halfway between the school house and the kitchen. Our plan included making a dash to the jeep, hitting the ground, then going the rest of the way as fast as possible. It worked great on the way over, but on the return trip, laden with our turkey dinners, we ran to the jeep, hit the ground as planned, but so did a lot of the turkey dinners. Soon the jeep was surrounded with turkey and trimmings!

Although we saw all types of injuries, some of the saddest patients were those suffering from combat exhaustion. I went to a house one day and found a GI seeking protection by trying to dig into the floor with his fingers. In Malmedy, I saw a GI walking back and forth in road ruts full of ice water obviously without any idea where he was or what he was doing.

We had the unforgettable experience of being assigned a Medical Administrative Officer who came to the Aid Station and told us he wanted to go to the front. I told him to just step out the front door! A few days later he came into the station carrying a live bazooka shell. He said he wanted someone to detonate it so he could have it as a souvenir. I reported this incident to Major Fyvie and needless to say, the poor fellow was gone the next day.

One day a German artillery shell came scudding through the front door of the school building, but didn't explode. I have always been thankful for that dud.

We didn't use the triage system during this time. We had about 12 medics, a doctor and a dentist in our outfit to take care of all the incoming wounded. We treated other ailments such as colds, diarrhea, and upset stomachs, as well as shrapnel wounds, bullet injuries, combat fatigue and frozen feet.

There was a big controversy over trench foot as opposed to frozen feet. Our aid station personnel received official notice that GIs in the field developed trench foot because they did not wash their feet and change to clean socks each day. We were instructed to designate the condition as "trench foot," which was considered a self-inflicted wound. Our major told me that we were never to use those two words on an evacuation card!

I admit to having had a problem with the liquor ration. We had four Aid Stations and we received three bottles per day to be used for medicinal purposes. There was scotch, cognac and some cheaper brands, but I was usually accused of keeping the best for our Aid Station. I should have documented the liquor distribution, for I really tried my best to divide it fairly and I thought that I did. Ironically, I didn't even drink liquor!

We remained in the school building until the breakout from Elsenborn in late January at which time we headed back toward the twin cities of Krinkelt and Rocherath. My experience in treating these soldiers seemed like a routine job to me at the time. I was able to accept the responsibility without it creating any lasting personal problems. Of course there were times when patience grew thin but a good night's sleep and some decent food took care of those times. We were always hungry for fresh meat and we butchered a cow and a pig during our stay at the school house. We greatly enjoyed the meat for as long as it lasted! Usually the wounded men and the others who needed our help did not complain excessively or give us a hard time. I feel honored to have served as a medic in the 395th, and shall always remember and admire the courage and inner strength shown by the men on the Elsenborn Ridge.

A SITE REVISITED

Vincent Meinhart
61st Chemical Depot Company

I was a 24-year-old GI with Patton's 3rd Army when the Germans approved a desperate plan on December 16, 1945 which we now know as the Battle of the Bulge. My outfit, the 61st Chemical Depot Company, was supplying the 90th Infantry Division with the 12th Corp at Saarlautern, Germany. At that time General Eisenhower diverted all the forces he could to courier attack.

Swinging northward with no sleep we boarded 6x6 trucks. As we moved through the night, it got colder, the snow got deeper, the fog got thicker and the tanks and trucks were slipping off the road. We were so cold we built a fire on the steel plate of the truck out of twigs to keep our hands and feet warm on the way up to Tontelange. Ten days later General Patton's 3rd Army broke into Bastogne. Our outfit later on went to Lorentzweiler, Luxembourg, where we billeted in houses with civilians.

Recently I went to Germany with my son, Lieutenant Colonel Richard Meinhart, who is in the Air Force. We went looking for the house where I stayed. Remembering the railroad station where the CP was, I found the house looking very much the same as in 1945.

I knocked on the door and a woman who spoke little English opened it. However, she was not the occupant of the house that I remembered. She invited me in to see the room where I slept. She took me to town hall, where clerks spoke English and they looked up the records and found the names of the 1945 occupants.

One was a guest at a nearby nursing home. I visited with her, but she was elderly and the conversation did not go so well. However, she gave me the phone number of her sister who also stayed there during the war. I talked with her for over a half hour, and she remembered me and we had an enjoyable conversation about the period 46 years ago.

I brought back many memories of the Battle of the Bulge that never can be forgotten.

WELCOME TO F COMPANY

Harvey S. Meltzer
42nd Infantry Division

I recall December 25, 1944 as a chilly, clear day as I was standing with my sergeant looking across the Rhine River at the German troops on the other side. We were bivouacked in a mansion along the Rhine River and war seemed like a very far off place to this naive 18-year-old kid from Worcester,

Massachusetts.

As we were standing and watching the Germans, I asked the sergeant why we did not shoot at them and he said, "If we shoot at them, they would shoot at us!" So both sides left each other alone! The sergeant then told me that I would not be able to look at a German soldier and shoot to kill him. He said I would be too scared! I think because I wore eyeglasses the sergeant was fooled by my looks, but I told him he had nothing to worry about, when the time came, my rifle would be fired, and it was.

In the evening we were served the customary Christmas dinner of roast turkey, cranberry sauce and the rest of the trimmings. It was very nice because there was a fireplace lit up in the mansion and it was all very warm and cozy. We then went off to bed ready for the unknown.

Sometime after midnight several of us were awakened and told to gather our things and move outside. We were then advised that we were being transferred to the 90th Division up north as replacements. (We found out later that heavy losses were incurred at the Saar River.) We rode in the dark and on into morning and I can still remember how beautiful it was as we rode through Nancy, all the trees lined up along both sides of the highway, as we headed for Luxembourg riding in back of the truck. As we rode further north it became much colder and snow covered the ground everywhere.

We arrived in late afternoon dusk and were lined up along the road waiting for instructions. As we waited we then heard an enormous explosion and hit the ground as fast as we could wondering what had hit us. We looked up and saw our new sergeant standing there and he told us that our own 240mm cannons across the street had fired a salvo at the Germans! I'm sure we all had red faces as we were welcomed to F Company of the 359th Regiment of the 90th Division.

We would all see much worse in the coming days as combat infantrymen, but to this young kid these two particular days stick in my memory. In the combat days ahead the occurrences are still vivid, but the actual date is not even in my memory.

A MORE DISTANT VIEW

Murray Mendelsohn
159th Engineer Combat Battalion

December 16, 1944, started off as a typical day at the 159th Engineer Combat Battalion Headquarters in Useldange, Luxembourg. It was a cloudy, cold day but not unusual considering the way the weather had been going.

I had had my breakfast at the schoolhouse where the majority of H&S Co. was quartered plus having the company's mess facilities. After my walk back from breakfast, I was entering into my morning office routine in the chateau headquarters facility.

Then serious news came in and in a spirit of great urgency the operations officers and enlisted men got their equipment together and left in a rush. Apparently the Germans had attacked along the German-Luxembourg border and were advancing in large numbers through the thinly held American lines.

The 159th had been assigned to the 4th Infantry Division as infantry reinforcements and the line companies, A, B, and C and the headquarters leadership and support group were hurrying to take up their positions in the Consdorf area.

Those of us left behind at headquarters were trying to sort out the details and prepare for our own emergency program. I saw one of the day-old intelligence memos stating that there seemed to be much greater movement along the German side of the border. It turned out to be all too true. I remembered that about a week before, while walking to lunch, that a German observation plane had flown over at a very low altitude. Useldange was no longer far from the impending action.

The group still in Useldange tried to take up the slack whenever possible. Guard schedules were expanded to cover a wider area and important facilities. We were all put on alert. That night I was assigned to guard duty at a Luxembourg water pumping station a few miles from Useldange. When I was posted I was told that the station operator would come along sometime in the evening to monitor the station.

It was pitch black, no moon or stars shone that night. The station was in an isolated spot off the main road. I walked around trying to keep warm and hoping that I would know when the station operator was coming. About an hour later I heard a motor bike coming closer. I went over to the pumping station and waited. I saw and heard a man approaching. He was tall, dressed in a black leather coat and did not expect me to be there and hailing him. I must say that I was nervous but I used a few words of German to determine that he was the man I was expecting.

He invited me inside the station and showed me the pumping equipment. We had a conversation for a few minutes and then I went outside to resume walking my post. From time to time I would go into the station to see that all was well, get a little warmer and have someone to talk to. It provided another one of my impromptu German lessons.

I found that most Luxembourgers spoke German so that I could at least make myself understood and find out what was happening. At least my school German courses had been paying off.

The time passed uneventfully and I was replaced several hours later, frozen but all right.

Battalion headquarters was located in a chateau built about the last 1920s. The exterior was in keeping with the style of the attached old tower and wall of the 11th century castle remnant. The interior was modem and spacious. I was happy to be able to sleep on the floor there for about two and a half months.

The operational officers and men were all up at the front. The personnel, supply and other support troops were given other tasks to take up the slack in the operation. This sequence of events went on for the next several days. Of course, there was constant concern about what was occurring at the front. Complete and accurate news was difficult to obtain. The bad weather conditions meant that our air force was not flying, a very important factor.

One morning, groups of us were sent to the line company quarters in the surrounding towns in order to pick up all the belongings and equipment that were left behind when the rush call came to the Consdorf area.

I was sent to nearby Bettborn to retrieve all the Company B Personal belongings. Nobody knew who was in control of Bettborn, in spite of its proximity. Our planes were not up there to do their usual scouting. We took several trucks and drove to Bettborn. On arrival, it appeared to be deserted with none of the local people to be seen. We went to the various buildings that B Company used for sleeping quarters. We started loading all the belongings that were there. We did not want anything to fall into German hands. It was a rush packing job and then we headed back to Useldange. Luckily the Germans were not in any of our billet villages and our mission was accomplished without incident.

This exercise showed up one of our major problems of not knowing how far the Germans had advanced on local levels. Of course rumors were rampant and usually not to be believed. Security was especially tight because of confirmed reports of German soldiers in captured American uniforms roaming around the area looking to cause confusion and worse. Fortunately, most of them were captured.

Then orders came to load up everything still in Useldange. While it was not a time for too much reflection, we felt a real tug about leaving the town and its wonderful residents. I am sure that we all said a silent prayer for Useldange as we left, heading for Rollingergrund, a suburb adjoining Luxembourg City on its northwest border. As an appropriate side, Useldange escaped unscathed.

In Rollingergrund we established our headquarters and barracks in a school. We unloaded and set up operations again. Then on December 23, with snow on the ground for the past several days, the sun finally broke through. The change in the attitude and outlook was magnetic. We all felt that the temporary setback was over. The line companies returned on Christmas night and then were all pulled back to the Charleville-Mezieres area to regroup. The battalion had lost strength in the heavy fighting and it would be some time before the wounded returned, where possible, and replacements would start arriving.

The battalion had been through a real ordeal in the intense fighting in the Consdorf area, but now we were going back to the engineering part of our mission. The 159th had been tested again in its combat role and had fulfilled its assigned tasks. As we headed to our next encampment and then on our steady northeastward push to Germany we felt our spirits rise again.

32ND ARMORED INFANTRY REGIMENT

Oda C. Miller
3rd Armored Division, 32nd Armored Infantry Regiment,
2nd Battalion, Co E

"Victory Or Death," the motto of the 32nd Armored Regiment, served as an inspirational order to this first of the 3rd Armored Division's two great battering rams. Commanded by Colonel Leander L. Doan, the 32nd contributed much to the powerhouse drive of the "Spearhead" Division through Europe.

Allied Counter Offensive
3–6 January 1945

On 3 January, VII Corps started a new offensive to the southeast with 2nd and 3rd Armored Divisions abreast followed by the 84th and 83rd Infantry Divisions. The objective of this attack was to drive rapidly to the southeast, with the armor leading, seize Houffalize and its vital road net; and join up with the Third Army coming up from the south, thereby pocketing elements of the German Army that had penetrated further to the west before they could be withdrawn.

In the zone of the 3rd Armored, the attack was made with combat Commands "A" and "B" abreast. Combat Command "B" was on the right (west) of the zone. Each Combat Command moved out to the attack in two Task Force columns:

C COMD. "A" (Brig. Gen. Hickey)
T F "Doan"
Hq 32nd Armd. Regt.

2nd Bn., 32nd Armd. Regt.

3rd Bn., 36th Armd. Inf. Regt.

1st Plat., A Co., 23rd Armd. Engr. Bn.

1st Plat., A Co., 703rd TO Bn

54th Armd. FA Bn.

T F "Richardson"

3rd Bn, 32nd Armd. Regt.

2nd Bn., 330th Inf. Regt.

2nd Plat., A Co., 23rd Armd. Engr. Bn.

2nd Plat., A Co., 703rd TD Bn.

67th Armd. FA Bn.

C COMD. "B" (Brig. Gen. Boudinot)

T F "McGeorge"

HQ 33rd Armd. Regt.

1st Bn., 33rd Armd. Regt. (-3rd Plat., Co A)

2nd Bn., 36th Armd. Inf. Regt.

2nd Bn., Co. D, 23rd Armd. Engr. Bn.

2nd Plat., Co. B, 703rd TD Bn.

3rd Plat., Ren Co., 33rd Armd. Regt.

83rd Armd. FA Bn.

TF "Lovelady"

2nd Bn., 33rd Armd. Regt. (-3rd Plat., Co. B)

3rd Bn., 330th Inf Regt.

1st Plat., Co. D, 23rd Armd Engr. Bn.

1st Plat., Co. B, 703rd TD Bn.

2nd Plat., Ren. Co., 33rd Armd. Regt.

1st Plat., AT Co., 36th Armd. Inf. Regt.

391st Armd. FA Bn.

In addition to the organic elements of the Division, the strength was bolstered by the attachment of the 330th Infantry Regiment (83rd Division) and three artillery battalions: the 83rd Armd., 991st (S.F. 155 Guns), and the 183rd (155 Hows.). Each Combat Command had two battalions of infantry and two battalions of artillery in direct support. If a penetration could be effected quickly it was felt that the forces were insufficient.

The plan for the day of 15 January called for Task Force "Orr" and Task Force "Miller" (Combat Command "A") to take over Baclain and Mont le Ban; Task Force "Kane" to pass through Yeomans and take the high ground south of Brisy; Task Force "Welborn" (formerly Task Force "Walker") to attack through Sterpigny, thence to Retigny, allowing Lovelady to come into Cherain under reduced pressure. However Task Force "Kane" was able to advance only a short distance and Task Force "Welborn" got only into the western edge of Sterpigny. Task Force "Lovelady" attempted to advance on Cherain. Again they ran into mines in a defile. Anti-tank guns caught the vehicles in column, and at 1530 they had no medium tasks left.

Adding fuel to a fire that was already hot enough, an enemy column moved into Sterpigny to reinforce the garrison there whereupon Task Force "Richardson" from Combat Command "A" was attached to Combat Command "B" and committed to the Sterpigny fight, but the situation remained virtually static. Only the western edge of the town was taken.

Task Force "Lovelady"" was relieved in place by Task Force "Bailey" (a Company of medium tanks and a company of Infantry from Combat Command "A" area to refit and reorganize).

When Welborn and Richardson continued the attack on Sterpigny on 18 January another enemy column attempting to enter the town from the east was dispersed by artillery. Antitank and small arms fire started coming into the town from the woods to the northeast which was thought to be clear. The town itself was secured, but direct fire continued to come in.

Task Force "Hogan" was ordered to send a force into Cherain the morning. He was able to get only Infantry into the town because of a blown bridge between Vaux and Cherain. This force met little resistance. Having fought stubbornly for days, the enemy then withdrew. Task Force "Bailey" was sent into the town to relieve Task Force "Hogan's" Infantry and secure the town to allow Hogan to assemble his whole force in Vaux for an attack on Brisy in conjunction with Task Force "Kane."

Task Force "Kane's" attack toward Brisy was stopped cold by heavy fire of all types. When Task Force "Hogan" got their infantry back out of Cherain they attacked toward Brisy to assist Task Force "Kane," but were also stopped after a very short advance.

Task Force "Yeomans" secured Sommerain, forcing the enemy to withdraw south.

By 17 January, Task Force "Hogan" was reduced to twelve medium and ten light tanks. The Infantry Battalion (1st Bn., 330th Inf Regt.) was down to one hundred and twenty-five riflemen. Task Force "Kane" had eleven medium and seventeen light tanks left. The infantry strength, including Battalion Headquarters Company, was three hundred and eleven. Both of these task forces held their positions as did Task Force "Yeomans" in Sommerain. Task Force "Richardson" continued operations over in Sterpigny.

Task Force "Welborn" attacked from Cherain to secure the first hill to the southeast there, a distance of about one thousand yards. On the first attack elements of the force succeeded in reaching the objective, but were forced to withdraw. The second attack carried to the hill and Task Force Welborn held there.

Elements of the 4th Cavalry Group took over the sector from Vaux west to the division boundary on 18 January relieving Yeomans, Kane, and Hogan.

On 18 January, Task Force "Richardson" continued to attack to secure the east edge of the woods east of Sterpigny. When they secured this objective line Combat Command "A" in two task forces. Task Force "Doan" and Task Force "Lovelady," assembled in the vicinity of Sterpigny preparatory to continuing division's attack south. It was planned that Doan should seize Rettigny, Renglez and the high ridge south of these towns while Lovelady screened his advance and protected his left flank along the wooded ridge southeast of Sterpigny. Task Force "Kane" of Combat Command "R" was to attack south from Cherain and take Brisy and the dominating hill to the south thereof, Richardson secured his objective and the scheduled attack moved rapidly against very light resistance. Both objectives were taken on the afternoon of 19 January. The next day the division started moving northwest to rest areas centering around Barvaux and Durbuy.

The portion of the German salient west of Houffalize had been liqui-
dated, but the enemy had conducted an efficient withdrawal. The effort had
cost him heavily but he had succeeded in withdrawing a very large part of his
forces not expanded in the fifteen days of bold offensive fighting in December
and the stubborn rear-guard actions of 3-16 January. In rare cases was he
forced to give ground where the loss would seriously endanger the extrica-
tion of his carefully-hoarded armor without inflicting severe losses on the
attacking force.

During a rest period there is plenty of work to do. The "rest" means that
you are not in contact with the enemy. New reinforcements have to be fit-
ted into their places and given additional training. New equipment has to be
tested, and there is maintenance work in whatever quantity time permits. It
is a time of rest, though. The tension of battle is gone. There is time for a few
movies and recreational convoys to nearby cities, and there is time to count
the score.

The decisive fighting in the Ardennes salient lasted from 16 December
1944 to 16 January 1945.

For this period there are two sets of concrete figures that can be juggled
at will to propagandize either our cause of the German. They are the losses of
men and material on each side. A third item for speculation: "what did Von
Rundstedt's gamble gain or lose?" does not concern us directly in this outline.

Taken separately, loss figures may be used to prove almost anything.
Together they serve only to emphasize that it was a hard fight. Here they are.

During the period 16 December to 16 January, the 3rd Armored Division
suffered 1,473 battle casualties. Of this number 21 officers and 166 enlisted
men were killed in action. The rest were wounded or missing.

Battle losses in vehicles were as follows:

Medium Tanks: 125
Light Tanks: 38
Artillery Pieces: 6
Other Vehicles: 158

A carefully prepared day to day estimate of losses inflicted on the enemy for this period totals up to:

1,705 estimated killed

545 estimated wounded

2,510 Prisoners (actual count)

The estimated vehicular casualties inflicted, counting only those known to have been destroyed, are:

Tanks: 98 (31 of them Mk Vs)

SP Guns: 20

Motor Transport: 76

AT or AA Guns: 23

Artillery Pieces: 8

AFTER THE BULGE

Oda C. Miller

3rd Armored Division, 32nd Armored Infantry Regiment,

2nd Battalion, Co E

Our crew consisted of Tank Commander Sgt. Raymond Juilfs, Driver Cpl. Joe Caserta, Assistant Driver Pvt. Joe Mazza, Loader PFC. Kenneth Banaka, and myself.

On the morning of 26th Feb. 1945, Units of the 3rd Armored Division were located on the edge of a small town preparing to attack across an open field to the town of Blatzheim, Germany. This area of Germany was called the Cologne Plains, which was supposed to be excellent tank combat country. But we were wrong, as the Germans had their anti-tank guns dug in and covered with camouflage nets which completely concealed them. Just a few hundred yards into the field was a series of slit trenches which needed to be cleared out before we started our attack. Three light M-5 tanks from "B" Company were sent out to accomplish this. All three were instantly knocked out causing a number of casualties. The main attack was to begin as soon as a group of farm buildings on our left were taken by "F" Company.

Thinking this had been accomplished, we were given the order to move out in a line formation. Just as soon as we moved out into the field, we were told to return as the farm had not been taken and there were a number of anti-tank weapons located there. Shortly thereafter we were again given the order to move out. Of course, because of our false start, the Germans knew exactly where we were and we immediately lost a number of tanks including the one that I had transferred from following the Battle of the Bulge.

Tanks from "F" Company joined with "E" Company and we continued our attack. We were about halfway across the field when, in all the confusion of battle, our tank suddenly dropped off into a large bomb crater. By the time I could get all the equipment that had fallen on me from the sponson and had turned off the main electrical switches, the rest of the crew had bailed out. When I got out of the tank I found out why the rest of the crew had bailed out; there was no way that the tank could get out of that hole without the help of a T-2 from Maintenance. When I crawled out of the crater I found the rest of the crew lying on the ground behind a pile of potatoes covered with straw. I immediately laid down next to our tank commander. We had not been there long when an artillery shell landed just a short distance from us in the middle of a group of "F" Company tankers who had also lost their tank. I watched as one tanker jumped up and started to run but suddenly fell to his knees and looked around at us. He had no face, and I am sure he was dead along with the rest of his crew.

I then told our crew that we should move away from this area and walk back to the town we had left from that morning. I nudged Juilfs, who didn't move, and I discovered that he had been hit in the head by a large piece of shrapnel and was dead. Joe Caserta was a little dazed since a piece of shrapnel had hit his crash helmet and made a hole but had just given him a bump on the head. He also had a small wound in his shoulder. With the rest of the crew we made it back to the starting point. My right ankle had been bothering me, but I couldn't see any problem until I finally peeled down my overshoe and saw the hole in the overshoe and my boot and the blood in my boot. A small piece of shrapnel had penetrated into my ankle joint. Joe Caserta and I were taken back to the medics located in Stolberg. The doctor probed for the shrapnel but could not get it, so he bandaged my ankle. Joe and I went back to the Company, and neither of us lost any battle time from our wounds.

After the war ended the Company was located in the small town of Munster by Dieberg. I was having trouble with my ankle, so I went to the 45th Med. Bn. They took x-rays and sent me to the hospital in Frankfurt where the shrapnel was removed. I spent about 10 days in the hospital and then returned to my Company.

If I may backtrack to how, in a very convoluted way, I eventually joined the 3rd Armored Division. I turned 18 on Nov. 9, 1942, and graduated from Northeast High School in Kansas City mid-term in Jan., 1943, then went into the Army in Feb., 1943. I took basic training with the newly formed 20th Armored Division at Camp Campbell, KY. After basic the Division down-sized from the old Square Division to Tank Battalions. That caused a lot of excess men who were formed into a provisional battalion, myself included. We were then sent out as replacements. I ended up being sent to a replacement pool in England in Feb 1944.

In May a group of us were detached to the 48th Ordnance Battalion and we spent our time water-proofing M-5 Light Tanks in preparation to take to Normandy as replacement tanks.

Shortly after "D-Day" we moved the tanks to Southhampton and loaded them on an LST. We landed on the beach with a one-man crew per tank about 11 PM on June 15th. I then spent the next couple of weeks driving a 2 1/2- ton, 6x6 truck picking up ordnance supplies from Omaha and Utah beaches. A replacement pool was finally set up in Normandy and we were recalled. Shortly thereafter I was sent to "E" Co, 32nd AR, 3rd Armored Division as one of their first replacements near St. Jean de Daye. (The 3rd AD had just seen their first combat and needed replacements.) I saw combat with three different crews during the five campaigns from Normandy to Dessau,

Germany, on the Elbe River. My crews lost two tank commanders, killed in action, on the way.

INSIDE A TANK

Oda C. Miller
3rd Armored Division, 32nd Armored Infantry Regiment,
2nd Battalion, Co E

My name is Oda C. "Chuck" Miller. I was a corporal Tank Gunner on an M-4 Sherman tank in E Company, 32nd Armored Regiment, of the 3rd Armored Division during WWII. My Tank Commander was Sgt. Bill Hey, Driver T-5 Roy Fahrni, Assistant Driver PFC Peter White and Loader Pvt. Homer Gordon.

Our unit was located in the small town of Buchbach, Germany, a suburb of Stolberg, preparing for future action in the Roer Valley when the German Army started its counter attack in the Ardennes Forest, better known as the Battle of the Bulge, in Belgium. Units of the 3rd Armored Division were pulled back into Belgium to help counter the German offense.

One morning in early January 1945 we were in a small town named De Staart, Belgium. We moved out in line formation over an open field toward the town of Grand Sart.

Our first bad experience was when we ran over a land mine. The explosion really rocked the tank and filled it with black smoke. We were lucky however and the only damage was a couple of flattened bogie wheels and the rubber tread blown off of a few track blocks.

We continued on and I was firing the 75mm gun at a German tank next to a barn. I had fired one round of armor piercing when all of a sudden we received a direct hit to the turret. The shell hit the cupolo ring and a flash of fire hit in my periscope. The shell blew the tank commander's hatch open, took part of his head off and then proceeded to blow off the anti-aircraft mount and gun. Bill Hey was killed instantly and he fell down on my back covering me with blood.

By the time I could get Bill off of my back the assistant driver had bailed out and the loader had crawled through the turret and out the assistant driver's hatch. All I could think about was getting out of the tank since when they hit you once they generally keep hitting you till the tank catches fire, instead of checking to see where the gun tube was located.

When I finally got Bill off my back and crawled out of the turret, I rolled over the duffel bag rack expecting to land on the back of the tank but ended up falling all the way to the ground. (The deep snow cushioned my fall.) I had mistakenly left the gun slightly to the left over the driver's hatch. When I hit the ground, I crawled to the back of the tank since we were receiving machine gun fire.

When I got back to the tank, the driver started backing the tank since he could not get his hatch open because of the gun tube. I had left the controls in power traverse and as the tank backed up the gun traversed to the left and he was able to open the hatch and get out. We made our way to a small creek bed and to the Town of Sart. Everyone thought I had been hit since I was covered with my tank commander's blood.

The next day Graves Registration people removed Bill Hey's body and we took the tank back to battalion maintenance for repairs. We then removed the good shells and cleaned the inside of the turret. Bill's brains were on my seat and blood covered everything including the radio. It was a very gruesome job.

THINGS I DID TO STAY ALIVE WHILE I WAS A POW

George F. Mills
28th Infantry Division, 109th Infantry Regiment, Company E

We had been in combat for seven months when I was taken Prisoner of War on December 18, 1944, approximately 1900 o'clock. The Germans started marching us east. About seven days from the day we were captured, we were in a small village where there was a German army hospital with a big red cross on top of it. At this time we still had no food. About noon we looked up and there were about 2500 B-24s dropping bombs on us and on this village.

The Germans wanted us to help look through the bombed houses for German citizens. We went looking, but we were looking for food or anything to eat. One house was bombed bad, on fire and it had a basement. Andy McLaughlin was with me. He and I went down in the basement of the house that was on fire, and we found potatoes. The fire had half cooked them, and we burned our mouths eating the hot potatoes.

I didn't keep up with the days of the month, but some days later we reached Stagliger IV B, where we were fingerprinted and given German P.O.W. tags. I had a gold ring that one of my sisters had given me, worth about $150 in 1943. There I met a P.O.W. from Denmark and traded him the ring for a loaf of bread. Andy and I ate the loaf of bread in a hurry.

We walked for five months. Two nights we were in Stagliger IV B, two nights we were in Stagliger VIII A on the Polish border. Some nights the guards would get tired, and would put us in barns in small villages. Sometimes we could steal sugar beets or a rutabaga, or barley if you could beat the horses to it. One night they put us in an old barn. At two or three o'clock in the morning I could hear a cow in the next stall. I worked until I could get one of the boards loose, then I got to the cow and I tried to milk her, but I couldn't get any milk. Andy's father ran a dairy in Kansas, so I went back and got Andy. I would hold my hands in my helmet to keep it from making a noise, and I milked that old cow all night and we'd drink it as fast as we could get a little in the helmet. When the old farmer came out with this bucket the next morning, he sat down on the stool and started to milk. Soon he was cursing the old cow because she would not give milk.

To survive as a P.O.W. you must be in good shape when you are captured, and you must have a good buddy, and you must take a lot of chances. Andrew McLaughlin and I had an agreement if anything happened to me, when he got home he would go to my mother and tell her what had happened to me, and I would do the same for his mother. We also had an agreement with each other about any food we got, how small we would divide it with each other, and we did that.

One night we were put in a brickyard building and I was really sick. They had fired the brick the day before, and the kiln was still hot. That night Andy put me up in the chimney of the kiln. The next morning I was all right. When you are a P.O.W. you have lice on you at all times. When you lay down and try to get warm, they start running. I had a vest sweater. Every time I could, I would take off all my clothes and pick off the lice and put the clothes back on. By the time I would get them all back on, the lice would start running around on me again. I traded the sweater to a German woman for a small bucket of potatoes.

One night we were put in a large barn with hay in the loft. About 2230 one night they moved a wagon in and had a small lantern by the wagon. I told Andy I could smell food in that wagon and I was going down to see. It was the guards' food for seven days. I ate some bread and sausage, and told Andy to go down and eat some, but be sure not to tell anyone else. When you are that hungry you can smell food for blocks. Before the night was gone the men in the hay loft had eaten all the food in that wagon.

When we got to Stagliger VIII A on the Polish border, we were there for two nights. There was a British P.O.W. who came down and wanted to know if anyone had any American money, that he had cigarettes for five dollars a pack. I didn't have any money because I had paid forty-seven dollars for one Camel cigarette, but I had some one hundred dollar money orders. He said he would go see. He came back and said he would take one money order for 20 packs of cigarettes, so I signed it the wrong way so they would have trouble getting it cashed. Then with the cigarettes Andy and I could trade for food. The first thing I did was trade one pack for one can of Eagle Brand milk. Andy and I drank that in a hurry.

The Germans had started the Americans back west because Russian artillery was coming. We had traveled some days and they put us in a big barn loft. The next morning about 0800 I heard a tank coming. When I looked it was a half-track and a command car behind it. When it got close to us the road made a bend and you could see the big white star on the side. By the time they reached us we had taken the German guards as P.O.W.s. The men were from the second armored. They gave us all the food they had, but it wasn't enough for some two hundred and more men, so we killed one of the farmer's calves. They had a pot in the bam yard, and potatoes in the barn, so we cooked the calf and potatoes until everyone had something to eat. We were then trucked back to an air field where there were about two thousand men. They were flying the British back to England and trucking the Americans to LaHarve, France.

Late in the afternoon I looked up on the hill and I could see a tent. I told Andy that they were feeding us up there. I asked them if Andy and I could have something to eat and they told us we could. When they would put food on the tray we would keep standing there for them to put more on. When we got to the end, the tray was headed up with food. Then all the help at the kitchen stood around us to see if we could eat that much. We did. I asked them if we could come back the next morning. They told us we could if we didn't bring the two thousand with us. From there we were trucked back to LaHavre, France to be de-liced and fed, and we got a shower. From there we took the boat to America. These are some of the things that you have to do and chances you take to survive being a P.O.W.

3RD ARMORED DIVISION MEMORIES

Marvin H. Mischnick
3rd Armored Division, Headquarters

I was a member of the 3rd Armored "Spearhead" Division. The division got its nickname because it was the spearhead of the Allied Armies across the European Continent. The Division under the command of Major General Maurice Rose, who was killed in action in Paderborn, Germany, while leading his men. The division that spearheaded all the way from Villers Fossard and St. Lo in France in June of 1944 to Dessau and the Elbe River in Germany. The division that closed the Falaise Gap in France and the Ruhr Pocket in Germany. (It was not any of General Patton's divisions or any part of his Third

Army, as has been mistakenly reported by some historians.)

The 3rd Armored Division was the first armored division to enter Belgium, the first to breach the Siegfried Line, and the first to capture a German town (Roetgen). The Spearhead Division was the pride of the 7th Corps Commander Lt. Gen. Joseph L. "Lightning Joe" Collins, and the U.S. First Army, at first under the command of Lt. Gen. Omar N. Bradley, and later under Lt. Gen. Courtney H. Hodges. I mention this because nobody seems to know that it was the U.S. First Army that spearheaded across Europe. Nobody seems to ever have heard the names of Maurice Rose, or Courtney H. Hodges. Everybody seems to think Gen. George Patton and the Third Army won the war. It's time that people knew about a heroic and creditable 3rd Armored Division, and about Gen. Maurice Rose. I recommend reading Andy Rooney's book titled *My War*.

I was the division photographer of the division headquarters, Forward Eschelon, during our participation in the Battle of the Bulge, and also during the whole liberation of the European Continent. My work was published in two editions of the books titled *Spearhead in the West*, which is the history of the 3rd Armored Division. One edition was printed in Germany in 1946 during our occupation there just after the war ended. The other edition was an up-to-date model of 1992, and also in the book *Death Traps*, by Belton Y. Cooper.

Going from the serious now to the lighter side. I'll tell you something a little humorous as well as newsworthy and a personal memory of the Bulge. Our division had a CP (Command Post) bivouac at the insane asylum at Lierneux, Belgium in January, 1945. In refreshing my memory of an incident there, I remember walking through a long dark and dank tunnel on the way to our kitchen truck to get chow. And after chow, we had to walk back through the tunnel. All through the tunnel were individual mental patients scattered about who looked at us as if we were strange creatures from the planet Mars. It gave us the feeling that they were in great fear of us, and perhaps suspecting that we would torture them. Our bivouac at the asylum at Lierneux was also the place were Cpl. George Stettinfeld and I had mixed a batch of home-made ice cream that we made with snow in George's GI helmet. Lemon flavored ice cream with the synthetic lemon powder (which we called "sympathetic" lemon powder) from our K rations. After we ate it, George remembered that he had previously washed his feet in that very same helmet.

I also remember a couple of other incidents in Hebronval, Belgium. When our CP bivouacked there, it was very cold. It must have been 30 degrees below zero. I had my fingers frost-bitten while taking pictures, because I couldn't operate the cameras with gloves on. (Now, to this day, whenever the temperature gets below 60 degrees, my fingers get numb.) I also had to carry the cameras underneath my overcoat and combat jacket to keep the camera shutters from freezing. There were not too many buildings around where we could sleep without freezing to death. I found one outbuilding. It was a small wooden barn about 10 feet square and about 15 feet high. Actually, it was a cow shed. In this very small cow shed was a stall with a bull in it. The bull was not very happy either, with a stranger coming in there. So I didn't stay in there too long. I decided to walk around the outside of the shed to look for any other possible place to sleep for the night. When I got to the side of the cow shed, I saw a closed wooden door up about 10 feet from the ground. After piling up a few things to stand on to reach that door, I opened that wooden door to have a look inside. It was the storage room for hay for the bull in the stall below. I climbed in there and bedded down for the night. It happened to be directly above the unpleasant bull. I didn't think the bull got too much sleep that night, because he knew I was still present right above him, and it made him nervous. Of course, I was a little nervous too with him being about two feet below me. I also kept worrying about how many rats or mice would be crawling over me in that hay pile. But one good thing came from that cold, cold night. The heat from the bull manure (proper civilian name for it) kept rising up to where I was sleeping and kept me as warm as toast, while it was 30 below zero outside. And that's no bull.

DECEMBER 24, 1944

John Mistler
75th Infantry Division, Headquarters

At that time I was a 1st Lt. in the 75th Infantry Division, Division Headquarters Company. I was the Division Traffic Control Officer and in charge of all vehicles for transportation at the Division Headquarters level. I was told to report to 75th Division Headquarters to General Mickel, Assistant Division Commander. When I reported he told me a battalion of the 106th Infantry Division has been entrapped by the Germans. They are completely encircled. One of our Division Regiments has been ordered to drive a wedge through the German unit so we can rescue that trapped battalion.

"I want you to prepare 20 trucks to go in there tonight and bring those men out. You pick an officer to lead those trucks in. There will be no headlights, no cat eyes, and our MP's will have a man or men at every road junction or intersection to direct the convoy. Have that officer report here at Division Headquarters at 6:00 pm for his instructions. You may go now. Have that officer here at 6:00 pm."

I responded, "Yes Sir. By the way can you tell me what regiment that battalion belongs to?" As I remember he said it was the 106th Infantry Division Regiment 426. (I may not be accurate on this).

I went to my unit and I told Staff Sgt. Elmer Rouse to prepare 20 trucks and my jeep for the in-the-dark convoy. I asked him to put one case of C-Rations and a case of ammo in each vehicle. I told him I would not need a driver for my vehicle. Sgt. Rouse told me he would have them ready. I knew he would and he picked the best drivers and trucks we had. A few minutes before 6:00 pm I reported to Division Headquarters for the briefing. General Mickel asked me, "Where is the officer who will lead this convoy?" I told him I was going to take the convoy as that is my brother-in-law's unit and I have more reason to go.

He said, "You cannot go," and he left the room.

The Division Chief of Staff, Colonel Herbert Powell said, "What are you going to do now?" He told me to pick someone. I said "I did; I picked me. My brother-in-law is in that unit. The General will come back and approve my decision."

He came in soon and said "Good Luck Lt.," and he touched me on the shoulder. After the briefing I left with the convoy about 6:30 pm.

As we proceeded, the Military Police had done a good job of placing the men at junctions and intersections. We arrived in the battalion area about 8:00 pm. It was a very desolate and depressing atmosphere with too much snow and no lights. When I had all the men on the trucks, I walked to the last truck and asked if there was a John Burke on this truck. One man responded and said Johnny had been captured three days ago. I asked if he was injured. The man said, "No he was not injured but he was wet, cold, out of ammo and very hungry as we all are." I thanked him. I went to the next truck and asked and someone said "I never heard of him." I went to the next truck and was told Johnny was not injured but had been captured. I thanked them and said, "We'll be out of here soon."

As I was walking to the head of the truck column where my jeep was, a man said "Halt, what's the password?" and he stuck his rifle in my stomach very hard.

I responded, "Soldier, you hit me so hard in my stomach I forgot the password."

He said, "I don't want any conversation, I want the password."

I said, "Take me to your supervisor." He told me to walk straight and I could feel his rifle between my shoulders. We went to a small tent. There was a captain and a First Lieutenant there. The guard told them this man doesn't know the password. The captain was a dental captain. He asked, "Why don't you know the password?" I explained what happened and also told him I was in charge of this convoy and we are ready to leave.

The captain asked if I had any dental work done in the army. I told him yes, a dental bridge. He asked me to hand it to him. He looked at it and asked my serial number. I gave him the number and he agreed it matched the number in my bridge. He said, "The password is ____. If you are ready to leave we will follow you out of here."

I told the security guard, "You did a good job but you sure startled me. You are a good soldier."

I moved the convoy out of that area (no headlights) and took the road I was directed to. I came to an intersection and took the road I was directed to. About a mile farther and at a fork in the road a guard appeared. He was very nervous and told me to go that way. Then he told me it sure was lonesome here. As I started on the road, I thought the road was very narrow and as I proceeded it became more so. I decided this road doesn't go anywhere. I stopped and told the driver behind me to pass the word back I was going to turn around. I cut wire on a fence and the field looked flat but heavy with snow. I planned to make a circle and then return on that road. As I progressed all seemed okay. The first two trucks behind me were near me and as I watched the third truck dropped about three feet in the front.

I found we were driving over a pond. We used two trucks to pull that truck out while I was finding the perimeter of the pond and made a new track for them to follow. We returned on the narrow road to the junction. The guard said "I'm sorry I directed you on the wrong road. I've been out here alone for so long, I'm very nervous." We proceeded on the other road and went to a small village where the 75th Division had established a temporary mess hall and medical facility.

Someone met me and told me to unload the troops and have them stand by the trucks. I did that and men were leaning on the trucks. One of the trucks began to slide sideways on the frozen packed snow and one wheel went over a retaining wall about four feet. I had the men hook two trucks on it and pull it back on the road. I told the men not to lean against any of the trucks. About that time a Major said "I'll take charge of the men now. You may leave." We left and started back to our unit, about an hour's drive with the roads as they were and no lights.

We were driving on a ridge and I saw a buzz bomb coming toward us. I could see the flame at the exhaust. It looked like it was coming right at us. I quickly pulled into a ditch and the trucks did the same. The bomb passed over us about 20 feet and then the motor stopped. As it started to drop it cleared the ridge and went into the valley below where there were some Allied Supply

Depots. We could hear it explode and see the flash.

I told the drivers behind me to pass the word back they could turn on the cat eyes on every other vehicle and we were going to our unit. When we arrived there I thanked the men for a good job. It was about 2:00 am. I went to Division Headquarters to make my report. A few days later General Mickel found me and said, "You tell your men thank you. They did a good job."

106TH INFANTRY DIVISION, 591ST FIELD ARTILLERY BATTALION, BATTERY C

Eugene Morell
106th Infantry Division, 591st Field Artillery Battalion, Battery C

Having relieved the 2nd Division near St. Vith, Belgium on December 10, 1944, we spent several days firing our 105mm howitzers at unseen enemy without receiving any return fire. This had been a rest area for the 2nd Division and was to be an indoctrination to combat to the green troops of the 106th Infantry Division.

Most of us were young men. I had just turned 19 in October. We were having a good time in our cozy little shacks which had been built by the 2nd Division men. Each shack had four bunks and a wood stove and each howitzer was just outside the shack entrance. Two five-man crews operated the howitzer. One crew for days and the other for nights. There were four howitzers all in line and situated behind a sloping hill just on the edge of the Village of Steffeshausen, Belgium. We found out later that our division should have been covering a five-mile front but instead we were spread out over a 27-mile front, this being a supposed rest area.

Just before dawn on December 16, we were called out for a fire mission. The five of us ran out to the gun just in time to be greeted by incoming artillery fire. We each started performing our duties in firing back at the unseen enemy. Of course we had to urge to find cover but kept following the orders for aiming and loading for what seemed like an eternity. We stayed at Steffeshausen until the evening of December 17 and were firing the guns continuously, not knowing that this was the start of the largest battle of World War II and that we were right in the middle of it. We had no idea what was happening to the other two regiments of the 106th Division. My battalion, the 591st Field Artillery, was in support of the 424th Infantry Regiment.

Just at dusk on December 17, we learned that the enemy was in the process of surrounding us and that we had to move out in order to avoid being captured. My Battery C stayed and fired covering fire for Batteries A and B while they withdrew along a secondary road which was the only road not in possession of the enemy and only 300 yards from German infantry. Number two gun was stuck in the frozen ground and although the crew worked hard to get it free, we had to leave it and take our turn along the secondary road after dark in convoy trucks towing howitzers.

We reunited with A and B Batteries at Burg Reuland, proceeding to Grufflingen, digging the howitzers in and continued firing. We were constantly under enemy artillery fire all day at Grufflingen. We were losing ground and on December 21st, we moved to Braunlauf during the night. This same night the enemy broke through at St. Vith, threatening our flank. We moved to Commastem at daybreak the next day and our C Battery was again left to cover withdrawal of the infantry. We fired a lot of rounds and they withdrew safely, partly because of the fog. On December 22 we were told that we were surrounded and in danger of being captured and also learned that two of our regiments had been captured after running out of ammo and supplies and trapped in the woods, having lost contact with each other and with division. Each regiment commander had decided to surrender to save lives and without knowing the other regiment was doing the same. This left the 424th Regiment with our 591st Artillery Battalion still fighting but low on ammo and equipment. Our guns were positioned at the edge of the woods and aiming across a clearing. Because of the possibility of being captured we were ordered to deposit all of our souvenirs of German origin into a hole that was dug especially for this reason and to be buried.

We ended the day low on ammo and with C rations again—mostly beans— for supper. We joked about not having to worry about being low on ammo after eating beans for the last few days. If our guns ran out we could shoot back at the enemy but were hoping it wouldn't come to that. We kept the guns silent that night but were ordered to use up all the ammo in a great barrage the next morning. Then we hooked our guns to the trucks and rode to the main road which was lined on both sides with disabled tanks and vehicles still smoking from the battle that had just taken place. There were dead soldiers from both sides along the road and as we stopped by a log building, we dismounted and walked over to a tarpaulin lying on the ground and it was covered with bodies of paratroopers from the 82nd Airborne Division. It was a touching scene as they lay there side-by-side in two neat rows—all young men.

Up until then we had seen a lot of dead men from both sides and were becoming accustomed to the sight. Somehow the sight of these men lying there together, who had lost their lives while helping to clear this road for our escape, remained with us as we crossed the Salm River at Vielsalm on our way to Ville for regrouping.

CHRISTMAS 1944 - BELGIUM

Eugene Morell
106th Infantry Division, 591st Field Artillery Battalion, Battery C

We had not shaved, bathed or even washed our hands since December 16th. We had been eating and sleeping in dirty holes in the ground and had not had time nor the urge to change.

Just at dawn on December 23rd, we opened fire at a road not far away. Our fire was being directed by a forward observer; consequently, we couldn't see our targets. We used up all our shells by firing as fast as possible, and then hooked the big guns behind the trucks. Our whole gun crew was riding on the back of the truck and was told to stick with the truck as long as it kept moving. But if the truck or its driver was disabled then each man would be on his own to escape any way possible.

We stayed with the trucks and the whole convoy emerged on the main road. At this point we could see what we had been shooting at and the damage we had done—with the help of our tanks and also the 82nd Division paratroopers. We saw disabled tanks on both sides of the road, mostly German tanks with dead German soldiers, lying along the road and several tanks had dead Germans on top of them, their clothing still smoking. There were dead American soldiers scattered all along and we stopped among this carnage by a log building to relieve ourselves.

I personally walked among the dead of the 82nd Division, who had already been gathered up and placed side-by-side on a canvas along the side of the road. There were two rows of them having been placed with their feet toward each other. There were eleven men in each row, all lying on their backs, most of them with their eyes still open.

By now we were becoming accustomed to seeing dead soldiers, but as I stood by 22 of them in one place, my thoughts were that there would be sadness in 22 families back home when they were notified of the death of their loved ones. I wished that I could talk to the family of each one and tell them what little I knew about his death and that they had died helping to clear this road which we were using to escape capture.

December 23rd: We loaded into the trucks and passed through Belgian towns and villages that had been devastated by fire from both sides. We had not been told that we were moving back to regroup, having lost so many men in such a short time.

We camped in an open field just outside Ville, Belgium. Our clothing included socks and underwear. Our feet were always cold. At Ville we camped in an open field near a large horse barn. The village was just down the road from us. We built a fire and melted snow in our helmets and stood by the fire, pulled up our shirts and washed our upper body, put clean T-shirts and shirts on, then lowered our pants, washed down as far as possible, changed our boxer shorts and pants.

We watched a German and American plane shooting at each other just above us and they disappeared from our sight. Some of us went into the horse barn and wrote our first letter since the start of the battle. I wrote home telling them that I was safe and not to worry about me.

We had come here to get replacements for the men that we had lost and to clean our guns and get ammo and so on. That night we slept in a warn barn loft and it was a comfortable feeling hearing the horses munching on hay and we expected to be there for Christmas Eve and away from the fighting.

We spent Christmas Eve fooling around and wondered what was going on in the fighting which was only a few miles away, for we could hear the shooting. Just before dark we were ordered to mount up and get ready to leave. There had been a breakthrough near Fays, Belgium, and our artillery support was needed.

It was Christmas Eve and we were on our way back to combat. It was a dark, cold night and there was a feeling of gloom as twelve of us rode on the back of a canvas covered truck with everything we owned riding with us. We wore overcoats and were wedged together so that our bodies were not freezing, but our feet were so cold that it was miserable.

Someone asked me to play a Christmas song. My harmonica and I started to play "Silent Night" and I could sense that everyone was thinking of home and their families, probably gathered round the Christmas tree. I was thinking of home also as I played and realized it was a sad song, so I started playing "Jingle Bells" and soon we were all singing as we watched our howitzer trail along behind us.

There is hardly ever a time that the army tells you where you are headed, and as usual we rode through the darkness until the trucks stopped and we had to jump down from the trucks and land on our cold feet. It wasn't long until we were warmed up by digging the big gun in and then our four guns started shooting at the unseen enemy. Our fire was directed by our forward observer who was in front of us and saw the targets and where our shells were landing. We spent the night firing the guns and trying to get warm and when daylight came we could see that we were on a hill and were shooting over a valley at another hill.

There was a battle going on out of our sight and we were doing a lot of shooting and no one was shooting at us. There was a Belgian farm house in the valley before us and we were shooting directly over the house and barn. There was smoke coming out of the chimney and chickens running around in the snowy yard.

It was Christmas Day and we were scheduled for another can of beans for Christmas dinner. Pvt. Katz, PFC Bermudez, and I stood looking at those chickens and decided to have chicken for Christmas dinner instead of beans. When the second shift came on to relieve us at the gun, we walked through the deep snow down the hill and approached the house. We couldn't be positively sure that there weren't Germans inside, so we took cover behind trees in the front yard and hollered, "Hello." The door opened a small crack and a man's voice was saying something in French. Katz stepped out from behind the tree and using sign language gestured that we wanted a chicken. He made a money sign with his fingers meaning that we would pay. The man waved his arm as if to say go ahead and no pay was expected, so we caught two old hens and started back up the hill. We guessed that the Belgian man had stayed to take care of their animals while the war was going all around over their house.

We took the chickens back to our gun position and wrung their necks and cleaned them and built a fire and stuck a stick through them and took turns holding them over a fire, all the time kidding the guys in the other gun sections about us having chicken for dinner and they were having beans.

We decided that the chicken was cooked enough and each of us used our trench knife to cut off a piece. It was burned on the outside and raw on the inside and not fit to eat but we were bragging how good it was and how smart we were to be having chicken instead of beans. Katz said, "Let's save some for supper" and took it to the truck and later on, when no one was looking, threw it away.

We continued firing all day and it let up sometime along toward evening. Chow time came and we walked back behind our position to the chow truck to get our can of beans and much to our surprise we were told to bring our mess kits. As we approached the chow truck we could smell turkey. The cooks were putting turkey and dressing in each mess kit as we took our turn at the tail gate.

We three chicken eaters were not hungry because of the raw chicken. Bermudez, who had a weak stomach, had been complaining about being a little sick to his stomach, but we took our turn and started to eat while standing around the chow truck with everyone else. We were to find out later that our Christmas dinner had been delivered by plane and dropped by parachute.

KATZ ON A MISSION

Eugene Morell
106th Infantry Division, 591st Field Artillery Battalion, Battery C

There were times when we would move from one place to another. There would be a whole convoy of trucks pulling our big guns, which came bouncing along behind four of the trucks which were loaded with the ten-man gun crew of each truck. Each truck had a row of benches in the back down each side for seating the gun crew. The back of the truck was covered with canvas for protection from the rain and the rear of the truck was wide open at the tailgate so that the crew could look at the countryside and at the truck following behind. There were jeeps and other vehicles in the convoy.

If it were to be a long trip the whole convoy would halt every so often for a nature break. The stops were usually made where there were no houses and the men would stand behind the trucks to relieve themselves. However, once in a while the problem would be a stomach ache for which the procedure would be for the unlucky fellow to take a shovel from a truck and a wad of toilet paper and hurry to the nearest cover, preferably the woods. After making sure that he could not be seen from the road he would use the shovel to dig a shallow hole in the ground, then squat over the hole and do what he came there for. Then he would use the shovel to cover the mess he had made, then bring the shovel back to the truck and join the rest of us in the truck. Nothing was said about it because we were used to the procedure and it usually worked out well except for one guy in our truck. His name was Katz; he was a jovial, easy-going guy who was built straight up and down with no athletic ability.

One day the whole convoy stopped and Katz grabbed the shovel and a wad of toilet paper and started across an open field toward small woods, with the shovel on one shoulder. He hadn't said anything and none of us paid any attention until the guy at the back of the truck drew our attention and said that Katz was in a mighty big hurry. We laughed and one said that Katz was hurrying because he was afraid that we would run off and leave him and someone said it was because he was afraid that it was because he was about to mess his britches. We were watching as he disappeared behind a bush but we could see his head until he sat down. For some reason the trucks started their engines earlier than usual and someone hollered, "Hey, How About Katz?" Someone said, "Here he comes." We all gathered at the back of the truck because we were sure that he hadn't been given enough time and here he comes from behind the bush with the shovel in one hand and holding his pants up with the other. He was trying to hurry but the shovel and trying to hold his pants up was holding him back, but he did reach the side of the road as the convoy started moving.

He entered the road just behind our truck still carrying the shovel in one hand and holding his pants up with the other. Meanwhile we were cheering for him and laughing, also, as he was losing ground and our truck was pulling away from him. Finally, he waved a short good-bye and stepped aside, for the next truck in line stopped for him.

As we watched he disappeared behind the truck getting ready to get aboard and suddenly the shovel went flying through the air and into the ditch.

The next time we stopped, Katz took his place in our truck amid a lot of joking and questions directed at him, while he kept a wide grin on his face as he went along amiably with the fun. Someone asked, "Did you finish your business? And, did you cover it up? And, did you use the toilet paper?" In response, Katz said, "No?" and jokingly tried to move over and sit on his lap. Someone asked, "Why did you throw the shovel away after carrying it all the way to the road?" Katz answered that he never realized he was carrying it until he was trying to find a place for it on the truck. Katz was a good guy and well-liked by all of us.

This is a true story that I thought was worth writing about.

BUTGENBACH, BELGIUM

Rocco J. Moretto
1st Infantry Division, 26th Infantry Regiment, C Company

On approximately December 10th we were relieved and it was rumored that the First Division would be returning to England for a much needed rest. By then we had been in combat for 6 months starting with the Normandy Invasion on June 6th. Our ranks depleted and badly in need of all sorts of equipment, the rumor sounded good. We were pulled back to the Leige-Verviers area.

After less than a week the Germans had broken through the U.S. defenses and my unit was immediately alerted and rushed to the breakthrough area.

"C" Company was attached to the 2nd Battalion of the 26th Infantry Regiment for the move. We traveled both on foot and by truck in a shuttle type move and our target was Butgenbach. On our way we encountered many American troops who had been overrun, were disorganized and in full retreat.

Some of the troops were on foot and some of the men related was going on. The one account which has always stuck in my mind was that tiger tanks were being dropped by parachute in the breakthrough area. On the way we had also been advised by S-2 the Germans had dropped paratroopers dressed in American uniforms who spoke perfect English. This and other stories we heard made us wonder what we were headed for.

We arrived in Butgenbach late at night on December 16th and immediately started to set up a defense.

The area had been occupied by an American field hospital which had very recently evacuated the area. They had departed in an awful hurry, leaving behind a few tents, partially eaten food and all sorts of clothing including women's unmentionables.

Outposts were set up along "C" Company's front with the main line of resistance approximately 75 yards behind the outposts.

At the break of dawn the following morning all hell broke loose. As far as your eye could see German tanks were coming over the rise firing their machine guns as they came.

German infantry followed the tanks on foot. After a short time the tanks overran our outposts. They ran right over the foxholes in some cases and in other instances the enemy tank personnel motioned for the men to surrender.

Everyone as far as I could judge began to withdraw piecemeal. I and some of the others finally sought refuge in the cellar of an extremely large building.

Col. Daniels, Commander of the 2nd Battalion, and his headquarters personnel were the occupants of this building.

Two tanks soon penetrated to within 20 yards of the building and by this time there appeared to be over a hundred soldiers in that cellar. At one point a rifle went off and someone yelled out, "They're throwing hand grenades down the cellar," and boy did that start a scramble.

Col. Daniels was personally directing artillery fire over the radio. He was in communication with all sorts of artillery units, including our own 33rd Field and division's 5th Field with their 155s. He even was asking for corps, artillery and at one point he yelled over the radio, "Get me all the damned artillery you can get".

There is no doubt in my mind that Col. Daniels almost single-handedly slowed the German advance until reinforcements arrived and began to build on our positions.

Thanks to Col. Daniels and fortunately for us, the German infantry had taken all sorts of casualties from the artillery fire and were unable to penetrate our defenses in any number.

When Col. Daniels was advised about the two tanks which had penetrated to within 20 yards of the building, he asked to be kept advised of their movements. I would inch up the cellar stairs and when the tank crews would spot me they would turn the 88's and fire a round. But before they did, I would come flying down those cellar steps.

The situation remained that way, it seemed, for an eternity.

Col. Daniels called for volunteers to knock out the tanks with a bazooka. One young soldier somehow with help managed to get on the roof of the building and miraculously disabled one tank. It seemed like an impossible task but somehow that kid got the job done. The remaining tank stayed for a while and then turned tail, probably realizing he was sticking out like a sore thumb without support.

It was fortunate for us that our artillery inflicted so much damage to the German infantry, otherwise we would have surely been outflanked.

During the Bulge, I understand that 43 enemy tanks were knocked out in the 26th Infantry Regimental area.

In succeeding days the Germans attacked our positions numerous times with artillery supporting their infantry, but by then we were solidly in place and never budged an inch.

Toward the end of December the action slowed somewhat and patrols from both sides operated in the area.

HOW INTELLIGENT IS INTELLIGENCE?

Ed Morgenstern
17th Airborne Division

The use of censorship by the military has been questioned on a number of occasions. Here is an example of the futile use of censorship during the Battle of the Bulge in World War II. I hope the incident will make the intelligence community think at least twice before imposing censorship.

On January 7, 1945, I was wounded in the fighting around Bastogne, Belgium, and was taken to a U.S. Army hospital (MASH unit) in the area. A week later, after recuperating from surgery, I asked for some V-mail stationary to notify my parents that my chest and abdominal wounds, although serious, would heal in time. I was aware that the then War Department would send them a scary telegram stating that I was "seriously wounded in action."

However, a medical officer warned me and the other patients in our ward that our letters were to be censored and we could not write that we were wounded or in the hospital. The reason we were told was to keep the Germans from knowing our casualties should the mail fall into enemy hands. I really could not see what harm could result from such information, but as a lowly PFC, I carried little weight.

By the middle of January the German advance had been stopped. Of course, I had to follow orders and could only write about harmless thoughts and incidents. I wrote that I was seeing new faces and new places. I did underline the date and requested that the letter be held for future reference.

Subsequent correspondence advised me that my parents had received my V-mail letter before they received the telegram and they were happy that I could write. My cousin who was shown the letter knew I was in the hospital. He noticed that the letter was censored and initialed by a "Capt. J. J. Jones, M.C." (not his real name). And since the Marine Corps was not in proximity to Bastogne, the M.C. must stand for Medical Corps.

Had all the mail from hospitals and the list of casualties been available to the German General staff at that time, it would have been useless. The German army was being pushed back and was in no position to take advantage of the situation, even knowing how high our casualties were. German casualties were even higher.

A REPLACEMENT IN THE 1ST INFANTRY DIVISION

Bert H. Morphis
1st Infantry Division, 26th Infantry Regiment, B Company

After completing infantry basic training at Camp Adair, Oregon, I crossed the country to Camp Shanks, NY in late March, 1944, and shipped to England in April, shortly after my 19th birthday. On June 13, 1944 (7 days after D-Day) I landed on Omaha Beach and joined the 1st Division as a replacement for one of the rifleman lost in the invasion.

After the St. Lo Breakthrough we quickly fought across France, Belgium, and into Germany. On September 13 I saw the Siegfried Line for the first time (It was not the last). On September 20, outside of Aachen, a German artillery shell buried me in loose sand, knocked me unconscious, burst an eardrum, and tore up both my legs.

After approximately 3 months in the 81st General Hospital in Cardiff, Wales, I made my way back to my outfit and joined them on Christmas Eve just outside Butgenbach, Germany. The First had been in reserve at the time of the initial attack and had been rushed back up to the front. I came into Butgenbach after dark on a bright moonlight night, and I shall never forget the sight of that war-torn city covered with a thick mantle of snow, silvery white in the moonlight. To top it off there was not a sound of war to be heard. Everything was deathly quiet in the snow. It was as if everyone was celebrating Christmas.

The next day we were served a Christmas dinner of turkey and the trimmings, and I ate it standing in a stable under the farmhouse which served as a command post, with the cattle looking on. It was great.

Sometime later we started pushing the Bulge back slowly. We would move forward a short distance and dig in, advance again and dig in, and so on, sometimes three or four times a day, if memory serves. And this was no ordinary "digging in." It was bitterly cold and the ground was covered with two to three feet of snow. The ground was frozen so deeply and so hard it was almost impossible to penetrate, so we carried quarter-pound blocks of TNT with detonators to loosen the frozen crust. With a pickaxe we would dig a small hole to accommodate the TNT, set it off then proceed to dig our foxhole. For this purpose we carried full size picks and shovels to expedite the frequent digging in. Moreover, since we were fighting in dense forest, we carried axes and crosscut saws. An open foxhole provided little protection from "tree bursts" from artillery shelling. Therefore, it was necessary to put a cover of logs and soil over our foxholes. Our practice was to dig a hole just deep enough to work in, cut logs to provide a cover, cover the logs with dirt, then crawl inside and finish digging the hole to size. Frequently we would no sooner finish a shelter then we would move and leave it. I don't recall ever being so tired! Once I had a hole just about deep enough to cover, but instead I woke up much later lying on top of my shovel where I had fallen sound asleep while digging. Fortunately there had been no "tree bursts" in my vicinity.

I think everyone's most vivid memories are of the numbing cold. Mine certainly are! The cold was enough of an adversary without the Germans. Just staying alive took all of one's ingenuity. I remember being on an outpost right in front of the German lines where the choice seemed to be between moving and being shot, or lying perfectly still and freezing to death. Somehow we survived, I with trench foot on only one great toe.

One of my saddest memories is of seeing German prisoners carrying bodies, both American and German, out of the woods. Most were frozen in such grotesque positions it was difficult to keep them on a stretcher. They had frozen stiff in the exact positions in which they had died.

Another thing I remember vividly is the snow. I had seen snow before, in Oklahoma and New York, but nothing like this. The evergreen trees were so thick you could hardly walk between them, and they were all totally covered with snow. If you happened to bump one too hard you found yourself totally buried in snow. Sometimes it snowed so hard that one would almost smother. You had to cover your mouth just to breathe. This was frightening to someone who had never experienced it.

Once we had an outpost, which was manned by three or four people, a great distance in front of our lines. We lost our communications with the outpost and feared it had been taken over by the enemy. Since I knew the way, I set out at night leading two wiremen who replaced the line as we went, until we discovered where it had been cut by a mortar round. As we approached the outpost, with no warning whatsoever, someone opened up on us with an M-1 rifle, wounding both wiremen. Not knowing whether it was being fired by a German or an American, I hit the ground and immediately began yelling. Sure enough, good old Private "X" had blasted away without so much as a challenge. Later he shot himself in the leg with a captured pistol and I never saw him again. So far as I know he never shot anyone other than Americans.

Food was always a problem. Our cooks were great about bringing hot food right up to the front lines when it was possible at all. However, most of the time during this period it was just not possible. I remember one two-week period when every morning and evening they brought each of us one Spam sandwich and a cup of coffee. When they started out it was all hot, but by the time it got to the front it was all cold. Surprisingly, I still like Spam! But I was certainly glad when we got some "C" rations we could heat up and have a hot meal. We got a large supply of rations at one time, and almost immediately got orders to move out. We had to leave most of the rations behind; so we ate all we could before left. I ate six cans of meat and beans and almost died from the overdose.

In late January, 1945 we hit the Siegfried line again. G-2 said the pillboxes were empty, but many of us old time squad leaders were skeptical. Unfortunately, we had a new platoon leader who had never been in combat, and he refused to listen to our pleas for caution. Early in the morning, when it was pitch black, he led the platoon on a combat patrol into an area where there were a large number of pillboxes. We passed by one without incident, until the entire platoon had passed by. Then a machine gun opened up from behind, killing about half the platoon, including the lieutenant. The poor guy never had a chance to learn, and he took a dozen others with him!

When it was light enough to see, the twelve or so of us who had survived discovered we were in an open area with German pillboxes to the left and right of us, one straight ahead, and the one we had passed behind us—almost totally surrounded—and all were heavily manned. Fortunately we discovered that another a few hundred yards behind us had some GIs rather than Germans, so we started making our way to it a few at a time. Finally everyone had escaped but me and one other. We made a run for it with me pulling him as best I could. I had finally gotten my first overshoes just before this action and they were almost the death of me. They were two sizes too big, and I could hardly run in the snow that was probably two feet deep. However, being fired at by machine guns and rifles from three different bunkers at the same time does add wings to the feet! Somehow we made it, even with the snow being kicked up at our heels all the way. We stayed in the bunker all day with the Germans firing at us sporadically. As soon as it was dark we took off to our lines which we had left hours before. We got there safely, but learned later that the field through which we had escaped was full of "S" mines—the kind which pop out of the ground then explode at about waist height. The only thing which saved us was that the mines were solidly frozen in the ground and couldn't pop out. I guess frozen ground can be a blessing sometimes!

Lots of other things happened which might be of interest, but my memory has faded considerably after 45 years, which is probably a blessing.

THE ATTACK BY THE GERMANS

Ian A. Morrison
106th Infantry Division, 422nd Infantry Regiment, 1st Battalion

The morning was foggy and cruelly cold. The heavy, wet snow was three feet deep on the ground and eight-to-ten inches deep on the bowing limbs of the fir trees surrounding us. As it thawed enough to drop from those limbs it sounded to the two of us alone in a forward observation post like enemy patrols sneaking up behind us. We shivered in the post, and in the grave-like claustrophobic sleeping bunker located fifteen feet away, on the very edge of a knoll on the Schnee Eiffel. There, for the third successive day, we observed across the steep wooded valley the massing of enemy infantry, tanks and butane-fueled trucks.

Our observation post was surrounded by grenades hung low in the bare bushes, their pins attached by trip wires to each other and to our open ground-level ports. They could be triggered by a foot, a shin or by us. We longed for the comfort of our squad's German-built bunkers a mile behind us—bunkers which recently had been evacuated by the veteran 2nd Division and occupied by our green 106th troops. Green, because the division not only was untested in battle, but filled with recent recruits and transfers from the ASTP and AAC ground training units. Our training together was, to say the least, minimal. Nevertheless, if, as Tom Clancy claims in his novel, *Clear and Present Danger*, there are only two types of fighters—the infantry and those who support the infantry—we were of the former.

We sailed to Scotland on the Aquatania in October as an infantry division, convened in the Cotswolds awaiting the transshipment of our heavy equipment finally located in Le Havre. The equipment had gone there directly from the States, cosmolene and all. In late November of 1944 we moved directly to the Ardennes Forest area in Belgium where we replaced the veteran

Second Division. We were told by the troops we were relieving that it was a very quiet place, and would remain so, since the Germans "were already defeated." We were delighted to hear that, since our 106th was to have two regiments spread out across a front of twenty-seven miles!

In the next three weeks we battled the elements, an occasional German patrol, and trench foot. Every day fifteen to twenty men of the regiment were sent to rear hospitals suffering from trench foot—the result of the combination of the cold, snow, inadequate boots and insufficient dry socks.

We didn't know then, nor for that matter for years to come, that the U.S. Army lost 12,500 men on the Belgian border in the winter of 1944–45 as a result of trench foot—the equivalent of a full, badly needed division!

As we worked in the heavy snow, immersed in the dense fog which prevented air surveillance of the enemy for days on end, we kept notifying our rear echelon by telephone that even our green untutored senses could hear and occasionally see that the Germans were congregating trucks, tanks and hordes of men on the opposite side of the Schnee Eiffel.

Our reports seemed to be treated with the contempt veterans of battle hold for the uninitiated. No one listened to us until December 16. By then it was too late. We then were rushing rearward, ordered by division headquarters to reform battle lines closer to St. Vith. In three days of rushing and fighting, encompassed in fog, we retreated about five miles and had dug at least seven foxholes each day, seeking protection from never-ending artillery tree bursts, or preparing to skirmish with the flanking enemy. Our intermittent rushing rearward was so great that some soldiers who had lost their units were running after our trucks, hopping on and straddling the barrels of our towed 57mm guns. Their screams, unheard by our drivers, as their testicles were pounded to treacle before they slid off, remained in our minds for weeks. For forty-five years.

On the morning of December 19th, in a narrow valley near the border village of Schoenberg, Tiger-tank-mounted 88's picked off the front and rear of our already massacred motorized column. More of the enemy were outflanking us from the heights with infantrymen who, unlike us, had plenty of ammunition and food, of which we then had none.

The war was over for us late on the 19th of December and, as it turned out, for the entire 422nd and 423rd Regiments. We were herded by our recent German prisoners to a barnyard in Schoenfeld where, crowded, cold, hungry and hurting we spent the next 24 hours before beginning the straggling, starving, scared march to a railhead in Germany where a hundred of us were shoved into each awaiting boxcar. The boxcars were known since World War I as "forty and eights," when they transported, in reasonable comfort, forty troops or eight healthy horses. One hundred men, many of us with deathly debilitating dysentery, determined that we could only survive standing up. Come what may. Some of us had to lie down between the legs of our comrades.

Christmas Eve, 1944 was a time to remember. Our train was motionless in the rail-yard of Limburg, Germany. The only sounds were the moaning of our comrades within our boxes, and those fore and aft of us.

About midnight the drone of Lancasters rudely reminded us that the British bombed at night. As the first bombs exploded around us in that strategic spot we found the strength in panic to break out of our confine to stumble as swiftly as we could across a frozen ploughed field where we huddled thankfully in the deep troughs. As dawn arose we realized that there was no room for escape so we laboriously lifted ourselves from the hard little gullies and reluctantly returned to the box cars.

We discovered that those of our group that had escaped the car on the opposite side, and thus had to scale a small cliff, had been obliterated by a direct hit from the British aircraft. A new war of survival as prisoners of the Germans lay ahead. Some of us made it. Too many didn't. That is another story.

A NIGHT IN THE WOODS

Joseph C. Nicollela
28th Infantry Division, 28th Quartermaster Company

Night marches. They were a training camp routine. However, no number of those controlled marches back in the States could have prepared my platoon for its night in the woods on the 19th of December 1944.

After sustaining heavy losses in the Hurtgen Forest, my division, the 28th, was assigned to the rest area in Wiltz, Luxembourg about mid-November. On Sunday night, the 15th of December 1944, our company's officer, Lt. Homer Sanders, called us together to outline what our next move would be. The Germans, he explained, were apparently planning a major offensive, and we had been ordered to hold them off until the 28th Division HQ could move all equipment to Bastogne. Some men light-heartedly joked that Christmas—a mere ten days away—would be ruined, but we had sensed for several days that the Germans were up to something.

Our initial plan was to break up and form defensive positions in and around Wiltz. My platoon, led by Lt. Sanders, contained about 50 men and left for its position just outside Wiltz on December 17th. Then, as the Germans began closing in, we were ordered on the 19th of December to move to the crossroads near Wiltz where some trucks would be waiting to take us to Bastogne.

However, when we reached the crossroads, the trucks were afire and the Germans were there waiting for us. As we ran for cover into the nearby woods, they opened fire. Flares emblazoned the sky directly above the woods. In the confusion everyone began running in different directions. Many, including me, lost helmets and weapons. As we lay on the ground, bullets whizzing by over our heads, Lt. Sanders shouted for us to crawl away from the gunfire toward the other end of the woods. The cries of others who had been wounded could occasionally be heard as the barrage of gunfire continued.

Somehow, after crawling on our hands and knees and, at times, our stomachs, about half of us made it to the end of the woods, the gunfire now audible just faintly in the distance. Unfortunately, the others were either captured or dead. At the woods' end was a road that Lt. Sanders had us carefully cross one man at a time into the woods on the other side. We regrouped and with the help of Lt. Sanders's compass made our way north to Bastogne.

After walking a few hours or so, we spotted a farmhouse in a clearing and cautiously approached it. As it turned out, three old people lived there. Walter Heinbach, the only one of us who knew German, approached them. They were terrified and pleaded with us not to harm them. We had no intentions of doing so and merely wanted something to eat and to get warm. They gave us black bread and some water, for which we were very grateful.

The rest of the night was spent walking some more through the woods. Conversation was minimal, and I remember trying to drive the idea of being shot or captured out of my head. Eventually, we assumed that we must be nearing Bastogne since the sound of fighting was beginning to be heard in the distance. Then, as dawn approached, we finally stopped to rest, groups of three taking turns as guards.

At daybreak we awoke to the sound of gunfire. German paratroopers, who had begun landing in the field next to the woods, began attacking us. After wounding some of them, we moved out again in the direction of Bastogne. We passed a Nazi paratrooper who lay wounded on the ground. He was dressed in full battle gear, including hand grenades that were attached to his uniform. "Helfen! Helfen!" he begged. We walked quickly by him, daring to get no closer for fear he was booby-trapped.

Sometime during that morning, the 20th of December, we met another group of lost GI's, or "stragglers" as we were being called. I remember a photographer taking pictures of us and asking us questions there. (One of the photographs from that day, showing a group of several displaced soldiers, has appeared in several Battle of the Bulge books.) It was also there, about midmorning, that some quick action had to be taken. Since additional confrontations with the enemy were inevitable during daylight, Lt. Sanders asked us if we wanted to surrender or attempt to reach our unit. We resoundingly chose to continue our efforts to reach the 28th Division. Later that day we were fortunate to be reunited with our company after a harrowing night march in the woods.

CHRISTMAS OF '44

Katherine Flynn Nolan
53rd Field Hospital

The third platoon of the 53rd Field Hospital arrived in a small village in Holland not far from the German border. It was early November, 1944, and bitter cold. A few women and children and one old man stood staring at us as we huddled under khaki blankets in the back of the truck.

"I can imagine what they are thinking of us. We are really a mess," said Marie, our platoon chief nurse.

"We sure are. What I wouldn't give for a hot shower," said Laura. "And a hot meal."

"The cooks should have the field kitchen set up tomorrow, but hot showers? Who are you kidding?" I said.

Then the trucks began to move again. We were on the main street passing houses and stores and finally a church. Then we turned into a schoolyard and stopped. An old priest stood on the steps of the school, a threadbare black coat over his cassock. Our commander approached him. They spoke for a few minutes and shook hands. Turning around to face us, the colonel shouted, "We'll set up in the school."

Our long journey had begun at five o'clock this morning. From somewhere in Belgium the convoy had bumped along potholed dirt roads and some paved ones also in bad shape hour after hour with frequent delays. If we got to a check point ahead of schedule it would be a wait there while another convoy with higher priority went through first. We had K-rations all day. Cold, tasteless cans—something that was called scrambled eggs and meat—and those dog biscuits they called crackers. Some powder to mix with water in the mess kit tin cup. Lemonade, it was called. Meanwhile the temperature kept dropping and it looked like snow. The tarp covering the top of the truck gave a little protection from the wind but that was all. We were dirty, weary and chilled to the point of numbness.

The school was a newly-built red rick one-story structure with four wings.

After living and working in tents since landing on Utah Beach in Normandy, we were delighted to be moving indoors at last. When the desks and chairs were removed it made an excellent hospital. Quickly, the cots were set up, IV paraphernalia in place, receiving, shock wards, post ops, and surgery were made ready just in time to care for the first casualties.

For the next fourteen hours there was no let-up. From time to time we caught glimpses of nuns peeking in the room as we worked. They were surprised to see us nursing the patients. They, like the villagers, had taken the six of us for prostitutes.

A company of the 84th Division (Rail Splitters) was pinned down at a railroad bed and taking heavy losses. Ambulances kept arriving with more and more until every cot and litter was taken.

An invitation was soon extended through the priest who spoke English. The nuns wanted the nurses to move in with them in the convent.

Several hours later two of us managed to get off duty to go over and see our room. The nuns had prepared a large store-room as our dormitory. Six of their beds were ready for our use. The nuns and 28 war orphans in their care slept in the basement. They at first expected us to join them there, but at this point we were ready to die in our beds if need be in comfort. To sleep in a real bed under a roof was such luxury that we felt spoiled and pampered. The doctors and corpsmen teased us about it and wanted us to ask Mother Superior when their turn would be. She spoke a little English and when she finally understood, she said they were welcome to come one at a time for a hot bath.

Now, in order to have hot water for the tub a lot of work was involved. Wood had to be gathered from the woods, broken or cut up with an axe to fit into a small furnace built under the water tank behind the tub. I still think about all this sometimes when I turn on a hot water faucet and wonder whether the nuns at our favorite convent still heat water in the same way.

Usually the hospital remained in one place about ten days. Then the patients would be evacuated to a general hospital in the rear, or to an evacuation hospital for an airlift to a general hospital in England. The packing up of equipment and supplies, taking down of tents, and getting our personal gear in order went swiftly and smoothly by this time, since we had done it over and over till it was routine. When the outfit we had supported went back for a rest period, we would be reassigned to a new outfit just going into action.

However, this didn't happen with the 84th. As Christmas approached, things quieted down on the fighting front. As the days passed, the orders to evacuate patients did not come. Tubes were removed, IVs discontinued, and for the first time we had convalescent men taking food by mouth, growing stronger and getting into the holiday spirit. There were still a few in serious condition, but they did not want to be moved to a quieter area. Perhaps they felt more secure surrounded by their buddies. I don't know. Whatever the reason, it worked, because every one of them made it.

A young Dutchman began to visit the hospital each day. He spoke English and soon was helping out in the wards. He finally moved in. An excellent organist, he would play the school organ, moving it from room to room, playing requests and Christmas carols until the atmosphere was really jolly.

Leo, our Dutch friend, went out to the woods to cut down little Christmas trees for the wards. The patients made silver stars from K-ration cans. The Red Cross gave out cartons of Life Savers. We used bandages to string them to add to the trees. Everyone had the Christmas spirit.

Meanwhile, the nuns were planning a Christmas treat for the nurses off duty. They baked some special Christmas pastry from ingredients our cooks scrounged up for them. They brewed herb tea from roots of some sort. The feast would follow three Christmas masses in the convent chapel starting at midnight Christmas Eve.

On the 23rd of December, orders came in for us to evacuate all patients. Wrapping them up warmly for their trip to a general hospital, much good natured kidding went on. We had grown close to them all and it was like saying goodbye to family. Several of them were from New York State as were three of our nurses: Laura Ball, from Syracuse; Marie Arsenault, from Schuylerville; and Virginia Stenson, from Brooklyn. They were getting all kinds of promises about visits when the war was over so we pretended to feel slighted until we got assurances of the same. This would mean a trip to Worcester, Massachusetts, to see me, Katherine Flynn; to Memphis, Tennessee for Ruth Nolen; and to Clayton, Alabama, for Ruth Stevens. Their intentions were sincere but never did these reunions occur.

Christmas Eve at the appointed hour, we assembled in the chapel. The masses seemed to go on forever. Finally, we went to the dining room. The best linen, crystal and China was on the table. Hand painted place settings with our names completed the beautiful scene.

It was a wonderful and strange little Christmas party with us speaking no Dutch and the nuns speaking no English, except for the tiny bit Mother Superior knew. Somehow, though, we communicated with gestures, nods, smiles or frowns; but we understood one another and that too was beautiful.

Just after the tea was poured, we heard sounds of engines. One of the drivers came and said for us to report at once. The tea was too hot to drink; yet we did not want to waste it. Also we would be on the road for many hours and might not have anything hot to drink or eat for days. We would not be cheated out of this last luxury.

"Please tell the colonel to give us a few more minutes," said Marie, our chief nurse.

"Yes, ma'am," he replied and left.

For some reason that tea took a long time to cool off. The driver returned to say we were holding up the convoy and must come immediately. Then the horns began to blow like mad.

Down the street the Red Ball Express was waiting. Trucks stretched out as far as we could see. Headlights blazing, horns blowing, the colonel shouting, "Those damned women are holding up the war." It was quite a sight.

The nuns followed us to the street, waving and saying Merry Christmas in Dutch. We wished them the same and thanked them for their kindness and hospitality through our friend, Leo. Then we were rolling along toward the border and Germany. That was Christmas Day in 1944, one I am not likely to forget.

MY LIFE IN THE 55TH ARMORED INFANTRY BATTALION

Homer Olson
55th Armored Infantry Battalion, Company B

On December 7, 1941 came the bombing of Pearl Harbor by the Japanese. This changed everything for the whole world and us. Our government rationed many things to the civilians; everything went to the military.

In March 1942, I went to work for the northern oil pumping wells with Ralph Bennett. That was a good job and we got along well together. Many of my friends were volunteering and being drafted into the military. I don't like water, so I didn't want the Navy. Because of my bad ears, I couldn't get into the Air Force. So I waited for the draft. I turned twenty years old on September 15, 1942. I was put in class 1-A and passed my physical in Erie, Pennsylvania on November 4. I left on the train November 18 from Ridgeway, Pennsylvania because we lived in Elkco. That day, I kissed my mother and hugged my dad for the first time in my adult life. It was a sad day for them and for all of us. Our induction center was at New Cumberland, Pennsylvania. We were there for three days getting our uniforms, shots, and etc. We were put on a train and four days later we were in Camp Polk, Louisiana. It was a big camp, with two armored divisions there. I was assigned to Company B, 55th Armored Infantry Battalion that I stayed in for the next three years. (They broke us up in August 1945 down in Austria.)

We took four months of basic training there at Camp Polk, and then went on the Louisiana maneuvers for two months. It was pretty rough on most of us; we were busy all the time. We learned to shoot and qualify with the M-1 rifle, all of the machine guns, pistol, mortar, hand-grenade, etc. We did a lot of close order drill and many road marches. The longest was a 30-mile hike with light packs. I didn't like the bayonet drill and was glad that I never had to use one.

The weather was wet and chilly there and I caught a cold and high fever. They put me in the hospital for a few days. That is where I spent Christmas of 1942. We learned a lot in those first few months. A big thing was learning to live together in close quarters. Most guys were great, but there are always a few "bastards." Some got homesick. I never did, but did get lonesome sometimes.

About once a month, everyone got kitchen, police, latrine duty and a twenty-four hour guard duty. This is where I learned to clean toilets. On one wall there were three long urinals. Another wall was the sinks and mirrors and on another wall were ten commodes. The showers were back in farther. That place was a madhouse. Every morning after breakfast, you had no privacy and you couldn't be bashful. Each company had their own bugler and all the calls were with a bugle. Reveilles, chow call for three meals, and work calls at 8:00 AM and 1:00 PM. Retreat at 5:30 PM and lights out at 9:30 PM with Taps at 11:00 PM. We got up at 5:45 each morning and breakfast was at 7:00. In that hour and fifteen minutes you got dressed, stood reveille, made your bed, mopped the floor around your bunk, made sure your clothes were okay and shoes shined, and fifteen minutes of calisthenics. It sure was a different lifestyle, but it went pretty well if you made up your mind to it. I got a ten-day leave and came home in April after the Basic Training was over.

Pay day was the first day of the month. Fifty dollars in cash was what you got paid. After deductions of insurance, bonds, and laundry, $35.25 was left. Sometimes they would pull a "short-arm" inspection on pay day. This was to check for venereal diseases. The uniform for that hour was shoes and raincoats. A doctor would be sitting on a chair in our day room. We lined up outside and when you got in to see him you opened you raincoat and squeezed you penis. If there was any fluid, you went on sick call and didn't get paid.

In May and June we were on maneuvers in Louisiana and West Texas. Lots of mosquitoes, snakes, and dust. When this was over, we moved to Camp Barkeley, Texas near Abilene. I was assigned to a half-track there and became a driver. I liked this better, as I always liked to drive anything. That fall, I was sent to Fort Knox, Kentucky to mechanic school for three months. Gene Foster of B Company, 55th AIB was also there and we got to know a couple of girls in Louisville. We would see them on weekends, sometimes.

While we were in Fort Knox, the 11th Armored Division moved to the Mojave Desert near Needles, California for desert maneuvers. When we were done with school, I got my papers, train ticket, and also a five-day "delay in route," so I went home for three days. On Christmas Day of 1943 I was on the train headed for Needles. We finished maneuvers in February and went to Camp Cooke, California near Santa Maria. We went to Los Angeles and Santa Barbara some weekends. Usually, we went to Santa Maria. Many of my friends were Italians and we would go to Santa Maria for Italian food on Saturday night and then to the Palomino Bar. If we didn't catch the bus back to Camp, we would sleep in the USO Club on a pool table or a chair.

Early in September, we were put on a troop train headed for Camp Kilmer, New Jersey and then overseas. That was a nice train ride. It was a long train with two steam engines in front and five steam engines pushing in the rear. We went through thirty-seven tunnels going from California to Denver. There were two kitchen cars in the middle of the train. The front one served the front half of the train and the back car, the back half. We ate well, two times a day. They stopped once a day and we got off to walk and exercise. It took six days and five nights to get to Camp Kilmer, New Jersey. After a few days passed, we went by train to New York and onto a ship, the USS Hermitage. It was an experience, having your name called and walking up the long "gang plank" and knowing that you were leaving your homeland. The duffel bag that we carried was quite heavy. They put us on a deck down below the water line. It was crowded. The bunks were five high. The lights were not bright enough so that we could read a little and play poker and shoot craps. These were on the floor wherever we could find a place to put a blanket down. There were poker games going on someplace twenty-four hours a day.

There were five thousand of us on this ship and they told us there were sixty ships in the convoy. Each ship was a mile apart so we couldn't see all of them when we were allowed up on the top deck. We had a Navy escort: the Destroyer Escorts. They would zigzag between the ships looking for submarines. I got a little seasick at times, but not bad. We got fed twice daily and I could usually eat a little. We ate standing up with our trays on a bar. You had to hang onto the bar and your tray and hit your mouth with your spoon. The ship was rolling in some direction all the time.

We were thirteen days on the ship and landed in Southampton, England around October 3rd. They put us on a train and took us to a small camp between Tisbury and Hinden, about ninety miles from London. We didn't do much training in England, just a few hikes now and then. Over a period of time we got our equipment, which consisted of tanks, trucks, jeeps, half-tracks, guns, ammunition, and rations.

We were given some two-day passes. I went to Bristol once and London twice. One pass that I had to London was the day before payday and then payday. An English pound was worth $4.09 at that time. The first night that we were there, the price for a woman, all night, was one pound. The next night (payday) the price was four pounds. We didn't bother the women that night.

Early in December, we crossed the English Channel. The drivers went with their vehicles, tanks, half-tracks, trucks, and jeeps in a "landing ship tanks" (LST). The front of the LST opened up and we drove up into it and turned around so that you faced out. This way you could drive straight out onto the beach when they opened up. We were on this ship for twenty-four hours and landed near Cherbourg, France. We drove to fields near Rennes, France. It took three days for our division to assemble there.

That night, out in the Channel, there was a submarine alert. They stopped the ship and killed the engines. We were "bobbing" around out there in that flat bottom ship. Each driver had to pull a two-hour fire guard in the tank deck with a guy on each end. My time was midnight to 2:00 am. It was hot down there and very strong gasoline fumes. I got seasick and threw up a few times, until there was no more to come up and I just gagged. I was sure glad when 2:00 am came so I could lie down again.

After the division got all together, we started to move inland. Then an order came down to change course and go north. When we got up to Rhiems, France we heard about the German breakthrough in Belgium—making what they called the "Bulge." We hit snow and cold weather up there. From here on things and places are vague and hazy. I know that we spent Christmas Day in Belgium somewhere. It was cold.

We were in reserve for a couple of days and then they gave us a small town to take. We didn't get it that afternoon. We had a counterattack that night and the Germans took nineteen guys from our company prisoner. I remember that one guy was taking twelve German prisoners back and one was wounded and couldn't walk fast enough, so he shot him there on the road. I thought to myself, "What the hell is going on here? This is terrible." After a while, you get used to these things and if you want to survive you can become pretty cruel.

The Germans had Bastogne surrounded for many days. Most of the 101st Airborne Division was in there. The 4th Armored got in there first from the south. We got in a day or two later from the northwest. That was a happy day for everyone.

We started moving again, taking small towns, clearing woods, and slowly closing the Bulge. It was cold and the snow was quite deep. There was lots of frostbite on the fingers and toes. We threw away our shoes and cut up GI blankets into strips about six inches wide and wrapped our feet and legs. We then put our feet into four buckle overshoes, which we had. I went to the Aid Station one time and they painted my toes with something. I just lost a couple of nails. At one time, I had on two pairs of long underwear, two pairs of pants, two shirts, a woolen GI sweater, and a field jacket. It is unbelievable what the human body can stand—both mental and physical. Some people are stronger than others are, so some "broke down"—it was nothing to be ashamed of. I know that prayers helped a lot.

Every letter that I wrote home, I asked Mom and Dad to send gloves, handkerchiefs, and socks. I carried them in my seat cushion, in my half-track, and gave most of them to my buddies. They nicknamed me "Mother Olson." One time, I asked Mom to send us a chocolate cake with frosting and walnuts on top. She did and it came in about five weeks. The walnuts were green with mold, so we threw them away and made quick work of that cake.

I remember one town near Longchamps in Belgium. We got the hell knocked out of us going in. We cleared the town and stayed there that night. The next day was bright and sunny. We could see some dead Germans lying in the snow, up in a field near some woods. We found a long piece of rope and went up there. There were twelve lying frozen in many positions. Sometimes the Germans would "booby-trap" their dead. We would tie the rope around a leg and drag them a ways and make sure there were no wires attached to the bodies. Then we looked for watches and pistols. I remember one that I rolled over. His face was gone from the forehead down.

One time, there were several of us "dug-in" along a dirt road, in some woods with lots of pine trees. A jeep came down the road and stopped. It was a Lutheran chaplain from another unit. He asked if we wanted a prayer and communion. Of course we did. We were Catholics, Jews, and etc. But it made no difference. We got on our knees in the snow with our helmets on and weapons slung on our shoulders. He had some bread and bottles of wine and poured the wine in our canteen cup. A few shells landed fairly close but no one ran to their holes. He never stopped pouring the wine. We all felt better after he left.

One time they pulled us back in reserve for a few days. We got some replacements, supplies and hot food from our kitchen. We were "dug in" (two man foxholes). Anderson and I usually dug in together (he was a swell guy). He drove second track and I drove first track. We were getting a lot of artillery and mortar fire. Also, the Germans had a weapon that fired a shell like a mortar or a small bomb. We called them "screaming mimis." They mostly came at night and scared the hell out of you. We were cold, wet, and lying in our hole one night when things were coming in pretty heavy. I started to shake and shiver and just couldn't stop. I said, "Andy, I can't stop this shaking," and started to cry. It was all getting to me—especially the cold. Andy held me, lit me a cigarette, and we talked. After a while I calmed down. Anderson was a great guy, as were all of our guys. We loved and depended on each other; you couldn't make it alone.

One night, at this same place, Andy and I were leaning against my halftrack. We could hear a mortar shell coming (they came slow). We didn't have time to get in our hole, so we dove under the track. The shell landed four or five feet away in the snow and mud. It didn't explode; it was a "dud." The book wasn't open on our page that night. We survived. One afternoon, later on, we had taken this small town and we were getting some machine gun fire from some woods. Our company went to clear the woods and had to stay there all night. They called on the radio to bring up some rations and ammunition. They said the field might be mined. Andy and I gathered up supplies and put half in his track and half in mine. We thought that one of us should get through. We ran side by side and both got through. We tried to follow our same tracks back and about halfway back, Andy hit a land mine with the left track and caught fire. I stopped, he jumped out and ran to me and we made it back.

Somewhere around about this time they had brought up a portable shower unit. They had big tents and many tank trucks with water, and it was hot. We went back and got showers and new clothes. Boy, they felt good. We hadn't taken a shower since we left England two months earlier. That is the only good thing about fighting a war in the wintertime. You didn't stink much and the dead bodies didn't stink either because they froze quickly.

We closed the "Bulge" late in January and hit the Siegfried Line in February. The snow was melting and there was lots of mud. I developed a fear and hatred for the snow and cold that winter and it will stay with me forever. After the Siegfried Line, we started the "spearheads" to the Rhine River. Our objective was the city of Andernach, a city north of Coblenz. We cleared the city with help from another unit.

They then pulled us back a few miles to a small town. We were there five days, while the engineers built a "bailey bridge" across the Rhine. Owens found a German motorcycle there. Each morning, he and I would ride it to Andemach and get wine that we had found in a cellar. We gave wine to anyone who wanted some and it tasted good. The house that our squad took over to sleep in had a radio, and we heard some music for the first time in nearly three months (American music from Paris).

They built the bridge across the Rhine under a smoke screen and we crossed it in a smoke screen—an experience that I'll never forget. We started the "spearheads" again and one time we were cut off for three days. They dropped us supplies from the air. Gasoline was the big item and we got that in thousands and thousands of five-gallon cans. I saw General Patton twice. Once in the "Bulge" and once on a "spearhead."

We had the Germans on the run now. They were running out of gasoline and food, so they were using a lot of horses to move their guns and supplies in wagons. They were being strafed by aircraft and shelled from our artillery and the roads jammed with dead horses, humans, and everything. At times, we could not go around them and had to run over the bodies. On these "spearheads," we came to and released prisoners from POW (prisoner of war) camps and slave labor camps. These were sorry sights. They were so happy to see us. We knew that the end of the war was getting near, and all of us were praying that we could make it now that we had come this far.

We were in the mountains before we dropped down into Linz, Austria, on the Danube River. A small town, Wegscheid, we came to in the afternoon. Lots of SS there and putting up a stiff resistance. We got some houses burning so we could see better when it got dark. We used our cigarette lighters on curtains, etc. S/Sgt. Elwood G. Cashman, my squad leader, got it here. We felt so bad with the end so near. We finished clearing the town. The next day they sent my platoon (five half-tracks) out on a mounted patrol, down a dirt road for a few miles. We hit no resistance and found nothing. While we were gone, they shelled the town with artillery. Another guy had pulled his half-track under a tree where I had been. He got a direct hit and the half-track was half-gone. He was lying on the ground dead. I thought to myself, "God still has plans for me. That could have been me."

The war ended for us at Linz, Austria, on the Danube River. It was a beautiful city. In spite of the pain and suffering of a war there is a good side. I had many fine friends while in the military and we had many laughs and good times. This friendship has lasted over the years. We can feel it at our reunions. I must say that we had fine officers as our leaders. Three of them were killed. Most were wounded. Captain George Reimer, our Company Commander, was and is a good man. I think he was wounded four times.

There was a concentration camp near Linz called Mauthausen. That was a terrible sight and smelled too. Dead bodies all over and the rest were half-dead. They must have killed and burned thousands of people there. We sat in a field for several days after the armistice was signed on May 8, 1945. We started "occupation duty" in a small town, Ried, Austria.

I got a three-day pass to Paris late in May or early June. We went to Munich, Germany by truck and got on the train there. The train was full of GIs going to Paris or Luxembourg. When we got to Paris, they had a place where they gave each man with a pass one carton of cigarettes, soap, razor, toothbrush, toothpaste, and a comb. Most of us had our own, so we sold those things to French civilians for a good price. We also had German pistols to sell. I had five. The Frenchmen took us to a cafe where we went back in a corner and piled our pistols on a table and ordered a drink. They were looking over the pistols and the fellow across the table from me (one of us) shot himself in the left hand. They called the military police (MPs) to take him to the hospital. We gathered up our pistols and got the hell out of there fast. It was illegal to sell these pistols. We went to a Red Cross hotel, got our room, and we never heard anything about it. I had a little 25-caliber automatic in a shoulder holster, which I wore under my shirt. We weren't supposed to have concealed weapons, but we weren't too well liked in Germany. So many of us carried something.

The three of us went to a club that night. Each of us bought a bottle of cognac and a bottle of champagne at $4.00 a bottle. One of the sergeants got pretty drunk and went with a woman for the night. Baldwin and I went back to our hotel room. We saw the sergeant at noon the next day. He was sick and broke. She had "rolled" him for all his money. We each gave him some money. We saw many of the sights in Paris and had a good time there. One afternoon, I was walking by myself; there was a park and it had benches along the sidewalk. Two women, professionals, were sitting on a bench. We talked a little in "pidgin English" and I went with the older one to her apartment. We went through a door, into a hallway, and got halfway up the stairs when the front door opened and a man came in. I thought that it might be a "set-up." I unbuttoned my shirt and took out my little pistol. When she saw it, she got excited and finally got through to me that he lived downstairs. I wouldn't have shot anyone, but I would have scared someone. Everything turned out okay. She was good and knew her business.

When I got back to my company in Austria, they were loading up the tanks and half-tracks onto freight cars and shipping them back to France. The 2-1/2 ton trucks they drove back in convoys. I got in on this and there were two drivers to a truck with an officer in charge of each twenty-five trucks. The convoy stretched out for miles. Weaver and I were together and we were three days getting to a racetrack outside of Paris. We got into Paris again that night and caught the train back in the morning. When we rode trains over there, we rode in 40 & 8 (40 men or 8 mules) boxcars. There were no passenger cars this time. We each carried our own bedrolls and rations.

We were then sent to occupy Freistadt, Austria. There was a "displaced persons" (DP) camp there (people from other countries that worked for the Germans). They were being sent back to their own countries. Wally Laudert and I got in on one trip that was hauling DPs to Yugoslavia. There were many trucks and each had two drivers. We went over the Alps into Northern Italy and then into Yugoslavia. Several times a day, we stopped the trucks for "piss call." This was quite a sight. We unloaded the DPs in a field, near a town; there Marshal Tito's troops set up machine guns around the DPs. We stayed there in our trucks that night and were sure glad to leave the next morning. We made this trip early in July and on July 4th we received snow—the first and only time that I have gotten into a snowstorm in July.

We now were sent to occupy Ebensee, Austria. There was a big POW camp there and we had ninety thousand German prisoners to guard. They had "work details" outside of the Camp each day and my job, on most days, was to go to the main gate and draw and sign for six prisoners. They would go to the "wood yard" and cut firewood all day. They cooked on wood stoves in the camp. I carried a submachine gun and they didn't offer to run away. They were eating pretty well there. In August 1945, they broke up the 11th Armored Division and we were sent in all different directions to other units. We had been together for three years. Some others and I were sent to Czechoslovakia to a town near Pilsen to the 8th Armored Division where I was there a couple of weeks and then went to Germany to the 83rd Infantry Division. I was put in a service company of the 329th Infantry Battalion. I was driving a truck again. John Singletary, who was "ration breakdown man," and I would drive to Deggendorf to the railroad each morning. We picked up the rations (food) for the 4th Infantry Company and delivered them to four different towns that they were occupying. This was good duty. John and I had our room up over the kitchen. The cooks slept there too. So we always had food like oranges, apples, bread, and peanut butter in our rooms. Some women would come each night and if they stayed too late, they would stay all night. Civilians had to be off the streets from 11:00 pm till 6:00 in the morning. This is where a woman slept in my bed one night when she stayed too late. I never touched her. She looked too rough for me. When I woke up in the morning she was gone. I have told this a few times and people don't believe it. But it is the truth.

We were being sent home on the point system—so many points for service in the States, months overseas, for each Battle Star (I have three), etc. Anyway, I had sixty points. The 358th Engineer Battalion was being filled with sixty pointers for going home. So they sent others and me to the 358th in some town in Germany. We did nothing there.

One afternoon, an old man was leading an old skinny horse up the street, followed by some old women with pails and pans. They went to the town square and killed the horse. They cut it up and divided the meat. I didn't go up to see this; it wouldn't be a pretty sight. I am fortunate and thankful that I have never been that hungry. In this land of plenty, most people will say that they wouldn't do this, or they wouldn't do that. But that is "bullshit." This county would be the worst, because we are used to having too much. They would get on their knees or kill for a piece of bread. On the day after Thanksgiving, we started our journey home. We were taken to the "tent city" camps, near Reims, France. These camps were named after cities in the U.S.A. There were units coming in and going out every day. I went into Reims a few times. Reims was pretty well cleaned up by this time. The Reims cathedral is a beautiful church and wasn't damaged much. We went in and sat down for a few minutes. We were here a couple of weeks and then were moved to a "tent city" camp near Le Havre, France. This was on the coast. We could look down and see the city and the ocean. These "tent cities" were called "cigarette camps" and named after cigarette brands. I'm not sure, but ours was "Lucky Strike" or "Pall Mall". I still had a couple of extra pistols and sold them here. We were allowed to take one home and they were going to pull a "shake down search" on the ship.

All around these camps were signs that said, "One drip and you miss the ship." So if you got the "clap," you stayed there for treatment. We had a "short arm" inspection the day before we boarded ship. One day they told us that our ship was in and we would be loading up in a few days. On the afternoon of Christmas Eve, 1945 we went down and boarded ship. No trouble walking up the "gang plank" this time. The duffel bag was lighter and we were going home. We left that evening and went up into the North Sea and around the north of Scotland. They announced over the speakers that there would be a turkey dinner the next day for Christmas. We hit a winter storm that night and all Christmas Day. So many got seasick and couldn't eat their dinner. I ate some but not much.

This ship was the SS Argentina. It was a nice ship and not too crowded. There were seven thousand of us on it. Our trip lasted seven days before we reached New York on the morning of Jan 1, 1946. Most of us were on the decks so we could see the Statue of Liberty and watch the tugboats pushing us into the pier. It was quiet; no one was around because it was a holiday. Later in the day, we were taken off and put on a train to Camp Kilmer, New Jersey again. From there the train sent us to our "separation centers" in our different states. I went to New Cumberland, Pennsylvania again. There, we were "processed out." They told me my gums and teeth were bad and if I stayed a few days they would fix my teeth. I said, "Give me that honorable discharge and I will get my teeth fixed at home, myself."

On January 5, 1946 I received my discharge, $300 mustering out pay, and a train ticket to Kane, Pennsylvania. This ended my short military career of three years, two months, and one day. I wouldn't take a million dollars for the things that I learned—things that I saw and did. I learned more about discipline, which we have to have in our homes, our work, and ourselves. I rode the train all night to Kane. I got home Sunday morning, January 6. I surprised Mom and Dad. We were happy and had a good cry.

SOLDIER LIVES BECAUSE RADIO DIED

Ray Olson
83rd Armored Field Artillery

It was bitter cold before daybreak on January 16, 1945. Under heavy enemy fire, our four-man liaison team from Headquarters Battery of the 83rd

Armored Field Artillery, a bastard battalion of 105s, entered Sterpigny, Belgium from the North.

The battered town, located on a road between Houffalize and St. Vith, was entered on foot by forward elements of the previous day. A Task Force of the 3rd Armored Division had also fought its way into Sterpigny.

The nearness of our guns was clearly evident, as we were using charge one. Radio was the only communication to the rear. Our team pushed forward, since many forward observer groups had been chewed up, and there were no replacements.

Normally our team was a liaison between F.O.s and the guns. During the Bulge, abnormal was normal. Consequently, our team found itself in a town predominately occupied by German infantry and tanks with strong artillery support. Tiger tanks, usually open country weapons, periodically roamed through the town, blasting anything foreign or moving. Some 75mm shells from American tanks bounded off the Tigers with little or no damage.

Finally, a tank was placed between two buildings. The 75mm gun was loaded and aimed point blank a few feet from a Tiger's path in the road. When the Tiger was abreast, the 75mm shell was discharged. The shell tore a gaping hole in the side of the tank. The Tiger gasped and then exploded violently. The rubble of scrap steel temporarily formed a welcome roadblock.

The Jerries also occupied or controlled the high ground. This was a massive, steep and thick range of deep snow covered forests overlooking Sterpigny. German artillery was pinpointing its fire on all areas occupied by us, while the Jerries pushed in strength from the east.

In an attempt to turn the advantage, we directed 105mm fire on all probable high German observation posts and the Jerry attack forces. Delayed fuses were used to penetrate and phosphorus shells to light up or burn. In a short time, the battalion had fired some 1100 rounds of ammo. Nothing was working effectively. The Jerries continued to pound our holdings with mortars and 88s. The artillery battle continued into January 17, 1945. The Germans, looking down our throats from the high ground, were trying to annihilate us. We were desperately trying to survive, destroy Jerry O.P.s and stop the fierce ground forces.

Late on January 17, we were down to one working radio to our 105s. That radio suddenly failed. At that time, artillery fire was being directed from behind a burned out tank. We hurriedly carried the radio into the hallway of a standing building. As we were attempting to repair our only communication, a Jerry 88 shell found its target. The shell exploded in the doorway about six feet away. The radio, sitting on a table, partially protected me, but the blast and blow rendered me unconscious.

I woke up in a field hospital the next day with a chaplain leaning over me saying, "You are not going to die." There were many casualties from the one 88 shell. My radio buddy was seriously wounded, a major standing behind me had both legs blown off and the radio that had protected me from sure death was demolished. None of the wounded who survived would ever return to combat.

Shortly after the dead and wounded were evacuated from Sterpigny, the Germans took control. Hard, bloody, ruthless and destructive fighting had raged continuously for three days. On January 17, the Germans decisively won the battle for Sterpigny. The Jerries thereby kept open a road for their comrades retreating from the Bulge.

IN THE BULGE

Harold J. O'Neill
83rd Infantry Division, 83rd Signal Battalion

The 83rd Division was pulled out of Germany and sent southwest across Holland into northern Belgium. Bumper-to-bumper military vehicles stretched for miles on a road on top of a dike surrounded by flooded fields. Air cover patrolled overhead and when a vehicle broke down it was pushed off into the ditch or field. I was transferred to a messenger jeep that now required three men instead of two. The MPs stopped us repeatedly to ask about the winner of the World Series or Betty Grable's leading man in some movie. This was to detect English-speaking Germans in our rear areas.

The jeep had chains on all four wheels and the windshield laid on the hood to stop reflections. We put up a ten-inch board for a windshield and drove with a bobbing motion, peeking over it to see the road. Welded to the front bumper was a six foot tall angle iron with a notch to catch and break cables strung across the road at night. We carried K-rations and sometimes Ten-in-One rations that we heated on the engine block. You had to remember to punch a hole in the can or it would explode and the jeep smelled of burnt eggs or Spam. Jeeps have no winch so larger vehicles had to pull or push us out of drifts or ditches.

We wore long johns, wool shirts and pants and mackinaws instead of overcoats. Finger gloves were useless, so we traded with German prisoners for their fur lined mittens and a rabbit fur vest. The cost was only a few cigarettes. I wore three pair of socks with size 12 boots instead of my normal size nine. Towels with eye holes protected our face. Wet feet meant trench foot and frostbite was a problem. We usually had a pair of socks drying from armpit warmth and growing a beard helped.

The messenger jeep ran between the division headquarters and the three infantry regiment headquarters. With units on the move the information was often out of date and we spent two or three days on the road before returning to division headquarters. Thirty-five-year-old Pop did most of the driving and I did the navigation. Teenaged Elmer did a lot of sleeping. We rotated sitting in the back seat since it was the coldest.

The army issued single blanket sleeping bags, so we stopped at an aid station to pick up blankets with the least blood stains. Outdoors or in a building we put six or seven blankets under us and as many above. Only our boots were removed to sleep.

One bitter night we parked between two blazing buildings for extra warmth and another time we slept on the second floor of a windmill. Heavy Elmer collapsed the staircase so Pop and I used our tow rope to get down. We threatened to put him on a diet.

Near the end of the Bulge we picked up an illegal trailer that had no lights or brakes. It carried a small pot-bellied stove, stove pipe, briquettes of coal dust and molasses or something, a 220 volt radio, all volt radio, souvenirs, wine for Pop, rations, a tarp for a ground sheet, army overcoats or mackinaws…

None of us even caught a cold and we were happy when told to head to a coal mine for delousing and showers. The lice came from sleeping in barns and were known as "mechanized dandruff."

TRAFFIC JAM

Harold J. O'Neill
83rd Infantry Division, 83rd Signal Battalion

During the Battle of the Bulge, I rode in a jeep of the Signal Company Message Center. We carried coded and non-coded messages between Division Headquarters and lower units such as the Regimental Headquarters. A fifty caliber machine gun mounted in the back fired over the heads of the driver and navigator in the front. The folding top could not be raised due to the gun, and the windshield was flat on the hood to prevent reflections that might draw enemy fire. The Regimental HQs that we were trying to reach was on the move and their radio gave us two possible villages for their stopping place. We had no radio, but were given the information at the Division HQ before we left. As navigator, I picked the most direct route, but the bridges were out and I relied on secondary roads. Some of these were jammed with vehicles and many had weakened bridges due to heavy trucks using them. I then went off the map to use small dirt roads that had intact bridges that could handle the weight of a jeep. Many road signs were down, missing, or had been rotated by the enemy to give the wrong direction. After two days, we came to a better road with military traffic crossing a small river at the foot of a steep hill. The road went up the hill through a village built along the side of the road. Many buildings were burned or abandoned. A line of tanks, trucks, half-tracks, and our jeep went up the hill and stopped near the top. The traffic had turned the snow into ice and a half-track slid sideways, block-ing the road, with houses on either side. A tank tried to go in back of a house, but the hill was too steep. The road had been built on the gentlest part of the hill alongside the river. The snow was too deep for the jeep, so the machine gunner and the driver went to sleep. We had K rations that we could cook on the jeep engine, but I went walking down the hill to find something better and to warm up by walking. The tanker and truck drivers were building fires from wood of wrecked houses and shared hot rations and coffee with me. A bunch of officers and some engineer troops were moving the half-track at the top of the hill and ashes from the burned houses were used as sand on the ice.

We reached the top of the hill and in a few hours arrived at our goal, the Regimental HQ, ate at their mess and slept for a few hours before heading back to Division HQ with more messages. We made the return trip in one day since some major bridges were repaired. During the entire four days we never drove over twenty miles an hour because of the windshield lying flat and the icy roads. When night came, we looked for a place to sleep. Night driving was out because you could only use the blackout lights. We used wrecked houses, cellars for shelter and a few times, slept in the open.

Whenever we saw a tank or truck stuck, we stopped to help, using man power to push or the winches on the larger vehicles. We were towed out of trouble more often than we helped since we had no winch on the jeep. It was so cold that it numbed your feet so you could not feel the clutch or gas. The driver used the throttle instead of the gas pedal. We wore towels over our faces and goggles or eyeglasses to block the wind of the moving vehicle.

THE BULGE

Merle Otto
99th Infantry Division, 394th Infantry Regiment

Late September 1944, our outfit crossed the English Channel (very rough) and waded ashore at Le Havre France. From there it was days of truck rides to our post in eastern Belgium. In late November our regiment moved up to the front line, to replace another group, near Losheimergraben on the old Seigfried line. We could see the German pillboxes about two hundred sixty yards ahead.

For about three weeks our outfit stayed here. We were well "dug in" in our foxholes and even covered them with logs. It was very cold and snowed off and on. One night I woke up, tried to light a cigarette, and "no light." Not enough oxygen in the hole. I was attached to platoon headquarters as a "runner." Carried messages and rations to outposts. Almost every night six to ten GIs were sent on patrol to see what the Germans were doing or try and pick-up a prisoner. I went on a few of these patrols. In the middle of night we could hear German tank movement but I guess the higher ups thought the Germans were powerless.

On December 16th, 1944 at 5:30 A.M. "all hell" broke loose. Heavy German artillery shells were falling all over our defensive positions. Luckily we had those logs over our holes as shells would break in the trees overhead and rain shrapnel down over our positions. Only one of our foxholes had a direct hit with two men killed (our platoon). The artillery fire lasted one and a half hours. Then we heard the men and tanks coming. No direct frontal attack on our platoon but next door was the 106th Division and they were hit directly. Two of our platoons from our company were sent to help the 106th (all captured, killed, or wounded). The Germans got in behind our platoon so we were trapped.

During the night we joined up with the outfit on our left where an officer led us up through a canyon which was being shelled by our artillery to keep the Germans from advancing. We would set up and run between shell bursts coming (you can hear them coming) then hit the ground during bursts. One time the guy next to where I was lying didn't get up. I kicked him, but no response. He was dead and had been hit earlier. Our platoon and battalion formed up on Elsenborn Ridge where we "dug in" and would hold this ridge for the next ten days against repeated German assaults. Many, many Germans were killed in front of our emplacement.

For this action our battalion received a "Presidential Citation" and a "Bronze Star." We went two days without food or water, except for snow. General Peiper and his soldiers and Panzers had been stopped. After three weeks we had taken back the ground lost and moved into Germany. About five miles south of our positions the Malmedy Massacre occurred when one hundred fifty American prisoners were massacred. A few "played dead" and survived. After hearing of this we took no live prisoners for a while.

Our food during this time and much of the time later consisted of three boxes a day, about "cracker jack" size, marked breakfast, lunch, and dinner. Inside were small cans of scrambled eggs, ground meat, crackers, four cigarettes, and two "0" bars (chocolate). Occasionally, if there was a jeep near, we would "bum" some gas, pour it into our steel helmets, light it on fire, and heat the rations. A little better that way, and we survived on this type of nutrition. During the months of December and January we did not take a shower or change clothes. Slit trenches were our latrines. The Belgian countryside must be full of good fertilizer!

AFTER ACTION VS. ACTUAL ACTION

Demetri Paris
9th Armored Division, 14th Tank Battalion

An "After Action Report" is a report after an action. It could be shelling by enemy artillery, moving the command post to a new location, an administrative move to a new bivouac area or a combat action by a platoon or company. The AAR, as it is generally called, is made by a higher unit, such as battalion or division headquarters or higher level command element.

The higher headquarters writing the report is not involved in the combat action nor do they witness the combat. They must rely upon other and limited sources for their report. Yet their AAR becomes part of the official U.S. Army combat history, which is the source of research by writers, historians and others. It may not be a complete nor accurate report; it reports only what the preparing unit knows about the action.

The After Action Report of the Headquarters 14th Tank Battalion of 1 Dec 44 to 31 Dec 44 is an example of such a report:

"At 201250 Company "D" called for artillery fire on the infantry in front of CR 515. The forward observer could not get contact with his battalion, so the fire was adjusted by a tank platoon leader who sent his commands to the Battalion CP. These were in turn relayed by telephone to the 16th Field Artillery Fire Direction Center. One battery was registered on the enemy by the fire direction center for use as a base point for future missions."

I assume the date/time of the AAR is correct—i.e. 12:50 noon on December 20, 1944. I was the tank platoon leader referred to in the AAR. I had five tanks widely spaced on a slight ridge before a large open field with forest in the background. I observed a large enemy infantry force preparing to attack across the open field and knew we would be overrun.

There was no forward observer present. I chose to radio directly to the battalion headquarters for artillery support. Generally, radio messages to Battalion Headquarters were answered by a staff officer or enlisted man. I was surprised to receive the following response:

"Hello—Squirrel—this is Gopher. Send your message. Over."

Gopher was the radio call sign for the battalion commander, Lt. Col. Leonard Engemen. I told him the situation and requested artillery support. He responded he would try to get it. Moments later he radioed they would fire a mission so I gave him my location to the best of my ability. I said, "Give me one round and I'll adjust the fire."

I then radioed my four other tank commanders to prepare for artillery support on our position. This was so the tank commanders who were exposed could partially close their turret hatches upon notice.

The next message from Gopher was, "On the way." That first round burst near a treetop a few yards in front of my tank. I immediately radioed:

"Gopher—this is Squirrel. Great shot. Up 100 and give me all the fire you can." At this time the large force of enemy troops was crossing the open field. The fire of our 16th Armored Field Artillery Battalion was devastating. The enemy troops that were able hastily returned to the forest. They obviously decided not to cross that field again. I reported the results to Col. Engeman.

That night I became aware that the enemy troops were apparently recovering their wounded comrades. We withheld our fire and I cannot explain why. Many years later I learned our 16th Armored Field Artillery Battalion had the new Posit fuse, which explains how the first round detonated at the treetop in front of my tank.

BATTLE OF THE BULGE CASUALTIES AT SEA: NOT ALL AMERICAN CASUALTIES WERE IN BELGIUM AND LUXEMBOURG

Demetri Paris
9th Armored Division, 14th Tank Battalion

There were more than 600,000 American forces in the Battle of the Bulge. American forces suffered 81,000 casualties which included 19,000 killed in Belgium and Luxembourg.

But these were not the only casualties. Troops in England were being rushed to strengthen the American forces—both individual replacements and complete units. One of those replacement units was the 66th Division.

On Christmas Eve, December 24, 1944, the 66th Division troops boarded the Leopoldville, a Belgian vessel named for the city in the former Belgian Congo. It had a crew of 237 and its officers were Belgian, Congolese and English.

This vessel had been a cruise ship capable of handling 360 passengers, yet it was packed with more than 2,200 66th Division soldiers.

The ship was bound for Le Havre, France via the cold and rough English Channel. But the journey was interrupted when a German submarine torpedo struck it. An alarm and abandon ship was sounded in Flemish, a language spoken in Netherlands, Northwest Belgium and Norwest France.

The ship's officers and crew abandoned the ship, taking the few lifeboats. About 1,400 or 1,500 of the soldiers managed to be saved by the destroyers which were to protect the ship. The others either drowned or were crushed between the Leopoldville and destroyers. It is believed that about 800 of the soldiers died yet none of the crew or officers. The survivors were taken to several Army hospitals in France where they spent Christmas Day.

This tragedy was not announced and, as a result, was not reported by the press. In 1959, 15 years after this tragic incident, a report was issued without the unpleasant and shocking facts. A 1960 report by the British Admiralty (navy) excused the officers and crew. A 1992 Belgian report claimed Americans were in the lifeboats, a claim denied by the soldiers who survived.

One might suppose that, for security reasons, the American Army command in Great Britain decided to withhold announcing this tragedy so as to keep the information from the German high command. But if the German submarine had any signal capability, they most likely reported it to gain credit for the hit.

MALEMPRE, BELGIUM REMEMBERED

Demetri Paris
9th Armored Division, 14th Tank Battalion

The following was presented at a memorial service in Malempre-Manhay, Belgium on March 10, 1995 by Demetri "Dee" Paris.

We are here today to commemorate our meeting 50 years ago when we joined to defeat a common enemy.

The Germans attacked on December 16, 1944. Combat Command B of the 9th Armored Division met their first attack, defended St. Vith against repeated German attacks before the 7th Armored Division arrived. Combat Command B continued fighting without relief nor rest for the next seven days.

Companies A, B and D of the 14th Tank Battalion and the 89th Reconnaissance Squadron were holding a defensive line from Grufflingen to Hohenbusch. Other units of Combat Command B were similarly engaged against the enemy.

The command post of the 27th Armored Infantry Battalion was captured by the Germans. The German captors allowed medical officer Paul

Russomano to use an ambulance to bring medical supplies to the command post and, later, to evacuate wounded German soldiers.

Glen Strange was one of those captured. He escaped, obtained a handgun from his supply officer and organized about 15 of his infantry soldiers. He joined with Lieutenant Duck of A Company and a platoon of tanks from B Company of the 14th Tank Battalion to rescue the men held in his battalion command post.

Lt. Colonel Engeman, 14th Tank Battalion Commander, reported constant pressure by attacking German units. He said that Company D, with an attached tank destroyer platoon, was especially involved in repelling German units.

Orders came to break off contact with the enemy and withdraw. But it was not easy. General Clarke of the 7th Armored Division called upon Combat Command B for assistance. The help came from Companies A, C and D of the 14th Tank Battalion, Companies A and B of the 27th Armored Infantry Battalion and Troop D of the 89th Cavalry Reconnaissance Squadron.

Company A of the 14th Tank Battalion covered the withdrawal. They lost two tanks and three command vehicles in destroying German antitank guns. They recovered several American vehicles which had been captured by the Germans.

Lt. Col. Engeman led the 14th Tank Battalion out of the bulge. They came under intense fire at Manhay. Company C of the 27th Infantry Battalion was ordered to withdraw to Malempre.

Dr. Walter E. Reichelt reports in "Phantom Nine" that the withdrawal did not mean rest for Combat Command B. The 27th Armored Infantry Battalion established a defensive position around Malempre. The 14th Tank Battalion established road blocks. Company D of the 14th Tank Battalion reported to the command post of the 82nd Airborne Division. Company C of the 14th remained in Manhay where the 3rd Armored Division employed in attacks and where they lost three tanks before the 82nd Airborne Division had been forced out of Regne and called upon C Company of the 14th Tank Battalion to recapture the town at a cost of three American tanks and destruction of five German tanks.

Peter Elstob's book *Hitler's Last Offensive* states, "There was little rest for the weary soldiers from the St. Vith defense because of the increasing pressure from new-committed German troops would not allow it..." Also, "Some of the troops who had just retreated from St. Vith were hurried forward again to form a blocking position from Malempre to Manhay." Elstob reports other combat actions in the Malempre-Manhay area by Combat Command B.

Combat Command B closed into its assembly area at 0530 hours on the 25th of December. It had been in continuous combat with the enemy from 0700 hours on the 17th of December until 1430 hours on the 24th of December.

There were trying times and casualties for the civilians. The 1st SS Panzer Division killed more than 100 Belgians in the Stavelot area. The village of Bande had 32 Belgian youths killed by German soldiers. The 2nd SS "Das Reich" Panzer Division threatened civilians in the Manhay area. The citizens of Malempre-Manhay suffered injuries and deaths. It was estimated that 3,000 German shells fell on this area.

American shelling and bombing also killed civilians, in some cases where there were no German troops. With no enemy in Malmedy, bombing killed 125 villagers and 37 American soldiers. American bombs killed 250 civilians in St. Vith. This is according to Danny Parker in his book *Battle of the Bulge— Hitler's Ardennes Offensive, 1944–45.*

Yes, those were trying times... for American soldiers and for Belgians.

On June 10, 1989, the citizens of Malempre, Belgium dedicated a memorial to the American soldiers who defended and later liberated the town during the Battle of the Bulge (Ardennes). One plaque was dedicated to the Americans and the second to the civilian heroes of the village.

The benediction by Father Choque at that 1989 ceremony recalled the sacrifices: "Belgians and Americans, fighting together, died together, and, from the earth fertilized by their blood, peace had sprung. You are here today because gratitude is a fundamental virtue among honorable men."

Many of you who are here today are those honorable people for whom gratitude is a fundamental virtue. Those of us who fought are grateful for having lived through that combat and for the privilege of being here today. We join all of you in gratitude to those American soldiers and Belgian civilians that gave their lives for this victory over an enemy who would have destroyed us. We are mindful of the 50 years of peace you have enjoyed and pray that it lasts forever.

REMAGEN BRIDGE

Demetri Paris

9th Armored Division, 14th Tank Battalion

Colonel Engeman sent one of his light tank platoons under my command to clean out the pocket on the Waldburg Hill. I knew if we approached the hilltop we would expose the belly of the tanks, which is the thinnest armor, so I dismounted my men, except for the drivers, and had the platoon sergeant take his section, two lank crews, around to the rear. He was to watch for me to cover my advance. I then advanced to the top and when he signaled he saw me. I rose and advanced on the guns armed with a .30 carbine.

The gun crews immediately surrendered, placing their hands on their head. Although I had two men with some knowledge of German and Polish we could not establish their identity. And since tankers cannot lake prisoners I simply pointed to the rear the direction from where we had come and they immediately marched away with their hands on their heads. Years later I learned they were Hungarians forced into the German army and so were glad to surrender to the Americans. I placed thermite grenades in the gun barrels, which took care of silencing them.

I could not reach Colonel Engeman by radio so I went into Remagen to report the results. I took Sergeant Taylor with me, walking on the opposite side of the street into the rear since there was still sniper fire. I suddenly came under fire, hit the ground and rolled under a 2-1/2 ton truck. There I found our company first Sergeant and the cook's crew cooking food. A great gang that was always with us!

I found Colonel Engeman where he established his command post in a wine cellar. He promptly sent me to stop all troop convoys that he knew would be coming and prevent their trucks from blocking the narrow streets of Remagen and in the approach to the bridge. He was right. As convoys started arriving I would get the convoy's leader, give him directions to the bridge, dismount the troops and send the empty trucks on the route we were supposed to be sending them to Sinzig and the Ahr River. I told the lead driver to proceed a half to one mile and then bivouac in a roadside field. I never knew how the operation ended or whether they ever got back to their units.

The tanks and half-tracks that crossed were stopped by the Erpeler Ley, which is so steep that infantrymen had to crawl up. Our mission was to protect against an enemy counterattack, which would be the logical defense. Of course we knew we had to move so as not to block the exit from the bridge.

When I reached the east bank and the town of Erpel I turned right and proceeded until a saw a cut, since I knew they would not try to attack over that ridge but would seek an opening. This was what I learned in desert training at Camp Ibis when my friend Lt. Copeland and I would use a jeep to survey the area where we thought the next maneuver would be held.

After two or three days I brought my five tanks back to Erpel so I can assume the infantry had secured the bridgehead.

TANK UNIT RECEIVES PRESIDENTIAL CITATION

Demetri Paris
9th Armored Division, 14th Tank Battalion

Combat Command "A" of the 9th Armored Division has been awarded the Presidential Unit Citation for action in stopping German attacks in the period December 16–23, 1944. The citation was issued June 12, 2001, 57 years after their gallant defense.

The Combat Command, which consisted of a battalion each of tanks, armored infantry and artillery, plus engineers and reconnaissance troops, repulsed constant and determined attacks by an entire German division. After six days and when other troops arrived, the surrounded survivors fought their way out of the German encirclement.

Their determined fight disrupted the German schedule and allowed the U.S. III and XII Corps to bring additional troops to hold Bastogne.

The three combat commands of the 9th Armored Division were widely separated and were the first to meet the December 16, 1944, attack by Hitler's Panzer forces. Combat Command B was in the north at St. Vith alongside the 106th Infantry Division, which had two regiments captured. CC "B" held the Germans from St. Vith until the arrival of a combat command of the 7th Armored Division. Combat Command "R" was in the center at Bastogne while Combat Command "A," which received PUC, was in the south at Beaufort.

The German attackers called the 9th the "Phantom" Division since their attacks were being stopped by the division's combat commands at three separate places.

The citation reads:

"The Presidential Unit Citation (Army) for Extraordinary Heroism to Combat Command A, 9th Armored Division.

Combat Command A, 9th Armored Division, is cited for extraordinary heroism and gallantry in combat in the vicinity of Waldbillig and Stavelborn, Luxembourg, from December 16 to December 22, 1944, by repulsing constant and determined attacks by an entire German division. Outnumbered five to one, with its infantry rifle companies surrounded for most of the time, clerks, cooks, mechanics, drivers and others manned the 10,000 yard final defensive line. Supported by the outstanding responsive and accurate fire of its artillery battalion this widely dispersed force stopped every attack for six days until its surrounded infantry were ordered to fight their way back to them. This staunch defense disrupted precise German attack schedule and thus gave time for the United States III and XII Corps to assemble unhindered and then launch the coordinated attack which raised the siege of Bastogne and contributed to saving much of Luxembourg and its capital from another German invasion. The outstanding courage, resourcefulness, and determination of the gallant force are in keeping with the highest traditions of the United States Army."

THE 9TH ARMORED DIVISION FOUGHT GERMAN ARMIES: THREE COMBAT COMMANDS WIDELY SEPARATED

Demetri Paris

9th Armored Division, 14th Tank Battalion

Units and elements of the 9th Armored Division were attached to or fought with more major commands during the Battle of the Bulge (Ardennes) than those of any other U.S. Army division.

This is based on military records and explains why the German high command called the 9th a "phantom" division after receiving reports from several German armies that they were attacking the 9th AD in separate locations.

The Battle of the Bulge Historical Foundation (BOBHF) has identified nine major American commands which fought in the Ardennes Campaign. The 9th AD fought under eight of these commands and, in addition, also fought under the command of the British 21st Army Group.

These findings were the result of studies by Maj. Gen. George Ruhlen, who commanded the 2nd Armored Field Artillery Battalion of the division. Ruhlen, now deceased, was known as an historian dedicated to accuracy.

The three combat commands A, B, and R were attached to three of the 18 infantry divisions, two of the three airborne divisions, and three of the eight armored divisions who fought in the Battle of the Bulge.

In addition, smaller units of the 9th AD were attached to or fought under another infantry division and another armored division.

Other 9th AD units supported elements of two other infantry divisions, a third airborne division, and another armored division.

The only critical Bulge areas where the 9th AD was not involved nor engaged in combat were the far north sector around Elsenborn and in the west from Marche to Celles.

Division Action Not Reported...

There are factors which resulted in the combat actions of the 9th AD not being reported.

1. The most likely reason the 9th AD actions were not reported in the

press nor in published historical books is the division was under "secret" classification throughout the battle. The attacking German armies knew the 9th was delaying their advance yet American correspondents were prohibited from writing about this combat. Unfortunately, the secret classification was not lifted until about January 5, 1945.

2. It is well known that an attached or supporting unit generally receives no mention in the After Action Report of the unit to which it is attached or is supporting. For example, Combat Command B which delayed the main German attack in the St. Vith area for six days was not included in the award granted the 7th Armored Division with whom they were fighting alongside. One exception is the 101st Airborne included Combat Command R in their award of the Presidential Unit Citation (PUC) for the defense of Bastogne.

3. Yet a third reason was that none of the 9th AD units were under division control. Maj. Gen. John W. Leonard, the division commander, did not have any of the three commands under his control. All were fighting in widely separated locations, the 9th AD did not fight as an entity as did other divisions except the 10th Armored Division.

Division Separated Before Bulge Attack...

On December 9, 1944, Combat Command B (CCB) was relieved from the 9th AD control and attached to V Corps to support the 2nd Infantry Division. The 2nd was to attack and open a gap through which CCB was to advance and capture the Roer River dams and prevent the Germans from flooding the Roer Valley, which would establish a geographical barrier to Allied advance.

The status of the three combat commands during the battle were: CCB fought in the north to delay the German capture of St. Vith, CCR fought in the center and, along with other troops, delayed the German advance at Bastogne until the arrival of the 101st Airborne Division and CCB of the 10th Armored Division. CCA was initially in the south at Beaufort, Luxembourg, and then at Bastogne with the 4th AD.

When attacking German armies reported action against the 9th in widely separated locations, the German high command dubbed the 9th a "phantom" division. Also, German armies twice reported they had destroyed the 9th AD.

They learned the 9th was not a "phantom" division on March 7, 945, when CCB captured the Ludendorff Bridge at Remagen, Germany, and were the first Allied troops to cross the Rhine River. It was not until January 8, 1945 that all elements of the 9th AD were joined again under the command of Maj. Gen. John W. Leonard.

PUC Delayed by Secret Classification...

As cited above, CCR of the 9th AD was included in the Presidential Unit Citation awarded to the 101st Airborne Division for the defense of Bastogne. The other two combat commands were denied the PUC because of the lack of records of their combat action caused by the "secret" classification. However, when the cold war ended, the German records were obtained and submitted to the Awards Branch. As a result, CCB and CCA were awarded their PUC 50 years after their Bulge combat action.

MEMORIES OF WORLD WAR II (1943–1946)

Oliver C. Parker
666th Field Artillery Battalion

I was inducted into the Army in July, 1943, at San Francisco, California. Next, I was sent to my induction center at Ft. Ord, California, near Monterey, where I was issued clothing and equipment, given a GI haircut, and received my shots. Also, there I attended several indoctrination classes and took various tests. From Ft. Ord, I was sent by train to Ft. Riley, Kansas, near Junction City, for basic training. I remained there until April, 1944, when I was assigned to the Field Artillery and sent to Camp Bowie, Texas, near Brownwood, for further training. After a few weeks, I received my first furlough and traveled by train to Oakland, near San Francisco, where my parents were living. In October, 1944, my unit, the 666th Field Artillery Battalion, and all our equipment was sent to Camp Miles Standish near Boston, Massachusetts, to await shipment overseas.

We were given additional clothing and equipment plus more shots. On the morning of November 9, 1944, we boarded the New Amsterdam, a Dutch Luxury Liner that had been converted to a troop ship, and sailed east. This was a fast ship that depended on speed to keep her out of trouble. There was no armed escort to help; neither was there a convoy to hinder her.

We then boarded an odd-looking train and headed south. Around three the next morning we arrived at our destination: Wightwick Hall, near Wolverhampton, England. We remained there until December 20 when we headed for the Port of Weymouth. After a one-day delay, we were combat loaded onto an LST and sat in the harbor that night waiting for the rest of the convoy to be made up.

The next morning at eight we sailed into the English Channel. Although the weather was clear, the channel was as rough as ever. We landed at the battered port of Le Havre, France, where we threaded our way through the litter of wrecked ships left from D-Day. A few minutes later we were rolling off the ramp, up the beach, and into what was left of the city.

We headed east and spent our first night in an open field near Fry, France. We almost froze the first week because we had not received our sleeping bags and combat boots. We moved on through France into Belgium where we were a part of the VIIth Corp Artillery, First Army, attached to the 83rd Infantry Division.

The first position we occupied was near Regne, Belgium. Our unit advanced through Belgium and Germany until the surrender of Germany on May 7, 1945. We then moved south through Paderborn, Kassel, Coburg, Nuremberg, Freising and Munich. Next, we turned east along the Bavarian Alps to Salsburg, Austria, then turned back north to Scharding, Austria, on the Danube River.

After the war, our job was primarily that of peacekeeper. We set up guard posts at various checkpoints and picked up DP's (displaced persons) trying to return to their homeland. We would hold them in fenced prison camps until we had a load, then return them to their homeland. We also guarded POW camps as well as continued training as we assumed we would be shipped to Japan where the war was still going on.

After Japan surrendered, while awaiting my time to return to the states, I received a pass to Great Britain for ten days plus travel time. I, along with two guys from my outfit, took off for London where we had a wonderful ten days. Among the things we saw were the Tower of London, Westminster Abbey, Big Ben, and the Changing of the Guards. On our way to London, we stopped in Paris for three days, then we stopped another three days on our return trip. Altogether, we were gone almost thirty days.

By March, 1946, I had enough points to receive a discharge, and I shipped out of Le Havre, France and landed in New York. I then passed through Camp Kilmer in New Jersey, and was sent to Camp Chaffee, near Ft. Smith, Arkansas, where I was discharged.

I received the following medals: World War II Victory Ribbon, Good Conduct Medal, American Theatre Ribbon, EAME Theatre Ribbon and Three Bronze Service Stars. I was in the following campaigns: Ardennes (Battle of the Bulge), Rhineland and Central Europe.

SHOT IN STOUMONT, BELGIUM

James C. Pendleton, Sr.
30th Infantry Division, 119th Infantry Regiment

Third Battalion, Headquarters Company, 119th Infantry Regiment, 30th Infantry Division was in Aachen, Germany, on December 16, 1944. We had been stationed at Aachen for several days; not much was going on at that time. Our battalion was among one of the first U.S. troops to enter Germany. The scuttlebutt was that we were waiting on the Russians to come in from the east.

Late in the evening of the 16th, the battalion started moving back toward Belgium, although no one seemed to know why. We travelled stop and go all night of the 16th and into the evening of the 17th. The roads were clogged with heavy equipment and heavy artillery and other troops were moving with us—some one way and some the other. A few German planes would make an appearance occasionally and strafe and bomb. This would cause us to be delayed for a couple of hours. Road signs were turned in the wrong direction.

Many times we would travel for several miles before we would realize we were headed in the wrong direction and would have to turn around and go the direction we had just traveled. After a day and two nights, we arrived in Stoumont, Belgium. Since we had previously cleared the enemy from Belgium, we felt we were in safe territory and did not need to have troops stand guard at night. We left our equipment and vehicles in the road and went into the buildings for sleep and warmth.

My group was the A and P Platoon; the platoon leader, Lt. Goodman, woke me in the middle of the night and asked me if I heard noises outside. I told him I did and why weren't those troopers sleeping and why didn't they wait until daylight before they started making so much noise. He informed me that the noises were German Tiger Tanks hauling off our 57 gun. The guys from my company were Jim (Red) Aldridge (Maryland) and Garrison (Memphis, Tennessee). I cannot recall the names of the machine gunners but they were from I Company.

We took 12 anti-tank mines with us; that was all we had available to us. We laid four mines across the street and were able to knock one tank out immediately. Then we laid out four more mines and destroyed another tank and were able to do that a third time. By this time it was getting daylight and more tanks kept coming, replacing the ones we destroyed. We ran out of mines so we took refuge in a store with a glass front. One of the tankers pulled up, stuck his 88 barrel in the window and in perfect English asked us if we wanted to surrender. We told him we would surrender to him.

I looked around, saw a side door, and told the others to run for it; there was a jeep 3-16 setting outside the door idling. I jumped into the driver's seat and the other guys piled in and we made a run for it out of the alley and down the road. We had gone about a 100 yards when we saw a German half-track in the middle of the road. The half-track started firing on us. When that happened, the front wheels were shot off the jeep and I was shot in the right forearm. The other guys slid down the road into the ditch and got away around the curve. I never saw those four guys again. I saw an open door and ran into the building. Unfortunately for me, the room was full of Germans. A German put a burp gun in my face and I was able to grab the barrel with my good arm and shoved it away from me. He either emptied the gun into the wall or it jammed—I'm not sure what happened. I then backed out, and ran to the corner of the same building. I was standing there when Joe Duvall, from my company, came by and applied a tourniquet to my arm. He then ran between two buildings and I never saw him again.

While I was standing there trying to decide what to do, I noticed an American tank down the road in a curve. He would shoot and then back up in the curve to get out of the way of the enemy tanks. He was close enough to me that I could holler and wave and he saw me. He said he couldn't get me in the tank but if I could use my good arm to hold onto the barrel, he would throw me over onto the other side and put the tank between me and the Germans and their small arms fire. He told me when I heard the tank rev up three times he would come in and throw the barrel in my direction. Somehow, I was able to wrap my left arm around the barrel and hold on while he backed out with me. I never knew the name of the company the American tanker was with. He dropped me off around the curve and I dropped and kept moving.

By this time, I was getting weak from the loss of blood. I would walk as far as I could and then stop to rest. At times other soldiers moving back would see me and carry me until they would become tired. About noon a medic outfit found me and picked me up in their ambulance. By dark of December 19th, I was in a tent city hospital. I stayed in a Paris hospital for a week or two and then transferred to England. I was sent back to the States in April on the George Washington hospital ship.

ONE HOUR IN THE BULGE

Joseph V. Pilliteri
5th Infantry Division, 10th Infantry, Company E

It was one day in December, 1944, in northern France on our way to Luxembourg. I was a scout walking knee-deep in snow. A TD came up to assist us in our push forward. The tank saw a Jerry run into a farm house about 300 yards down in the valley. They fired one round into the house. My buddy and I ran into the house. (My buddy, James Mitchell, was killed a few days later.) We went through the front door. Mitch went down the hall to clear other rooms. I went into the first room—that's the room that the shell entered. In the room were two German soldiers. One had his head half blown off—you could see his brains moving. The other one had both legs blown off and was in shock. As I entered the room, he raised his arms and was saying over and over something that sounded like "Soney, Soney." After 50 years those words still haunt me. I thought he wanted me to shoot him, but he was unarmed so I did not.

I went out the front door and into another at the corner of the building. As soon as I entered the room, six German soldiers put their hands on their heads and surrendered to me. That could have been my last day. It was a radio room. The room had large radios all over the place. My first thought was to put a few bullets into them. Then I thought they might be of some use to us. I lined my prisoners up and started to take them back to my unit.

Just as I got the last one out the door, another Jerry (he must have been behind the building) ran into me as I went backwards. I came down with my machine pistol. It was a German gun that I had picked up at the other end of the building. Thank God it was not on safety. I shot a burst of bullets through his shoulder and collar bone. He started to cry and wanted to pick up his overcoat. I spun him around to join the group. Now I had seven prisoners. When I got back to my squad the prisoner I had shot was still crying—he wanted to see his mother. When my sergeant heard him, he wanted to kill him, saying he was thousands of miles from his mother. I got between them, told the sergeant he was my prisoner and I didn't want any more harm to come to him.

I lasted until January 20, 1945, when I was wounded in Luxembourg.

ELSENBORN RIDGE

Charles R. Posey
2nd Infantry Division, 9th Infantry Regiment, Company M

I was en route from Camp Chesterfield to be a replacement in M Company, 9th Infantry, 2nd Division. While we were being transported we heard rumors of a German breakthrough. By the time we got to Elsenborn Ridge, the story began to unfold. Col. Hershfelder had managed to retreat from the German breakthrough; however, there had been a lot of casualties. The first I heard about was "Whitey" had been run over by a German Panzer. Everyone thought he was dead. To our surprise when the war was over in Europe and we got to Ft. Sam there was "Whitey." He had been taken prisoner.

I arrived at M Company as a machine gunner, 30 caliber, water cooled. The first evening I was in the camp I had dug a foxhole. We were being shelled constantly. Tree bursts scattered shrapnel everywhere. Then to my surprise Capt. Man, company commander, came to talk with me. He had received a battle field commission. He spent a little while giving me encouragement. He was part of a historical unit—the Honshu Regiment. I do not really remember what he said but when he left I went to sleep.

I don't know if any of the men I served with are still alive. I have lost touch. I remember a Sgt. Flores. He got a Silver stsar for bravery. Satoff was our Medic. I remember a Sgt. Figero. One guy who came to the front with me was named Perry.

We were shelled night and day and strafed by Messerschmitts.

The cooks said they would come up to our forward position if we would dig a kitchen for them. A funny thing happened while we were working on it—there was a tree stump we could not pry loose. Someone in higher Headquarters had decided to issue 1/4 sticks of dynamite for us to dig foxholes in the frozen ground. "Ha Ha—not a good idea." Anyway, someone suggested that we use a few sticks to dislodge the tree stump. We used 4 or 5. When it exploded the stump went into the air like a rocket. We finished the kitchen. We even fixed a shelf not so deep for the cooks to sleep on. A few days later a very angry artillery officer came up. He wanted to talk with our CO. It seems the stump hit one of his trucks. He was furious. But when he met Capt. Man, they knew each other and had gone to the same high school, I think in Pennsylvania.

To complete this story about the 1/4 sticks of dynamite, when we began to advance someone drilled a hole and ignited the stick—"Bam!" This was followed by a series of explosions. The German observers had triangulated on the explosion and dug a few more foxholes for us. Needless to say, immediately they took all the rest of the dynamite away from us.

We should have known better because even when we had dropped a mess kit the German artillery would guess we were eating and shell us. I am grateful that John Eisenhower mentioned the stand at Elsenborn Ridge in his book *The Bitter Woods*.

MY NUMBER ONE MEMORABLE EVENT

Harry Reed
3rd Armored Division, 53rd Armored Reconnaissance Battalion

The most memorable event for me in the Battle of the Bulge was around the Hotton-Soy area. On December 23 about 3 o'clock in the morning we heard small arms firing at our roadblock about a mile from the small town where we were. So we took two jeeps, one armored car, and one light tank. I was in the lead jeep about halfway to the roadblock when we ran into Germans on both sides of the road. They were cross-firing on us. We finally made it through to our troops. Our lieutenant was in the front seat; he was hit in the neck and killed. The jeep had bullet holes all over it and all the tires were flat. I had a 50 cal. machine gun mounted on the jeep; I fired it till it burned up and two other automatic weapons till all the ammo was used up. I do not remember firing them. My driver told me I was sure mowing them down. The driver and I were the only ones to come out of the twelve men. All the vehicles were destroyed. I was awarded The Bronze Star and Purple Heart.

413TH AAA BATTALION, BATTERY B

Kenneth L. Reiter
413th Anti-Aircraft Artillery Battalion, Battery B

Staff Sergeant Reiter (90mm gun commander) and Sergeant Lashley Martin would like to share our experiences endured while in the Battle of the Bulge.

Our battery was stationed 1-1/2 miles east of Bullingen several days before the Bulge attack. Our main mission at that time was to shoot down incoming buzz bombs and missiles. This was supposed to be a stalling front and sort of a rest area for our unit and all of our extra trucks for hauling supplies were loaned out to other units to help bring up the line of defense.

So we were left as sitting ducks to march and retreat. So in the overall deal, we had to leave all our personal belongings, such as duffel bags and some supplies, for the Germans.

At 5:30 a.m., the Germans opened up with search lights and artillery and we had about 16" of snow on the ground. I called it a wakeup call. My outfit was alerted to retreat to a safe area, in Steinbach and Sourbrodt. There were three 90mm crews that had ammunition and left with me and my gun crew to fire armor piercing and air bursts on incoming tanks at a road intersection; one machine gun crew and one 90mm crew were left behind to cover our main retreat and hold back the incoming German tanks and infantry. As daybreak appeared, we spotted eight or ten German troops with white uniforms crossing the terrain about 3/4 of a mile behind our firing line and between them and our retreat unit. The Germans directed fire on the retreat convoy. Several of the unit were injured, also Major McGain. At the same time we were in hot action with incoming infantry and tanks. My 90mm crew and machine gun crew held off the Germans some seven hours. We piled up six tanks, blocking the roads, and Martin and his machine crew killed 21 out of 25. They took four prisoners (one SS officer). I disarmed them, finished firing all the 90mm ammo, and somehow escaped capture and made it back to our unit about 3:30 p.m.

Now I'm 85 years old and thank the good Lord for his protection.

The following is from the progress report of Battery B (during the Battle of the Bulge period:

TD

Dec. 16 1-1/2 mi. East of Bullingen

Dec. 17 Biv. at Steinbach & Sourbrodt

Dec. 19 Elsenborn

Dec. 20 2 mi. So. West of Monchau

AA

Dec. 25 4 mi West of Eupen (Xmas)

Jan. 3 2-1/2 mi No. of Verviers, Belgium

SURROUNDED

Kenneth L. Reiter
413th Anti-Aircraft Artillery Battalion, Battery B

The 413th Anti-Aircraft Artillery 90mm Battery "B" gun number two was stationed approximately 3 miles east of Bulligen, Belgium in an area known as "Buzz Bomb Alley." At that time it was like a powder keg and we knew it. On December 10 we moved into this area, being attached to the 106th Infantry Division. We were told it was a static area and our first rest area. With Christmas coming up our spare supply of trucks and drivers were loaned out to haul up supplies to the first Army.

So in this condition at the time we were caught with our pants down. However we did wipe out the Germans on December 12. They fired a buzz bomb in the alley about 20 feet from my gun crew and when the motor shut off we hit the dirt and slid some 100 yards and a cloud of dust, probably a dud. On the 14th of December it was about zero degrees and we got hit with snow, which thanks to the wind blowing came halfway up to the peak of our tents.

Then on December 16 at 5:30 a.m. all hell broke loose. Searchlights lit up the sky and the artillery began to fire with shells coming into the trees overhead. Now about this time the battalion commander arrived from head-quarters and ordered us to march to Monchau. Our gun crew was given orders to fire until all our ammunition was used and then blow up the gun if we were surrounded.

The spearhead attack by the Germans came between 8:00 and 10:00 a.m. So help me, only God saved us from being massacred. During our retreat I could see off to our right many Germans with white uniforms moving across the snow-covered field about 400 yards away and about five yards apart. Germans headed for the rear of the road where our convoy had just left. I expected to encounter tanks followed by infantry. Our machine gun crew would protect us if the enemy would come around by my left flank. Sure enough we were surrounded!

On the other side of road German tanks began to appear and I gave the order to open fire. The third armored shell scored a direct hit, resulting in a fireball and black smoke. We could not see much, therefore we immediately went to firing bursts parallel with the ground in hopes of stopping the German infantry. We fired numerous rounds and when the smoke cleared our machine gun crew had captured some Germans; one of them was an SS officer. All were taken to be interrogated. We were able to take all our equipment, with the exception of 50 duffel bags and some personal belongings, to our next destination.

ALTERNATE POSITION "AMBUSH"

Clayton I. Rice
106th Infantry Division, 589th Field Artillery Battalion, Battery B

The gun crew of Battery B, 589th, was busy taking over the Howitzer positions that the 2nd Infantry Division had vacated when the kitchen truck and the supply trailer, driven by Pvt. Clayton Rice, came to a stop just short of where the observer wanted it to be.

Captain Brown, who was watching the operation, gave the order to pull ahead. The right wheel of the trailer was in the mud pretty good and as the truck inched ahead, the left wheel of the trailer rolled up on some unforeseen object and over the trailer went, spilling supplies, including a lot of loose potatoes, into the mud. Captain Brown did a well-executed military about-face and left, washing his hands of the entire mishap. He had more important things to tend to. The 589th was here to furnish the 422nd Infantry Regiment with artillery support.

The 11th of December, 1944, went well with the boys settling into positions. The men were informed that they would be served two meals a day by the kitchen helpers who were set up in a big tent. Needless to say, the men of the 2nd Infantry were not too happy about leaving "the quiet sector" and the comfort of their quarters which consisted of partial dug outs and well-constructed camp-like tops, a good place to spend the winter of 1944 and 1945.

The lonely guard duty out on the perimeter was spooky, with the buzz bombs going over one after another and with one's eyes glued on the clumps of brush that seemed to change into shapes of men and at times seemed to move. Once in a while a big rabbit would be seen running across a large open space.

The bottom of the foxholes had water in them and it was very, very, very cold. Early in the morning of December 16, 1944, the men sleeping in their huts were jolted from a sound sleep with dirt from the roof falling on their faces and by the earth below shaking and making lots of noise. The men were experiencing the first incoming mail: heavy shelling delivered by the Germans. Unbeknown to the boys, this was the beginning of the "Battle of the Bulge." The attack came as a big surprise and created a lot of excitement among the group.

The gun crew went to work and everything seemed to be okay. About mid-morning, a casualty from "C" Battery was carried into our position and the word was that "C" Battery was hit hard. "B" Battery had escaped with little damage. It was not yet noon and it was reported that the German tanks and soldiers were close by.

A bazooka team was dispatched and after a short time one of the team members returned. The soldier was out of breath and white as a sheet. He reported that the Germans had taken his partner's head off with an 88 fired from a tank. It was plain to see, even to the privates, that the 589th was in trouble, but at this time no one could have guessed how bad!

There was a strong, eerie feeling of bewilderment and shock that settled over the young men. The gun crews stayed active and, as the day progressed, at intervals fired just over the hill, which would suggest that they had lost contact with any forward observers. It was reported that a couple of enemy tanks had been knocked out.

As daylight faded, it was plain to see that "B" Battery had made it through the day in good shape. The word was that we were to pull out during the night and proceed to an alternate position.

About 3:00 a.m., Battery "B" could be found out on the road proceeding to the next position in complete blackout (not even the Cat's Eyes were allowed). The light equipment was up front. Next came the gun trucks followed by the kitchen truck. The maintenance crew in their Dodge was in the rear.

The convoy was to travel real slow, but had only progressed a short distance on the main road when someone up front got in trouble and the column came to an abrupt stop. Evidently the night vision of the GI driving the kitchen GMC was not too good because that truck didn't stop until the gun barrel was through the radiator, stopping at the dashboard. "Hope the gun isn't damaged," blurted the truck driver and the Great Old Cook riding next to him shot back, "To hell with the gun, how about the truck?"

You know, he was right. That Jimmy was inoperable and had to be abandoned. The crew jumped up onto the truck ahead with the help of the gun crew riding in the back. The kitchen truck was burned so it would not fall into the hands of the enemy. Being out on an open hill, the fire could have been seen for miles.

"B" of the 589th Field Artillery Battalion made it to the alternate position as the day broke on the 17th of December. The gun crew didn't even get the guns in place and the trails spread when a jeep came flying in with the driver shouting that the German tanks were right behind him. But that's another story, a very sad story for many.

188TH COMBAT ENGINEERS IN BELGIUM

Wilfrid R. Riley
188th Combat Engineer Battalion

In mid-December the Battalion was performing all the tasks that are peculiar to being a combat engineer. However work on all of these projects ceased when we were ordered by Third Army Headquarters to join the other units that were ordered north to stop the massive German penetration of our lines in the First Army area.

We departed from Keskastel in the Saar Valley on the morning of December 20th and joined the thousands of American soldiers heading for Belgium. Several times during the move north we had to move to the side of the road and permit armored units to pass through us. Armored units were apparently needed ASAP. During one of these halts I was asked about our final destination and said that information had not been given to me before our departure. The look of concern on his face told me that he was very concerned. I told him: someday "Grif" if we survive all of this we will be sitting in our rockers with our favorite libation in our hand and we will smile as we remember moments like this. I hope he did because I have.

We stopped for a day in Longuyon, France and then on to Martelange, Belgium on the borders of France and Luxembourg. Martelange was to be the base of our operations in the Battle of the Bulge. That night B Company was given the assignment of outposting Martelange as the next town north, Bigonville, was held by the Germans. A company was to build a Bailey bridge across the Sure River to provide two way traffic across the river. C Company was to be held in reserve.

My platoon moved out of Martelange toward Bigonville with the arrival of darkness and as we neared our assigned location to set up a defensive position we were commanded to halt. In the darkness I could not see the source of the command. Then a voice commanded the soldier wearing the long coat to move forward. That was me and after a few steps I was again ordered to halt. Then there was the request for the password followed by questions about cities in the USA and questions about baseball, etc. When the challenger was satisfied he told me to advance once again. I did as commanded and very soon I saw an American battle tank sitting next to a small building under a tree, well concealed for such a large unit. Looking up I saw the muzzle of the cannon and in my mind's eyes it was at least twenty four inches in diameter. The voice coming from the tank said, "Soldier, if I was in your shoes I would get rid of that long coat you are wearing because in it you sure as hell look like a German soldier." In the freezing weather I could not discard the coat so I tucked it into my waist and inquired if that looked better. An affirmative reply was received. (Our supply sergeant gave me a mackinaw coat to wear the next day after I told him the story.) I was given permission to move on by the voice that I never did see.

We moved on to our assigned location which was close by and the platoon was soon located in the best positions to defend the area around the road crossing. Nothing unusual occurred during the night but at first light a column of tanks approached us from the East and stopped when they saw us. Up went the hatch on the lead tank and an officer asked our identity after identifying himself. He asked if we had seen or heard anything during the night. He was told that we heard a lot of vehicle movement in Bigonville during the night. With that the hatch closed and tanks proceeded toward Bigonville. In a very short time the sounds of battle were heard. We remained alert for whatever might happen.

The first group of prisoners the armored infantry brought out of the town included an officer, a captain. He was dressed in a dark red uniform and wearing an overseas cap of the same color. He seemed to be dressed for a classroom rather than a battlefield. All of the other prisoners were in battlefield gray uniforms and wore a steel helmet or were bareheaded.

Other groups of prisoners were brought out of town and into the midst of the area we were defending where they were thoroughly searched by the 4th Armored Division soldiers. Later they were loaded into trucks and taken to a collection point (that is an assumption on my part). They did not say and I did not ask. In mid-afternoon the town was in the hands of the 4th Armored Division and our mission was finished and we returned to Martelange for the night.

On December 24th, Christmas Eve, the 188th Engineers and the 249th Engineer Battalions were placed in the line east of Martelange. The 4th Armored Division had progressed nearly to Bastogne and was ready to breach an opening in the German defense. The two Engineer Battalions and two Artillery Battalions were to take the positions now occupied by the 4th Armored Division. When the Engineer and Artillery Battalions were in place the 4th Armored units would move back through them and move east and sweep around the left into Bastogne.

We began the process of digging in, which was very difficult if almost impossible, as the snow was thigh deep and the ground was frozen solid. Where is the TNT when you really need it? All night the friendly fire from the artillery was reassuring, especially when the familiar sound of incoming whistling shells was not heard throughout the night. However the Germans did launch flares all night long and they illuminated the area as if it were daylight. We froze in place to avoid detection. The Germans did not attack and we were perfectly satisfied to hold our position. At noon on Christmas Day we were relieved by elements of the 6th Cavalry Division. We moved to an area in the rear where our mess personnel had a wonderful Christmas dinner prepared for us.

The maneuver of the 4th Armored Division of moving out as we moved in was a successful one. The next day, December 26th, they smashed through the German defenses and the siege of Bastogne was ended. On that day we were briefed on our next assignment, but that is another story for another time.

A FEW LUCKY BREAKS

Richard Rizzio
374th Armored Field Artillery Battalion

My experiences in the Battle of the Bulge will be a bit different than most. Being wounded previously, I was transferred from forward recon and fire battery duty to service battery—one of many lucky breaks that seemed to follow me throughout our four major campaigns.

Captain Olson and I were on a FO post and caught in an 88 barrage. We continued our fire mission. I was slightly wounded and received the Purple Heart. We both received Silver Stars. Captain Olson had saved my life with the words "Duck, Rizzio." A two inch piece of shrapnel hit where my head had been positioned.

As to the Battle of the Bulge, our battalion was settled down in a small French town of Merchweiler, east of Metz. Enjoying a break in the race across France, it seemed like the war was winding down. Up north, things were starting to liven up. Being on radio duty, I received the order around midnight on December 18th to move out. It took us the rest of the night, the next day and the following night to reach the combat area of Stocken, Belgium. What a drive and oh so cold. Short on manpower, I was both radio operator and jeep driver. The only other person in the jeep was a newly assigned 90-day wonder, a 2nd Lieutenant who never offered to relieve the driving on the entire trip. Consequently, I fell asleep momentarily on the second night's drive, running off the road and into the bushes. God knows what the results would have been if the bushes had not been there. I have often thought if I ever met this officer, it would be the right time for an ex-noncom to tell an ex-officer what he really thinks of him.

Our battalion was assigned to the famous 4th Armored Division as support artillery and started our fire mission at Martelange on the Belgium-Luxembourg border.

On Christmas Day, our battalion fired 1,691 rounds of 105 shells, the largest number to date. I remember how bitter cold it was.

However, we did enjoy a complete turkey dinner as our mess truck caught up, along with our Christmas mail from home.

General Patton visited our command post but I didn't get to see him. A few days later, the siege of Bastogne was broken.

My comment of a lucky break refers also to my transfer to Service Battery. Had I remained as a FO or Fire Battery, I question being here today. We suffered a good number of casualties. At another time, I had an 88 shell go under me and not explode. Thanks to slave labor, it was a dud.

I knew we did not endure many of the hardships other units suffered, especially the 101st and 28th Infantry Division. None of us will ever forget those days. The real credit goes to those stalwarts who held the line while reinforcements came from all directions.

ATTACHED TO THE 18TH AIRBORNE CORPS

Luis R. Rodriguez
240th Field Artillery, C Battery

I served in "C" Battery, 240th Field Artillery Battalion as a cannoneer with 155mm guns often times referred to as "Long Toms." We were in the area of Stolberg, Germany, and preparing to move to Duren, Germany, when we got word of the German offensive. On the night of December 23 we made our move to assist in the Battle of the Bulge, arriving in the early hours of December 24 in the town of Stavelot, Belgium. We set up our guns and we fired 4,051 rounds of ammo in the first ten days in support of the 82nd Airborne Division and attached to the 18th Airborne Corps.

Our guns had fired many rounds of ammo, having gone into combat in the Falaise Gap August 18 in France, so a rush was executed to supply us with new gun barrels or "tubes." It was a one day operation, so by evening we were back in action again. I will have to say that as artillery men, we did not have the discomforts that our front line troops experienced but the cold was equal. We had poor winter clothing, especially sleeping bags. I made a sleeping bag out of two GI blankets plus two civilian blankets wrapped with a piece of tent material. This worked out quite well.

The extreme cold weather raised problems with our guns; it would freeze the hydraulic oil in the rams that assisted in raising and lowering of the barrel plus also the recoil mechanism. One time we had only one gun operable. So 24 rounds of ammo were fired with the one gun, all in rapid fire. I will mention that in the snow we painted our guns with powdered milk to blend with the snow. After all this firing the barrel was brown in color from overheating. A short time later this same gun blew up, scattering pieces for one-half mile.

BATTLE OF THE BULGE AT HOUFFALIZE

James E. Sammons
2nd Armored Division, 17th Armored Combat Engineer Battalion,
Company E

After fighting to bridge the Albert Canal in Belgium and our battle for Maastricht, we regrouped in the November, 1944, wet and cold and then moved near the German border in the City of Aachen for assault.

The German Army broke through the line about 100 miles to our south at Bastogne. We back-tracked with the entire division about 75 miles in black-out at night to meet head-on and stop the German 2nd Panzer Division and 560th Volks Grenadier Division at Houffalize, in its drive to split the Allied and cut off our supply.

The pick and shovel platoon of our company in 10 degree weather cleared a path over the steep hills of blacktop roads covered with 10" of snow over 2" of ice for our tanks to engage in battle.

I was driver and Morse Code radio operator of Command half-track for the company commander. After four days of battle, the 2nd Armored Division completely destroyed the 560th Panzer Division. Hitler's SS Storm Troopers called the 2nd Armored Division "Roosevelt's Butchers."

A night later (the password was Geronimo), we continued to pursue the Germans and after daylight the next morning, one of our half-tracks with 12 men on board came to a bridge in the road. Before they could check the bridge for explosives a German 88 bullet crossed the bridge and hit the center of the armored windshield—went through and out the rear door. Not a soldier was hurt.

It was Christmas Morning.

A SOLDIER'S STORY

Dominick Daniel Santagata
5th Infantry Division, Company B, 7th Engineer Battalion

My name is Dominick Daniel Santagata. I was born on August 23, 1924 in Woodhaven, Long Island, New York, New York. My parents were both born in Italy and came to America to find a better life and were very proud to become American citizens. I was the eldest of eight children. The family moved to Stamford, Connecticut when I was two years old. The extended family resides here to this day.

My childhood was one of school, family holidays, carefree days of growing up in a tight knit community with a strong sense of our love for America. When World War II broke out I was a senior in high school, age 17. All able-bodied young men had to register with the draft board. By late 1942 all my school friends were being drafted into branches of the service. At that time, I decided it would be best to volunteer in order to join the Army which was my first preference.

Upon signing up I was sent to New Haven, Connecticut for my physical and passed with flying colors. Then it was on to Ft. Devans, Massachusetts for processing for an additional three weeks. My next assignment was Ft. Belvoir, Virginia to begin my training as a combat engineer. After tough training at this engineering fort, I was then sent on to New Castle, Pennsylvania, awaiting reassignment to Camp Shanks, New York. While stationed at Camp Shanks I got a chance to return home for a week's leave. I bid my mother goodbye and said I would see her again and upon returning to the Camp, was instructed we were shipping out the next day for Europe. We left New York Harbor on the Queen Elizabeth and landed in England. We traveled to Scotland, then boarded another ship to Northern Ireland.

By now it was the fall of 1943, the sea was very rough and men were becoming seasick. It was a very unpleasant trip. The troops landed in Belfast, Northern Ireland. We trained in New Castle for eight months and one month in Portadown, and at that time I was assigned to the Fifth Infantry Division, and then we trained for all kinds of warfare. We took part in bridge building, laying mine fields, handling all kinds of explosives, flame throwers and constructing barbed wire fences. Most of our maneuvers took place along the sea coast and up into the mountains. The long winter months were cold, wet and very dark. On one occasion we were map reading and the whole platoon got lost. Each one of the men was to use the compass and this did not work out very well. While the platoon was trying to find out which way to go, I saw a phone booth in the area and decided to go in and keep warm. I picked up the receiver to try the phone and a young operator answered, "May I help you?"

I explained who we were and that we were lost. She told me she could not divulge this information. Somehow I convinced her that we were American soldiers and she gave me the information and we all got back safely to camp.

After completion of our training the Fifth Division put on an exercise for General Patton and General Eisenhower. The picture of this exercise is displayed in General Patton's Museum in Ft. Knox, Kentucky. In early July we left on a ship to Cherbourg, France, first landing on Utah Beach. A few troops waded ashore in deep water, the rest left from a steel ramp, then walked ashore. There were mines everywhere, dead horses and cows and debris. At that point we were assigned to the First Army, relieving the First Engineer Battalion in the Caumont Sector. This was hedgerow country; we never knew what was on the other side of the hedgerows. The Germans laid heavy 88mm on the highways and fields and there was heavy fighting. At this time, our division was taken from the First Army of Gen. Omar Bradley and assigned to the Fifth Division under the command of General George S. Patton, Jr.

My first river crossing occurred at the Vire River at night. This was a night to remember. When the first boat reached the other shore all hell broke loose, and it looked like the Fourth of July. Enemy fire was coming from all directions. We then had to return to get another boatload of men. At Anger the Division moved on to a railroad bridge. Our mission was to make the bridge a highway bridge for tanks and other vehicles. The German snipers kept us under heavy fire and we were always running for cover; however, we were successful in completing our task.

We then rapidly deployed across, the men riding on M-10 tank destroyers and any other vehicle available. As we traveled through many towns and villages we fought and killed Germans, as well as taking prisoners. We were on the outskirts of Paris, fighting the Germans in foxholes, when the word came we would not be liberating Paris; rather we were assigned to Reims. This was not too disappointing as this was the Champagne city of France. Upon our arrival we filled our canteens with the "bubbly."

Onward to Metz! The city of Metz contained five forts, the toughest of which was Ft. Driant. This fortress had underground connecting tunnels and was heavily fortified by the Germans. Much of the fighting was done underground. There were times when I walked over dead bodies going in and coming out. An order came down that the next day we were to attack using flame throwers. Later on this order was cancelled due to the fact that the risk of losing many men was too great. To this day I believe that if I had entered the fort with a flame thrower I would not be alive today. I can remember clearly in Metz after fierce house-to-house fighting, the American troops talking to the Germans to give up. We were billeted in a large home. Upon entering, I observed a large picture of Adolph Hitler hanging on the wall in an office. I picked up an inkwell and threw it at the picture, destroying it.

During one of our Moselle River crossings, Capt. Manos asked me to take six stretcher bearers down to the river to pick up a wounded soldier, Lt. Taylor. We found the Lt. badly wounded and headed back up the hill with him. The Germans began to fire machine guns through the trees at us. On the way up the hill, I lost my helmet and when we got to the aid station Lt. Taylor told me to take his until I could secure a new one. We now entered into the Battle of the Bulge phase of the war.

On December 10, 1944 the Germans made a big thrust into the American lines into the Ardennes Forest. A meeting was held in Verdun by Gen. Eisenhower, Gen. Bradley and Gen. Patton. Patton was asked how soon he could have his army ready to halt this major attack. Gen. Patton replied, "I will have three divisions ready in two days' time." This was thought to be an impossible task. Within two days all the troops were ready and the men went at top speed on every vehicle available. Patton's Fourth Armored Division headed the attack. They found a hole in the German's line of defense and relieved the troops that were trapped in Bastogne.

Another important river crossing was the Sauer River at the town of Diekirch in Luxembourg. We wore white bed-sheets to camouflage ourselves. I was the platoon radio-man that day when my best friend, Donald Ickes from Chicago, was killed on the bank of the river. To this day each year the town reenacts the river crossing of the 7th Engineer Battalion of the 5th Division, who was responsible for liberation of their town.

After securing the town of Diekirch, the troops scattered into homes. We all went to mess call and lined up to get our chow and I came upon a container filled with pounds of butter. This butter was to be used for the officer's pancake breakfast the next day. Lo and behold three pounds of butter was missing. The order came down that the company had to stand outside in the cold every half hour in formation until it was returned. Two pounds of butter came back, one remained missing.

When I attended my first reunion many years later and met up again with Col. Manos in Kokomo, Indiana, he was reminiscing about the missing butter and he often wondered who had taken it. At that point, I said, "Do you really want to know who took the butter? I did!" The reason it was never returned was due to the fact we had all eaten it. At the conclusion of the reunion I handed him a wrapped gift. Inside was a pound of butter.

Our last major river crossing was the Rhine River which occurred on March 22nd at 2200 hours. There were to be 25 assault boats to each engineer company. On the first return trip Frank DiTommasso and I were being shelled with mortars. As we approached the shore and got out of the boat, a mortar shell came between us but did not go off. It had landed in the soft mud. The good Lord was watching over us that day.

All in all our division made a total of 26 river crossings. We fought in five major campaigns: Normandy, Northern France, Rhineland, Ardennes (Battle of the Bulge), and Central Europe. On May 8th when the war ended we were in Czechoslovakia engaged in removing road blocks. There were two Fifth infantrymen killed because the Germans didn't know the war was over. I believe these were the last two soldiers killed in our division.

In July we returned to France and left from the Port of Le Havre for

America. We arrived on the Hudson River on the Liberty Ship LeJeunes, sailing past Lady Liberty. It was the best feeling in the world. Home at last. There were welcome home signs on the shore and people were cheering. We were transferred by truck back to Camp Shanks, New York and all the troops were given a 30-day recuperation furlough. Home at last to Stamford, CT after almost three years. What a wonderful feeling. I stepped off the train and my mother and father came running down the platform to me. What a great family reunion we all had!

I had to report back to Ft. Devans, Mass. And then on to Camp Campbell, KY. After six weeks, I received an Honorable Discharge from Ft. Knox, KY. After returning home, I trained to go into the construction field and worked throughout New York and Connecticut on commercial buildings for over 50 years. I married, had two children, seven grandchildren, and three great-grandchildren.

I never spoke of my war experiences for more than fifty years. It was only when I attended a 7th Engineer, Fifth Infantry Reunion in Kokomo, Indiana that I reunited with my war buddies. From there I joined the Veterans of the Battle of the Bulge organization and have enjoyed traveling throughout the United States to their reunions. Each December I travel to Washington to join the Battle of the Bulge organization ceremony to honor this historic battle and the men who lost their lives. We place a wreath at the WWII Monument. The ambassadors from Luxembourg and Belgium are in attendance.

At that time I was given an application stating that the French government was presenting veterans who fought in France an award for their service in the liberation of their country during WWII. I completed the necessary paperwork. The French government advised that I have been awarded a Chevalier in the Legion of Honor. The Ambassador of France will be presenting me with the insignia of the Legion of Honor at a ceremony on May 8, 2012 at the West Point Military Academy, in West Point, New York. To think that a young 17 year old soldier who fought a war so many years ago would have such an honor bestowed on him is more than I could have imagined. This will be the final chapter in my military service.

CHRISTMAS EVE IN AN OLD BARN

Dominick Daniel Santagata
5th Infantry Division, Company B, 7th Engineer Battalion

After reading Harold Storey's article, "Christmas in Luxembourg," it brought back memories of my experiences during the war. We left Metz and drove all night to stop the German attacks. The weather was one of our enemies and the snow made it hard to move our jeeps, trucks, and tanks. The roads were covered with ice and snow and when we arrived in Luxembourg our company was also billeted in an old barn.

It was Christmas Eve and there I was standing guard duty; it was bitter cold and I can still remember the full moon shining down the landscape.

Many Christmas Eves have gone by; however, my thoughts still go back to the old barn and Christmas Eve in 1944. Moving on, we had to cross the river at Diekirch in Luxembourg and this is where I lost a great friend, Don Nickles from Chicago. He was wounded and died there on the riverbank. Each year the townspeople of Diekirch reenact this river crossing that resulted in the liberation of their town.

This crossing was one of the 26 that the 5th Infantry Division made in France, Germany and Luxembourg. I too was blessed to return home after five major campaigns and begin my life. As long as I live I will never forget the men who were left behind.

UNDER A TIN ROOF

L. D. "Whitey" Schaller
28th Infantry Division, 110th Infantry Regiment, Company B

In combat, the life and mood of infantry soldiers is full of rapid unexpected change. The 28th Division left the Hurtgen Forest on the 10th of December for rest and rehabilitation. Twelve men went to guard an observation post located in a deserted mountaintop village overlooking the Our River. Hurtgen was a terrible, deadly place. I was so jumpy that eight more days passed before I became aware that my shins were cold and my feet had been frozen. In this hyper-alert state of mind we assumed the on-two, off-four duty assignment. We were comfortable sleeping in the conditions of a previously shelled house. We weren't shooting at anyone and the Germans weren't shooting at us. We might even doze a few minutes in a watchful nap in the warmth of an afternoon sun.

We moved in under super dark conditions on a rainy night. Within minutes I was located at a BAR post in a shed and under a tin roof attached to a barn. The shape of the outpost indicated the direction of the front and we understood a mine field and booby traps surrounded our position. You know it had to be too good to last. Soon ordnance personnel arrived, loaded repair weapons, fired them at German positions, and then quickly departed. Of course, German forces took offense and responded in kind. They shelled us two days in a row after the jeep carrying war chow appeared. On the third day, American artillery took care of the German Panther.

Soon after, dog and owl calls were heard at night as German patrols probed the territory. "Have no fear; we are enclosed in a safe area." But then one night we heard and recognized enough German to know someone fell into our slit trench. They had safely penetrated our mine field. Soon after, again on a rainy night under the tin roof, a big black and white cow jumped up on the sand bags immediately in front of me. An amazing feat! I did calm down and return the grenade to the safety of its nest at the BAR post. On succeeding days we eliminated stray cats that prowled the area setting off explosives. As the Germans became more aggravated, a heavy weapons section moved into two houses below us. With remarks of, "You guys are just jumpy," they ignored our warnings. Two wisps of smoke curled from two chimneys. Two 88 rounds neatly removed the chimneys at the roof line and put the fires out. It was quiet after that until the day we left.

Noticing the increased activity as units arrived preparing to jump off, German artillery saluted us. Two shells relocated a machine gun nest and the BAR post. A third round rang the bell in the church tower. We left that place and occupied positions in front of Marnach and were well forward and center when the Bulge began.

ATTACK ON MANHAY, CHRISTMAS DAY, 1944

Milton J. Schober
106th Infantry Division, 424th Infantry, 2nd Battalion, Company F

After a week of fighting in the area of St. Vith, Belgium, at the onset of the Battle of the Bulge, German forces had compressed the American defenders into an oval-shaped area which became identified as the "fortified goose egg." Units within the "goose egg" were the 7th and 9th Armored Divisions, the 112th Regiment of the 28th Infantry Division, and the remnants of the 106th Infantry Division (essentially the 424th Regiment and attached artillery). These troops were incorporated in the XVIII Airborne Corps under command of Major General Matthew Ridgeway. Being a paratrooper, Ridgeway believed that the troops in the "goose egg" should attempt to hold their positions until friendly forces could fight forward to reinforce them. Field Marshall Montgomery, Ridgeway's superior officer at this time, thought otherwise and ordered that the battle lines be "tidied up" by withdrawing the more than 20,000 troops from their nearly encircled positions on December 23, 1944, through an opening held by the 82nd Airborne Division. The withdrawal was successful and the troops were repositioned north of the bulge created by the German Panzers driving to the west in an attempt to reach the Meuse River.

My unit, Company F, 424th Regiment, reached a position in the woods well north of Manhay in the area of Werbomont as darkness approached on the 23rd. We had not had a decent meal in a week, we hadn't had shelter from the weather, and we weren't able to get more than a few hours of sleep here and there during the preceding week. Because we had retreated many miles, we had difficulty accepting the fact that the Germans were still near at hand, not realizing that our withdrawal was largely parallel to the German thrust. At any rate we were miserably cold on that night of the 23rd—it was cold enough for the drinking water in my canteen to be a solid block, around zero. To get some sleep a number of brush fires were started by the troops, not exactly a brainy decision in a combat area, but nothing came of it and we did get sleep.

Colonel Dupuy in St. Vith: *Lion in the Way* reports thusly: "It was a battered, disgruntled, groggy aggregation which finally found billets and bivouacs up in the vicinity of Werbomont during the night of 23 December. But for the 424th Infantry, dead on its collective feet, there was only the windswept, snow-covered wooded area around Houssonloge, north of the Werbomont crossroads. No wonder that Reid, the regimental commander, to this day sets his jaw in bitterness when he talks about it—"What did they do? They did what might be expected—they chopped down trees and lit fires to bring some warmth into their frozen bones. Damn the enemy! Damn the blackout! After all, there's a limit to what flesh and blood can stand. And Reid approved."

December 24th, Christmas Eve, dawned beautifully. Blue sky was showing and the sun, which we hadn't seen in some time, perhaps since we landed on the Continent, was dazzling us by its appearance. The clear weather was extremely important to us because it gave Allied planes an opportunity to bring destruction to the enemy. The German tank columns had been able to make their huge penetrations without the interference of our planes for the entire first week of their attack.

The sun's appearance had a great buoying effect. The next lift was from the opportunity of the first shave since early December. A woman in a farm house near the bivouac area offered "chaud d'l'eau" (hot water) and the use of her kitchen for shaving, I had barely dampened my face and daubed on lather, when the woman came dashing in screaming, "La Boche, La Boche, La Boche!" I grabbed my rifle and ran outside, lather dripping down my face. Overhead a formation of B-17's was moving east on a mission over Germany. And then I noticed several parachutes descending from a very high altitude. What the woman had guessed were German paratroopers were in fact the crew of a B-17 which had been disabled—back to the shaving chore, and all's well on Christmas Eve in 1944, or so I thought!

Later, sometime after dark on Christmas Eve, some higher authority must have taken sympathy on the rugged lifestyle we had been following and had us trucked into a nearby village, probably Werbomont, where we were quartered in homes for our first protection from the weather elements since the German offensive started. We sacked out on the floor, crawling into our sleeping bags. We had barely pulled up the bag zippers and started to doze off when all hell broke loose—"Everybody up—we've got to move out quickly—the Germans have broken through our lines." The absolute disgust of tired men is hard to project. Profanity, cursing, oaths floated through the air. Stumbling outside in the coldness of night, we were loaded into trucks of the 7th Armored Division and headed south in the direction of the important road junction of Manhay. We were dropped off on the highway, perhaps a mile north of Manhay. We walked a short distance down the road and then cut off into the woods on the west side of the Liege highway. Still in somewhat of a stupor and cursing the bad luck and once again being denied a decent night's sleep, we were brought back to reality by Captain Cassidy's screaming that the Germans may be coming over the nearby hills at any moment and we had better start digging foxholes. I was very confused as to what was going on, and it wasn't until months later that I became aware of the facts.

It seems that the 2nd SS Panzer Division had commenced an attack at 9:00 p.m. Christmas Eve in the direction of Manhay. The German tank column had a captured American Sherman tank in the lead. The 7th Armored Division defenders had assumed the column was the American 3rd Armored Division, which was known to be changing its positions. When the Germans suddenly began firing the surprise was absolute and the 7th Armored fell back in chaotic state. The Germans captured Manhay; the fear of American commanders was that they would head north toward Liege and in the process outflank American positions. Hence the hurry-up alert in bringing us to the vicinity of Manhay to thwart a northern thrust from the Germans.

So here we were in the early morn of Christmas Day, 1944, digging foxholes as protection against the German onslaught which never came. We dug and anxiously watched the nearby hills for signs of the enemy. Hours passed, nothing happened and we began to wonder if our leadership knew what was going on.

With such inactivity, we were told to move closer to Manhay at midday and we were treated to a bombing exhibition. We could see American P-38 fighter planes, those with the distinctive twin fuselages, dropping bombs in the hazy outline of the village of Manhay. Our visibility of the targets was poor, but we later learned that the planes were zeroing in on Panzers of the 2nd SS Panzer Division.

We didn't know it then, but Maj. Gen. Ridgeway, our corps commander, had ordered Brig. Gen. Hasbrouch, of the 7th Armored Division, to retake Manhay by darkness on Christmas Day! In the mid-afternoon we learned that our 2nd Battalion of the 44th Regiment and units of the 7th Armored Division were selected for this task. We were given no briefing as to objectives or anything else, but merely told to lighten up for the attack, that is, to leave such things as sleeping bags behind to improve our mobility.

We moved out along the edge of the tree line in a single file on the high ground. In the process of this movement, the activity was noticed by the Germans, who started some machine gun firing, not too intense, but enough for a couple of men to receive leg wounds.

It was late afternoon, in twilight, that we reached the positions from which we were to begin our attack. Word was given for us to emerge from the woods and begin our race downhill across open farmland toward houses along the main highway. As we began our attack and picked up running speed, not a shot was fired by the Germans. Our confidence increased as momentum picked up, and whooping and hollering started, with the troops firing wildly to the front. It was as if we were playing a game of "cowboys and Indians." The open area that we were traversing was 300–500 yards, in my recollection, and the only cover provided along that route in our area was a sunken farm road cutting across the fields. I remember running down on to the road and up the mound on the other side with barely a pause. Still no fire from the enemy. But then, about 30 yards behind, it started. Rapid fire machine guns began their stutter and traversed the field from my right across my front. It wasn't difficult to spot their source because of their use of tracer bullets whose entire trajectory could be followed. Forward movement stopped as if by command, and we hit the ground.

Thirty or forty feet ahead my squad leader, Mike Jerosky, was hit as he reached a wire fence 100–150 feet behind the house toward which I was moving. George Buansco, close to Jerosky, also was hit but much more seriously. I'll never forget his screams for a medic followed by the words, "I'm dying!"

As I lay on the ground trying to be as inconspicuous as possible in the absence of a hole to crawl into, many thoughts go through my mind—What do I do now?—Do I docilely take the enemy's fire without retaliation—Isn't it my duty to fire my rifle—After all, I know where the enemy's fire is coming from because of the tracers. So I slowly bring my rifle to firing position and fire the eight rounds in a clip toward the source of the tracers. By now it is quite dark and I have no idea of the effect of my fire, but then the Germans fire a flare high into the air. It looks as bright as the morning sun and seems to take an eternity to descend to the ground to be extinguished. I guess it drops on a parachute principle to extend its life, but at any rate it appears so bright that I feel certain that all enemy eyes are focused on me and that I must even minimize breathing to appear completely motionless, expecting the "coup de grace" at any moment.

When darkness again settles over the area. I feel I have to do something to improve my position. But then an artillery barrage starts, and I didn't know if it was German or American fire. I'm now convinced it was so-called "friendly fire." The shells land behind me and they are not coming from my front. Fear again enters my heart as I lie completely exposed. I don't know how close the shells are landing, but the ground is trembling as I hug it as tightly as I can. When the shelling subsides I crawl over to the only soldier I see. I don't remember his name, but he is in the same squad as I. He says that he felt something hit his shoulder. I look at it and see that his field jacket is tattered at the shoulder but no bleeding is in evidence. I ask him if he swallowed any "wound tablets." He says "no," so I give him some, along with water from my canteen. Then I suggest that we make a run for it back to the recessed dirt road that is some 30 yards behind us. He agrees and we get up and run as fast as we can, expecting machine gun fire to sweep the area; it doesn't happen as we reach and collapse on the sunken road. We see no other men from our company and learn later that the order to withdraw was given which never reached us. Dozens of wounded men are on the road and the medics are doing what they can to alleviate their pain. We assist in moving the men on makeshift stretchers to bring them closer together for eventual evacuation; it is very cold out and the wounded keep asking for blankets or something to keep them warm. I have no idea where the rest of our company has gone but I suggest to my fellow squad member that we walk toward the area and see if we can find anyone. No one is in sight as we come to a road, but a short distance away we spot a house. We have no idea who might be inside, friend or foe. We rap on the door and see the front window shade slowly curl up as a soldier's face appears. Thank God, it's an American. The door opens and we see perhaps eight or ten men sleeping on the floor. We prostate ourselves, alerted periodically by the sound of vehicles passing in the night, wondering who they might be. We hardly give thought that this is our observance of Christmas as we fade off to sleep.

Manhay had not been captured by us, but the Germans withdrew, so for the night it was a "no man's land." One of our wounded who rejoined our company months later, said a German patrol came through the area where the wounded were lying and an English-speaking member of the patrol told them the Germans were withdrawing and that they could expect help from the Americans soon. This seemed rather remarkable to me since our opponents in this area were an SS Panzer division, and compassion is something not generally associated with the SS.

Today, if you visit the northern edge of Manhay on the main highway to Liege, you will see a marker which indicates the furthest point of German penetration in the Bulge and I have the satisfaction of knowing that I contributed to the location of that mark.

KEEPING WARM

Donald Schoo
80th Infantry Division, 633rd Antiaircraft Automatic Weapons Battalion

In December, I sewed a pair of wool socks together and wore them around my neck like we did in the winter of 1944 to keep them dry and warm in the Battle of the Bulge. Every day we would change socks to keep from getting trench foot. Now I wear them to remember the longest, coldest winter of my life!

BATTLE OF THE BULGE – ALONG THE SURE RIVER FRONT

Arthur Schreckengost
4th Infantry Division, 12th Infantry Regiment

After four weeks of constant attacks against a well-entrenched enemy in the Hurtgen Forest, the Fourth Infantry Division was in dire straits. I mention this because I am convinced the Germans used this delaying action to set up the forthcoming Battle of the Bulge! Some of our most experienced infantry divisions, including the 4th, 28th, and 9th, were depleted by second line enemy units (mainly German allies such as Hungarian and Romanian) who in well-developed defenses and in horrible weather conditions made the advancing American forces pay a heavy price for every yard gained! By December 4th we were no longer a viable fighting force. HQ recognized this and on December 5th pulled the Fourth from action and sent it to Luxembourg for refit. Under the assumption that the war was in its final stage and that the German Army on the western front was incapable of mounting any serious threat, this was done in a leisurely fashion. The 12th Regiment, which I was assigned to, was posted north of Luxembourg City along the Sure and Mosel Rivers. The north and east banks of these rivers were part of the famed Siegfried defense line!

I was with F Company at Berdorf on December 16th when our morning patrol reported heavy enemy presence on our side of the Sure River. A mixed bag of infantry, heavy weapons and forward observer specialists made up our twenty-four man unit quartered in a large farm complex. We were ill prepared for any form of major defensive action since most of our supporting artillery and armored units had much of their equipment in maintenance or scheduled for replacement. However, we did have fairly potent infantry capability consisting of three mortars, several water cooled 30 cal. mgs, one 50 cal. mg (jeep-mounted), several BARs and a mixture of rifles and grenades.

Our situation was further complicated by a very limited supply of ammunition and radios that had been so damaged by the wet conditions in the Hurtgen Forest that they were all but useless. This left us with only portable communication equipment with a maximum range of a few kilometers! All our other outposts were beyond this range since F company was responsible for about five/six kilometers of front. This was equivalent to what an entire division would normally control!

The Germans had intentionally kept the front quiet by not sending patrols to our side of the river (heavy snow cover would show their tracks) and by lightly manning the Siegfried fortifications. Thus when they hit us at dawn on the 16th of December we had to quickly react to keep from being overrun. Here our experienced infantry cadre saved us from being overwhelmed! Like all seasoned units they had prepared for the unexpected. An MLR had been set using the outer wall surrounding the farm buildings and positions on the upper floors of the house and barn. Here riflemen supplemented our strategically located mgs, BARs and mortars. When the enemy forces advanced through the cultivated fields surrounding the farm complex they were devoid of most cover except for a few apple trees. I was on the second floor of the house with a clear field of fire on both the north and east sides of the MLR. When the enemy advanced reached within approximately 200 yards of our position the order was given to open fire!

The heavy volume of fire must have shocked the enemy. I'm sure they only expected light resistance. Here their lack of information (no recent patrols) on our strength put them at a temporary disadvantage. They reeled back, then showing they were experienced troops, quickly recovered, and taking their casualties along, they fled back to the safety of the forest! During the remainder of the day, the enemy probed our position several times to ascertain our strength. Each time we easily repulsed their advances. We had one meaningful encounter when oddly enough nearby enemy fire, on our west flank, seemed directed away from our position. Years later I learned this was a result of one of our patrols, under the command of SGT Potts, trying to take haven with us! Luckily they changed course and made it back to F Company HQ and eventual freedom.

Finally, about 3 PM, two German officers appeared, under a white flag, at the edge of the forest. We replied with a similar party outside the compound gate. After a parlay, our reps returned with the ultimatum to surrender or have our position destroyed by artillery fire. To emphasize their point several half-tracks, armed with high velocity 75 mm cannon, were stationed on the main road about a half mile from the farm! We had hoped to maintain our position until dark (about 4 PM) then attempt to escape in small groups to safety. With our ammunition almost gone, and with the knowledge of how destructive enemy artillery was, we knew our fate was sealed. After destroying our weapons, and burying any "loot", we marched into captivity! Were we victims of poor command decisions? I choose to believe the Hurtgen was a major snafu that set-up the Bulge and caused many more casualties than if the half dozen divisions decimated there had been at full strength during the Bulge!

DEFENSE OF MONSCHAU BY THE 38TH CAVALRY SQUADRON

Alfred H.M. Shehab
38th Cav Recon, 102nd Cav Group

By mid-December 1944, the United States 1st Army had made tremendous advancements since the landings at Normandy not six months earlier. Sitting at one of the easternmost penetrations of the 1st Army was the town of Monschau, Germany, of which the 38th Cavalry Reconnaissance Squadron, 102 Cavalry Group (The Essex Troop) was assigned to defend. The defensive line extended from just south of the town, northwest, then north along the Mutzenich Ridge to the train station on the north side of the village of Konzen. It was a very large sector, giving the squadron commander, LTC Robert O'Brien, no choice but to employ the entire strength of the squadron in the line, leaving no reserve. It was here that I commanded the 3rd Platoon of Troop B, now numbering about 30 men, occupying a front about 1,300 yards in front of Konzen.

Through the months of November and December, the sector was relatively quiet except for ceaseless and aggressive dismounted patrols, which gave us patrol dominance. The usual clashes with enemy patrols were frequent and deadly. I had found a hunting lodge at the edge of the woods, and there established my command post from which to base our patrols. The short spurts of battle continued through the first weeks of December, as further advancements were slowed by the gasoline shortage the entire Army was experiencing. Sometimes, at night, a few of us would slip into Konzen and leave copies of *Stars and Stripes* just to let the Jerries know we were there. I must have been an absolute fool! But, when you are young, you do things that you look back on and wonder how you survived them. At the time, it was just something to do to pass the time and mess with the enemy's head.

On the night of 15 December 1944, we heard a huge number of airplanes flying overhead. Running outside to see what was happening, I saw loads of people dropping. The Jerries had dropped a bunch of paratroopers. Standing outside the hunting lodge that was now my command post, I grabbed an M-1 rifle and started shooting at them. At the same time, our .50 calibers mounted on armored cars opened up, spraying the sky with fire. Receiving an order from command to take out this battalion of paratroopers, my driver and I headed out into the woods to see what we could find. We picked up a couple of them, each of whom was carrying a bottle of rum. After hearing this, I had difficulty keeping my lads in. Now they all wanted to go out and capture paratroopers!

The next morning, 16 December at 0530 hours, which is an un-godly hour to start anything, much less a war, the Germans opened up with an intense barrage of artillery, mortar, and rocket fire. We holed up in our defenses, hoping not to suffer a direct hit. Communications had been nearly severed, and there was a confusion as to what exactly was happening. In that, I was lucky in a sense. From what I understand, at headquarters, they had become rather distressed as to what was going on. They were actually worried. But we young lieutenants didn't know any better. To us, it was just another fight. It was not until later in life when I started reading the history of this thing that I got frightened about what went on.

A few hours later, enemy paratroopers became active behind our lines. A large-scale assault was developing on the B Troop front, with a platoon of Jerries attacking our rear. I was forced to draw on my already lightly held main line and send a combat patrol to ward off the German attack. Entering the forest, my men flanked the Germans and drove them south, killing several and taking two as prisoners. Still, the enemy refused to relent, and escalated its attacks against our thinly defended position.

The attacks continued for the next few days, and though a number of observation posts were overrun, we had held out. At one point, one of my lads came running in and said, "Lieutenant, I don't know what's going on behind us, but boy, there is something out there!" At that, I went out, and sure enough, heard a lot of noise coming from the woods. Crouching behind a tree, I hollered, "Who's there?" A voice came back, "Well, who the hell are you?" So I replied, "Well, who the hell are you?" We finally made a deal. We would each get an officer and meet him in an open space. It turns out it was the 49th Infantry, which had sent two companies from about twenty miles up the road. They had been told that we were wiped out. At that, they moved in and relieved the 30 men I had, assuring that the Germans would never gain control of Monschau. For its defense of Monschau, the 38th Cavalry Squadron received the Presidential Unit Citation.

MY WAR EXPERIENCE

Oliver W. Siebert
220th FA Bn, 324th Inf. Regiment

I was an artillery forward observer with the 220th FABn, 324th Inf. Regiment. My brother worked for the local electric utility and I worked as a machinist and tool and die maker—we were both working our way as students of electrical engineering at Washington University, in St. Louis. The day after Pearl Harbor, we went to join the Navy. He was immediately selected and I was rejected as being 'clinically blind' (I could not see the chart without my glasses, let alone the Big 'E'). I kept trying different branches, all the same answer.

Eventually, my draft notice sent me to the induction center for my physical. It was cold in the morning in an open sided tent; the morning tests were done while undressed (so for the first and last time the Army used logic), i.e., we would take the afternoon tests in the AM and the AM tests (but with clothes) in the PM; except we were not given the morning tests (when they normally tested for eyesight). As desired, I was suddenly in the Army—as an Artillery Forward Observer (which relied heavily upon good eyesight)!

After basic, I was sent to the ASTP (Army Specialized Training Program) for some GIs who had considerable college. When the ASTP was stopped I was short of my degree by one semester; they needed more bodies for the European invasion more than they needed more engineering officers. During the battle for France, we were short of Artillery Forward Observers 2nd Lieutenants (who were the second to Infantry Platoon Leaders for highest casualty rates); I received a field promotion.

After I was injured, and awaiting a medical discharge, I was advised that I had also received an appointment to complete my degree at West Point. Even with my bad eyesight and messed up leg/body, they would offer a dispensation (at that time, they had no idea how high would be the casualty rate to invade Japan). The Army offer was, i.e., "—accept West Point or be discharged as an enlisted GI." I actually gave the offer several days' serious consideration.

I met with the orthopedic MDs and they said my prognosis was not good, with one leg an inch shorter than the other. With my hips tilted, my spine twisted, my future was going to be questionable for even walking, let alone for running across a field/beach firing an M-1 held at the hip (as a pistol), etc. As it came to pass, their medical judgment was correct—I limp, I walk with a cane and while I have been able to compensate for those difficulties (which also led to Paget's Bone disease, etc.), my original 6'-1-1/2 " height is now only 5' 5" short. It would not have been a reasonable choice.

We fought across France; after we took Strasbourg (on Thanksgiving), as a full division, we motored to Sarreguemines; during that trip, almost two weeks before the 12/16/1944 Bulge began, I was captured by blond, blue-eyed German S.S. officers, in U.S. GI uniforms, speaking 'good' English (acting as MP's, redirecting some limited number of 'younger' 2nd Lieutenants (driving alone in their own Jeep), off a side road (for interrogation). After three days, I was very fortunate in that I was able to escape (my captor was not so lucky).

On Christmas Day, 1944, while at my Artillery Forward Observation Post (a large shell hole, on the top of a hill, about 1/4 mile in front of my infantry regiment), I was wounded in my right leg. A German shell landed about 5 feet in front of me (it should have torn me into lots of little pieces)—my guardian angel saved me again—it only broke my leg.

It took many hours to crawl back to where aid men were able to carry me back to the 9th Evac. hospital (sort of a Korean War MASH type temporary hospital. They patched my leg together with a full leg cast). On either December 26 or 27th, 1944 (I was pretty well doped with self-imposed morphine during my several hours long crawl back to our lines—I can't be sure), while being taken by ambulance to the 35th Station Hospital, we were strafed and I was hit again in the same leg (at a different place). My good luck held as it had for me for all of my combat exposure, when I should have died every day on the line. Our outfit had the record for WWII: 24/7 x 144 days without any rotation off the line.

This time, at the 35th Station Hospital, I was taken directly to the operating room—the damage was found to be more extensive—and they did as good a job as could be expected (the 35th Station Hospital, at Chalon-sur-Saone (south of Dijon, France) was short of help—most non-commissioned medical help had been sent to the front as infantry replacements (huge casualty rate during the Battle of the Bulge). Later, by train to the 3rd General Hospital (Aix-en-Provence) "for my photo"—then a three-week hospital ship trip along the equator, up to Charleston, SC, to rehab and discharged before the war was over.

130TH GENERAL HOSPITAL IN THE BULGE

John J. Stamos
130th General Hospital

The 130th General Hospital was located at Ciney, Belgium. Its primary mission was to treat "combat exhaustion" casualties from the First and Third Armies.

The tactical situation had constantly affected the mission and operation of this unit. Initially, when the Roer River offensive started 16 November 1944, 1,000 cases were sent here from Liege to relieve the burden in the then-incomplete hospital center there. These were lightly wounded "ten-day" cases. They were well triaged and by 1 December most of them were back to duty, a long evacuation having been avoided. From 1 December to 19 December the unit performed its primary mission. The events from 19 December to 31 December can best be recorded in the wording of the daily journal kept at the time.

19 December 1944: Battle casualties begin to pour into the hospital.

20 December 1944: Surgical teams from the 12th Field Hospital and 3rd Auxiliary Surgical Group assist in handling large numbers of battle casualties. Over 600 admitted in past 24 hours.

22 December 1944: Prisoners of war returned to central stockade. Litter bearers pulled from all elements of unit. Flow of casualties between 500 and 600 per day. Patrols of enemy tanks and a few infantry troops have appeared south of the hospital less than three miles away. The 207th Engineer Battalion, only U.S. troops in the area. Because of the enemy advance, the NP personnel,

hospital dieticians and physiotherapy aids evacuated to the 99th General Hospital Total of 54 people involved in this evacuation. Unit transportation and trucks loaned by the 1233rd Engineer Fire Fighter Platoon utilized.

23 December 1944: Number of casualties entering station less than 200 during 24 hour period. Some ambulances en route to station reported captured. Heavy gunfire heard east and south at an estimated distance of five miles. By use of hospital train and ambulances, evacuation down to non-transportables accomplished. Evacuation of all non-essential personnel recommended to Surgeon ASCZ. All personnel other than minimum essential number to care for patients evacuated to Ecole Athenee Royale, Charleroi, Belgium. At 2200 hours a jeep was fired on by German patrol between hospital and Sorrines, approximately two miles from hospital. Small arms fire heavy on the southern and western end of the rehabilitation camp reservation. Trucks were ordered out at once to avoid loss of critical transportation. Remaining at the station were only sufficient personnel to care for the non-transportable patients. Total evacuation: 9 hospital trains in past four days, approximately 2,700 patients. To duty at 11th Reinforcement Depot 850 patients. Loaded directly from clearing station on train 200 patients.

24 December 1944: During the night two casualties brought in from two miles away with severe injuries (one with an arm and leg blown off and the other with half the face blown off and multiple chest and abdominal wounds) died as did one non-transportable case with multiple GSW of the head. Today we are out of contact with either our own or the enemy forces. Two men joined us during the night, Privates Buchanan and Ditzler from a clearing company of the 84th Division. These men had been held prisoner by Germans but were released some three miles away and directed by the enemy to, "Go to the big hospital. There the Americans will take care of you and we'll be along when we have time!" The three dead were buried in the cemetery attached to the hospital at 1100 hours today. The priest of the school, M. Monat, after being assured all three were Christians, officiated at the burial ceremony. Graves were marked as prescribed by Graves Registration. Heavy firing east, west, and south all day.

25 December 1944: A few vehicles have come through the Namur

today. No casualties, message sent to Surgeon, ASCZ, as to status of station. Advance elements of the Second Armored Division arrived during the afternoon. Artillery fire heavy at times. Deputy Surgeon, ASCZ, visited station and took CO for conference with Surgeon. Agreed station was to hold for the time being and one surgical team added to holding unit. CO proceeded to rendezvous point at Charleroi, collected personnel and returned to station at Ciney, Belgium.

26 December 1944: Active combat throughout the day and night, south, west and north of the hospital. The 41st Infantry preparing to jump off from a line 500 yards SW of the main hospital building. Artillery set up behind the hospital, firing over. Machine guns and mortars firing from the rehabilitation camp. Approximately 40 casualties during the day. One birth early in the morning, a girl baby being delivered. The parents, local town people driven from their home by the enemy. During the night a German paratrooper landed in the medical detachment bivouac area. This landing was two point—directly upon both testicles astride a fence post. Paratrooper was made a prisoner at once and immediately hospitalized. In the evening a call from Lt. Col George Rand, MC, Office of the Surgeon, ASCZ, advised that it was the surgeon's desire that all critical items of equipment be removed during the night. This was accomplished by unit vehicles. In the meantime, because the battalion aid station and clearing stations were still behind the hospital, the patients came to the station. Those who had been non-transportable, were now out of shock and were transportable. By midnight small arms fire was falling about the hospital grounds. Artillery fire from both sides was almost constant, the triangle Celles, Dinant, Ciney being a mass of fire of various calibers.

27 December 1944: By 0600 hours, no patients remained in the station. All critical items had been removed. Fire became more instead of less intensive. The bulk of the personnel holding had been at 0100 hours marched out, through the woods to Assesse, the rendezvous point. This group was guided by a party of natives, members of the resistance movement. At 0640 hours the station was abandoned. The Commanding Officer reported to the Surgeon, ASCZ at 0730 hours and, after a conference, proceeded to Charleroi.

28 December 1944: Station reoccupied at 1400 hours. The clearing station of B Combat Command (B Company of the 48th Medical Battalion) was found to be occupying the floors previously considered as suitable and guarding government property. An interval of some five hours had passed in which the station had been abandoned. In this period combat troops, and some civilians had taken small items and thoroughly rummaged through much of the plant. Inventory, however, showed less than $500 of government property loss and no large personal item loss. Quarters were remarkably messed up, but few items were actually missing. Cigarettes, candy and the rare bottle of liquor had been searched for diligently by all concerned in the five hour period.

29 December 1944: Hospital being cleaned, shelves repacked and stocks re-inventoried.

30 December 1944: Hospital clean, minimal equipment available, one surgical team standing by. No patients.

31 December 1944: Standing by. Some small assistance rendered to Clearing Station. Air attack tonight with one stick of bombs on village and repeated strafing of roads—no damage to hospital or personnel. Enemy apparently recognize site, strafes road to hospital, cuts off guns and goes over at tree-top level, reopening fire on road and village immediately after clearing hospital.

Summary

The year 1944 for the 130th General Hospital saw its activation, shipment, reorganization into a neuropsychiatric unit, reshipment, operation, evacuation, abandonment and reoccupation. It saw the hospital serve as a general hospital, an evacuation hospital, a field hospital, a clearing station, a battalion aid station and then, sitting between the lines, holding its non-transportables for either the U.S. Army or the Wehrmacht—whoever came first. It saw the hospital in the United States, England, France, and Belgium. In all, less than eight weeks of hospital operation was accomplished, but almost 7,000 patients were admitted and disposed of in this brief period. This (1944) was a year of packed activity for the 130th General Hospital.

Because of constantly changing tactical demands the primary mission of the hospital—the treatment and rehabilitation of soldiers with combat exhaustion—cannot be said to have been accomplished in 1944. The fact that a special neuropsychiatric hospital was flexible enough to change its function with constantly changing needs is worthy of note, because it could not have done so if it had been too specialized. The big lesson that 1944 taught us was that a special type hospital can do an efficient job in the advanced section of a theatre of operations only if the principle of flexibility of function is maintained.

BELGIUM BREAKTHROUGH

Phillip C. Stark
84th Infantry Division, 334th Infantry, 1st Battalion, Company A

It was the day before Christmas of 1944. In the previous month we had fought in Holland and Germany. Those had been slow moving days and nights. In that time we had moved forward about five miles. One month of daily attacks had cost our company about 175 in dead or wounded of the original 200 men that had left the United States as a combat team. But this is not a true measure of our casualties. Periodically we had gotten replacements and they were equally expendable. It didn't take long to break in a new man on the front. After one of the artillery or mortar barrages that came on an average of once every 15 minutes, and after one attack, each new man became an experienced veteran. "A" Company of the First Battalion was a seasoned outfit.

And then one night a new outfit replaced us on the line. We thought we were being relieved for a 24 hour rest that would take us behind the lines about five miles. Experience had accustomed us to one of these rests for roughly every seven days of fighting. These were the times when we would sleep, because there was no real sleep on the front. But this time we were disappointed. We were informed that the Germans had broken through the 106th Division in Belgium, were gaining territory in a rout, and we were being thrown into the gap.

This was how it came about that on the morning before Christmas we were dug in on the outskirts of the small town of Bourdon in Belgium, on the northern flank of what was later to be known as the "Bulge." Our position was beside a railroad track on the edge of the town. The snout of my machine gun stuck through a hedge that ran along the tracks. We could thus cover the front through the hedge and the flanks of our position down the tracks on both sides. We also had to be vigilant to our rear because the Germans were spread throughout the whole area. No definite front line had been established.

An incident that illustrates this point occurred after our arrival in a truck convoy. When we disembarked from the trucks, we were supposed to be well behind the actual line. We started our march forward while the trucks turned back to retrace their route. We were later informed that they never reached the rear safely. The whole company was captured. This convinced us that a "front line" did not exist.

Near our position was an old railroad switch house. In it we had stored some precious food we had received in one of the very few Christmas packages that reached our company. We hoped that on Christmas Day we could split our watch into two sections and while one section stood guard, the other could enjoy rest and a good meal in the little brick switch house.

But this was never to be. On this same morning, and just after a particularly heavy incoming artillery barrage, a runner came to order us to move forward to clear a company of Germans out of the woods directly to our front. We were assured that we would return to this position as soon as the task was completed. So we left our treasured food to rot in that switch house.

Upon arrival in this sector we had been ordered not to take any prisoners. They didn't say, "Shoot any German who surrenders," but there was no alternative. The Germans executed their prisoners because, were they to take those who surrendered or were wounded, they would not have any way to take care of them. We had the same problem. Our forces were spread thin. Few people back home were aware of or could understand the necessity of these tactics. We were forced to use the same dreadful measures that our enemy used. When a prisoner was taken, often the officer or "non-comm" in charge would order that he be taken on a "short trip back." The men thus assigned would take the prisoner back a couple of hundred yards, do what was expected of them, and be back with their unit with little time lost. I thank God that, because I was not a rifleman, I was never ordered to take a "short trip back."

These were the conditions under which we moved forward to clear out the woods. At 5:00 p.m. we entered the dense forest under heavy fire from the Germans within. As I ran forward I would hit the ground periodically when the whiz of a bullet sounded too close or a psychic urge befell me. Once I landed next to a clump of brushes only to have an enemy bullet clip off a branch not five inches from my head.

One of my short runs brought me to a wounded German lying on the ground. Because I carried the machine gun on my shoulder, my sidearm was a 45 caliber pistol. He saw me and frantically reached for a white handkerchief in a plea for mercy. He knew what he would do if our positions were reversed. We both knew what I was supposed to do. I aimed the pistol at his head and he began to cry.

No matter how much hate I had gathered from seeing Germans kill cold-bloodedly, I could not bring myself to shoot this young, good-looking blond boy. I had made him suffer just by my threat. My hate consoled my conscience in this. I passed on, leaving him unguarded in our rear. To this day, I wonder about him. Did some other GI come across him lying there and do what I was supposed to have done?

FOXHOLES AND CHRISTMAS OF LONG AGO REMEMBERED

Phillip C. Stark
84th Infantry Division, 334th Infantry Regiment, Company A

It was Christmas Eve, 1944, and our Company held a position just west of the Belgian town of Verdenne. As Wib Theuerkauf (my 2nd gunner on our 30 caliber light machine gun) and I sat huddled in our foxhole listening to the sounds of German soldiers singing and celebrating in the town, a runner informed us that we would be attacking at about midnight to take the hill 300 or 400 yards directly in front of us. My machine gun squad was to go with the 1st rifle platoon and Howard Shore's squad (the other machine gun) was to go with the 2nd.

While the heavy pounding of the enemy by our artillery was still going on, we took off, running blindly (as usual) and trying to dodge the German machine gun tracers we could see, yet knowing there were others we couldn't see. We reached the top of the hill too soon and sustained casualties from our own artillery.

We had been told that we would find foxholes at the top of the hill because the position had been previously occupied by our troops. We found them but unfortunately there were dead GIs in each one. So we moved back a bit and dug furiously for the safety that a hole can give. We immediately ran into shale rock, but we dug till dawn and, even then, we were only just barely able to get my 6'6" frame below the surface (and then only in a tangled position).

Christmas morning was beautiful, clear and crisp. We persuaded ourselves that this day would be different, that war might be set aside in honor of the birth of the Prince of Peace. And so I walked down to the holes of the dead GIs in front of us to pick up useful items strewn around their holes. As I bent to pick up an unused aid packet, my hair literally stood on end—I saw movement in the hole. I had been trying not to look at the mutilated bodies but here was what I thought was a dead body, turning his head to look up at me. He must have been lying in that position ever since the Germans overran this position a couple of days before. He pulled himself out from under another (really) dead body and asked me what outfit I was from. He ignored the obvious hole in his leg and struggled out of the hole. I quickly knew that he was not wholly "with it."

At this precise moment a German armored car, escaping from the town on our left, drove right across our front and opened fire on me and my new friend. Howard Shore, who had been watching my little drama, was walking down to join me when he was hit in the leg (literally somersaulting him in the air). When the aid man came to help Howard, I sent the other wounded GI with him (still ignoring the hole in his leg).

For the rest of the day the Germans blasted our position and the spirit of Christmas. Their purpose was clear—Germans retreating from Verdenne and crossing our front had to have cover. As each German vehicle was hit by our anti-tank guns, the riders in it jumped out and ran for the woods far to our front. I fired (with tracers) till the rifleman in the next hole (with an 0-3 rifle and telescopic sights) told me they were not moving. It was a bloody Christmas for us in 1944.

The only good news for us that day was that a rifleman nearby had somehow come across a pickaxe and gave it to us so that we were able to penetrate the rock to the extent that we could kneel in our hole.

Just before sun-up the next morning, at a time when the front had suddenly become very quiet, Wib (who was on guard) anxiously whispered, "Phil." It was just getting light and we could see many silent figures coming up the slope toward us. They had traversed the field in front of us in total darkness and were not more than 100 yards away. I slammed my gun in full cock and opened fire, pinning them down quickly.

I had to fire and then duck to avoid the return fire that my muzzle flashes drew. Once when I was up, a bullet pierced the ammunition box to the left of my gun and continued through the material of my overcoat shoulder, but didn't touch me. Wib could not keep down and as the duel continued, a bullet went through his helmet, his wool knit cap and out again, only pulling his hair out through the holes.

We had been so completely absorbed by our continual fire fight that we had failed to see three German tanks heading right for our hole. We yelled frantically that tanks were coming but there was probably nobody there to hear; our troops were either dead or had retreated.

We had no choice but to keep on firing; the enemy was too close and we would have been cut down in an instant had we attempted to run. We heard tank sounds to our rear and, for a fleeting moment, thought that friendly tanks were coming to our rescue.

I was firing when Wib came up to take his last look at what was happening. A bullet hit him in the middle of the forehead. I was now alone and knew that I too was going to die. Wib had been there to help reload after the first "ammo" belt was gone, but now I was almost at the end of the second belt and I knew that it would take too long to reload alone. If I stopped firing for only a moment, the enemy would overrun me.

I was firing the last of that second belt when I felt that my head had been torn from my shoulders. I now know that a bullet had ricocheted off the left side of my gun, had broken up and smashed into the left side of my face. I found myself in the bottom of the hole, my head in bloodied hands. This had to be the end.

I lifted up to look out and saw an explosion on, or in front of, the middle tank. It must have been our own artillery. Whatever it was, it saved my life. There was a lot of smoke and almost instinctively I scrambled out of the hole and ran for the rear. I ran right into a burning German tank—the tank we had heard and thought might be coming to save us.

I continued to run almost blindly over the hill and found two GIs who bandaged my head. Then we all took off across the open, flat terrain toward the woods from which we had attacked on Christmas Eve. By this time, the German tanks had reached the top of the hill and were firing at us as we ran. I believe that one of the other fellows was hit, but to stop was to die.

Needless to say, I reached the woods and our troops. My memory from here on is dim—my head was "splitting." Aid men picked me up and sent me off to what proved to be six hospitals in two-and-one-half months and full recovery (except for my permanently blind left eye).

I have always wondered what miracle, what twist of fate, allowed me to survive in the face of such odds, when so many others died.

BRIDGES IN THE ETO

Ralph Storm
11th Armored Division, 21st Armored Infantry Battalion, Company B

Some decisive battles were fought over bridges in the European Theater of Operations in 1944–45. A number of battles were fought for possession of large bridges over the Rhine as at Arnhem, Holland, and Remagen, Germany. Other bridge operations, mostly in the Bulge, we aimed at denying bridges to the Germans by blowing them.

Lienne Creek Bridge. In the Ardennes, American strategy dictated the demolition of bridges to deny their use to the Germans. The Ardennes rivers are relatively small, however the valleys are often V-shaped. Many rivers can be forded by foot troops, but they have steep rocky banks which restrict tank crossings to bridges.

On December 18, 1944, or Day Three of the Bulge, Kampfgruppe Peiper of the 1st SS Panzer Division was heading toward the Meuse River with an armored force of nearly 4,000 men. On Day Two, or December 17, Peiper's men had captured and gunned down nearly one hundred men with machine guns. The place was Five Points, as the engineers called it. On a map the crossroads hamlet is listed as Baugnez and is near Malmedy.

A number of bridges had been blown by the 291st Engineer Combat Battalion on December 18, but there was a timber trestle bridge over Lienne Creek at the hamlet of Habiemont. If Peiper could capture the bridge over Lienne Creek at Habiemont, the way seemed open to Werbomont and the Meuse. It was a case of who would get to the bridge first: Pieper and his armored column or an engineer demolitions crew. As it was, the German column was delayed by sixteen P-47 fighter-bombers that strafed and bombed the column, knocking out one tank and two half-tracks. The raid forced a delay for the Germans as wrecked vehicles had to be pushed aside and the wounded tended.

Meanwhile at Werbomont, a dozen miles west of the bridge, fifteen engineers were loading a truck with explosives and wire. Their truck had a damaged engine from having made a furious trip the previous day. The engine valves were burned and the truck could only do ten miles per hour. Arriving at Lienne Creek bridge the demolitions crew under Corporal Fred Chapin began setting up charges and wiring them. The men had mixed emotions about blowing a bridge that they had built in September. But the men also knew that they could build a new bridge, a Bailey or a treadway-pontoon, in a few hours or days.

The sun set on that dark cloudy day at 1635 hours but the explosives—2,500 pounds of TNT—were set and wired by then. As a precaution, a backup charge was set and wired to a second detonator. Corporal Chapin stood with the detonator in an old German sentry box from where he had a good view of the bridge and its eastern approaches.

And where were the Germans? Two Belgian farmers spotted the Germans three miles east of the bridge and ran across country to warn the engineers at the bridge. At 1645, after sundown and before it was completely dark, Corporal Chapin saw the lead German tank, a monster Tiger Royal with a long-barreled 88mm gun, creep around the bend in the road. The Tiger fired its main gun at a mine-laying crew near the bridge. The engineers scattered. Watching the German tanks near the bridge, Chapin turned the detonator key and saw "a streak of blue lights, the heaving blast of dust debris, and knew he had a good blow." With a thundering detonation the timber trestle bridge was reduced to scrap wood and sawdust.

Earlier that day the three bridges at Trois-Ponts had been blown in Peiper's face as he advanced with his vanguard. Now at Lienne Creek, for the fourth time that day, Pieper was denied access to a bridge that might have gotten him to the Meuse. Charles MacDonald wrote of the Kampfgruppe leader's anger after the bridge had fallen: "Joachin Pieper reputedly pounded one knee with his fist in sheer frustration and muttered: 'The damned engineers! The damned engineers!'"

LIFE AND WORK OF ARTILLERYMEN IN THE BULGE

Ralph Storm
11th Armored Division, 21st Armored Infantry Battalion, Company B

The writer believed that in order to do a story on the life and work of artillerymen in the Bulge, one should seek out former artillerymen who served in that battle. After advertising in *The Bulge Bugle*, a number of Bulge veterans responded with their stories. The writer was more than pleased with these responses and is most grateful to the artillery men who shared their memories and made this writing possible.

The Battle of the Bulge was different from other campaigns in Western Europe in that it was fought during a particularly cold winter in which the troops were not adequately equipped with cold weather clothing and boots. Second, in contrast to the summer and fall campaigns, when American units were continually on offensive, GIs in the Ardennes were on the defensive for much of December 1944. In some areas, the Germans continued their offensive into January 1945.

American artillery battalions played a major role in squelching the German offensive of December 1944. Compared to the great masses of German troops collected behind the Ardennes front in November, the American front lines were relatively thinly manned. However, behind the front were an impressive number of artillery battalions. Backing up the Losheim Gap, for instance, were at least eight battalions of artillery. General Gerow of V Corps could depend on more than 500 artillery pieces which could be directed at some point in the Ardennes.

One of the most deadly tactics used by American artillery was the time-on-target concentration, which involved combining the gunpowder from several batteries or battalions onto a single target on which the shells were timed at nearly the same moment.

As a result of the employment of many guns, the time-on-target technique, and the proximity fuse, the American artillery was a fearsome weapon which had an immense psychological effect upon Wehrmacht troops.

Charles MacDonald, in his *A Time for Trumpets*, described the effect that massed artillery fire had on some young German soldiers in the Bulge: "Inside Bullingen before daylight the next day, December 21, twenty-some young SS troops of the 12th SS Panzer Division, quartered in a house belonging to a farmer, Albert Kohnenberger, were sleeping in the cellar. Most were boys, 15 to 17 years old, and had already participated in the attacks on Dom Butgenbach and experienced the wrath of American artillery. Kohnenberger was with them in the cellar when noncommissioned officers arrived to order them back to the attack. The Belgian farmer watched in silent pity as the boys began to weep. As they gathered their gear to move out into the cold night, tears streaked down their faces."

Stephen Fritz, in his study of German soldiers' letters and diaries in World War II, had this quote in regard to the German soldiers' fear of U.S. artillery: "We're all sick to death of it and scared to death of it, all of us. Our fear reached grandiose proportions, and urine poured down our legs. Our fear was so great that we lost all thought of controlling ourselves."

Another opinion on the effect of American artillery is Francis Balace, a specialist on World War II history at the University of Liege, Belgium. Balace concluded that "It was American artillery which definitely won the battle." With American air power largely neutralized by clouds and fog, what could keep the Panzer forces from seizing the Meuse bridges? An incredible number of U.S. artillery shells were fired in the Ardennes. For the period of December 16 to 31, 1,250,000 shells were fired by U.S. artillery battalions in the Ardennes.

A much remembered feature of the Battle of the Bulge was the unusually cold Ardennes winter, and Mike O'Connor of the 965th Field Artillery Battalion (155mm howitzer) recalled the dark, cloudy weather: "The weather was terrible from the 26th to the 31st of December, 1944. We had only one clear day where our forward observers could adjust their fires, six days with haze or light fog, and nine days with snow, rain, or fog. Many missions were fired unobserved because of the weather; some of these were very successful, allowing our infantry to gain ground that had been captured."

Mike also wrote of how the cold had a "telling effect on the men, frost bite on hands and feet, exhaustion in deep snow, (poor) visibility in snowstorms, and cold food. The equipment would not function properly due to the congealing of the lubricant in the guns and vehicles."

Mike served as a T/5 jeep driver and radio operator in the 965th first at Weweiler, Belgium, on December 16, and later as the battalion was ordered westward to the "Fortified Goose Egg" near St. Vith, and again to Heyd, Belgium. At Weweiler, the 965th supported the 106th Division, later they supported a number of units including the 7th Armored, 82nd Airborne, and 75th Division.

John Kalagidis served as a truck and vehicle mechanic with 552nd Field Artillery Battalion (240mm howitzers). The 240mm guns were heavy artillery and were the army's largest field pieces. The gun would fire a 365 pound shell a distance of 15 miles. John wrote of the effects of the cold: "Very cold, but we managed. I had every bit of clothing on that I was able to wear. Some GIs were crying, it was so cold. On top of that I had the GIs. ...We had to dig spade pits and recoil pits to put our guns into position. It was hard digging in the ground."[1]

The 552nd was not attached to any division or corps but was used wherever needed. During the Bulge, the battalion moved from Stolberg, Germany, to Jalhay, Belgium, near Eupen.

John Grant was a front rodman with the 16th Field Artillery Observation Battalion which on December 16, 1944, was at Binsfeld, Luxembourg. Binsfeld is east of Troisvierges, which is roughly east of Bastogne. John recalled the cold days in the Bulge: "One man had bad trenchfoot in my section. Learned later that he lost both feet. I had minor frostbite in my feet... We were always cold and never did receive the new 'Shoe Pac' for cold."

GIs familiar with Bulge events will recall the Malmedy massacre in which nearly 100 members of the ill-fated 285th Field Artillery Observation Battalion were executed by a German SS unit. These sound and flash men did not come to shoot, but rather to locate enemy guns. John Grant recalled: "We had sound and flash OPs out front. Many times ahead of or with infantry outposts. I only pulled OP duty a few times since I primarily was the jeep driver for the lieutenant in charge of our sound survey section."

Leonard Schafenberg served as message center chief with the 174th Field Artillery Battalion (155mm self-propelled M-12). Leonard recalled the snow-covered, icy roads, "how guns skidded on roads, breaking tracks. Men seemed to take the cold pretty [well], lots of shoveling snow from vehicles stuck."

The 174th was at such Luxembourg towns as Lauterborn and Berdorf, and also at Neufchateau, Belgium.

Bud Lauer was a driver and gunner with the 907th Glider Field Artillery Battalion at Bastogne. Bud recalled much snow and cold temperatures: "Some places 4 feet of snow and down to 6 below zero, and never was in a building for our 42 days in Bastogne."

The 907th supported the 501st Parachute Infantry of the 101st Airborne Division, and their guns were sited roughly where the Bastogne Museum stands today.

Leonard Kyle served as executive officer of the 490th Armored Field Artillery Battalion (105mm, self-propelled), 11th Armored Division, which first saw action west of Bastogne. Leonard recalled his frostbitten hands and feet and also how a cook in his outfit suffered from frozen feet after standing in a steel bedded truck frying pancakes for two hours.

Ralph Balestieri was also with an M-7 unit, the 58th Armored Field Artillery Battalion, which when the Bulge began was located east of Bastogne. Ralph remembered how the extreme cold "froze the dead like cordwood, like logs... After Logvilly there was a shortage of blankets. I made a special run with a 2-1/2 ton full, some donated by service battery men."

Jerry Eades served with the 62nd Armored Field Artillery Battalion in North Africa, Sicily, and the Normandy Campaigns. During the Bulge, the unit was located one mile east of Roetgen, Germany supporting such units as the 102nd Cavalry Group and 78th Infantry Division. Jerry recalls some of the effects of snow and cold on men and equipment: "Recoil slow on guns for first few rounds, men reacted slow, due to snow and ice covered ground and equipment."

Al Alvarez, of the 7th Field Artillery Battalion, had served with the 1st Infantry Division through the Mediterranean and Normandy Campaigns. During the Ardennes Campaign, the battalion was on the northern shoulder of the Bulge at such places as Sourbrodt and Hosfekl, Belgium. Al recalled, "We wore layers of clothing, and many of us had foul-weather gear from U.S. Navy at Normandy Beach." Lacking shoe pacs or overshoes, his "FO party used straw, wrapped with blankets over the boots and wrapped with common wire for traction on snowy trails."

The nearness of an artillery unit to the front varied with the situation. The artillerymen's responses to this question ranged from 300 yards behind the front to as much as 9,000 yards. Leonard Kyle, of the 490th Field Artillery Battalion, recalled that as part of a marching column, the distance behind the moving units would be about 1,500 yards, but in fixed positions, the range would be about 2,500–3,000 yards. Leonard Schaffenberg recalled that his unit's M-12 self-propelled guns would "on special jobs be located forward with the infantry."

Counter-battery fire was a hazard to be avoided, and John Kalagidis wrote how on one occasion the 552nd's 240 mm howitzers were forced to displace when the German artillery had them "zeroed in." On the other hand, Mike O'Connor remembered how in the fall of 1944 in Belgium, his commanding officer selected a site behind a steep hill which shielded the guns from enemy observation and the unit received no counter battery fire while at that position.[2]

Most of the artillerymen in this survey said that their unit forward observers remained at the front with their radios and phones until relieved. One officer would serve in an OP and all battery NCOs were required to take their turn. Leonard Schaffenberg, of the 174th Field Artillery Battalion, reported that his unit's FOs would return each night.

Forward observers needed to carry sufficient supplies for several days in forward positions. Al Alvarez recalled that he typically carried: "Foreign legion neck cape and white camouflage sheet over my radio, extra batteries, 1/4 mile reel of wire, #10 can of blackened grease (for frying), hunks of cow meat (to cook), bottles of wine, all suspended from my web equipment, with submachine gun with many clips, grenades, 1/4 hunk of dynamite (to blow open foxholes)."

In the event of enemy breakthroughs, forward observers were in vulnerable positions. One artillery battalion supporting the 106th Infantry Division in December (the 333rd) lost nine of its twelve howitzers, all of its forward observers, and about 250 men including the battalion commander as a result of the breakthrough.

Ralph Balestrieri, whose 58th Armored Field Artillery Battalion also lost substantial amounts of equipment, recalled the move back from the front: "From Longvilly to Bastogne, lost about half of everything in firing batteries and my battery. When ordered in new position by 9th Armored Division elements, lost rest of equipment in tank battle... the men escaped in small controlled groups."

There were a number of massacres or prisoner shootings inflicted upon American artillerymen in the Bulge. The largest number of victims were from the 285th Field Artillery Observation Battalion at Baugnez, but another eleven men of the 333rd Field Artillery Battalion were executed at Wereth, Belgium. Mike O'Connor of the 965th recalled how two missing men of his unit were later found to have been executed during the December breakthrough.

There was much back-straining work for members of a gun crew. The 155mm shells weighed 95 pounds and each shell had to be hand-carried to the gun pits. The 105mm shells weighed 33 pounds each, and came in 120 pound boxes. Bud Lauer wrote that once at Bastogne, his battery was "down to 83 rounds and had only one "K" ration each day for 3 days. That didn't go far handling 120 lb ammo boxes. I lost 25 lbs in those 42 days."

In such extreme weather conditions, the human body burns more calories than are being replaced, and the body literally feeds on itself. The result is weight loss, fatigue, and more vulnerability to frostbite and disease.

One of the chief worries felt by artillerymen was incoming artillery or counter-battery fire. During the Bulge, the Germans located American battery positions with patrols, sound and flash methods, and particularly in German-speaking eastern Belgium, with information from civilian spies.

There were other serious concerns on the minds of artillerymen. Leonard Kyle recalled the thought of "being maimed. Death is final. To have lived without legs, hands, eyesight, or brain damage, would have been difficult."

Bud Lauer recalled, "Not seeing the end of this great war. I am one of the so-called lucky ones... Our wire man was from Wisconsin... close friend. He got killed Christmas Eve, splicing a phone wire. He was married and had two small girls."

Leonard Schaffenberg wrote of the respect he had for the "German 88mm gun with its very high muzzle velocity, when you heard it fire it was already on top of you, a very distinctive sound, never forgotten by me."

John Grant spoke of "incoming artillery and screaming meemies. Also because we had a lot of cross country survey work, we were always fearing mines, while carrying survey control."

As a section chief, Jerry Eades was concerned about how his men thought of him as a combat leader:

"My greatest fear was being caught being afraid by the men in the gun crew. I was afraid of losing my cool while under fire, and I had a fear of being hit in the stomach."

A number of artillerymen who responded remained in the army after World War II. Al Alvarez did tours of duty in Korea, Vietnam, and elsewhere before retiring with the rank of Lt. Colonel. Jerry Eades had served in the pre-war army horse artillery as early as 1936. Jerry was seriously wounded in both legs in March 1945 and this ended his 10-1/2 years of army service. John Grant served another 16 years in counter intelligence before retiring. Ralph Baliestrieri was called back to a tour of duty in the Korean War.

Among the various branches of service in the European theatre, artillery casualties were third highest with 5.4% of the Bulge casualties, behind air forces with 9.36% and infantry with 75%. On the other hand, the greatest majority of decorations, some 82.32% were awarded to army air corps personnel in the ETO, while only 3.5% were awarded to men in field artillery. Another 9.3% went to infantrymen.

Footnotes: (1) Moving a 240mm howitzer outfit was no small task, as the complete unit (gun and carriage) weighed 19 tons and required the use of a crane. The 240mm shell weighed 365 pounds. (2) Counter-battery fire was a common hazard in WWI and a future U.S. President, Harry Truman, experienced this in August 1918. In Alsace, France, Truman was a battery commander of a 75mm horse drawn howitzer unit of the Missouri National Guard. The outfit had recently arrived overseas, and was about to have its first combat experience. It was a pitch dark, rainy night when incoming enemy shells began landing in the battery position, terrifying many of the men and causing them to panic and run. Truman was on horseback when a near miss knocked his horse into a shell hole with Truman pinned underneath. He was able to squirm out from under his mount, and with blasts of profanity was able to get things under control. In later years, this incident came to be known as the "Battle of Who Run."

THREE DAYS AND A HERO TO REMEMBER

Derk Strikwerda

17th Airborne Division, 513th Parachute Infantry Regiment, Company C

As the years pass so rapidly now, it is amazing how clearly I still remember three particular days during those indescribable months. January 4th, 7th, and 26th, of 1945, have lived indelibly in my mind and have been recalled so many times since that time. During those days it seemed that we would all surely die, and on the 26th of January, I saw a man step up and prove himself to be a hero.

On the night of January 3rd, as Operations Sergeant of Company C, 513th Parachute Infantry Regiment I, accompanied by Company CO Captain Kendrick, to the Battalion CP to mark up the appropriate maps for the attack we would make the next morning. Seventeen troopers in C Company were wounded during the night before the attack by tree bursts, and we had no information by battalion of the hailstorm that we would encounter in this first big attack.

When we jumped off the next morning at 0830, we had two platoons forward with Company Headquarters in between. The enemy fire we faced was unbelievable. In minutes, the Company 356 Operator was killed and Captain Kendrick was severely wounded. Everything went downhill right after leaving our main lines of departure.

It was part of my job to hang on to the company records, and afterwards to piece together the information concerning exactly what happened since the day of the 4th. It was early morning of January 7th before I got everything unscrambled. The sorry truth of it all was that we lost 100 men out of the total company strength of 160 men!

While we were still reeling from this day in hell, we attacked again on January 7th. We attacked over the same open ground, losing half of what had been left of Company C. Thirty more of our guys were KIA, MIA and WIA! I jumped in a jeep with a kid named Falconer from HQ, 1st Battalion, and we were hauling ammunition to the attacking companies.

As we sped up toward the Bastogne Highway, an artillery round came in and exploded near us. Falconer was hit and the concussion actually blew him out of the jeep. The jeep was still running and I finally succeeded in getting Falconer back into the jeep trailer, driving him back to the battalion aid station.

I never saw Falconer again. I thought sure that he had died of his wounds, as he appeared to be seriously wounded. [I later learned] that he had survived despite a piece of shrapnel that had entered his lower back and exited out of his sternum. Falconer died in 1993 and I deeply regret that I hadn't made an effort to contact him before that time!

January 7th became the second day of agony for C Company. My morning report turned in on January 8th showed 30 more casualties. One hundred thirty brave troopers were casualties in two attacks. It was all unreal!

On January 26th, Lt. Clark informed the Battalion CO that we had taken our objective and according to our map, a patrol would enter territory a mile behind the German lines. I joined the small patrol that was ordered to scout out the situation in enemy territory. We had no cover and were in plain sight when we were about 400 yards from our destination. Much to my surprise, we made it to a row of trees and it was a miracle that we weren't all wiped out because the Germans were only a few hundred feet on the other side of that row of trees!

When we reached the trees, Lt. Clark sent James G. Smith, a machine gun sergeant, and three of his men to set up a gun 200 yards to the right of the Company CP. In minutes, the Germans brought them under fire with one being killed and another, John Erdman, being hit five times by a sniper.

One trooper with me was hit while we were routing out two Germans in a machine gun nest and a tracked vehicle started up nearby. Lt. Clark sent word for us to "get the hell out of there." Noble Eagle, my 300 radio operator, and I took off through the trees. We were running back over the same open ground, bullets snapping everywhere—I can't understand how they missed us.

We had run several hundred yards when I spotted an incredible sight. There was Jim Smith plodding through the knee-deep snow carrying John

Erdman on his back. He and another trooper had already helped Erdman for about 200 yards when the other trooper couldn't help anymore, so Jim carried him alone. Eagle and I finally reached them. We made a litter of sorts and got Erdman back where he could get medical aid. Jim had carried Erdman on his back for almost half a mile before we reached them to help. We were all under enemy fire over halfway back to our own lines.

There is no doubt about it. Jim Smith was solely responsible for saving John Erdman's life. It really didn't soak into me at that time, but I had never seen anyone put someone else's life above their own. I had never really experienced what "love for one's fellow man" or esprit de corps really meant until that day. I do now and I'll never forget the two terrible days of January 4th and 7th, and the day I saw a real-life hero!

IN THE VICINITY OF ECHTERNACH

John J. Sweeney
10th Armored Division, 61st Armored Infantry Battalion, Company A,
1st Platoon, Machine Gun Squad

Our Company A on December 18 was deposited in a very dark, cold and wooded area for the night in the vicinity of Echternach. We were told to dig in and stay quiet and alert because there was heavy enemy activity in the rear. The night was so dark you couldn't see your hand in front of your face. The ground was made up of heavy wet clay and our entrenching shovel couldn't dig into it, so we had to sleep on top of the ground and take our turns at guard duty and listening posts. It was so cold that the rear echelon brought up some overcoats (2 for every 3 soldiers). We placed one overcoat on the ground and 3 of us lay on it and covered ourselves with the 2nd overcoat. The only one who was warm was the middle guy so we changed places every 20 minutes or so.

The next morning was dark, cold and dreary and we were told that we had to attack through the woods and up a hill to knock out some rocket emplacements. The 1st platoon was to make the frontal assault and the 2nd platoon the right flanking movement. We moved out after eating some K-rations for breakfast and we were immediately shelled mercilessly for what seemed like an eternity. When a lull in the shelling occurred (which only meant the enemy was reloading) we started up the hill again, only to be shelled even more mercilessly. Enemy shells hit the trees above us, burst and rained shrapnel from above, which was devastating. The casualties were unbelievable and everyone figured he was next. My machine gunner, Pfc. Willie Wilson, was shot in the stomach by a sniper and killed just 10 feet in front of me as we were moving up. I then became the sniper's next favorite target but the closest he got was an inch or two above my rear end.

Another lull in the shelling and another move up only caused the shelling to increase. Looking desperately for some cover, I jumped into a large tank trap only to find it full of enemy soldiers and other Company A men trying to protect themselves from the shelling. When the shelling stopped for a moment or two both the enemy soldiers and ourselves scrambled out of the tank trap and went our respective ways into the woods with not a shot fired at each other. The woods were at this point so thick that if you went a few feet you couldn't see each other.

What was left of our platoon started forward and up again only to receive more shelling. It seemed like an eternity in hell with no way out. The screams of the wounded, the noise, the smoke, the awful weather and the feeling of helplessness only confirmed that war is hell and beyond anyone's imagination. At this time I was hit in the left arm by a piece of shrapnel but it didn't do too much damage so I bandaged it and ignored it.

All of us were wondering why our artillery didn't respond to the enemy's attack and try to slow them down. Someone said there was a strike back in the U.S. and there was a shortage of artillery shells and that our guns only had three shells apiece. We didn't even hear any of the three shells per gun respond and it left us with a very helpless and abandoned feeling.

Somehow after many hours of this unbelievable and awful battle three other men from Company A and myself reached the top of the hill. Guess what? No enemy rocket launchers. At this point I had one of my squad's machine guns but no ammunition as the ammo bearers were either killed or wounded. The four of us congratulated each other on reaching our objective and decided to consolidate it when we saw a group of enemy soldiers in the valley below us running along the tree line. We all opened up with our M1 rifles but the bullets barely reached the tree line and we hit no one. Then the 2nd platoon leader arrived and ordered us off the hill even though we tried to convince him otherwise. However, he told us there were enemy tanks behind us and that we'd probably be cut off. We were convinced and immediately left our hard fought position on the top of the hill.

On the way down the hill the shelling had stopped and the silence was very eerie except for the moaning and crying of the wounded. I saw Pfc. Pitt, one of my machine gun squad buddies, sitting against a tree, obviously seriously wounded and in a state of shock. I tried to talk to him but got no response. All of a sudden an enemy tank appeared about 25 yards away, slowly making its way through the woods and headed towards us. I fired my rifle at the tank but it didn't even notice my shooting at it. I then proceeded down the hill and saw the most horrible sight imaginable: almost my entire company strewn about the hill either dead or seriously wounded.

When I got to the bottom of the hill there was a dirt road running alongside it, which was the same roadway we jumped off from. Only this time there was absolute confusion with tanks and half-tracks knocked out and burning, wounded and dead soldiers everywhere, a few ambulances and soldiers wandering about looking for some leadership. The calls for the medics were desperate and heart rending.

I met Pfc. Santofalco, another member of our machine gun squad, who looked very worried and perplexed. He said to me that he had to do something about the wounded and the situation. I agreed but had no idea what to do. He told me had found two ambulances and two working tanks and that we could fill the ambulances with some of the wounded and along with the tanks for protection drive them to the Aid Station which was in the town about two miles down the road.

Falco also told me that there was a road block down the road before we got to the town that had to be dismantled and that there were enemy troops all around. I never understood how Falco knew so much and how capable he was under such terrible conditions. It was now late in the afternoon and getting dark and it looked like we were in a very desperate situation. Time was running out, particularly for the wounded.

Between Falco and me, we were able to round up ten other men willing to try and break out of the situation with the two ambulances full of the wounded. We also convinced two tankers with their crews to join us and lead the ambulances down the roadway. Our convoy took off for the Aid Station in town as fast as we could go with the two tanks in front, each with six infantry soldiers riding on the back of each tank. Falco and I were riding on the second tank along with four others. He was on the right side and I was on the left side.

After we travelled about 1/4 mile down the road the enemy soldiers started to fire at us from about 100-200 yards away and from both sides of the road with small arms fire and machine gun fire as well as what appeared to be anti-tank fire. The tanks were buttoned up and we were firing our rifles as fast as we could from both sides off the back of the tanks. Our tank was hit by enemy fire and three of us on the back of our tank were wounded, including Falco and myself—Falco in the knee, the other soldier in the shoulder and I in the face. The other tank and the ambulances were also being fired on but they appeared to be okay.

Our plans were to dismount when we got to the road block and clear it. However, when the lead tank was about 100 yards from the road block, it didn't look very formidable and we decided to drive right through the road block. We hit it with our lead tank as fast and direct as possible and the tank broke right through it. Hooray! The rest of us followed safely and we arrived at the Aid Station, which was later captured (so I was told). Confusion in this area reigned supreme, with all types of military vehicles moving in all directions in the dark, and wounded soldiers everywhere. No one would listen to our pleas that our Company A lay wounded and dead two miles down the road. I suppose they already knew about it, but didn't have the resources to do anything.

The medics sewed up my jaw and wrapped my head in a large white bandage. I met Pfc. Sam Stahlman, my closest buddy in the machine gun squad, at the Aid Station and we had a joyous reunion. Sam had been wounded in the leg and was hopping around trying to find out what was going on. Eventually, we went that night by ambulance to a field hospital in Thionville (I believe). Sam and I no sooner lay down on a couple of stretchers in what appeared to be the gym on the main floor of a school building right by the rear exit door, when someone ran down the middle of the gym screaming that the Germans were coming through the front door.

Sam and I, remembering that the Germans were taking no prisoners at this time, got up from our stretchers and limped out the back door and pulled ourselves into the rear of a moving 2-1/2 ton truck full of medical personnel escaping capture. I passed out in the truck and the next time I woke up I was lying on my back in a large white hospital ward with the sun shining through the windows and a beautiful nurse standing over me. I thought I was in Heaven. After leaving the hell of the battlefield, I was in Heaven! I have never seen or heard of Pfc. Santofalco since that date. Thank you, Santofalco, wherever you are; you are one brave soldier.

HOW IT ALL BEGAN

Gustav Swiersz
28th Infantry Division, 112th Infantry Regiment, 2nd Battalion, Company E

After a grueling and devastating encounter in the Battle of Hurtgen Forest (early November 1944) the 28th Division was deployed to the Luxembourg/German border. "E" Company was dispatched to Lieler, Luxembourg, located on the west bank of the Our River. (Germany being on the east bank.) Our line was a series of outposts on the Our River. In what perhaps may have been the first shots fired as the BOB began, they also, with hindsight, may be deemed to be prophetic of the campaign that followed.

That brief encounter is best described by two young GIs in my squad. The two GIs, James Norris of Conley, Georgia and Robert Farmer, of Bluefield,

West Virginia, were manning an outpost dugout on the Our River's west bank. This is how, in his own words, Jim Norris describes how the Battle of the Bulge began in our sector:

"He (R. Farmer) and I shared an unusual experience that morning of December 16th, 1944 (5:30 a.m.). We were in the outpost dugout, doing double guard duty. He was resting, I was looking at the beautiful scene, the moon on the snow all 'quiet and serene.'

"But this changed quickly. All at once big searchlights hit the sky; we could hear tanks running so I woke Robert and we called the Company C.P. The Company Commander told us to come back to the C.P., that the Germans had attacked the 110th Regiment and were coming in mass attack towards us.

"As we got our gear together we looked up on the hill in the moonlight and there was this German Tiger tank and he spotted our dugout position. He fired one shell over us then one in front of us. Robert looked at me and said, 'You know what this means; the next one is coming in.' So we laid there and could hear that third shell coming in. After a little time nothing happened. We raised up and saw the third shell sticking just a few feet in front of us, in a direct line with us. It was a faulty shell.

"I had always believed that God was taking care of us. Anyway you talk about two boys moving through the snow to get to the company—there was no stopping us. We were able to hold our position until sometime in the afternoon, then we had to go. They were making it so hot for us that we just had to retreat. But, thank God, we lived to fight again."

FROM THE HURTGEN FOREST TO THE BULGE

Martin Sylvester
4th Infantry Division, 12th Infantry Regiment, Company G

During the winter of 1944, I was front line infantry with the 4th Infantry Division in the Hurtgen Forest, Germany. We suffered heavy losses from constant shelling and mortar attacks. We were wet, cold, and exhausted. In

early December, word came that we were to be relieved and sent to a holding position where there had been no activity for several months. It would
be rest and rehabilitation. We were sent to a town called Echternach, which
may have been a resort town. It was alongside the Mosel River in a valley
surrounded by hills. The Germans were on the other side of the river, apparently also on vacation, and apart from an occasional shell—I guess to
remind us that they were still there—there were no hostilities. It was an
abandoned town, and for the first time in months we would be indoors with
showers, hot food, and no fighting. Weapons were collected in order to be
serviced and reconditioned, and fresh clothing was supplied. We were told
that the Germans were also in a non-combat position and that they occasionally crossed the river to wander the area, perhaps to loot or spy on our
activities; no one was sure. We did, however, carry a rifle whenever we left
town to explore the area.

On December 15th it was my turn to spend a few days at the observation post, a dugout on a high cliff overlooking the German positions across
the river. With our binoculars we had a panoramic view. We could see the
Germans lining up for exercise and chow. It seemed they always had hot food.
They often gathered in large groups for a kind of camaraderie and socializa-
tion. Sometimes, when the wind was right, we could hear music and singing.
There were three of us at the outpost. We took turns at watch.

On the morning of December 16th, I had just awakened and opened a
K ration tin of bacon and cheese when I heard "Red! Red! Come here; look
at this!" My buddy handed me the binoculars and I could hardly believe
what I saw. It was cloudy and foggy but through the haze were thousands
of Germans crossing the river. They were walking across pontoon bridges
which they must have put in place overnight. We then heard small arms fire.
We got on the phone and it was a while before someone picked up. Whoever
answered said they couldn't talk. "We're up to our ass in Krauts; we have one
rifle for every five men, one automatic, and our guys are getting hit all over
the place," he shouted. "We have to find a way out of here. You guys better get
out while you can."

It was the beginning of what would later be called "The Battle of the

Bulge." I learned later that my outfit was surrounded and lost three companies. In the town of Echtemach there were face-to-face encounters as the Germans moved into the town at dawn and the awakening Americans were surprised to find Germans in the street and entering their billets. I heard that one G.I. was frying bacon for breakfast when a German opened the door and walked in. They were both startled, and the G.I. acted first, hitting the German in the face with the hot frying pan. He then ran out the door, down the steps, and into the street, leaping over and dodging Germans who were sitting on the steps and loitering around the door to the building. The Germans began to shoot at him, and he weaved and dodged, somehow avoiding the shots, and reached our headquarters where our guys were watching from a window and cheering him on. He made it to the building and through the front door without a scratch. (This incident was told to me later when I ran into some of the men who had been there.)

We were unsure about how to get out of there. Small arms fire increased and seemed to be coming from the west. There were men approaching from that direction. They were American medics carrying a wounded officer on a stretcher. They put him in our dugout and left to retrieve more of the wounded. We asked if we could help and were told that we had better get out. We headed east. It sounded like there was fighting everywhere. While walking along a dirt road I spotted a soldier about fifty yards away at the edge of a wooded area. At that distance I couldn't tell if he was American or German. We were pointing at each other when he dropped to the ground and there was a spray of bullets at our feet. We started to run and an American ambulance, coming from that direction was speeding toward us. We tried to wave it down. It would not stop. We ran and ran. There were men and vehicles all moving in our direction. No one would stop. I don't know how, but we ended up in Liege, Belgium, exhausted.

In Liege people seemed to be going about their lives, and except for the presence of American military and occasional buzz bombs you would hardly know there was a war. There were stragglers everywhere, all from different outfits. We kept asking about the 4th Infantry, and where to report, but no one knew. We were actually getting bored with Liege when we found an officer who was gathering stragglers to form a line of defense against an anticipated German attack. He put us in touch with remnants of the 4th Infantry that made it to Liege. It was Christmas Eve, 1944 on the outskirts of the city of Liege. We were placed in positions some fifty feet apart from each other and told to dig in. The Germans were expected to attack at dawn, Christmas Day.

We were at the edge of a wooded area about a hundred yards from another wooded area were the Germans were waiting, with an open field between us. It was obvious that we were far below strength and would be overrun. I did not believe I would survive this one. At dawn, on December 25th, there was the most spectacular and beautiful sight. The Americans began shelling the wooded area where the Germans were waiting to attack. The sky became illuminated with brilliant, colorful explosions, one after another and some simultaneous. It was brighter and more vivid than I had ever seen. A welcome sight! The noise was deafening. It lasted only a few minutes and then hordes of Germans came running toward us. They were about halfway across the field when we opened fire. They were moving fast and it did not look like we could stop them, when suddenly, from behind us, fresh American troops came running out to meet them. It was the "bucket of blood" infantry, coming to relieve us. There could not be a more welcome sight. We jumped out of our foxholes and cheered. An officer passed the word that we were to withdraw, but we just stood there and watched the Germans falling like flies, and those that could were running back to the protection of the forest. The 28th Division was called the "bucket of blood" because of their arm patch. It was red and shaped like the state of Pennsylvania, which looked like a vase. We then found and joined what was left of our respective outfits. There were quite a few of the 4th Infantry and we were gathered into a fighting unit to return to the front.

OH, TANNENBAUM

Sam Tannenbaum, son of Henry I. Tannenbaum
83rd Infantry Division, 331st Infantry Regiment, 2nd Battalion, Company F

[Sam Tannenbaum sent us the following article regarding his search for what happened to his father, Pvt. Henry I. Tannenbaum, who was killed in the Battle of the Bulge.]

The first time I saw the picture was when Tony Vaccaro, 83rd Infantry Division, 331st Infantry Regiment, 2nd Battalion, Headquarters, sent me a catalog of an exhibit of his photographs that had been touring France in December, 1996. The caption read, "White Death: Photo requiem for a dead soldier. Private Henry I. Tannenbaum. Tannenbaum means Evergreen Tree; it was taken during time of year when the name Tannenbaum evokes thoughts of snow and Christmas."

Private Henry I. Tannenbaum was my father, a member of Company F, 2nd Battalion, 331st Infantry Regiment, 83rd Infantry Division, who was killed on January 11, 1945, during the Battle of the Bulge. He had returned to the front line after being wounded in the Hurtgen Forest. I became a war orphan at two and a half years of age. Tony was a soldier with a camera who knew my father as a fellow New Yorker.

Tony credits "White Death" with the start of his photojournalism career. "White Death" appeared in *Stars and Stripes* magazine. The walls of Tony's home are covered with his photographs of presidents and kings, world renowned painters, authors and movie stars. Many of the photographs have appeared in *Life* and *Look* magazines. Tony has had an amazing impact on my life.

I had "White Death" inserted at the end of a chapter I wrote for *Lost in Victory: Reflections of American War Orphans of World War II*, published by the University of North Texas in 1998. The VA estimates over 183,000 American War orphans as a result of World War II. In 1994, I helped form a group now known as the American World War II Orphans Network (AWON). For more information about AWON and how I met Tony, thanks to a Luxembourger named Jim Schiltz, readers with internet access can visit http://www.awon. org/awtannen.html. In 1999, "White Death" was selected as Photograph of the Century by ZEIT magazine published in Frankfurt, Germany. In presenting the award, Josef Haslinger, an Austrian novelist who was active in the anti-Waldheim movement, wrote about the story behind the picture:

"The photograph was taken the morning of January 11, 1945, near Ottre, in Belgium. The name of the dead soldier was Henry I. Tannenbaum. He was part of a raiding party of four tanks and twenty soldiers that ran into a German ambush; some of his comrades were killed outright, but most were left wounded. Then a German soldier came out of the woods and executed each of the injured men with a shot through the head. The surviving witness was Sergeant Harry Shoemaker. He pretended to be dead and brought the photographer (Tony Vaccaro) to the scene of the event that next morning."

Tony Vaccaro wrote *Entering Germany* in 2001, published by Taschen, and in it he included a two-page spread of "White Death" at the front of the book. In *Entering Germany*, Tony tells of returning to the scene some 50 years later and discovering that the Belgian landowner had planted evergreen trees in the former wheat field. Where one Tannenbaum had fallen, there was now a forest of Tannenbaums.

In June, 2002 citizens of Belgium and Luxembourg, forever grateful to American soldiers for their liberation, erected a monument to my father near the place where Tony shot "White Death." The memorial plaque reads in part: "We remember Private Henry I. Tannenbaum, New York, killed in action near Ottre, January 11, 1945." It is signed by U.S. Veterans Friends Luxembourg and the Community of Vielsalm (about 20 miles north of Bastogne, Belgium). For more on the memorial, readers with internet can visit http://awon.org/memorials/ottre.

July 10, 2002, I visited a Tony Vaccaro photo exhibit called "The Last Battle," in the George C. Marshall Museum in Lexington, Virginia. The signature piece of that exhibit is a Larger than life-sized reprint of "White Death." The caption reads: "The last battle took place east of the Elbe River in Germany. It lasted 26 days and abruptly halted 45 miles outside of Berlin."

As a member of the 83rd Infantry Division, Tony Vaccaro recorded "the last battle" in startling black and white photographs. Here they speak of the horror and irony of war. The photographs are not retouched, so they appear, as the artist states, "to show that they are not only images of war, but they also went through war."

"The Last Battle" was also on display at the Mighty Eighth Air Force Heritage Museum in Savannah, Georgia, in June, 2003. For more on that display, readers with internet can visit http://www.awon.org/pooler.

In addition to Tony, I have spoken to many wonderful members of the 83rd Infantry Division: Manny Lamb, Stew Barrick, Cliff Wooldridge, Jack Straus, Larry Dalton, David Hume, Robert Sessions, Bernie Cove, and Ralph Gunderson. Unfortunately, none of these men remembered my father. I am still searching for another war buddy of my father's named Dave/David Brooks of the 83rd Division, who wrote to my aunt about the massacre at Ottre in February, 1945. They met at Fort Meade, Maryland, in July 1944. He recalled my father conducting religious services for soldiers of the Jewish faith in England. They recovered from wounds in Aachen, Germany, in December 1944.

THE BEST YEARS OF OUR LIVES

Joseph A. Tedesco
4th Infantry Division, 377th Antiaircraft Artillery Automatic
Weapons Battalion

I was 21 years old when I went into the Army. I took my basic training at Fort Eustis, Virginia. I was sent to Camp Stewart, Georgia. It was an anti-aircraft outfit. There were four batteries to a battalion and I was put in Battery D. They made me a gunner on the 50 caliber machine gun. There were two sections to a battery and each section had 40 millimeter guns. They had a Sergeant, 2 Corporals, 2 truck drivers plus 12 men in each section. We would go to the firing range and shoot at a sleeve target that was towed by an airplane. It was pretty hard to hit the target, but the more we shot, the better we got. We also had to learn how to identify German airplanes. One day we loaded all of our guns and trucks on railroad cars and went to Camp Carrabelle, Florida where we were to begin amphibious landing training. They would put us in LCI or LCP Boats and go out into the Gulf of Mexico about a mile, then they would turn around and head for shore. Sometimes the landing crafts would hit a sandbar, and they would let down the ramp and we had to get off. Sometimes the water was two feet deep and other times it would be up to our chest. While we were there, we went through the infiltration course. We had to crawl under barbed wire while they were shooting live ammunition over our heads. One night, they took us to a tall building that had a cargo net over the side. We had to get on the net and go down it into a boat that was at the bottom. They had some soldiers at the bottom that would swing the net simulating a ship that was sinking. We went back to Camp Stewart and our Colonel made us pitch our pup tents on the ground in the open field.

In July, we went to Tennessee for maneuvers. It was hot and dusty and our Colonel would not give the drivers any rest so they had a bad time staying on the road. One day, a truck with some soldiers in it from another battery went over a cliff. Two soldiers were killed and the rest were sent to a hospital. Then our Colonel decided to change out drivers. We stayed in Tennessee awaiting orders to go overseas. We finally went to Camp Shanks, New York and got on a ship that took 14 days to cross the Atlantic. We landed in England and took over a vacated school that we used for our barracks. In March, we became part of the 4111 Division area and my gun crew was sent on maneuvers with them up in Wales. We had to waterproof all of our guns and trucks and then we went out into the channel. One night while we were out, we were attacked by German E-Boats and lost 749 soldiers and sailors. The Army kept it a secret for 40 years. Today there's a monument in honor of all the men that lost their lives that day.

While we were in Wales, my Sergeant got sick and went to the hospital. He never came back, so the Captain made me acting Sergeant. When we got back, I saw some strange trucks in the motor pool. They were called half-tracks and had four 50 caliber machine guns mounted on a turret. These guns could turn all around as well as up and down. An officer and a Corporal came over to me. The officer said he would like me to take command of one of the tracks but said I would only be a Corporal. He said he knew I would be a Sergeant soon, but he still wanted me to take the half-track. He said I had to make up my mind what I wanted to do. I told him I would take the half-track, so the Corporal that was with him became a Sergeant instead. Now I had to pick my own men for the track. There would be only five of us and a driver. I picked men that I knew were good with the machine gun and also a good driver.

The invasion began on June 6th and my battalion went in at Utah Beach on the 12th of June. The 4th Division had gone in on D-Day, June 6th. My half-track was sent to the 42nd Field Artillery. They had four tanks with 105mm Howitzers. Their Captain treated us as one of his own soldiers. He made sure that if we needed anything we got it. We would get all our rations and our clothes if we needed any from them in convoy. After we took Cherbourg, we were in what they called the hedgerow country. The Germans had dug into the hedgerows and had good cover in which to hide. Our infantry was losing a lot of soldiers and could not make any headway. General "Teddy" Roosevelt was given the job to get the infantry moving. The General got the idea of using the half-tracks up front to strafe the hedgerows because we had so much fire power. Each one of our guns would fire 500 to 600 rounds a minute. So on July 12th we went up front. I set up in a field and had my men dig their foxholes about 30 yards from the track. My Captain came up to see how we were set up and asked me where my foxholes were. I told him where and he said to "dig them around the half-track". I told him I thought it was a bad idea because the Germans would try to knock out the half-tracks and a near miss would put my men in danger. He said "that's an order." So while he was still there, I had my men start to dig. As soon as he left, I told my men to use the holes they had first dug. The Captain went to another track that was two fields away from mine and he told that Corporal the same thing he told me and that's what the Corporal had his men do. We were hooked up by phone to an officer who was up front and could see the Germans and he would tell us when to shoot and when to stop. We would shoot so much and for so long that sometimes one of the barrels would burn out. We had eight extra barrels that we had tested on the firing range. With special gloves, the men would change the burned out barrel and keep on shooting. That first day, my driver started to cry. He couldn't take it so I put him in a foxhole and told him to stay there so he would feel safer. When we got back that day to a safe area, I told my Captain that I wanted a new driver. I told him why and so he gave me someone else. We went up again the next day and did the same thing. That night, a good friend of mine who was on the track two fields away would not say anything. He was always joking around and laughing, but this night he wouldn't say anything. I asked him what was wrong and he said he felt funny and could not explain how he felt. He said he wasn't sick or afraid, he just felt funny. I told him to stay behind the next day but he said he was going up anyway. By this time the Germans knew just about where we were and the shells were getting closer. One exploded pretty close so I told my men to get into the foxholes. The next volley came in and a shell hit a tree two fields away. When it exploded, it covered all of the half-track and the foxholes. The driver was hiding under the track so he didn't get hit and he came running to me and said all the men were wounded. I told him to stay with my men and I ran over to the track. The first hole had the Corporal in it and he had a big hole in his hip. I used both my first aid kit and his to bandage his hip and he said to look after the rest of the men. I checked the holes on that side and they were empty. I ran around the track and the last foxhole had my friend in it. I knew he was dead because he had shrapnel holes in his back and his helmet. I took him out of the hole, dragged him away from the track, and covered him with a blanket. By this time, our Captain heard about it and came up. Well, I was so mad at him that I made a lunge towards him but he held out his hands to stop me and said, "I guess you were right about digging the foxholes away from the track." But it was too late... I lost a good friend. We heard later that Teddy Roosevelt asked our officers, "What are your half-tracks doing? They are killing all the Germans by themselves," so I think we did a good job because now our infantry was starting to gain ground.

Next came St. Lo. This time the big brass got the air corps to help. Three thousand airplanes were to leave England and bomb the Germans. The artillery was to mark the front lines with smoke shells and the planes were to drop their bombs beyond the smoke onto the Germans. Well, the first wave of planes did, but somehow the wind drifted back blowing the smoke onto our soldiers. Before the big brass got word to the planes, we lost a lot of soldiers and also a general, N.C. Near.

The Falaise Gap is where we had thousands of Germans surrounded and the English were to close the gap to the north of us, but they must have stopped for tea because thousands of Germans got away to fight another day. We were now getting close to Paris and the 4th Division could have gone into Paris but the big brass wanted to give the honor to the French's General Leclerc. So the 4111 Division had to wait for them to catch up. They got in front of the 4th Division and marched into Paris. We were the first Americans in Paris and the people went crazy. We could not move our track because we would have run over someone. The people were wall-to-wall on the streets. They would give us wine and flowers and the girls would climb on all the trucks, jeeps and half-tracks kissing everyone. They were so happy to be free from the Germans. We spent the night in the park but no one slept because the French would come over with gifts and wanted to talk.

We left the next morning and had the Germans on the run. It was open country and our tanks were moving right along with no trouble. We set up one day near a town called San Quentin. A boy and girl about their teen years came by and were looking at our track. I got talking to them and they made me understand they came from Italy and they wanted me to go see their parents. So I went and their parents were very happy to see us. They made us some coffee that was made of roasted wheat and chicory. It was awful, but we said it was good. The father asked us if the Germans would come back. I told him they were gone for good. He then took me outside and started to dig until he uncovered a long box where he had hidden two bikes. He told us that if the Germans knew he had the bikes they would have taken them. He told us there would be a street dance that night and we should go see it. Two of us went and the people were singing and dancing and, of course, drinking. The men came out to the square and they had two women with them. These two had been collaborating with the German soldiers so they put them in the center of the square and shaved the hair off of their heads.

We were on the move again. We were in convoy when a German airplane came out of nowhere and began strafing the convoy. My men and I jumped off the half-track and jumped into the ditches and empty foxholes that were near-by. It was dusk when this happened and by the time it was over and we were able to get back into our track it was dark. There was a smell like someone had crapped in their pants, so we looked at everyone on the track and we saw that one of my men had jumped into a foxhole that a soldier had used as a latrine. This poor guy was covered all the way down the front of him so he had to throw away his clothes and put on clean ones. We had a good laugh over that.

It was stop and go all night and in the morning we found out why. Our airplanes had strafed a German convoy that was using horses and wagons to move... the road was full of dead Germans and horses. We finally got a tank with a snow blade on it to push everything off the road. The word came down that if we saw horses that were badly wounded to shoot them rather than make them suffer. It was hard to shoot some of the horses because they were so beautiful. It was 2:30 PM when we finally got to set up. We dug our foxholes, ate our C-rations and now it was getting dark. My men asked who was going to start pulling guard. I told them no one because we could see the battalion headquarters in a field near us. I said if they're here, we must be miles from the front. Besides, we would be up early. The next thing I knew, someone was shaking my foot. I looked up and it was my platoon Sergeant who I hadn't seen since we left England. He asked me who was on guard and I told him no one. He said the Captain was on the road and wanted to see me. So I reported to the Captain and he wanted to know who fell asleep while on guard so he could court-marshal the soldier that fell asleep. Well that's all I had to hear. My men and I had been together for two and a half years and we were like brothers so I wasn't going to tell him anyway. When I told the Captain I didn't post anyone, he told me, "You're a buck private; who's next in command?" Each one of my men was called up to the Captain and they all said if Tedesco was not good enough, neither were they. He got red in the face and said he would find someone to take command. We got a new Corporal from one of the 40 millimeter guns. He was with us two weeks and one day he was up in the turret of the gun when off in the distance we could hear anti-aircraft firing. It had to be a German plane so I told the Corporal to get ready just in case the plane would come within our range. Well the plane did come and I am yelling at the Corporal to shoot, but he never did. The phone rang and they wanted to know how many rounds we fired. I gave the phone to the Corporal and he said he did not shoot because he thought they were friendly planes. Later that day, he took me aside and said that he did not know how to operate the guns. I said, "You mean to tell me that for two weeks our lives were in your hands and you're just telling me now you don't know how to operate the guns?" So I had to teach him all about the guns. The war was something else. Back home the only time we would see someone dead was at a wake. Now all we would see were dead soldiers every day, both Germans and Americans, so it's hard to see what the war was like. When the weather was hot, they would bloat up to twice their size. Between the smell of all of them, plus the dead cows and horses, it would make you sick. But as time went by, you got so used to it that you forgot what fresh air smelled like. You also had to get used to seeing just parts of bodies and soldiers so burned up you couldn't tell if they were Germans or Americans.

Our Division was then sent to the Huertgen Forest. This place was hell. You were afraid to put your foot down because the Germans had put mines under the leaves and many soldiers lost their feet and legs. When the Germans would shell us, the shell would hit the tree tops and explode, raining iron shrapnel down on us. I was lucky to get the engineers to clear a path up a hill. Once they cleared the path, they put white tape around the trees on both sides and we had to stay inside those white tapes. We were so high up, one day German planes flew by and we were eye level with them. I was the first one to get into the gun turret. I picked up the first plane in my sights and although we were taught to shoot short bursts, I shot almost all my ammunition at the first plane because if I was short, the bullets might hit one of the planes that were behind the first one. I saw smoke coming out of the first plane so I knew he was hit. He made a right turn and headed towards his front but it was too far to hear if he crashed. We were there from November to December and then we finally got a rest. We drove to Luxembourg and for two days we thought the war was over.

We got to Luxembourg on the 12th of December and on the 16th of

December the Battle of the Bulge started. The Germans broke through our lines killing and capturing thousands of American soldiers. There was a lot of confusion because some of the Germans could speak perfect English. They knew all our slang words, all our ball players and movie stars. They would turn the road signs around so we would be going the wrong way. It was sad to see so many of our soldiers running to the rear and throwing their guns away. One officer surrendered 7,000 of his men because they just came from England and did not have time to set up in a good position so rather than have his men killed, he gave up. Our outfit went out in the country about two miles from the town we were in. There we found a mansion that must have belonged to a duke or baron. It was beautiful and we made it our command post. The Germans were shooting at us for two days and never hit the mansion. An officer told the Captain to give him a jeep and a radio operator and he would go see if he could find where the Germans were. The Captain said okay and the officer took off. For three more days the Germans were shelling us and we heard nothing from the officer who left. Each day we changed codes for the day. Our radio operator asked the officer radioing in for the code for the day... the answer he got was the wrong one. So he told the Captain that a German was on the radio who could speak perfect English and that maybe the officer that had left to go up front must have been killed or captured. Our Captain said, "Let's get out of here." He then came to me and said for my crew to take the tail end of the convoy... we would be the last ones out. On the way back to the town that we were first in, a truck went into a ditch and couldn't get out. Being the last ones out, I couldn't just leave him in the ditch so we got out our cable, pulled him out and he took off towards the town. We still had to rewind our cable and when we got to the town there was no one there. We came to a crossroad and went across, but that was a mistake because the Germans saw us and started shooting at us. We made a fast U-turn and went back to the crossroad. This time we took a left turn and two miles down the road we found our artillery set up and they were shooting at the mansion we just left. Our Captain had left an officer and a radio operator in a patch of woods near the mansion. The officer said ten minutes after we left the Germans were in the mansion. Our artillery shot at the mansion most of the day and when we went back, the mansion was nothing but rubble. There were dead soldiers all around the place and trucks were burning up. The American soldiers started to loot anything they could find but our Captain had them put everything back.

During the Bulge, one of our half-tracks got hit. The men were slightly wounded but the track was in good shape. All they needed was a driver. The motor pool Sergeant remembered that I used to drive one when we were in England. So they came looking for me and I went back to the command post. It was there I saw my Captain for the first time since he busted me and he gave me a choice. I could drive a truck or drive the half-track, so I took the track. Now I had to wait for a crew. There was a house and a barn there and I killed three chickens and gave them to the kitchen section to cook. They had made a kitchen up in the barn. An American tank came by and the Germans where shooting at it. They missed and the shell hit the top of the barn. I ran to see if I could help and I met two soldiers coming out of the barn. They said that two soldiers were killed and some were wounded. Just then, I got a funny feeling like someone was telling me to get into the house. So I grabbed the two soldiers by the shoulders and said, "Let's get in the house!" We had just made it to the house when another shell exploded. I hit the wall on one side of the hallway and the other soldier hit the wall opposite me. I could feel my right leg burn and my left hand. I looked at the soldier opposite me and his right leg was gone. I looked at myself and I was covered with blood and chips of bone. It was from the other soldier. I yelled for medics and the soldiers in the back rooms came running out and looked after the soldier whose leg was gone. They looked at me and said to run to the barn because there was a medic there. I made it to the barn and they stripped me and bandaged my leg and then took out the shrapnel that was holding my gloves on my hand. They put me in a jeep and I went to a field hospital. I was there for two days and then I went back to the command post. I found out that the two soldiers that got killed were cleaning the chickens that I killed. I never heard what happened to the soldier who lost his leg.

We finally got a crew and a new corporal so we moved out. Now we were near the German pill boxes. The mess Sergeant had a kitchen set up in a pill box that was 200 yards from where we were. We would take turns to go eat two at a time. The Corporal and one of the men were the last to go. The mess Sergeant told the Corporal that he wanted a soldier to help with KP. The Corporal got back and told the soldier who was with him to go back and pull KP. That meant that he had to walk all the way back when he was just there a few minutes ago. That was the last straw. This soldier picked up a hammer and was going to hit the Corporal on the head. The Corporal saw the motion and he ran looking for the First Sergeant. When the First Sergeant came, the men told him all of the crazy thing this Corporal made them do since he was put in charge. The First Sergeant told the Corporal to get his gear and leave. He turned to me and said for me to take over and he would see that I got my rating back. This made the men happy.

We had a mission to go up front again and one of my men said he didn't want to go. He said I could either shoot him, or have him court-marshaled, but he wasn't going to go up front. Well I knew this soldier had been in the room where all the men got wounded and he did not get a scratch. This happened twice to him so I told him to stay behind and we went up without him. The next day, we had to go up again, and this time he said he was coming with us. The day before, he just had a feeling that something might happen to him. During the war, there was snow on the ground and one day as the snow was melting we saw a hand sticking out of the snow. We didn't know if it was an American or a German, so two of us pulled on the hand and out came a dead German soldier. His face was white and wrinkled. We took out his wallet and there were pictures of him and his family and here he was dead at our feet. That's when we would feel sorry because it could have been one of us. What happened at that place will always be in my mind. There was a creek nearby that we would get our water from. We would always put pills in our drinking water, but this time the pills did not work. The reason they weren't working was because we did not realize that under the snow that was melting and going into the creek, were dead soldiers, cows and horses and we all got dysentery. I was sick as a dog for eight days.

By this time the Bulge was just about over. We had pushed the Germans back to where they started from. We had 19,000 soldiers killed. I don't know how many were captured or how many were wounded, but I know that the Germans lost twice as many as we did. Our outfit was sent back into France to clean up some pockets of Germans that we bypassed. We were with an outfit whose captain told me there were 500 German soldiers in a town that was over the hill from him. He said that I could shoot at any time during the night at any movement we saw on the hill because it would not be any of his men. It was here that I almost got shot by one of my own men. That night, we were all sleeping in a large tent when I had to go to the john. I left the tent and when I tried to get back in, I couldn't find the opening so I was making a lot of noise. All at once, I heard someone from inside the tent say, "Don't move or I'll shoot." That scared me so much that I think my voice changed. I said, "It's me. Look at my bed roll and you will see that it's empty and I am outside." So they let me in but one of my men still had his gun pointed at the opening of the tent.

During our last move, we ended up with the Japanese-American soldiers from the 442nd Field Artillery that had come up from Italy. The Captain called me over and gave me a bottle of whiskey. He saw the gun I had and he said he had one just like it but it was all apart. He found it on a dead German who was in the water and he did not want it to get rusty so he took it apart and could not put it together again. We worked on it until we got it firing again and he wanted to buy mine. I told him no, I was taking mine home. We came to a farm and we had to cross a wooden bridge. The old farmer came out and said the bridge was "kaput". I didn't believe him so I got my driver to start across. He was nearly across when the bridge gave way. The bumper caught the bank on the other side and the trailer was holding up the rear of the track. My driver got so mad at me he said, "You got us into this mess so now you can get us out" and he left. I got two trucks to pull me back out. It was time to leave and I could not find my driver so I drove and got in the convoy. Good thing we had to wait because now I saw my driver and he was drunk. I put him in the track and while we were waiting and old man was picking up all the cigarette butts that the soldiers threw away. When he got near my track, my driver got out and hit the hands of the old man and the butts went flying and the old man ran away.

I had a good friend in the artillery that was a forward observer. He and an officer would go up front and direct the artillery when to shoot, how far and left or right until they hit what they were shooting at. He only had to go up front when his name came up, but instead he would take the place of another soldier whose name came up if that soldier would give him his months' pay. I told him he was nuts to do that, but he said that if he had my cigarette lighter it would bring him good luck. So I would give him my lighter and he would give me his wrist watch. I don't know what happened that one day, but he went up front without my lighter and he got killed. They told me they couldn't even find his shoes, so it must have been a direct hit by a shell. So once more, I lost another very good friend.

As we kept going south, we reached Austria and started to see a lot of slave laborers. They were skin and bones. We gave them all the c-rations that we did not like and they were happy to get them. I saw some slaves skinning what I thought was a deer, but it was actually a police dog. One of the slaves could speak English and he told us that they started out with 3,000 slaves and as the weak ones would fall, the German guards would club them to death. They didn't want to shoot them because they were afraid that the Americans would come to investigate the shooting.

The war ended while we were with the Japanese and we had to find our battalion. The Japanese-American soldiers got on both sides of the road and began making snowballs. As we drove off, they threw all the snowballs at us. I guess it was their way of saying good-bye and good luck. To me they were the best. We found our battalion and our battery in a small town. We had 500 German prisoners in a stockade. Another Corporal and I got the job of going to the farmers and asking them how many prisoners they needed to help on the farm. Each morning we took them to the farms and dropped them off with a guard and picked them up at 4:30 PM.

When the point system came out you had to have 85 points to go home. I had 120 points so I and some others left for England. We got stuck loading low point men to go to the Pacific theater. This was in July. The war with Japan ended in August and we were still in England. Finally we were put on trucks and went to Wales where they put us on a ship that took 14 days to cross the

Atlantic. We landed at Camp Dix on the 23rd of October and it took three more days before we got discharged. A group of us that lived in upstate New York got on a train that would stop at all the towns to let off the ones that lived there. We got on this train at 2:30 AM on the 26th of October and I got to Rochester at 2:30 PM. It was a happy day because my family was waiting at the station.

The funny part of this story is that I left home on the 26th of October 1942 and got home on the 26th of October 1945.

This is my story of an old soldier...

The men on my half-track came from different parts of the United States. We would share our last cigarette and share the last bit of food. We showed each other pictures of our loved ones that we left behind. We would write to the wives and girlfriends (and, of course, mom and dad) and tell them how brave we were and not to worry about us. We would comfort the ones who lost a family member back home and we would feel sorry for the one who got a Dear John letter from his girlfriend and we would comfort each other when we were getting bombed or shelled by the enemy. We were together for three years, and I never heard anyone say a bad word about one another... we were like brothers. I was happy when the war ended because now my men could go home to their loved ones, but I was sad at the same time because I was thinking of all the soldiers who weren't going home.

I and millions of soldiers gave the best years of our lives so that our children, grandchildren and those to follow would live in a free world. Thousands of young soldiers gave their lives for the freedom we have today.

We were brothers... may they rest in peace and God bless them all.

TANK BATTALION ESCAPES ST. VITH TRAP

Meron J. Thompson
9th Armored Division, 14th Tank Battalion

After participating in combat action night and day from December 17–23, 1944, in the vicinity of St. Vith, Belgium, we received an order on the morning of December 23rd to withdraw from the area to a line set up by the 82nd Airborne Division.

We had been in St. Vith four or five days before I realized that there was a general attack other than the combat in our area. I heard on BBC radio that the brightest spot on the whole front was at St. Vith, to my surprise. Then, I realized there were attacks up and down the line.

On the morning of December 23, 1944, about 5:30, I heard orders on the radio and the plans and orders by which we should disengage and withdraw from the area.

I understand at this time that Combat Command was using our 14th Tank Battalion Headquarters as its command post since it was not safe to have the company commanders meet at CCB Headquarters to receive orders because the enemy was in the whole area.

The order was for my Company C to lead the 1st platoon under Lt Morrison's leading. We withdrew to an area to the west and to a line being held by the 82nd Airborne.

We expected to have a little rest that night but, after servicing our tanks, gassing up and cleaning our guns and eating a warm meal, we received orders to move out shortly after dark. Again, the 3rd platoon was leading. I did not know our destination at that time but on the way we met a Colonel Swift, who flagged us down and asked to speak to the commanding officer who was directly behind the 3rd platoon. This was Lt. Col. Engeman, who commanded the 14th Tank Battalion.

Swift told Engeman who he was and that he had orders from Corp Headquarters to get any outfit he could find and use them. He told our CO he could get authentication by radio from headquarters. Swift then wanted our CO to give orders to the leading platoon leader, Lt. Morrison.

Swift told Morrison that the Germans had broken through with Tiger tanks and SS Panzer grenadiers. He ordered us to go to a village and set up a road block to stop the Germans. We arrived at the village, set up the roadblock and waited all night with no action. We were still there at noon on December 24th.

Sometime after lunch, Lt. Morrison told me he had orders to support the 82nd Airborne in the village they were trying to recapture. Later that afternoon, we moved forward in a line with Lt. Morrison on the extreme right and my tanks on the extreme left. As we moved in this formation, we received orders from Lt. Morrison to turn left 90 degrees. We were then in a column with my tank leading and Lt. Morrison bringing up the rear. Three tanks were between us.

We had moved a short distance when I received the first hit which was on the barrel of my tank gun. The second one hit the motor, the third was underneath my feet. Then I heard the explosion of shells in our ammunition. That is when I gave the order to bail out.

As we got out, I saw three other tanks being hit consecutively—that is, all the other tanks except that of Lt. Morrison. There was a small ravine and all the men gathered there with me. I gave the order for the men to scatter out and make it back to our lines.

In all, four tanks were knocked out. I was the only one wounded in a tank. My gunner was wounded after he left our tank in withdrawal. I was on the extreme right, came to an 82nd Airborne position and they evacuated me to the hospital.

When the first round hit my tank gun, small fragments of the AP shell hit me in the face and numbed it. I had not shaved for several days and the blood from the wounds froze on my face. Even though only slightly wounded, I had the appearance of having been through a sausage grinder.

The sun appeared on December 24th. This was the first day the air force came out in mass formation. I think they were bombing Manhay. There were so many airplanes and so many groups that I could not attempt to count them.

As for our physical condition, we were very tired, having no sleep nor rest for some time. We were not particularly hungry since we were given two hotcakes with a spoonful of jam and lukewarm coffee that morning.

I was evacuated by the 82nd AB medics, as was my gunner, Leo Sobrisiki, who had also been wounded. Our own company did not know what happened to us with the result that we were carried as missing in action for a while.

I was evacuated to Liege, Belgium, and then to the first General Hospital in Paris, arriving on January 1, 1945. I returned to my tank company and was wounded again seriously on April 12 and remained in the hospital for more than two years. My platoon leader, Lt. Morrison, was killed in action on April 19, 1945.

Addendum: In his account of this combat action in which four tanks were knocked out, Meron Thompson reported he was wounded and evacuated by medics of the 82nd AB, but this was not known by his Company C commander nor by the 14th Tank Battalion Headquarters. As a result, the following telegram resulted:

"Govt-WUX Washington DC Jan 13, 13 100 rP. Mrs. Katherine B. Thompson, Route 1, Jacksonville, Ala Rte Anniston. The Secretary of War desires me to express deep regret that your husband Staff Sergeant Meron J. Thompson has been reported missing in action since 24 December in Belgium. If further details or information are received you will be promptly notified—Dunlop Acting Adjutant General."

But a second message followed later:

"Washington DC 251A Jan 21, 1945. Mrs. Katherine B Thompson (sic). Reference my telegram thirtieth Jany, and a letter of fifteen January report now received your husband stall (sic) Sgt. Meron J. Thompson was slightly wounded in action twenty four Dec in Belgium and is not missing in action as previously reported. Mail address follows direct from hospital with details. J. A. Ulic, The Adjustant (sic) General."

ON PATROL IN EUROPE

Gilbert Troxell
28th Infantry Division, 112th Infantry Regiment

When I went overseas, I joined the 28th Infantry Division somewhere in France. I was in Company F, Second Battalion, 112th Infantry. We were in Luxemburg on December 16, 1944 when the Battle of the Bulge broke loose. We went through the Battle of the Bulge. It ended January 25, 1945. After that they pulled us back near Colmar, France.

One night, about 1:00 in the morning, they sent us out to make contact with another outfit about a quarter of a mile away. They wanted us to see if the enemy was penetrating through. We made contact with the outfit and were on our way back when we met a German patrol.

The Germans walked within four feet of us. We had our rifles on them, and they had their rifles on us. Nobody fired a shot. The Germans went on, and we got up and went back to our outfit.

On January 31st, I got wounded. They got me to the hospital on February 1st. I stayed in the hospital about forty days before they returned me to my outfit. The sergeant and a lot of my buddies had already moved on.

RIDING SHOTGUN ON GERMAN PRISONERS

Dean VanLandingham
26th Tanker Division, Military Police Platoon

One day during the first week in January, a Corporal Davis and I were assigned to ride shotgun on a couple trucks of Germans being sent from the line to the P.W. compound in Arlon, Belgium. After delivering the prisoners we decided to do some recon work in the bars and cafes of the city. We were successful. So much in fact we forgot which road to take back to our regimental H.Q. (the 328 of the YD Division). Being adequately filled with anti-freeze we finally asked an M.P., "Which is the road to Groshus?" Maybe we didn't pronounce the name any better than I can spell it, but he pointed out a road. We started down using only the cat's eyes of the jeep for help in keeping on the road.

After about an hour one of us began to sober up somewhat. Somehow the road didn't seem right. We should have gone through a small burg named Ell and crossed a stone bridge then a sharp right turn. After some discussion we agreed the M.P. was probably right. We kept on.

Suddenly a "Halt," cracked out at us. Then "You dumb — turn out those lights." A sergeant came up and stuck a B.A.R. in my face. After some discussion while we tried to explain who we were and what we were doing and going the sergeant said, "You dumb drunk, you are in Bastogne with the 101." That didn't mean a thing to us. So we turned around and returned to Arlon. By that time it was beginning to get light we found the right road to our outfit.

It wasn't until I was in the hospital in England (I was shot through my neck January 20) that I became aware of the Bastogne situation and realized that Davis and I had driven through fifteen miles of German held territory.

As it is said, "God takes care of children and drunk damn fools." He sure did take care of us that night.

254TH ENGINEER COMBAT BATTALION

Ed C. Vickstrom
107th Engineers, 255th Engineer Combat Battalion

[This document was previously listed as SECRET.] At approximately 162400 hours December, 1944, a message was received from the 1121st Engineer Combat Group that the battalion was on a two-hour alert as infantry. The report also directed our commanding officer to report to the G-3, 99th Infantry Division at once.

At the 99th Division Headquarters, the commanding officer was told that the enemy had broken through and were coming up the Honsfeld-Bullingen highway. The G-3, 99th Infantry Division also instructed the commanding officer that all roads leading into Bullingen were blocked with tank destroyers and light tanks and this battalion was to form a defensive line south and east of Bullingen, Belgium, to protect these blocks. [Overlay is not attached.] The battalion was then formed into two echelons; the forward set up a command post in Bullingen with the companies dug in on the south and west side of the town and the rear echelon commanded by Captain Fairfax of Headquarters and Service Company, moved to the vicinity of Waimes, Belgium, to await further orders.

After setting up the command post in Bullingen all guards of units stationed there were notified of the situation and runners were sent to locate the positions of the light tanks and tank destroyers. The runners returned and reported that no light tanks or tank destroyers could be found.

One sergeant of a tank destroyer outfit was brought in by Company B and he stated that he had been captured at Honsfeld, escaped from the Germans, and wanted to report German armor heading toward Bullingen in strength. He said that he had seen twelve (12) tanks and could hear more coming.

A short time later a 1st lieutenant walked into the command post, stood around to get warm, asked several questions, and stated that he had a platoon of armored infantry in half-tracks. His identification was checked and was satisfactory. When asked where his command post was he said that he was mobile and that the Germans were coming and he was leaving. This didn't seem unusual as they usually accompany tanks and the tanks had apparently also left.

At approximately 0600 hours four flares, blue, white, red and white, were observed to the right of our Company B front. About five (5) minutes later tracked vehicles were headed in our direction. These were not positively identified as we presumed that there were still some division units in front of us. The first positive identification was shouts that were heard in German. The fire order was then given by 1st Lieutenant Huff, Company B, who opened fire with rifles, rifle grenades and machine guns.

The German infantry then piled off the vehicles, one (1) Panzer tank and six (6) half-tracks, got within 15 yards of our positions before being driven back. They pulled back and reorganized and in about twenty (20) minutes the infantry charged our Company B positions under supporting fire of the tanks. The tanks fired a few large caliber shells but most were 20mm high explosive shells and machine guns. This attack was in greater force and in spite of the tanks and shouts of their officers, they were driven back after sustaining heavy losses. The next ten (10) minutes gave us time to evacuate our wounded but now it was getting quite light.

Then, after about ten (10) minutes they charged again, but this time the assault was led by their tanks. As no heavy anti-tank fire was encountered, the tanks spread out and overran Company B positions crushing two machine guns. The men stayed in their foxholes and only three (3) men were injured by the tanks passing over them.

The German infantry was still unable to over run our positions due to the intensive small arms fire. The German infantry then withdrew and maneuvered around our flank which was exposed. In this action one (1) tank was knocked out and two (2) of the twelve (12) damaged while many Germans were left lying on the battlefield.

Having been overrun, the battalion was instructed to fight a delaying action falling back on Butgenbach, by G-3, 99th Infantry Division. Orders were issued by battalion for Company C to fight back out of town and northwest along railroad tracks. Company A, towards Wirtzfeld, and Company B and Headquarters down Bullingen-Butgenbach Road.

Company C fought back through town and took positions north of Bullingen. Company A as yet had not been pressed and held, and the battalion took positions on the ridge west of town. Company B having been cut off could not reach the road. Headquarters men were moved from position to position to give the appearance of a strongly held line with favorable terrain in front of them. This line could be seen from the town and when their point reorganized it took the St. Vith road south. The enemy point, on reaching crossroads of the St. Vith-Butgenbach road, halted for approximately ten (10) minutes and finally moved south. Our objective had temporarily been accomplished.

After the enemy point passed, the support, at about 0800 hours, sent tanks toward Wirtzfeld where the 2nd Infantry Division met them with tank destroyers. They also knocked out one (1) tank flanking Headquarters position west of town.

At about 1200 hours, two (2) platoons of Company B had worked their way through the woods and joined Headquarters west of town and three (3) anti-tank guns were found located at CR K93002. The Germans brought up artillery and shelled the position west of town, and at, approximately 1300 hours, the line, under several light tanks which had just arrived, dropped back to the crossroads.

At about 1500 hours the 26th Infantry relieved the unit and took over this position. At 1545 hours Company A was subjected to shelling and strafing by our own troops. Because of this, the company commander ordered the company to withdraw toward Wirtzfeld. En route the 23th Infantry was contacted, told of the situation, and they formally relieved Company A of the responsibility of their front.

After being relieved the battalion returned to Camp Elsenborn where we reorganized and prepared for our next missions.

A CHRISTMAS TO REMEMBER

Margaret Hammond Walenski
16th Army General Hospital

There was snow, plenty of snow. The air was cold and crisp and clear—a picture perfect setting for the Christmas season. But this was December, 1944, and this was Belgium. Located between Liege and the German border, the 16th Army General Hospital was in a most precarious position at this time. Row on row of army ward tents clearly marked with big red crosses on each roof stood in the field at the top of the hill. The chateau, which housed female personnel, was about a quarter mile away. Although the chateau appeared to be a medieval fortress, even surrounded by a moat, we were well aware of our vulnerability.

For weeks, we had watched the glow from artillery fire light up the horizon and had followed the track of anti-aircraft fire as it streaked across the winter skies. The V-2 rockets sputtered at intervals every night. It was when their put-put-put stopped that we held our breath waiting to hear the blast of the landing. When on night duty, someone would race out of the tent at the sound of an approaching buzz-bomb to see what track it was traveling. Once seen beyond our area or on either side, we knew it was not our route and we were not doomed for destruction with that one.

The bombs and V-2s from Germany were directed at the bridges of the

Meuse River in Liege and there we were right in the middle. Casualties continued to roll in. Work continued and so did the snow and cold. That week before Christmas could hardly be called festive but we did manage a few decorations for the wards and a party of sorts at the Officers Club. The enemy had been advancing steadily. We had been ordered to pack our musette bags with supplies for three days and be prepared to leave all else behind should we be forced to evacuate the area. Some nights we would go to the top floor of the chateau to watch "dog fights" or the trails from anti-aircraft guns as they repelled the attackers. Christmas Eve was different. It was not too noisy. Or had we not heard as we tried to enjoy ourselves?

Laughter was there but underneath was the yearning for home and Christmases past. The feelings were not expressed, but each one was aware of what could happen should the Germans suddenly move closer to their objective, Liege. In our room at the chateau, a tall slender tin water pitcher was bedecked with a few scrawny green boughs and decorated with an odd assortment of small items—a sad imitation of a Christmas tree, but loaded with Yuletide spirit.

Since mail from the States had been delayed, there was little hope of presents from home. Each of us managed to find some small token for the others, although we knew that the gifts would be left behind if we had to move out. Poems and stories accompanied each present and lifted our spirits for a while as we shared them and laughed together.

The roaring sound of approaching aircraft interrupted our masquerade of merriment. The planes, too close and too low, very definitely were not ours! Repeated rounds of machine gun fire echoed through the Holy Night. Seven stalwart army nurses became motionless and speechless. Slowly conversation resumed with questions tumbling over one another, wondering what was going on. Had the enemy reached our area? Was anyone hurt? Would we be loaded into trucks and moved? We sat and waited.

It was not until the evening nurses returned to the chateau at midnight that we heard the grim facts. Two enemy planes had made a fast run over our tented hospital, raining down their deadly missiles as they flew. A couple of German renegades had disregarded Christmas Eve and all the rules of the game, using the big red crosses for targets. Two corpsmen were killed as they carried coal to fill the potbellied stoves in the ward tents. Others were injured, but the toll could have been worse. This tragic news was all we needed after an evening of suppressed sadness. One by one we wept, clinging to each other or sobbing quietly alone, huddled in a blanket. The tears flowed without shame. All of the loneliness of Christmas away from home and family, all the fear of imminent invasion, all the weariness of long hours of work, and all the stress of being brave and courageous were released in the streams of tears as we mourned for our dead and wounded comrades.

Not your traditional holiday season, but then the worst was over. We began to hear good reports from the incoming wounded. There was a breakthrough and our forces had the Germans on the run. The holidays were over and we had survived the Battle of the Bulge!

Now, in a land far away, where there is no snow and no cold, crisp air, Yuletide will see only sun, sand, and heat. Thousands of young men and women will again struggle with loneliness and thoughts of home, not knowing when they will be called upon to give their all. Perhaps this present time of Silent Night, Holy Night will bring a breakthrough as it did years ago and they will survive and again give thanks for Peace on Earth, Good Will to all.

"M" COMPANY MEMORIES... THE LOAF OF BREAD

George M. Watson
87th Infantry Division

Lou Balin was the mess sergeant. He was a solidly built man with a round face who reminded one of Babe Ruth.

The weather was miserable. Road traffic was nonexistent. The Air Corps said, "Ceiling's too low for flying." The Germans had a secret weapon. How else could we be strafed when the "ceiling's too low to fly?"

The line of troops of "M" Company, 346th Regiment existed on K-Rations.

K-Rations made you do things… like open the waxed box and discard everything except the high energy bar, the four cigarettes, heat tab, and toilet paper that had been colored khaki. (The dictionary defines khaki as brownish yellow.)

The cooks took turns standing guard as Lou Balin sought a way to get something hot to the line troops. Rations were low and with weather conditions continuing to worsen, he ordered the kitchen truck to park alongside a low, stone farm building.

During the night the snow stopped and the winds diminished. Shortly after dawn the barn door opened and out stepped a farmer leading a cow. The cow was staked out with a bale of hay. That night as the cooks walked past, Balin said, "I'm going to look about." Fifteen minutes later a shot rang out…

The next morning a messenger came up to the dug-in line troops. The messenger said, "Small groups should take turns going behind the hill for food." Miracle! The cooks were there with warm cans of food. And what food—Swiss steak!

Balin said, "I was checking on the farmer and decided to enter the barn. A large, dark shadow moved toward me. 'Password,' I said three times. Still there was no answer and the figure came on. I squeezed the trigger. Some sort of clanging occurred as the form fell." One of the cooks mentioned how compassionate Balin was concerning the missing cow, as he handed the farmer a loaf of bread.

BRIDGE AT HEIDERSCHEIDERGRUND, LUXEMBOURG

George Whitten
166th Combat Engineers

Late in the afternoon, the 2nd Squad, 2nd platoon, Company "A," 166th Combat Engineers was ordered to a town called Heiderscheidergrund, a little village in a valley between Luxembourg and Belgium with a great road to Bastogne. They wanted to bring troops to stop the Germans who were putting pressure on Bastogne.

We began to erect a Bailey Bridge, but every time we drove a pin, we were shelled by the Germans because the sound echoed throughout the valley. The officers decided to take the Bailey Bridge apart and erect a bridge made of the treads we used on rubber pontoons. Because someone had blown up two of the arches we had to put up two bridges of treads. We got the first set in, but could not lift the second one high enough to get over the first set.

The lieutenant said he was going to wire down for the lumber to come from the depot to lift the wheels of the truck. I told him I could build it without the lumber. He told me to "shut up." He was sick and tired of me. (We had known each other for over a year and a half; he was my original platoon leader.) He went into the guard house, on the border between Luxembourg and Belgium, to have a cigarette.

I went to the truck driver (not a member of my outfit so not subject to court-marshal) and asked, "Will you help me build the bridge?"

He said, "Gladly, soldier."

We lifted the tread to the truck, undid the crane, and lifted the back up. Now we were four feet in the air. We did not need any lumber so we backed over the first bridge and were ready to erect the second. I said to the driver, "We'd better awaken the Canadian infantry who are sleeping on the side of the road waiting for us to construct the bridge." They crossed on foot over the bridge and protected us so the Germans couldn't get to us. After the Canadians were across the river, we put the second tread in place. So now the two bridges were complete. The waiting tanks could cross. This took all of twenty minutes, instead of waiting three hours for the blocking.

When we put the last section down, the truck driver did not hear me and he put it down on my foot so we had to tug at a crow bar to lift the bridge.

Then, the lieutenant came out and said, "I'm going to court-martial you for disobeying orders."

The captain said, "The hell you will!"

The Canadian infantry played the bagpipes while crossing the river.

CHRISTMAS EVE 1944

George Whitten
166th Combat Engineers

I was on a machine gun post with two comrades when a gentleman who lived behind our foxhole came out and offered us some "schnapps" to celebrate Christmas. One of our comrades was French Canadian and spoke fairly good French and asked him to take a swig first. He did. Then we all had a sip because being on duty we could not drink.

I then asked him how many "Kinder" he had. He held up three fingers and said "three." I had in my pocket three peppermint patties from Schrafft's candy company, because a friend of my father's was Chief Engineer at the factory and had access to the candy, of which he sent me a package. In our trucks we each had a compartment where we kept our things, and I also had three oranges, which I gave to him.

A few moments later he returned and asked us to Christmas dinner. The lieutenant returned at that moment and gave us permission. We had rabbit, potatoes, and peas. I don't remember the dessert.

We then gave the farmer a package, which contained one day's meal and other necessities for ten men: canned bacon, coffee, scrambled eggs, beef stew, crackers, toilet paper, hard candy, and cigarettes.

That was the best Christmas dinner I ever had, or will have.

MIRACLES DURING THE BULGE

Lillian Voigt

My father, Elvin H. Wilken, was in the 7th Armored Division, HQ 129th. He drove a half-track from Normandy to the Baltic Sea, along with his brother soldiers in the 7th Armored Division. My father's Battle of the Bulge story had a somewhat different facet to it.

After being in the bulge for several days, his unit was ordered to Louveigne, Belgium on Christmas Day. While trying to get to their destination, he proceeded to cross a stream only to discover he was in the sights of a German gun. As he started to reverse the half-track the German soldier called out "Merry Christmas" in German and allowed the half-track to pass unharmed. My father being of German decent and fluent in German answered the soldier with the greeting of "Merry Christmas" and left the area before they could change their mind. That was his first Christmas miracle.

After arriving in Louveigne, they were told by their officers that they could sleep in the homes of the townspeople if they were invited, as you know the winter was severe that year. The young couple and their 4 year old daughter that invited the half-track crew to stay in their home eventually became my aunt and uncle. That evening after dinner the woman's sister came home after helping their parents with the chores on their dairy farm located behind the church in Louveigne. She was staying with her sister because a relative's home had been bombed and they were using her room at their parents' home.

Dad's second Christmas miracle happened when he met his hostess's sister, Angele Gonay, who would become his wife. After a wartime courtship and letters back and forth from wherever my father was as the war front moved on through Germany, they were married in Louveigne on November 10, 1945. They arrived back in Illinois in March of 1946, where they began their life, farming together west of Ashkum, Illinois.

They truly did live happily ever after together. I had a wonderful upbringing with these two people for my parents. They had many happy reunions with my father's army brothers and it was a privilege to know these men and their families. I accompanied my parents on trips back to the Bulge battlegrounds during trips to see our family in Belgium. I am so proud of the role my father played in WWII. My daughters and I accompanied my parents to the 50th reunion of the Battle of the Bulge in St. Louis, which was a wonderful event. My mother met Prince Philippe of Belgium and members of the Belgian underground, which was quite an experience for her.

454   True Stories

My mother passed away in 2005 and my father joined her in heaven in 2008. I have become an associate member of the Battle of the Bulge organization so I can continue to read *The Bulge Bugle*, which I enjoy.

AFRICAN AMERICAN SOLDIERS IN WWII

Joseph F. Williams
4049th Quartermaster Truck Company, Third United States Army

This letter to you is prompted by my reading Mr. Eugene Morell's "Letter to the Editor" in your February 2008 issue which refers to John McAuliffe's account of "The Invisible Soldiers of World War II," which appeared in the November 2006 issue of *The Bulge Bugle*.

I was a truck driver in the 4049th Quartermaster Truck Company, Third Army, under General Patton. Our responsibility was to deliver infantrymen to and from the front lines. Our 2-1/2 ton trucks were traveling day and night. I, like most of those who served under General Patton, state that if I had to go into war again, I would prefer to serve once again under General Patton. He was indeed a warrior. He did not stay in the rear in a safe place. He was always visible, in his jeep, standing up, holding on to the front window and checking on his men.

During the time I was in France, just before the push into the Ardennes and while we awaited supplies, I met a French family and was reunited with them in 1998 after 53 years. What an experience that was! My wife wrote a book about my life prior to the war, during the war, and how we found the French family.

Yes, African Americans were (and still are) the Invisible Soldiers of World War II, and in that regard, I recommend Spike Lee's recent movie, *Miracle at St. Anna*. The actual problems experienced by African American servicemen had never been exposed in any American movie until *Miracle at St. Anna*. I sincerely refer anyone interested in the history of World War II to view this movie. Thanks for the opportunity to send this to you.

BARBED WIRE

George Wilson
10th Airborne Division

An article in the November 2010 issue of *The Bulge Bugle* by Lester Schwann of the 82nd Airborne who cut his finger on a K-Ration can is a story that I can relate to because I had a similar incident happen to me. If you have read the *321 Mission Accomplished* history book, it tells about that move but doesn't tell any details.

On about Sept 24, 1944, we, the 321st, made a night march back up Hell's Highway to Veghel. They said it was 8 miles but it seemed more like 40. We got to our destination just at daybreak when all hell broke loose. I had already looked around and found a foxhole close by left by the Germans. It was nearby but on the opposite side of a hedge. I made a run for it but forgot about the barbed wire that ran through the hedge. I hit the wire and went headfirst into the foxhole. I don't know if the Germans had seen me go into the foxhole or not, but they were cutting the weeds and grass above my head and it was falling in on me. I never did know if it was machine gun fire or shrapnel from mortar shells. When I hit that barbed wire, I cut myself and it was bleeding quite a bit. I was told to go to First Aid and I could get a Purple Heart. I told them I didn't want one because someone might ask me how I got a Purple Heart and I wouldn't want to tell them I got it for running into a barbed wire fence. I used my own first aid kit and made it just fine. There were 4 more guys out there and I never did know if they found a hole to get in or if they were lying flat on the ground, but all 5 of us were okay after the shelling stopped.

I, too, was short on points when the war was over and had to stay another 3 months. I think a lot of us had enough points but had to wait for transportation back to the United States. All the cooks in our mess hall were older men and had more points and left real soon. I got drafted to take over the mess hall. I had 2 weeks' training before the cooks left and then it was turned over to me to prepare chow for the 40 or so men left. I guess it worked out okay because I didn't hear of anyone getting sick from the meals I fixed.

BREAKTHROUGH AT THE SCHNEE EIFEL

Robert K. Wineland
106th Infantry Division

The time is December 15, 1944. I am 20 years old, a first aid man with the 106th Infantry Division. We are just now taking up positions along the Siegfried Line—some of us are on the Belgian border, others are dug in amongst the dragon's teeth. We are in rugged mountainous terrain, and snowy grey clouds hang low. It is very cold. Ours is a young, untested division composed mostly of college kids. We have never been in combat.

December 16th, our first day on the line. The captain tells us: "A German patrol has slipped through our lines—let's get 'em." I was standing talking with two young soldiers. I left them, saying I needed to get my hat. One minute later a Tiger Tank came over the hill and fired point blank at them. They were blasted to pieces and I put identification tags on each of them. Then the war really started for me.

December 17th, one day later. There was terrible fighting all yesterday and all last night there were flares floating out of the sky and artillery shells coming in. I learn that our Golden Lion Division, the brave 106th Infantry Division has been wiped out and most of my comrades have been killed or captured. Survivors are wandering, lost like me in the snowy ridges of the Schnee Eifel, hiding by day, moving by night. Von Runstedt's Wehrmacht has overrun our thinly held lines and now after just one day of battle my division no longer exists as a fighting unit!

Three days later: I am alone, lost in deep woods somewhere in the mountains. Cold, hungry, feet frozen, I wander into a small clearing in the evergreen forest of the Schnee Eifel. I am so tired and hungry, I am thinking about lying down in the snow and resting a while. I suddenly I see a most wonderful sight. Here are two paratroopers of the 82nd Airborne, submachine guns in their hands and fragmentation grenades hanging about their belts. These guys could stop anything and anybody. The top guy is a colonel. Looking at me, he tells his sergeant, "This soldier needs a lift; give him the bottle from the jeep."

The sergeant reaches into a canvas bag and hands me a tall bottle of green liquid. I take a long pull, and then several more. It burns all the way down and when I return the bottle it is more than half empty. But I am no longer cold or tired. I study a map with the colonel, then turn and head off alone into the woods. Several days later I link up with some of my comrades. Together we make our way back to the lines just as General Patton's Armored Division comes up to stop Von Runstedt.

Ever since that meeting deep in the forest of the Ardennes, I have kept a bottle of green chartreuse in my closet in memory of that snowy encounter and the two paratroopers who helped me keep going.

A TIME TO REMEMBER

Harry Wintemberg
87th Infantry Division, 347th Infantry Regiment, 3rd Battalion

It was before sunrise on May 6, 1945. The day before we had raced some 30 miles through Central Germany heading for the Czechoslovakian border. Except for an occasional sniper, we had encountered no resistance, but instead were greeted by many villagers with hugs, kisses, flowers, fruit, candy and loud cheers as we passed through their small hamlets, no longer than one block in length. Our platoon of about 30 men had outrun the main elements of the division, including support artillery and the kitchen trucks. Fortunately, we were well stocked with the usual cold field rations. The lieutenant decided to select our squad of eight men to immediately proceed due east toward the German-Czech border. Our instructions were clear. We were to take two 90mm self-propelled tank destroyers (like a tank without heavy armor) and two jeeps with 50 caliber machine guns mounted on a swivel base. We were to proceed at maximum speed until we either encountered German resistance or the advancing Russians. If we met a large contingent of Germans, we were to immediately turn back. If we met the Russians, we were to wave an American flag and wait for them to come to us. We had a very crude map of the area. It showed a few fanning hamlets and very secondary roads for the next 50 miles.

At about 7:00 a.m., our group of eight took off—a jeep in front with two men, the two TDs with two men in each, and a follow-up jeep in the rear. I was riding in the 2nd jeep manning the 50 caliber. It was a beautiful spring day with the sun shining brightly and the temperature in the mid-70s. After a short distance we passed through a very small village and were advised by the residents that the last German soldiers had left about 24 hours before. By noon, we had advanced about 20 miles and had reached the Czech border. The guard house at the border had been abandoned. We stopped for lunch and enjoyed our "picnic" in the country. The next 10 miles was very slow going. The retreating Germans had blasted a number of trees down across the road in areas where the road was narrow and passed through a ravine. We had to stop and with chains had the TDs pull the fallen trees off the road. We lost much time. As the afternoon sun began to fall to the horizon, our sergeant decided to pull off into a small wooded area and settle in for the night. Guard details were arranged and we had supper and stretched out with our bed rolls for a good night's sleep. It was a quiet night, except for the distant rumble of artillery. We were up before dawn and took off at sunrise.

We had traveled only a short distance and we came up a small rise in the road. Suddenly, the lead jeep abruptly stopped and motioned for us to do likewise. Since we couldn't see over the knoll, we walked up to where the lead jeep had stopped. Never in my life had I ever had such a terrifying experience and certainly I haven't had one like it since. Before us was a stretch of open farmland with a long gradually curving road that could be seen almost to the horizon. The road was clogged with hundreds of vehicles crawling along, bumper to bumper. There were countless German tanks, artillery pieces, small vehicles, large trucks, ambulances, ox carts, and thousands of well-armed German infantrymen.

The lead vehicle was a staff car usually used by high ranking officers. Our sergeant had binoculars, but could only determine that the occupants of the staff car had stopped and held up the entire column of troops. They had obviously seen us through their binoculars. We held a panic conference and were about to turn around and make a hasty retreat, when the sergeant yelled that the staff car had what appeared to be a large white pillow case or sheet on a long pole that had been raised. (Note: We had not had any communication with our base unit since leaving the morning before. It was now May 7, 1945.) The staff car left the convoy and rapidly closed the 1 mile distance as it approached us under a truce flag. We pulled the two 90mm TDs and the two jeeps up in a line separated by about 15 yards and waited while our pulse jumped to at least 150 beats per minute. When the staff car came within about 100 yards, it stopped and a German officer got out and approached our position with a white sheet on a pole.

Respecting this international symbol of a truce we took no aggressive action. When the officer came within talking range, he said in perfect English, "I would like to speak to your commanding officer." Our sergeant simply replied that he was the ranking non-commissioned officer. The German said, "I am Colonel So-and-so (name forgotten) and am the regimental commander of these troops you see before you. I am prepared to honor the agreement reached this morning between the German High Command and the American forces under the command of General Eisenhower and unconditionally surrender my forces immediately." Having said that, he immediately removed his revolver from its holster and gave it to the sergeant. I remember him saying, "Our war is over and we want to go home under true supervision of the Americans... not the Russians." The eight of us looked at each other with one common look... "What the hell do we do now?" We never had the chance to celebrate the fact that the war was over and this would be officially known as V-E-Day. Our minds were so mixed up with fear, panic, and uncertainty what to do, coupled with the elation it was over and we survived what seemed to be the impossible.

The German Colonel, sensing our dilemma, made the suggestion that he order his troops to dismount all their vehicles and discard all their weapons along the road. He further suggested that they take their field packs with blankets and food rations and set up a massive camp in the farm land surrounding both sides of the road. He was obviously very worried about the approaching Russians, as he asked if we had an American flag they could set up on a pole in the middle of the encampment. Acting like we knew exactly what we were doing, we agreed with the Colonel's suggestions, including setting up the American flag as protection from the Russians. The sergeant directed that the two of us in the rear jeep take off as fast as possible back toward our main unit. So this other fellow (name forgotten) and I left. As we passed through one hamlet, the residents were out yelling and waving little American flags (source unknown) and wanted to stop us. To avoid running over them, we were forced to slow to a crawl.

Suddenly, a shot rang out and ricocheted off the side of our jeep. Everyone screamed and pointed to the hayloft of a nearby barn. I swung the 50 caliber machine gun around and let go with about 100 rounds spraying the whole side of the barn. Accompanied by some of the locals we ran over to the barn and found our sniper laying on the floor dead. While the farmers released their vengeance on the corpse with their pitch forks, we jumped back on the jeep and left. After about 30 minutes (distance uncertain) we encountered the main body of our unit heading east in a parade-like fashion. They were yelling and drinking liberated German schnapps and wine and having a great time celebrating the end of the war. We located our lieutenant and briefed him on what we had experienced.

Within minutes we were headed back east toward the area we had left our six guys watching over a whole regiment of Germans. Again, we were in for quite a surprise. The German colonel had moved all vehicles off on to the shoulder of the road. Looking like a campground for the Barnum & Bailey Circus, there were hundreds of small tents being erected, campfires burning and in the middle of it all mounted on some type of pole was the American flag flying over this German encampment. Our battalion commander, a Lt. Colonel, proceeded to discuss formalities with the German colonel. At this point, our group of 2 jeeps and 2 TD's were instructed to proceed to a nearby intersection and set-up a crossing guard until further advised. I never did learn how they disposed of the thousands of prisoners we had "captured!"

A DAY IN THE ARDENNES

Charles Woodman
75th Infantry Division, 291st Infantry Regiment, Company B

This is one those days I will always remember. The 75th Infantry Division had relieved the 82nd Airborne Division near Vielsalm, Belgium, during the Battle of the Bulge. I was a member of Company B, 291st Regiment of the 75th, and on this morning a group of us had gathered behind the hill on the high ground where we had our foxholes to build a small campfire to have some coffee. The weather had been miserably cold but this morning was bearable and I had removed my shoes in an effort to dry them out over the fire.

We had received mail earlier and some of us were reading letters from home when Freddie McCarthy came over the hill to show me a picture he had just received of a very attractive girl in a nurse's uniform. After I congratulated him, he asked if I wanted to go on an easy patrol with him, Harvey Pendergrass, Mickey Dutton, and one other man whose name I do not remember. He said this was like a stroll in the park and the mission was to find a decent spot to cross a stream which was east of our position for a large patrol planned for later in the day. Since my shoes were off and the water for the coffee was heating up I told him I would see him later when they returned.

This "walk in the park" turned out to be a disaster. Perhaps a half hour later we heard a firefight erupt in the direction that the patrol had taken. It didn't last long and the man whose name I cannot remember returned to say they had been fired upon by enemy troops before they reached the stream. The other three members of the patrol had all been hit.

We had a medic we called "Pop," who went into the open field on our side of the stream to help the wounded. "Pop" was much older than most of us and my guess is that he could have been over 40 years old. I believe he was from the State of Connecticut. He found Pendergrass had been killed, McCarthy was hit in the neck but was still alive, and he could not find Dutton.

While two stretcher bearers went to get McCarthy, the rest of us took up positions on the top of the ridge from where we could see a house on the other side of the stream. This appeared to be the point where the enemy fire originated. As I lay there watching the house and waiting, the medics carried McCarthy up the slope, and when they got to my position they set him down for a moment to rest. I had a chance to speak to him but he did not answer. One of the medics put some snow on his lips and he was able to lick it. It was at this time that we opened fire on the house, not knowing if we were hitting any of the enemy but relieving a lot of frustration and hoping that some of those rounds found a target.

Three days later, at about three in the morning, we moved from that position to start the attack that would end the German advance into Belgium. The name of the town that we moved to was Grand Halleux. The attack started with a fifteen minute artillery barrage and then we were off heading south across an open field, but that is another story.

The troops attacking to our west, which I believe was A Company, found Mickey Dutton's body in the creek, which we later learned was called the Salm River. They also discovered the remains of several dead German soldiers in the house that we had fired upon. McCarthy is buried in Henri Chappelle Cemetery and I have visited his grave four times starting in 1991. Harvey Pendergrass and Mickey Dutton were eventually returned home for burial as was true of 60 percent of the men who were killed in Europe. Pendergrass came from Mississippi. Dutton's first name was Carl and he came from Ohio. McCarthy was from Elmhurst, a part of Queens County in New York City. I did write to his mother and told her that when I saw him on the stretcher he was not in pain. She wrote back and told me that he was an adopted child and that they naturally would miss him. That is what I remember of one black day in the white snow of the Ardennes Forest when we lost three very good men.

INDEX OF AUTHORS

CPSIA information can be obtained
at www.ICGtesting.com
Printed in the USA
BVHW080158191221
624344BV00007B/546/J

9 780991